D1488414

Stardust and Shadows

STARDUST

—— AND ——

SHADOWS

CANADIANS IN EARLY HOLLYWOOD

CHARLES FOSTER

DUNDURN PRESS
TORONTO · OXFORD

Editorial Co-ordinator: Anthony Hawke
Editor: Don McLeod
Design: Jennifer Scott
Printer: Friesens Corporation

Canadian Cataloguing in Publication Data

Foster, Charles, 1923-
    Stardust and shadows: Canadians in early Hollywood

Includes index.
ISBN 1-55002-348-9

1. Motion picture producers and directors – California – Los Angeles – Biography. 2. Motion picture actors and actresses – California – Los Angeles – Biography. 3. Canadians – California – Los Angeles – Biography. 4. Motion picture industry – California – Los Angeles – History. I. Title.

PN1998.2.F67 2000   791.43'02'092279493   C00-931695-7

1   2   3   4   5   04   03   02   01   00

We acknowledge the support of the **Canada Council for the Arts** and the **Ontario Arts Council** for our publishing program. We also acknowledge the financial support of the **Government of Canada** through the **Book Publishing Industry Development Program**, **The Association for the Export of Canadian Books**, and the **Government of Ontario** through the **Ontario Book Publishers Tax Credit** program.

Care has been taken to trace the ownership of copyright material used in this book. The author and the publisher welcome any information enabling them to rectify any references or credit in subsequent editions.

J. Kirk Howard, President

Printed and bound in Canada. ⊕
Printed on recycled paper.

www.dundurn.com

Dundurn Press	Dundurn Press	Dundurn Press
8 Market Street	73 Lime Walk	2250 Military Road
Suite 200	Headington, Oxford,	Tonawanda NY
Toronto, Ontario, Canada	England	U.S.A. 14150
M5E 1M6	OX3 7AD	

TABLE OF CONTENTS

PROLOGUE

"There was a magic in those early days that made it easy for us to believe that stardust fell only on the paradise we knew as Hollywood. We worked hard all day, and played harder at night. The world was ours for the taking. We thought it would never end ... but it did!"

(Mack Sennett, 1958)

It was the summer of 1943 when I first became aware of the important role Canadians had played in the early days of the motion picture industry. As a member of the Royal Air Force, spending nineteen days leave in Hollywood, I was directed to the home of Sidney Olcott on Bedford Drive in Beverly Hills. Olcott had advised all the area's service clubs that visitors from Canada would be welcome in his home.

There were few Canadian servicemen or women in Hollywood at the time, and Olcott's invitation to dinner was extended to an eighteen-day stay. For the first few hours of my visit I was unaware that Olcott and his wife, the former Valentine Grant, were in any way connected to the film industry. But on the first evening, when I spoke of my hope to see inside one of the major studios, I discovered the amazing range of their influence.

Next morning the Olcotts drove me over to Canadian-born Mary Pickford's mansion, Pickfair, at 1143 Summit Drive in Beverly Hills. Mary greeted me with open arms and a great big hug and asked if I had any preference for my studio visit. "Metro-Goldwyn-Mayer, please," I said hopefully. A two-minute conversation on the phone between Mary and MGM chief Louis B. Mayer and everything was arranged. "My chauffeur will take you to Metro right away," she said. "You'll like Louis (everyone pronounced it Louie) Mayer. He is from Canada, too."

Mayer proved to be an incredible host. He insisted on escorting me personally into every nook and cranny of his immense studio.

"You are fortunate to be the guest of Sid Olcott," he said. "A genius. A great director. But he won't make any more films, did he tell you that?" I didn't want to tell him that this was the first I knew that Olcott was, or had been, a director. He continued, "We've all tried to bring him back but he is as stubborn as a mule." Others, when told where I was staying, intrigued me with more stories of Olcott's exploits in the film industry.

Mayer introduced me to so many of his stars that I lost count. But it was the Canadians he sought out who stayed in my memory. They were all so proud to talk about their former homes in Canada.

Allan Dwan, the veteran director from Toronto, Ontario, stopped shooting and introduced me to everyone on the set when we visited. We found Sam De Grasse, from Bathurst, New Brunswick, eating in the studio restaurant. How Douglas Fairbanks, Sr., could ever call this genial man "the slimiest and most evil villain on the screen" I found it hard to believe — until I saw one of his films.

Norma Shearer, from Montreal, Quebec, had been retired for several years but still used the cottage Mayer had built for her on the MGM lot. There she served tea for me and called her brother, Douglas, chief of MGM's sound department, over to join us. It was a day I will never forget. Mayer had his driver take me home at five. Later that evening he called and invited me back to MGM the following day. "I have a little surprise for you," he said.

The surprise was a luncheon party in my honor. All the guests were Canadian. Imagine sitting down to dine with Fay Wray from Cardston, Alberta; Walter Pidgeon from Saint John, New Brunswick; Jack Carson from Carmen, Manitoba; Rod Cameron from Calgary, Alberta; Fifi D'Orsay from Montreal, Quebec; Deanna Durbin from Winnipeg, Manitoba; Walter Huston from Toronto, Ontario; Ann Rutherford from Toronto, Ontario; Cecilia Parker from Fort William (now Thunder Bay), Ontario; and Mayer's biggest rival, Jack Warner, from London, Ontario. Mayer told me later that it was the first time in ten years he had sat down with Warner without arguing.

Jack Warner insisted on my visiting his studio next day. The following Monday I was Deanna Durbin's guest at Universal Studios. She called for me at 7:30 in the morning at Sid and Valentine Olcott's home and drove me to the studio where she spent the whole day showing me the Universal lot before driving me to her home for supper.

Richard Day, the brilliant set designer from Victoria, British Columbia, had called while I was at Universal to invite me to spend the next day at the 20th-Century-Fox studio. Day introduced me to George Cleveland (later to become famous as Grandpa on the "Lassie" TV series) from Sydney, Nova Scotia. Cleveland invited me to dinner and added another guest, Montreal-born Mack Sennett, founder of the Keystone Kops.

Sennett suggested we visit the Columbia studio next day to meet Del Lord, from Grimsby, Ontario. "He was my greatest custard pie thrower," said Sennett. "Now he's directing many of Columbia's comedies. He is working on a Three Stooges film right now." I found out that Sennett was right about the custard pies when one thrown by Lord from ten feet away hit me right in the face. Sennett set me up for that "moment to remember."

It was a fun time. For a while the war was forgotten as these wonderful people, so proud to be Canadians, gave me the vacation of my life. There was magic — then — in Hollywood.

Throughout the war I kept in touch by letter with many of my new found friends. When the fighting ended I visited Hollywood again, living and working there for a while. Now and then I was able to repay, in a small way, their generosity and kindness to me back in 1943.

Over the years I made notes of the startling, sometimes incredible, things they told me. As, sadly, each of my friends died, I was left with many wonderful memories that I could read over and over again.

I opened files on other Canadians I was not able to meet, but whose memories lived on in the stories I listened to with ever-growing fascination.

Joseph De Grasse, Sam's brother, a fine director and writer, had been dead for three years when I first arrived in Hollywood in 1943, but he was not forgotten. Florence La Badie, an early star who died tragically in her twenties, was mentioned many times by her friend, Valentine Olcott. Was there something about her mysterious death that she was reluctant to put into words? It took me many years to discover the secret.

Mary Pickford, who became a good friend, confided in me with many stories of her early days in silent films and constantly talked about her younger brother, Jack, then dead for several years. Was her belief in his talents justified? His story is perhaps even more remarkable than hers.

Marie Dressler, from Cobourg, Ontario, dead for a number of years when I first saw Hollywood, was often spoken about by Louis B. Mayer, who had adored her and was proud to discuss her life. Her name even got me an interview, in 1980, with Greta Garbo, who told me a secret about Dressler she had guarded for almost sixty years.

Mayer's friends told me how he had put a lot of former silent stars, down on their luck, under lifetime contracts with MGM so they would never go hungry. One was Florence Lawrence, the movies' first real star, the "Biograph Girl" from Hamilton, Ontario.

I had little time in the 1950s through 1980s to do much more than put my notes in some semblance of order. My library of show-business books, from which I gleaned every word I could find about Canadians in Hollywood, had grown, by the 1980s, to more than 500 volumes. But when January 1, 1990, came around I made a firm resolution that it was time to start telling the world how much the early film industry in New York, and later in Hollywood, owed to Canadians.

Over the past fifty years I have sought out and talked to more than 500 veterans of the early days of motion pictures. Many were in their late eighties. One, with an incredible memory, was ninety-eight.

I have travelled to many cities in every corner of Canada and the United States looking for people with memories they were willing to share. I studied thousands of files in libraries, newspapers, and private collections, making photocopies of aging and flimsy clippings where I was permitted.

The result is this tribute to eighteen talented Canadians. It will, I hope, make a lot of people wonder whatever would show business have done without them.

MAY IRWIN

"Why this distinguished actress and pillar of New York society should choose to exhibit herself in this passing fad of moving pictures is beyond my reasoning. She has, undoubtedly, done her career in the legitimate theatre irreparable harm."

(Charles Frohman, 1896)

Most film historians record Florence Lawrence, a nineteen-year-old actress from Hamilton, Ontario, as being the first motion picture performer to be named alongside the movie title as its star. That was in 1909, when the fast growing motion picture industry gave in to public pressure and told the world the name of the actress millions only knew until that time as the "Biograph Girl."

In fact, thirteen years earlier, another Canadian, May Irwin, had her name on posters advertising a fifty-second film, *The Kiss*, a scene from the Broadway hit play, *The Widow Jones*.

In 1896, no reputable actor or actress would acknowledge having been inside the primitive film studios of the era. But May Irwin changed all that when she yielded to the pleas of the motion picture camera inventor, Thomas Edison, to give "a real professional performance" for the benefit of the struggling industry. Until that time, all film actors were rank amateurs, more often than not people grabbed from the streets near the studios.

On June 26, 1896, May Irwin and John Rice, both appearing on Broadway in the Charles Frohman comedy, *The Widow Jones*, stood in front of a camera on the roof of a warehouse on 28th Street in New York City and recorded the kiss scene from the play.

The plump and jolly Irwin and aging Rice played a part in the birth of the film industry that is still on record in the United States film archives in Washington, D.C.

When the film was shown publicly two weeks later, Charles Frohman was very displeased. "I shall have to consider replacing Miss Irwin," he told the New York newspapers. But one week later he was talking to the film's producer, Edson Raff, pleading that future advertising for the Vitascope short should contain the words: "Starring the distinguished actress, May Irwin, now appearing in the Charles Frohman comedy on Broadway, *The Widow Jones*."

What had changed Frohman's mind? The standing ovation given to May Irwin on her first entrance each night at the theatre. "There are hundreds waiting at the stage door each night to catch a glimpse of her," reported the *New York Times*.

May Irwin

May Irwin, born June 27, 1862, in Whitby, Ontario, went on to much greater fame in a stage career that spanned fifty years. But only once again did she step in front of a film camera. In 1914, at the height of her stage acclaim, she made a two-reel film, *Mrs. Black Is Back*, for the Famous Players Corporation, a company in which Charles Frohman was a major stockholder.

"I was too old then for a film career," she told the *New York Times* when she officially retired from the stage in 1925. "How I wish I had been born thirty years later. I think I would have enjoyed working before a camera."

Her grandchildren recalled some years ago that she never tired of reading, to any member of the family who would listen, a critical review of her 1896 film debut. The writer was Herbert S. Stone, editor and publisher of a literary magazine, *The Chap Book*. Stone denounced her as follows: "It [the scene] is an outrage to decency and good taste. Neither participant [in *The Kiss*] is physically attractive and the spectacle of their prolonged posturing on each other's lips was hard to bear. When only life size on the theatre stage it is beastly. Magnified to gargantuan proportions on a white sheet it is absolutely disgusting."

May Irwin's successful stage career deserves more space than this brief story of her film fame. Possibly that can be done in a later book about the many Canadians who played major roles in the growth of the New York stage.

She married happily and became a wealthy woman. When she died, in 1938, she donated much of her money to theatrical charities. On the day of her funeral, New York theatres turned off their marquee lights for one minute as a tribute to her accomplishments and generosity. Obituaries did not forget her early role in motion pictures.

Riverside Memorial Chapel, in New York City, was packed with the elite of the theatre world to pay tribute to her career. Among those present were Raymond Massey, Alfred Lunt, Lynn Fontanne, Ruth Gordon, Jack Buchanan, Gertrude Lawrence, Lucile Watson, Orson Welles, Mary Martin, and Ethel Barrymore. They broke into the traditional theatre response, spontaneous applause, when the Rev. John Merrithew reminded them that she should surely be described as "the mother of the motion picture industry."

The Kiss was not forgotten forty-two years after it was filmed. Thousands of enthusiasts of the era of silent movies still remember it today.

AL AND
CHARLES CHRISTIE

"Most people think it was Mack Sennett who offered me the toughest competition back in the 1920s, but in reality it was Al and Charles Christie with their sophisticated Christie Comedies. The Christies, like me, used a more classy style of humor than Sennett. He was the best slapstick comedy man of all time. But whether the Christie Comedies or the Hal Roach Comedies were best in the more subtle style of humor, only time and history will tell."

(Hal Roach, at age ninety, in 1982)

Unfortunately, history will never have a chance to compare the Christie Comedies with either Roach or Sennett. Few of the films the brothers Al and Charles Christie made are still in existence, and to all except the real silent era buffs, the Christie Comedies are almost forgotten.

Sennett's Keystone Studio output, principally because of the Keystone Kops, Charlie Chaplin, the Bathing Beauties, Gloria Swanson, and Marie Dressler, are still being shown at silent film festivals.

Hal Roach Comedies have survived thanks to the longevity of Roach as a producer, the Our Gang films, and Laurel and Hardy, whose contributions to Roach in both sound and silent eras can still be seen on Saturday morning television programs in countries around the world.

But few of the great Christie Comedies made between 1915 and 1932, well into the sound era, are around for the world to judge their entertainment value.

The Wall Street collapse of 1929 wiped out Al and Charles Christie. "Very few of our negatives or prints survived," said Al Christie in 1943. "We couldn't afford to keep that old emulsion film in the cold storage it needed to survive."

The Christie brothers were an oddly matched pair. Al's sole interest in the film industry was directing stylish comedies that would make people fall off their seats laughing. Charles rarely watched one of the Christie Film Company's productions or visited the sets where the one- and two-reel films were being churned out at the rate of two or three each week. His job was to look after the books of the company.

Charles recalled his memories of the Christie brothers comedy studio in 1943. "There had to be financial control or things would have been chaotic, as indeed they were at both Sennett and Roach studios. Sennett admitted he often didn't know whether a film made a profit because he could never give a real estimate of the production costs. Roach had a succession of business managers; some ripped him off, others didn't know their job. I was an accountant, with film costing estimates from my days in New York, and when Al needed more than his genius at devising, writing, producing, and directing, I hopped the first available train to California to join him."

Charles Christie was born in London, Ontario, on April 13, 1882. His brother Al followed him into the world on November 24, 1886. Their father, as manager of the city's Opera House, was a highly respected man in the community. Their mother was the Opera House's box-office manager and accountant.

Despite its glamourous name, the Opera House was for most of its time before the turn of the century a burlesque and melodrama theatre. When visiting performers found it tough to get good accommodations in the city, the Christies took them to their large home where they became temporary boarders for the duration of their show's stay in town.

So the Christies' two sons, Al and Charles, grew up in the midst of the glamour, and despair, of the world of entertainment. In 1943 Charles recalled his early days in London. "I liked the show people. But even when I was only ten I couldn't understand their inability to handle money. I watched mother spend hours with them trying to work out budgets that would allow them to save a few dollars for the rainy days that came all too often to performers. I admired my mother's ability to control our family's spending, and grew up realizing it was her achievements that enabled us to live in a beautiful home without always worrying where the next penny would be coming from."

When he was fourteen, Charles graduated from school with a final mark in arithmetic of 99 out of 100. He was proud of his graduation report, which he kept until the day he died.

His parents immediately enrolled him in an accountancy course at a local business college. There he completed a four-year course in two years, and once more, at sixteen, was the star student. "My first job," he recalled, "was as an accounts clerk in a candy factory. At seventeen, when the accountant died, I was promoted. Much to the dismay of the factory owners I volunteered to revolutionize the company's entire system of accounting, but when I proved to them how much time and money they were losing with the old system they told me to go ahead."

Charles was asked by his former accounting school to set up a similar method of accounting that could be adapted to all types of industries. "They called it the Christie Method of Accounting, and before I knew it I was spending half my time teaching the system to young students, and half my time travelling all over Ontario introducing my method to other accounting schools. One of the first students to graduate from the London school, using my method, took my place at the candy factory as my teaching was now more than a full-time job."

Al also liked the theatre people who visited his home each week, but for different reasons. In 1943 he was always happy to talk about his childhood in London. "I couldn't have cared if the performers had money or not," he said. "Even when I heard mother tell them not to worry if they hadn't enough to pay for their board and lodging, that they could send it along later, I thought this was one of the great things about the theatre. You just didn't have to worry about money or the lack of it.

"And I loved the performers' ability to laugh at adversity. If they were booked into the Opera House on a sixty-forty share with the theatre management, and because of poor attendance their sixty percent didn't even pay all the performers, let alone the board and lodging, they still shrugged their shoulders, smiled, and went on stage bravely even if the theatre was three-quarters empty.

"I spent most of my evenings backstage watching them perform, or I would slip through the pass door and watch from the front. Before I was fourteen I was able to understand why some routines were funny and others were not. Somehow I analyzed their material and knew immediately what was wrong. I tried telling some of the comedians how they could improve their skits. Some listened, others told me to run away, but not that politely. The ones who did listen would try changing a bit of their act each night and, often, by Saturday night, when the theatre was always full, good or bad show, they got gales of laughter and lots of applause.

"Some of the acts would slip me a coin after the second show on Saturday, saying 'thank you' for the ideas I had passed along. Word of mouth in the show business of those days was more often than not the way items of interest to the performers reached their destination. So after about a year performers I had never met before would greet me on Monday nights. 'So you're the young man who put a bit of life in so-and-so's act. Go out front tonight and let me know what you think of my routines.' And more often than not they added that wonderful word, 'please.'

"By the time I was eighteen I was known as the 'act doctor.' I had expanded my advice from just changing the pratfalls and funny business, to rewriting their comedy skits. Before I knew it I was getting paid for my work.

"In those days the stage manager did just about everything that concerned backstage. He hung the drapes and set the scenery, sometimes with the help of just one assistant. He read the lighting plots the acts brought along and operated the lighting from a huge switchboard just off stage left, where he stood throughout the show. There were no fancy lighting experts as there are today; the stage manager of that time did the lot. Of course, he didn't have to worry about microphones and amplifiers because there were none. If a singer or comic couldn't be heard at the back of the stalls or up to the top of the highest balcony, he or she wouldn't get much work.

"I started rewriting the lighting plots the acts brought with them, and before long I was doing most of the stage manager's job. When our stage manager, Fred Mitchell, had a heart attack, I was automatically given the job.

"Suddenly I was in my element. I controlled the entire backstage. At nineteen I was getting very cocky, telling performers what to do, where to stand, and how to deliver lines. Surprisingly, I had very few problems. One act told me the word got around that playing the London Opera House was worthwhile, even at a reduced salary, because the 'act doctor' would give you free advice.

"A young fellow, perhaps eleven or twelve, kept coming around backstage, looking for any odd jobs. I gave him the task of brushing the stage before and after every show. George Summerville, that was his name. He told me he was originally from New Mexico, but had run away from a farm in nearby St. Thomas, where he was staying with his aunt and uncle. He desperately wanted to get on the stage, which his parents had promised he could before they were killed in an accident in the United States. When I discovered he had no place to stay I took him home and mother gave him a bed and fed him for several months.

"One day he said he was going to leave town with one of the travelling companies. He was tall, and very thin, and was the perfect foil for the usually portly, red-faced comics. I was sorry to see him go, and told him I hoped we'd meet up again someday.

"We did meet again, in 1916, when I was visiting the Sennett Studio. This very familiar-faced young man came over to me and asked if I remembered him. Suddenly I did; it was George Summerville, from London. When we had told each other the adventures that had led us to Hollywood, I suggested he come over to the Christie Studio when he needed work. He said, 'Great, I will, but you'd better know, Al, that I've changed my name. I dropped the

George because of what everyone called me, as I am so thin and scrawny. Now my name is Slim.'

"Slim Summerville played many parts in Christie Comedies, but his biggest successes were on the Sennett lot. That is, of course, until he played the one role people still remember today, the soldier Tjaden, in *All Quiet on the Western Front*. He got an Oscar nomination for that role."

Charles Christie was only twenty-three and Al Christie just nineteen when they decided to seek fame and fortune outside Canada. "I had an offer from Liebler and Company, a New York production outfit, to be the stage manager of one of the travelling road shows they cast and rehearsed in New York, but which played theatres as far west as Chicago," said Al. "I'd heard tales of life in the big cities and when this reputable company made me an offer, I knew I couldn't refuse. I told them I'd move to New York if they could find a job for Charles. I ballyhooed his financial achievements and they made him a very reasonable offer, too."

"We had our parents' blessing," said Charles. "Sure, we had more than a few qualms about going so far from home, but after long evenings of talking things over we decided to go. Once we'd made the decision we took two weeks to find replacement people for our jobs and then we hopped a train for the big city."

Within two hours of their train arriving in New York City both Al and Charles Christie were working. Harry Liebler, the senior producer of the company who had paid their rail fares from London, had also fixed them up in a clean theatrical rooming house near the company's rehearsal rooms and offices.

"Once we were settled in our rooms we were ready to work," said Al. "It was exciting to be in New York, but we both wanted to get going. We walked over to the company's office block and introduced ourselves."

"Glad you're here, boys," said Liebler. "You," he said to Charles, "can take that office in the corner and help sort out the financial mess one of our companies is in." "You," he said to Al, "can come with me to the rehearsal rooms. We are just a week away from putting out a new touring show. We need your advice on lighting and staging."

"We were a hit from day one," said Charles. "I sorted out their financial problems in short order, and Al had everything in place for their new show in only three days. Boy, did we think we were clever. We were in clover right up to our ears."

For three years Al Christie travelled the United States as stage manager, sometimes company manager, too, of Liebler's shows. During his spare time he wrote a complete comedy show that the company staged, allowing him to be assistant producer in the credits. "I liked the extra money and the recognition by the company, but I told them any more shows I wrote I wanted to produce myself," said Al. "There was very little opposition to my dream, and within a few months I had a second show ready for production. After that I stayed in New York writing and producing as many as ten shows a year. They weren't spectacular but they had comedy bits in them that no one had tried before that time. If I say I added a little bit of sophistication to vaudeville I don't think I'm boasting too much."

The word spread in New York theatrical circles that Liebler and Company had a remarkable accountant who had devised simplified bookkeeping systems for the company and its touring shows. Most touring managers had found the earlier methods of reporting income and payouts to be beyond their ability. Charles had a number of offers from top managements in the city, but he felt none of them offered the challenge that he was seeking.

"Not until I was approached by the Horsley brothers, William and Arthur, who were making the primitive films of that era in Bayonne, New Jersey, under the name Nestor Comedies, did I begin to get enthused," said Charles. "They made the new industry sound exciting. I soon began to realize this was the future career for me.

"I had visited friends at two of the small studios in the city and had been horrified by the tremendous waste of film, materials, and manpower. Half the time they didn't know what they planned to shoot next day, sometimes even the next hour. People being paid to act or build sets just sat around playing cards and, far too often, drinking themselves into a state where they were useless when the director was ready.

"I told the Horsleys that I was interested in their proposition, but that I had to have complete control of all financial matters. They agreed to give me this assurance in writing, and offered me more than double what I was getting at the theatre office. So, perhaps with a little doubt inside me, I left to join this new moving picture industry. I was a little concerned because I knew, at that time, no reputable actor on Broadway wanted any part of the industry, and because a lot of doubters were writing stories that said moving pictures were just a fad that would pass away very quickly."

William Horsley told the *New York World*, in a story printed in 1911, that "there was absolutely no control over costs in our early days. We were much too busy playing with our new toy, the motion picture camera, to worry if we were wasting a few dollars here and there. I wonder if we would have survived as a viable industry had not Charles Christie arrived to put our finances in order. It took him two months to straighten out our mess, during which time he often worked seven days a week and eighteen hours a day, before providing us with a realistic financial picture of the company. We didn't know it, but we were bankrupt before we really got started. He saved the studio from disaster and invented a stock and purchasing control system that I still use today. I doubt if it can ever be bettered."

Al Christie visited his brother at the Nestor studio on one of his breaks between productions and found himself enthralled with the new industry. "But it was rather like seeing those early comedy skits that used to horrify me with their crudeness at the Opera House in London," he said. "These were not professional comics, just ordinary people trying to be funny and they weren't. I asked Charles if there was any chance for me to write script outlines for the company and show some of the amateur comics how to react and get the most out of funny situations. In effect, exactly what I had been doing with the stage shows, except that there I had real pros to work with. Charles said he would approach William and Arthur Horsley with the idea. But he warned it might be a little time before he got an answer as they were very busy, not only with production, but with their film laboratory and distribution house."

While he was waiting for an answer, Al Christie wrote two or three rough ideas for comedy scripts. "Actually they were variations on skits I'd written for the touring vaudeville shows," he said. "When Charles passed the word that Arthur Horsley had approved my idea, I was so excited I even forgot to ask if I would be paid. But I trusted Charles. Wherever money comes into the picture he deals with it the right way. I was to get $15 for each of the two one-reel script ideas, and was to work with the director and the actors to get the most out of what I had proposed."

When the second film was being made, the director suddenly stomped off to William Horsley's office. Horsley told this next part of the tale. "He came to me in a fury. Asked who was directing this film, Christie or him. I told him he was, so he told me to get Al Christie off the set or he would walk out.

"I promised to talk to Al, but before I had an opportunity to get him alone I was called away to see a rough cut of the first film Al had written. It hit me right between the eyes. This was comedy with style. Gone were all the grimaces and grotesque make-up that we'd thought so funny in the past. He had real people doing real things and yet it was hilarious.

"I knew I had a problem. The director who had complained to me obviously hadn't directed this excellent comedy. This was a style I'd never seen before, and I doubted if anyone else had. And it was quite obvious that the real director, Al, must be given complete control of the second film. If you don't believe in fate, I do. That very afternoon a piece of wood crashed from the top of the set and knocked the official director out cold. He had to be taken to hospital and by the time he returned, next day, the film was finished and I knew we had a new director with totally new ideas."

With Charles Christie handling the finances and Al Christie turning out one successful comedy after another, it wasn't surprising that the one existing trade paper at the time called Nestor Films "an advancement in our industry which must surely give heart to those doubters who think we will be gone and forgotten in less than a decade."

The Nestor studio flourished until the fall of 1911, when William Horsley announced his intention of moving "lock, stock, and barrel to California."

"We cannot waste another four months this winter in New York, with our cameras freezing and our actors suffering frostbite," said Horsley. "I shall take Al Christie and a small contingent of actors to the West Coast at the end of October." He added that his distribution office and accounting offices for his three companies would remain in New York.

Before leaving for California, Al Christie married actress Shirley Collins. She was added to the small party who boarded a westbound transcontinental train on October 20, 1911. Others in the group were William and Arthur Horsley and actress Dorothy Davenport. Davenport was later to become the wife of the first-known victim of director William Desmond Taylor's drug ring, actor Wallace Reid, who died from an overdose of cocaine in 1923 when he was only thirty-two.

This was the first time in their lives the Christie brothers had been separated for more than a month or two. "I was tempted to tell Bill Horsley that I was quitting and heading out west with Al," said Charles. "But he convinced me to hold on to the good-paying job I had. 'When it's time for you to join us in California, I'll tell you' he said."

The quintet that represented Nestor Films in California moved into the Blondeau Tavern on the corner of Sunset Avenue (now Boulevard) and Gower Streets in an area that later became the heart of Hollywood. Al Christie convinced the hotel owners to allow them use of the hotel gardens and their large unused back lot for location shooting.

"We made a lot of films on the streets of Los Angeles and in the surrounding mountains, especially the westerns," he said, "but we must have made close to fifty films just outside the hotel's back door. They charged us $30 a month and threw in the interior of the tavern, including the bedrooms. They even talked other guests into playing small parts, or standing around as extras, and it didn't cost us a cent."

Nestor Films, with their California settings, became so successful that Carl Laemmle, then head of Universal Films, convinced the Horsley brothers that a merger of the two companies would be profitable for both. "We had still maintained our distribution house in the east, but Universal had, from 1913, been distributing all our films to every other place in the world," said William Horsley. "The merger seemed good sense and put a lot of hard cash in the pockets of Arthur and myself.

"So we moved everything we had, and that probably was little more than a couple of cameras, over to the Universal lot. Al came with us but within weeks I could see he was unhappy being part of such a large outfit as Universal had grown to be. A month after our arrival at Universal in July 1915, he came to me and told me he had made a decision to form his own company. I wished him well and promised him any help he needed."

"I remember telling William that I had wired to New York for Charles to quit his job there and head out west to join me," said Al Christie. "I had no idea where we would set up shop, but the owner of the Blondeau solved that problem. We were still living there, of course. He told me he wanted to sell the tavern and grounds as he was retiring. I told him we only had a few thousand dollars, and for some amazing reason he accepted our offer of $3,000 as a down payment with $15,000 more to be paid over the next three years.

"When Charles arrived we closed the tavern down to outside guests and pooled our cash to buy the newest available camera. The Horsleys convinced Universal to do our distribution and William promised to do all our developing and printing in the film laboratory he had built two years after we arrived from New York. He even offered us the chance to defer all payments for six months, and he threw in film on the same basis, as much as we wanted.

"Universal agreed to release up to fifty one- and two-reel films for us in the first year and Carl Laemmle gave us an advance of $5,000 to help pay for the actors and the sets we would have to build. Originally, we planned to make as many westerns as comedies, but Charles convinced me that the audience enthusiasm for westerns was dropping, but there was no limit to the demand for comedy.

"So the Christie Film Company's name went up and the Blondeau Tavern sign came down. We announced our plans through the trade press, and Universal helped by promoting our films through flyers they sent out to every exhibitor. It was Universal's word that Christie Comedies were going to be the big thing in the coming year that gave us a wonderful boost.

"We needed actors, and we needed them fast. The Horsleys allowed us to use many of the people we had found in the four years before we became independent. Everyone was so helpful that the Christie Studio soon began to exist in bricks and mortar, no longer just a dream in our heads."

The Christie brothers didn't realize it at the time, but the studio they slowly enlarged over the years that followed 1915 was the first permanent studio to be erected in Hollywood. "All the earlier ones were in places like Glendale and other suburbs of Los Angeles," said Charles. "When Hollywood was given its name in 1903 by Daeida Hartell Wilcox, after she built a beautiful home in the centre of an orchard, it was nothing more

On the set, from left: Harry Edwards (actor), William Beaudine (director), Alice Lake (actress), and Al Christie (producer).

than a fifty-acre lot. Later it became a subdivision centred around Hollywood Boulevard and Wilcox Avenue. Hollywood was actually listed as a city when we arrived, and there were a number of studios built outside the city limits. Sunset Avenue was the official outer boundary of the city, and when we located at Sunset and Gower we were the very first studio inside the city limits.

"Where we were located later became the site of the Columbia Broadcasting System's radio studios. Before we left we had expanded our land holdings and stages to cover a full city block. When they finally pulled our studio down, Charles and I attended a ceremony at which they installed a plaque on the wall of the CBS building saying this was the location of the Christie Film Company, the first permanent studio in Hollywood."

"What a lot of people don't know," said Charles, "is that in 1916 the residents of the City of Hollywood decided they would be much better off being part of the fast-growing Los Angeles. And that's what it is today, just a sub-sector of Los Angeles. There is no such place as Hollywood any more."

"Our entire bankroll to start the Christie Film Company in 1915 was $6,000," said Al. "When we didn't have enough money to pay for all the actors we needed we moved them into the hotel building and let them sleep and eat there while they were working for us. A lot of them were delighted to get out of the dingy one-room apartments they were living in, and often we had trouble getting rid of them. We had a Chinese cook we inherited with the hotel, and he made magnificent meals at a cost so low we couldn't believe it could be done, but he did it. In the first year he was probably the main reason why we were able to stay in business. And when he wasn't cooking he became a regular actor in our films."

Immediately the Christie brothers started operating on their own, Al Christie produced the first silent films with dialogue printed along the bottom of the film that coincided with the words the actors spoke silently on screen.

"Until Al invented this system," said Charles, "film captions were totally separate from the story. There would be perhaps thirty seconds of action and then a full-screen caption with a few words that explained the progress of the plot. Doing it our way cost more and meant we had to have complete scripts ready for every film before shooting began. But it was new and audiences loved it."

The Christies persevered with their on-screen captions for more than a year before any other company followed suit. "What perhaps decided

Universal to copy us was the huge success of our films," said Al. "The *New York World* pushed every other company to copy us with an article that said 'Christie Films have made it possible for audiences to believe they are actually hearing the screen speak. After a while you can almost hear the voices of the actors in your head.' In effect, what we did is what is still being done today with foreign films brought to the United States. They are captioned over the picture in English just as ours were twenty-five years earlier."

The Christie studio gathered together a group of twenty-four comedians, foils for the comedians, and young and beautiful heroines to add romance, even if the romance was sometimes spoiled by the fair young lady receiving a pie in the face, or a bucket of water dampened the ardor of an overzealous swain.

Al Christie disputed Mack Sennett's claim to have thrown the first custard pie in the motion picture industry. "We were so far ahead of Mack that I still recall the day he dropped by our studio to ask what we were using as the content of the pies.

"I told him we had them made by the hundred and they cost ten cents each. They were filled, I explained, with egg white and enough flour to make them gooey. I even told him we bought them from a bakery just across the street from the studio. A few days later I walked across to the bakery to order more pies and was surprised to see hundreds of boxes, similar to ours, stacked in a corner. 'You got them ready even before I asked?' I said. 'No sir,' said the baker. 'Those are for Mr. Sennett.'"

Sennett snorted when told that Al Christie claimed to be the first custard pie thrower. "Rubbish," he said. "We were throwing them before he was in long pants. And we had the best thrower, Del Lord, the very best. Tell that to Al Christie."

Al Christie laughed when he was told about Sennett's reaction. "Actually, neither of us was first; they were using them in burlesque years before motion pictures were invented. My recipe, which Sennett stole, came from my mother. She made them for the comics at the Opera House in London. Her recipe went far and wide. I passed it on to the baker and he produced hundreds of mother's custard pies!"

But custard pies were not the big thing at the Christie Studio. "We were more concerned with story lines than sheer slapstick, and I don't think we would have been nearly so successful if we had tried to copy Sennett. He was the master of slapstick. He dressed his people up in odd-looking clothing that no normal person would be seen dead in outside the studio. We dressed ours in street clothes and gave them funny situations that were, in our eyes, much more acceptable to the more sophisticated audiences the theatres were drawing by 1920."

Included on the payroll of the Christie Film Studio between 1915 and 1928, when sound films were beginning to be heard, were comedians Bobby Vernon and Billy Dooley, both forgotten names today, but big favourites with silent film audiences for many years.

If Sennett had his Bathing Beauties, Christie Comedies had the likes of Vera Steadman and Molly Malone. Malone moved into radio in the 1930s and into television in the 1950s, constantly working until she died at the age of sixty-three. Dorothy Devore, considered by many to have been the most beautiful girl of the silent era, and Ann Pennington, the girl who created the famed Black Bottom dance in the late 1920s, were two more of their discoveries.

Pennington, who was born in 1894, died at the age of seventy-seven in Hollywood. She weathered more than a few scandals but kept working until she was in her sixties. She remembered the Christie brothers in a 1963 interview. "It was a crazy world. But it was fun. I threw a few custard pies myself, in fact I got quite clever and while they usually never showed the thrower, they used to show me. Looking at me now you'd never believe I was beautiful in those days, but I was. The Christies helped me out when I had problems and I've never forgotten them. When Charles died eight years ago I went to his funeral. There was nobody there from those old days, very few people of any kind. But it could be I didn't recognize any of my contemporaries. I'm sure they didn't recognize me.

"If those days could have gone on forever I would either have been dead at thirty or a big star today. Those Christie days were mostly happy days. Everyone in the studio knew, as I did, that if you had a problem you could go to either Charlie or Al. They got dozens of people out of scrapes. They were good boys, those Christies. And wonderful, talented filmmakers. Their ideas were way ahead of their time. But the stock market crash got them, as it did lots of us. I don't regret one minute of my life, and I'll bet they didn't regret one minute of theirs."

In 1919 Charles Christie started a sideline that paid dividends for more than a decade. "By 1919 the use of cars in films was becoming the big thing," he recalled. "There were more real chases, accidents, and speedsters to fascinate filmgoers. It seemed like the boys coming back from the war wanted to do everything twice as fast as they did before.

"At the studios we found getting the older cars for comedy films was more and more difficult. Most were on the scrap heap or had been wrecked during filming. So I formed a company, Christie Cars, Inc., and hired a first-class mechanic to refurbish all the wrecks I could buy. Very soon I had two garages working round the clock on restoration and hundreds more cars sitting under little weather shelters in a five-acre lot behind the garage.

"Everyone thought I was completely crazy until they tried to find the cars they needed for their pictures. I had everything from Model T's to Cadillacs in my collection, and before I knew it every studio in California was lining up to rent them from me.

"I soon had an office staff dealing with queries, and a number of drivers, actually actors who knew how to drive but didn't get much action in the studios, who were on call to deliver the cars wherever they were wanted. I had days when I would have more than 200 cars rented out to different studios. Some of my drivers became the first stunt men in the industry. They doubled for just about every star in the industry. I even had to hire two female drivers just to double for the big women stars who didn't want to get injured.

"My stunt drivers soon became a separate business. I kept both companies going until 1929, when they began taking up far too much of my time. I sold the stunt business to two of my drivers and the car supply company to three of my mechanics. Under new names, both of them were still operating in the late 1940s."

Among the special memories of the brothers was their sound film version of *Charley's Aunt*. Made in 1930, it was the first of many versions that followed over the years. "We starred Syd Chaplin, Charlie's brother, and Charlie Ruggles in the film, and it was a great hit in the theatres," said Al. "Reviewers were suddenly calling Syd the next big comedy star. We kept the two actors together for five more films, all big box-office hits. We wanted to keep Syd for more films, because I felt we had discovered the talent that Sennett had missed. But it wasn't to be. Syd was disillusioned by his treatment at Keystone and when his brother offered him a full-time job as his financial manager, Syd said goodbye to acting forever. Now we will never know if he could have been as good as brother Charlie in his own way."

Many of the performers who made Christie Films famous between 1915 and 1928 are forgotten today. Some, like Julian Eltinge, probably the greatest female impersonator the industry has ever known, is not even mentioned in such superb reference books as Ephraim Katz's *The Film*

Encyclopedia, and receives a scant five lines in Evelyn Mack Truitt's *Who Was Who on the Screen*.

Others gone and forgotten, as far as most histories of early Hollywood are concerned, include Viora Daniel, one of Hollywood's loveliest and most competent actresses; Jack Duffy, a great comedian whose career was cut short by cancer; and Natalie Joyce, a young performer who gave up her rising star to become the wife of the boy she left behind at home. No records show if she lived happily ever after.

Josephine Hull, born in 1884, became the leading lady in early Christie films, moving into the sound era with a voice that matched her beauty. But she is perhaps best remembered for her Oscar-winning performance with James Stewart in the comedy, *Harvey*, which is still shown on television today.

In 1943 she had decided her film career was over. "I'm happy now with my memories," she said. "The Christie days were my best days. We had fun making pictures then. I made my last one in 1942. Really, I much preferred the stage. I was a star on Broadway when I was sixteen, did you know that?"

Producers decided Josephine Hull should not remain retired. She gave a glorious performance in 1944 in *Arsenic and Old Lace*. She told the *Hollywood Citizen-News* that "Al Christie coached me for that part as I felt I was out of touch and needed help. Al made my performance unique."

In 1950 she was again coaxed out of retirement by Jimmy Stewart to play in *Harvey*. In 1980 he recalled the performance that won her an Oscar. "I had seen her in *Arsenic*," he said. "But we had to find her before we could sign her for *Harvey*. It was Al Christie who located her, and he was there on the set every day coaching each line she spoke. Maybe that should have been a double Oscar in 1950, one for Josephine and one for Al as coach."

The Christie Film Company became so successful that it had its own fan mail department long before such departments were invented. "We had as many as ten secretaries typing answers to letters eight hours a day, six days a week, and often there was lots of overtime work. They were trained to pick out items from letters and make that the focal point of the reply to that individual fan.

"Each one of our regular stars had notepaper specially printed. I remember Helen Darling demanded that hers be scented with lilac. Then once a week the actors and actresses spent several hours signing the letters personally.

"Sennett let other people sign his studio replies, even photographs, but we never allowed that. The stars took stacks of photographs home with them and brought them back autographed. Would you believe that we actually sent out 8 x 10 glossy pictures to the fans? It cost us a lot but it was worth every penny."

The Christie fan mail department also spawned the publication of a monthly magazine, *Film Follies*. It was written by a staff of scriptwriters who were waiting around the studio for a new assignment.

The magazine developed from an initial eight pages to sixteen pages before it ended a twelve-year run in 1929. "We sent a copy out with every photograph and letter, and in the bigger cities it was sold in the theatres, at the candy desk, for five cents at first, but that had risen to ten cents by 1929," recalled Charles. "Each edition was printed in two colors on quality paper. We didn't make any money on it, but we gained thousands of regular readers and I'm sure it drew many more thousands, perhaps millions, to see our films. No other studio ever followed our lead."

The Christies claimed to have a lion as their studio's mascot long before Louis B. Mayer put his lion on screen to open every MGM film. "We originally had a friendly lion in the studio for use in dozens of films, and he became so well known we decided to adopt him as our mascot," said Al. "Everyone loved him and he walked around the sets when and where he wanted.

"He was a placid old cat and when he died suddenly, from what we later learned was eating poisoned meat, the entire studio was heartbroken. If we could have found out who poisoned him we would have lynched him, or her, on the spot." He laughed, and added, "With the cameras rolling, of course!"

In 1919 the Christies decided to break with Universal and go to Educational Films for distribution. "Universal was getting so big that only their own films got top promotion. We felt Educational, a much smaller company, would suit our style of pictures better and we were right, we stayed with them for twelve years," said Charles. "Of course we remained with the Horsleys for all our printing and developing. They had built a huge laboratory right next to our studio on Sunset and by 1920 they were serving most of the independent producers with superb work. William's son, known as William C., had joined the company after years of training and ran the technical side of the operation better than anyone else in the industry."

In the late 1920s the Christies purchased the former Metropolitan Studio on North Las Palmas Avenue to supply the space needed to handle their ever-increasing production load. When it became apparent that sound was going to be the big thing in the industry, they spent more than half-a-million dollars soundproofing all the stages at both studios.

"We were still number one with our silent comedies," said Al Christie. "By 1928 we had reached a level of sophistication that the other studios had difficulty equalling or copying.

"We were ready when sound equipment became available, and received considerable help from Douglas Shearer who was then working at MGM. We had known him for several years and he had earlier shared some of his lighting inventions with us.

"He asked if we wanted to try something that MGM had turned down, and because we knew how clever he was, we said 'yes.' So we were up and running with good quality sound almost as fast as Warners, MGM, and Universal. You have to remember that they were the giants of the industry, producing all kinds of films, and although we were small and specialized we more than held our own in the marketplace."

The Christies' first sound film, shot on the stages of the old Metropolitan Studio, was *Dangerous Females*, a comedy starring Marie Dressler and Polly Moran. "The other studios were looking to make an impact with sound through spectacle and musicals, but we were the only studio to concentrate exclusively on comedy," said Charles. "*Dangerous Females* was such a success that we had thousands of letters asking for more of the same with the same stars. So we produced the first series of sound comedies featuring two females in the lead roles. We made seven films in the series and were repaid handsomely at the box office."

The duo produced more than fifty full-length sound features in their two studios in 1929 before they really felt the effects of the 1929 stock market crash.

"Suddenly it was cash on the line for everything. And cash we didn't have," recalled Charles. "We had overreached ourselves buying the Metropolitan Studio and other real estate and when land prices dropped to zero we were left with bank loans to pay on property that was virtually worthless. Nobody was buying anything, at least at prices we could afford to accept. The bank wanted its money, and we hadn't got it. We continued making as many films as we could. The Depression brought millions to the theatres. Our comedy films were in terrific demand. But even more in demand from the banks was the money we hadn't got."

"We struggled through to 1932 and introduced people like Jack Benny, Milton Berle, Lucille Ball, and Bob Hope to movie audiences for the first time," said Al Christie. "Charles was so good at accounting that he could tell me from day to day where we stood. On February 1, 1932, he told me that if we sold all our assets we could just pay our creditors, so we decided to call our attorney, Paul Lowenthal, to convene a meeting of all our creditors.

"We made an assignment of everything we owned to the three companies, Christie Films, Metropolitan Sound Studios, and the Christie Realty Company, which held the deeds to most of the properties we had bought. Charles presented his financial statement to the meeting. It showed that our debts were $2.5 million dollars and our assets were slightly in excess of that figure. That, of course, depended on our being able to sell, in the still-depressed markets, those assets.

"The creditors agreed to be patient in view of our assignment of our personal property, which included both our houses. Charles had never married, and I had been divorced from my wife, Shirley, for quite a number of years, and had no children, so we had no concerns in that direction. We continued to make films over the eight months it took us to liquidate our assets. We ended up about $70,000 short of paying all our creditors. The Horsley brothers came to our rescue. 'Don't bother about us,' said Arthur. 'We don't need money. Pay everyone else then pay us whenever you can.'"

It is interesting to note that the Christies' Metropolitan Studio still stands at 1040 North Las Palmas Avenue. Today it is known as the Hollywood Center Studios, and some of the tenants have included Jeopardy and comedies like Empty Nest, Wings, and the John Larroquette Show. They still use the same sound stages that the Christies put together so well more than seventy years ago.

When all the creditors were paid, Al decided to go east to the city in which his career started, New York. Charles decided, after his experience in selling the company's assets, to go into real estate sales. In New York Al lived for several months in a small apartment that had no heating. In Hollywood, with somewhat better weather to help the situation, Charles lived in similar circumstances. "Al bet me," said Charles, "that he'd be in a first class house of his own before I could buy mine. I beat him by three months. I suddenly realized I was a great real estate salesman, and commissions came in at a tremendous rate. Because Al and I had paid all our debts honourably, and never did go bankrupt, as the papers at one time suggested, I was able to go to a bank and get a loan on a beautiful home in less than three months. Al had to wait a little longer, but he was back in production in New York within days of arriving there."

A 1932 article by Marguerite Tazelaar in a New York newspaper had the headline, "Queens Lot Ready for Comedy Under Pioneer of Pie-Throwing." It told how the film studios located in the Borough of Queens had thrown open their doors for Al Christie's return to New York.

It continued: "Christie has received the backing of the Atlas Corporation and the Guaranty Trust Company to make a series of independent feature films to cost $250,000 each. The first is to be Frank Adam's *Fathers of Madelon*, which was published earlier this year to great acclaim in *Red Book Magazine*. The rights to the story belong to Bernard J. Steele, president of Odesco Productions, Inc. Mr. Steele bought the story especially for Al Christie, whose comedic talents he believes are unequalled."

Over the next nine years Al Christie made thirty-two profitable sound films in New York. He refused to vary from his intention to make comedy the base of all his productions. "But I didn't make a great deal of money," he recalled. "Someone else did! Working for other people isn't like working for yourself. You don't keep the profits. I did well enough to buy a penthouse apartment, but something important was missing from my life."

That something was Charles Christie. In 1941, Al made a decision to return to California and get right out of the motion picture industry. "It was too big, too impersonal by the early 1940s. Money men were running the industry. Creative people were slowly but surely taking second place. I had no idea what I wanted to do, but I knew I could earn a living somehow."

By 1941 Charles Christie was living in a beautiful home at 460 South Bedford Drive in Beverly Hills. Now a top real estate broker, he had prospered in his new profession and proudly claimed to have sold Lucille Ball, Jack Benny, and other big stars their first Beverly Hills homes. He had three servants to look after his needs — a gardener who maintained the grounds, a housekeeper, and a butler, the latter an actor who came in each evening to serve dinner.

He welcomed Al back from New York and opened his home to the man with whom he had shared thirty years of his life in the film industry.

Al found work within a week. "A friend told me that morale at the huge Douglas Aircraft Company plant in Santa Monica was at an all-time low and production was suffering," he said. "It took me twenty-four hours to decide to drive to the plant and offer my services at minimum wage. I had no difficulty getting in to see the company heads, apparently my name still meant something in the industry, and when I laid my proposal on the table I was hired on the spot."

Al Christie's idea was based on Douglas putting him in charge of plant entertainment. "Not the usual kind where volunteers are found among the employees and made to look like idiots singing and dancing before their fellow workers," he said. "I told them I could deliver the biggest names in Hollywood to give daily lunch-time concerts for the workers, and at no cost to the company. When I named people like Bob Hope they were delighted. Now I hadn't asked Hope, or anyone else if they would do the shows, but I believed I knew enough about them to know this was something they wouldn't turn down. Although I'd been out of Hollywood for nine years I still had enough friends to get me the unlisted telephone numbers of the top stars. And in days I had set up a roster of entertainment that set my heart thumping and the workers at Douglas cheering."

Among the stars who appeared for Al Christie at the Santa Monica plant over the next few years were Bing Crosby, Bob Hope, Jerry Colonna, Dorothy Lamour, Lucille Ball, Milton Berle, Betty Hutton, and Gracie Fields, visiting from England. Hope made more than a dozen appearances in three years. Actors like Jimmy Stewart and Robert Taylor, who couldn't sing or dance, went to the plant to have lunch with the workers and sign autographs. Big bands like Glenn Miller, Jimmy and Tommy Dorsey, Duke Ellington, Les Brown, Cab Calloway, and Louis Armstrong appeared as often as their schedules allowed. Fred Astaire and Ginger Rogers danced for, and with, the workers.

"Every Monday and Friday we had a show," said Al. "Absenteeism that had always been at its peak on those two days dropped to near zero. The company had ten professional musicians on call to play for singers like Dinah Shore and Dick Haymes. It was such an incredible success that other plants tried to copy the idea, but, though I say it myself, nobody else was able to get the stars I took each week to Santa Monica."

When the war ended Al retired to the South Bedford Drive home. Charles continued to sell houses in Beverly Hills until 1950. Al didn't work again. Both brothers gave much of their time during World War Two to provide entertainment for servicemen and women in their home, running them back and forth to the film studios which always welcomed the Christies and their uniformed guests.

On April 14, 1951, Al Christie died at the age of sixty-five. He suffered a heart attack at home and though he was rushed to hospital immediately he died in the ambulance. There was no service; he had much earlier requested that his body be given to medical science.

On May 1, 1951, the *Los Angeles Times* reported that a petition for letters of administration had been filed in Superior Court. The petitioner was Charles Christie. He informed the court that the man who made millions for himself and others three decades earlier had left only $2,597. "Of this," said Charles, "there is $1,697 in cash and other personal property that had been valued at $900. No will has been found." He declared himself to be the sole heir as the last surviving member of the Christie family.

Four years later, on October 1, 1955, Charles Christie died at his beautiful Beverly Hills home at the age of seventy-three. And so ended a dynasty that had given the world of entertainment more than thirty years of laughter. His funeral service, held at the Hollywood Cemetery, where he was buried, was attended by a handful of the old-time stars who remembered the days of glory at the Christie Film Studio. There is no record of their names since no newspaper reporter considered the occasion important enough to be covered. His grave is marked with a simple plaque offering no more information than his name and dates of birth and death. The plaque commemorating the site of the first Christie studio in Hollywood is twice as large.

Charles Christie left a considerable amount of money, said to be in excess of a quarter of a million dollars, his home and all its contents, to the housekeeper who, he said in a one-page will, had "stood by me for more than thirty years, through good times and bad. I wish her to have everything of which I die possessed and hope she may continue to enjoy good health for many years to come." Unhappily, that was not to be. She died in a car accident only three months later.

JOE AND
SAM DE GRASSE

"Joe and Sam De Grasse are two of the most talented personalities in today's film industry. Joe, a very skilled actor, is also the consummate director, firm in his demands yet gentle in his ways of dealing with many different temperaments to be found in the motion picture industry. Sam is the only actor I know who can horrify an audience without make-up and without grotesque posturing and playing to the camera. He is also the only actor I know who pulls teeth on the set in between takes. A rare pair, they have given the industry not one but two new dimensions."

(Lon Chaney, Sr., 1924)

On May 4, 1873, when Joseph Louis De Grasse was born in Bathurst, a small community in northern New Brunswick, and two years later, on June 12, 1875, when his brother, Samuel Alfred De Grasse arrived, and had his birth registered in the same town, the motion picture industry was still a dream in the minds of pioneers like Thomas Edison.

The wooden shipbuilding industry, in which the boys' father worked, was slowly dying, and the De Grasse family, although they loved the simple life of the small town in New Brunswick, decided if there was to be a future for their children it was not to be in Canada.

They heard from friends who had already moved south that steamship building in New England was a fast-growing industry, and that Boston was a city that badly needed experienced shipbuilders.

Despite their French-sounding name, the De Grasse family, three generations earlier, had arrived in Canada not from France, but England.

But when Joe and Sam's parents, Ellen and Lange De Grasse, moved the family to Boston in 1882, they had no idea they were taking their children into a dream world not yet invented.

Little is known about the early years of the De Grasse family in Boston. But in 1886, the *Boston Globe* told of a "remarkable feat of heroism by thirteen-year-old Joseph De Grasse, who risked his life by diving into Boston Harbor to rescue a five-year-old girl, Jessie Tinkerman, who had fallen and vanished under water." The gold medal Joe received for his courage was found in his home when he died more than five decades later.

In 1943, Sam talked about his family. "Dad was a metalworker in the Boston shipyards," he said. "He was a hard worker, and even when times were tough he was never out of a job. Mother worked as a day maid at the home of Eben Jordan, who later founded the Jordan-Marsh department store chain. She was happy there. The Jordans were considerate employers who treated their house staff well."

Joe, who had turned out to be a wizard with figures, didn't protest when his parents enrolled him in a special school to learn accountancy. In turn, they didn't object when he spent his evenings at local theatres. He helped build scenery, painted sets, and — occasionally — graduated to playing large and small roles in plays ranging from Shakespeare to melodrama.

Sam, with no theatrical ambitions, entered the Boston Dental College from which he graduated as an honours student. For five years he practiced dentistry with surgeries in Boston and nearby Providence, Rhode Island.

Joe, a first-class graduate in his accountancy courses, was to find this training very valuable in the years ahead. But by 1903, when he was thirty, he had abandoned his full-time job as a bookkeeper with the City of Boston and was earning a good living as an actor.

His first real break came in 1905 when Ernest and Fred Shipman arrived in Boston with the cast of their new play, *Cavalier of France*. Their scheduled final week's rehearsal before the play's opening was halted two days before the first night when the leading man had a heart attack and was rushed to hospital.

Local theatre producers suggested Joe's name to the Shipman brothers as a possible replacement. Joe accepted the challenge and in only two days had mastered the script and was ready to face the opening night audience.

Sam never forgot that evening. "All the family and as many friends as we could round up were in the audience. We all believed in Joe but we kept our fingers crossed just the same."

They needn't have worried. The night was a triumph for Joe De Grasse. At the final curtain he received a standing ovation that was, said Sam, "at least five minutes in length." Next day's newspaper reviews called his performance a "triumph," "the debut of a giant," and "the local boy who has earned his right to centre stage."

When the play moved out of Boston, Joe De Grasse went with it. For ten months he starred in the touring show. Shipman plays were staged in first-run theatres in the larger cities of the United States. "As the star, Joe stayed in good hotels and was received by the big-wigs of each community," said Sam. "I remember him writing to tell us of the grand houses he visited, and of the important people he met, including President Theodore Roosevelt."

In Milwaukee, Caleb Johnson, head of the B. W. Johnson Soap Company, selected him to be the first member of the public to test and comment on Palmolive soap, the company's latest product. "A wonderful feeling of total cleanliness," said Joe in the newspaper advertisement caption that ran alongside his face looking in a mirror, removing his make-up after a show with, of course, the new soap prominently displayed.

In Chicago, he took part in a promotion to introduce the first issue of the Spiegel Mail-order Catalogue. His picture was on the front page of a Chicago newspaper, studying the catalogue, together with the mayor of Chicago and the president of the Spiegel Company. "He sent us the very first copy issued," said Sam. "Can you imagine, they were offering top quality furniture for seventy-five cents down and fifty cents a month! Joe presented the catalogue to a museum in Chicago in 1935, and as far as I know it is still there today."

Late in 1906, Joe De Grasse and the cast of *Cavalier of France* arrived in Los Angeles. The company was scheduled to play for two weeks at the Grand Opera House, but audience approval demanded the play remain for a third week.

In a letter to his parents, Joe talked of the "royal reception" he received in Los Angeles. "The Shipman brothers were publicity mad," he said. "As my success grew on tour so did my 'theatrical background' in the eyes of the Shipmans. One press release said I had appeared on Broadway, both as an actor and director, and that I had appeared for a successful season playing Shakespeare in London, England. It was all rubbish, but people lapped it up and the ovation I received on my first entrance was overwhelming, but totally unearned in reality."

Before the end of the play's second week at the Grand Opera House Joe De Grasse had been offered the position as resident director and performer in a stock company due to open at the Grand in three weeks. He accepted and signed a six-month contract at the princely salary of $150 a week, far in excess of anything he had ever dreamed of earning.

"He was hired without ever having directed a play in his life," said Sam. "But he didn't let the company down. He chose all the plays, which ranged from melodrama to comedy and audiences packed the theatre every night."

Six months later the people of Los Angeles and the drama critics were still applauding Joe De Grasse. A *Los Angeles Times* story of April 15, 1907, said: "Joseph De Grasse has, to the delight of theatre-goers and performers, accepted a new offer from management at a salary greatly in excess of that paid to him for his remarkable creative talents to date. Mr. De Grasse will stay a further six months at the Grand Opera House."

The story continued: "His long and extensive classical training has proved invaluable to the other members of the company who have had the excellent fortune to learn from his skilled mind. A few of the laggards in the company have greatly benefited by his total control of each production."

In June 1907, the *Los Angeles Times* theatre critic had this to say: "This non-artistic play, notwithstanding awfully silly dialogue, was enhanced and made very acceptable by the outstanding acting of Mr. Joseph De Grasse in the lead role and by his intelligent direction of the other actors. A poor play, but a resounding success, thanks to Mr. De Grasse."

In September of that year, Joe made a decision to make California his permanent home. "I have become very enthusiastic about the future of the motion picture industry," he told the *Los Angeles Times* in an interview. "I am spending most of my days at the studios watching and learning. By the end of the year I expect to make my debut as a film actor."

In November, he did make his debut at the Pathé Studio, but not as an actor. One of Pathé's resident directors was so enthused with the way De Grasse handled his actors at the Grand Opera House that he convinced the company to put Joe under contract as a film director.

Joe decided against cutting his ties with live theatre, agreeing to direct one out of every three of the stock company's productions. He later told the *Los Angeles Times* that he did this to further the career of Florence Barker, a seventeen-year-old actress he had introduced to the company a few months earlier. When she was not needed at the theatre, Florence accompanied him to the Pathé Studios and in a very short time was offered — with perhaps a little pressure from De Grasse — small acting roles.

Joe and Florence had by now moved into a home Joe had purchased on Wilcox Avenue in Hollywood. "Can you imagine the shock mother and dad had when we received a letter telling us this?" said Sam in 1943. "Things like that weren't done in 1907, at least not in Boston."

Joe's enthusiastic letters home helped make a big change in Sam's career. That same year he, too, resolved to head to California. "I figured even actors needed a dentist, perhaps more than ordinary people," he told the *Los Angeles Times* some years later. "I was tired of the cold winters in the east, so I sold my dental practices and bought a first-class ticket on the fastest train I could find that was heading for California. With me went as much of my dental equipment as I could pack in a large suitcase."

By the time Sam reached Los Angeles in 1908, Joe was well established and well respected in the motion picture industry. He had appeared in half-a-dozen films and directed two dozen more. Two days after Sam's arrival, Joe took him along to the Pathé Studio where he was working. "I was wandering around when a man I later discovered was a director came up to me and looked me over like I was a piece of meat on a slab. 'Are you on call for anyone?' he asked. 'Not so far as I know,' I replied. 'Then stand over there with those five fellas and when I shout 'go' you charge into the bank waving your gun. Pick one up from that table.' It all seemed a lot of fun so I did what I was told. And that's how I entered the movies."

Sam lined up with the other extras at the end of the day and received eight dollars for his debut. "I used it to take Joe and Florence out to dinner," he said. "When we got home there was a hand-delivered message waiting for me in the mailbox asking me to return next morning for more work. Well, that was it. I was hooked. If getting work in the movies was this easy I figured my days as a dentist were over."

A few weeks later Sam moved out of Joe's Wilcox Avenue home. "I was well set financially from the sale of my dental offices in the east and suddenly I had all the acting roles I could handle. I was making more money doing a job for which I had no qualifications than I had earned from years of dentistry experience in Boston. So I moved into a first-class apartment nearby."

For four years the De Grasse brothers worked steadily in the ever-growing number of Hollywood studios. Sam, who decided directing was of no interest, concentrated on tough guy roles and was so much in demand that on numerous occasions he worked in two different films, at different studios, in one day. "The good old Ford Model T I had purchased was the secret," he recalled. "Few actors had cars and I was able to get around so easily that some of the companies paid me not only to act but to transport other actors to locations miles out of town. My car became so well known that on one occasion I recall being asked to sign a contract made out to Sam Ford!"

Joe's fame grew rapidly as studios realized they had a real director on their hands. In 1928, he told the *Los Angeles Times* that "most directors were just actors who had made the transition by watching others direct. My stage experience gave me the knowledge I needed to create scenes artistically. I worked on scenes at home every night and when I arrived at the studio next morning I knew exactly where each actor was going to stand and what he or she was going to do."

Florence Barker's career had skyrocketed under the guidance of Joe De Grasse, and it was not long before she was billed as the star of the films she made. Joe coached her for every scene. In five years, she made twenty-nine films, sixteen of which Joe directed. "By 1912 her fan mail had grown so large that it took Joe, Florence, and myself several hours each weekend just sending out autographed photographs in answer to the letters," recalled Sam.

Christmas 1912 was a memorable one for the De Grasse family. The brothers had convinced their parents that they should visit California for the festive season. In October Joe and Sam sent them first-class rail tickets to Los Angeles. Two days before Christmas the family was reunited.

"It was a wonderful time," recalled Sam. "Our parents could see we were doing well. By then I had bought a house close to Joe and we both had new, quite expensive, cars. We had made friends among the elite of the film industry, and I'll never forget the look on my mother's face when Mary Pickford, her sister Lottie, and brother Jack came over to see us on Christmas eve. They knew our parents were coming from Boston and they brought them special Christmas gifts.

"And they were even more impressed when Mary waved a contract under our noses that she had signed that day with Adolph Zukor's Famous Players company. It was for $700 a week. We all found it difficult to believe that anyone could earn that sort of money. The only blot on that otherwise perfect evening was Jack Pickford. At sixteen he was already drinking heavily and was becoming a problem for Mary. He drank far too much, and long before the evening was over he had to be carried out to their car where he slept until they were ready to go home."

The year 1912 ended on a high note, but 1913 soon became one the De Grasse brothers would have liked to miss. On January 13, still in California enjoying the sunshine, Ellen De Grasse had a heart attack and died before she could reach the hospital.

More tragedy followed. On February 13, Florence Barker, who had been working at the studio against doctor's orders, determined to finish the final day of shooting, collapsed and was taken to hospital. Diagnosed with pneumonia, she died within a few hours of being admitted. Ironically, the film she had managed to complete was called *A Dreamland Tragedy*.

Worse was to come! On June 13, Joe's house burned to the ground. Ignited by flames from a neighbour's home torched by an arsonist, it was totally destroyed within an hour. "Joe must have had a premonition that something like this was going to happen. On the morning of the fire, for no apparent reason, he took with him to the studio a small suitcase in which he kept souvenirs like the gold medal from Boston," recalled Sam.

On July 13, Lange De Grasse, who had decided to stay permanently with his sons in Hollywood, was killed when he was struck by lightning in a freak electrical storm.

It was from that day on that the De Grasse brothers insisted on a new clause in all their film contracts. The clause stipulated that they would never be called on to work on the thirteenth day of any month.

In 1943, Sam recalled their feeling in 1913. "For at least a couple of years we awaited the thirteenth of each month with more than a little fear," he said. "We called each other several times on each thirteenth to see if everything was O.K. It may sound paranoid but there was real fear each time the thirteenth came around."

But good fortune returned early in 1914. The brothers discovered that their parents had invested the support money they had sent east each month in what at the time appeared to be a rather dubious gold mine. "The doubts vanished when we received a telegram saying the miners struck gold," recalled Sam. "For the next eight years, until the mine petered out, we received sizeable royalties every six months. By 1919 we were both wealthy men."

Joe De Grasse, with his accountancy training, had always been accepted as the financial expert of the family. "I entrusted all my financial affairs to him and he invested large sums in California property," said Sam. "When I decided to retire in 1930 I had more money and more sound investments than I knew what to do with."

The De Grasse brothers at one time owned the land along Summit Drive in Beverly Hills on which Mary Pickford and Douglas Fairbanks, Sr., built their dream home, Pickfair, and the vast area further down Summit Drive on which Charlie Chaplin built his sprawling mountain-side home.

Joe stayed with Pathé for several years, becoming one of the company's top directors. Sam moved from studio to studio, accepting as many of the roles offered as possible. He had contracts with Pathé, Amex, Majestic, Reliance, and Fine Arts. "I could have worked twenty-four hours a day if I had wanted, but since money wasn't the driving force I simply picked the parts that appealed to me. By 1913 I was playing nothing that wasn't a principal role."

Joe decided directing was not enough for him. Frustrated by some of the untrained actors he had to control, he started accepting acting roles in western films. His abilities as a rider soon earned him the title "The Pathé Bandit" and the studio sent out hundreds of publicity pictures to newspapers with him astride a bucking horse. "He looked strangely like The Lone Ranger, who arrived many years later," recalled Sam.

"For some time he considered abandoning directing and making a career playing masked bandits holding up stagecoaches. In fact, I wondered more than once whether he would have enjoyed being a real bandit, had he been born a few years earlier," said Sam. "Audiences loved the way he treated the ladies so gallantly when he held up the coaches, that he became almost a folk hero. So much so that some women's organizations, who felt idolizing a bandit as a hero was not the American way of life, marched around the theatres where his films were playing, trying to stop people from entering. The attempted boycott only made him more popular than ever."

Late in 1913 when the great silent director D. W. Griffith left Biograph, he selected Sam to be a member of his new acting company. "I knew I would make less money with Griffith than I could working independently," recalled Sam, "but one didn't turn down an invitation from Griffith. My contract left me the freedom to work elsewhere when Griffith didn't need me, yet I was on full salary all year long."

In 1913 Joe was once again in the headlines. A story supposedly written from interviews with him was printed in the *Atlanta Daily Journal*. He was quoted as saying: "I love horses, but wild horses would never drag me back to the east, particularly New York City. I don't ever want to see dirty old New York again." The remarks were repeated in papers coast-to-coast and editorials in New York newspapers demanded that exhibitors not show any more of his films. Once again the boycotts backfired. Despite picketing, there were line-ups to see his films in the city. Sam believed the initial story was planted by the studio and was designed to do exactly what it did — stir up trouble. "As far as I know, Joe had never been to New York City," he said.

Later that same year Joe, then working at Triangle Studios, asked Sam to meet him there. "He wanted me to meet Douglas Fairbanks," he recalled. The meeting set in motion a series of events that shaped Sam's career for his next twenty-two years in the film industry, until his retirement in 1935 at the age of sixty.

"Fairbanks thought it would be a great publicity stunt having two brothers fighting each other on opposite sides in his new film, *The Half Breed*," said Sam. "It was the first time we had acted together in the same film and Fairbanks was right, it got lots of newspaper space."

But it was not his acting that earned Sam a lifetime contract with Fairbanks. "I'll never forget the second morning on the set when Fairbanks was writhing around in pain with toothache," he said. "We were all set to abandon shooting while he went to the dentist when I had an idea. 'Doug,' I said, 'I do a little dentistry for my friends in the industry and have all my equipment in the back of my car. I can probably fix your tooth so we won't have to lose a day's work.' Fairbanks looked amazed. 'You think I'd trust my aching (that wasn't his word) tooth to an actor? You're crazy, let's close up shop so I can get to a dentist.' I finally convinced him that I was a fully qualified dentist and reluctantly he agreed, probably thinking of the salaries he would have to pay to the actors and crew if he cancelled the day's filming."

Sam and Fairbanks retired to the actor's dressing room where Sam set up his equipment. "Well, I'd never seen so many bad teeth or such shoddy dental work in my life," he recalled. "It was difficult to know which tooth to work on to stop the pain. Finally I settled on three teeth and filled them while he made terrible sounds of agony. It took me thirty minutes before I told him to wash out his mouth and see how it felt. I've never seen such a look of gratitude on any man's face before or after. He slapped me on the back and I recall clearly his remark: 'So I bought myself an actor and a dentist,' he said. 'I'll put you under personal, permanent contract. Name your price.'"

Fairbanks and Sam De Grasse agreed on a price. Fairbanks's lawyer was shooed away when he tried to tell Fairbanks he was offering too much. "No price is too high to pay for the disappearance of pain in my mouth," he said. The duo agreed on a long-term contract. Sam was to appear in all the Fairbanks films from then on and was to be available at any hour of the night or day — except on the thirteenth day of any month — to ensure the Fairbanks smile never faded. Griffith was consulted and both agreed to the new contract.

"As far as I know I was the only actor in Hollywood who was being paid year round by two different companies. Fairbanks obviously had the power to dictate because his contract, and an amended one with Griffith, gave him first call on me as a dentist while Griffith retained first call on my services as an actor. Fortunately we never did have to find out what would happen if both needed me at the same time for their individual priorities.

"Within a few months I had every tooth fixed and capped," recalled Sam. "The famed Fairbanks smile had never been more prominent. I never did find out who his previous dentist was, but I doubt very much if he ever had any training. Fairbanks's mouth was a mess. He even had me build a small dental surgery, complete with chair and the latest equipment, in the basement of the home, Pickfair, he shared with Mary Pickford. He had a western saloon downstairs and while Mary was away making personal appearances he had part of one wall taken out and the secret dentist's alcove built in behind. It wasn't until this year [1943] that Mary knew it existed. It was hidden when the original wall was replaced and could only be opened by a person with a key, and that meant Fairbanks and myself. The keyhole was hidden behind a moveable wooden beam. Whenever he needed a check-up we went down to the saloon, and locked ourselves in. I would spend an hour checking and rechecking the teeth but only occasionally did we have any problems from then on."

Since Fairbanks only worked for three or four months out of every year, Sam had ample time to take other acting roles he was offered. In 1913 he appeared in fifteen films directed by D. W. Griffith, and three with Douglas Fairbanks.

In 1916 Griffith told the *Motion Picture Herald* that Sam De Grasse was "so thoroughly experienced as a stage actor and so well trained by the best directors on Broadway, that I found him so easy to direct. I used him principally as the 'bad man' because, without the benefit of make-up, he was able to convince playgoers that he was really evil." He added: "In reality, Mr. De Grasse is a charming gentleman with impeccable manners, showing courtesy on the set at all times to everyone." The latter part of his statement is true. The first part was a figment of Griffith's imagination. Sam De Grasse never had any dramatic training.

Thanks to Griffith's statement, studio publicists sent out dozens of press releases extolling Sam's "Broadway experience." New York directors, when asked for quotes, agreed with Griffith that De Grasse was a competent actor who had blossomed under their tuition. Asked many years later why he had told the press that De Grasse had been in his stage company when, in fact, they had never met, producer-director David Belasco said: "If he was that good why should I deny myself a part in his success."

Sam De Grasse had many memories of both Griffith and Fairbanks. "I recall perhaps most vividly playing the role of Senator Charles Sumner in Griffith's *The Birth of a Nation* in 1914. It made my name into a household word across the country. And it made stars of many performers like Lillian Gish, Mae Marsh, and Wallace Reid. It was the first time I had been involved with a director who shot scenes with more than one camera at the same time. Despite all his careful rehearsing, there is one battlefield scene in *Birth of a Nation* in which you can clearly see the second cameraman cranking away in the background.

"Working with Griffith was working with a perfectionist. We were not allowed to improvise our own dialogue, despite the fact that there were no

Sam De Grasse as Senator Charles Sumner in D.W. Griffith's *Birth of a Nation* (1915), with Miriam Cooper and Jennie Lee (left, rear).

microphones to pick up the words we spoke. We had scripts and had to stick to them. Perhaps that is why so many of Griffith's films are still considered masterpieces. And, of course, he was fortunate to have the incomparable Billy Bitzer as his master cameraman. It is interesting to note than any Griffith films without Bitzer lacked the technical skills that Bitzer provided."

It was Griffith who made a comment that led to the only confrontation between Sam and Douglas Fairbanks. Griffith told Sam the reason he insisted on actors sticking to the written dialogue was simple. "There may be thousands out there in our audiences who are able to lip-read."

"I mentioned this to Fairbanks because he never stuck to the correct dialogue," said Sam. "He would whisper quite obscene things to his leading ladies, and funny things in death-bed scenes trying to get the other actors to laugh." "Rubbish," he said. "No one could ever read my lips. I've always done it this way and I always will."

At the next premiere of a Fairbanks film, De Grasse proved his point. He hired twenty people who were capable of lip-reading to attend the opening night performance. It was a dramatic film, and Fairbanks was horrified to hear yells of laughter and derisive hoots coming from one part of the audience at most inappropriate moments. He stopped the film and demanded to know why they were making a mockery of his appearance. "Simple," said the leader of the lip-readers, "we could tell exactly what you really said in that death-bed scene. It was hilarious."

"Fairbanks offered each of the offenders $50 to leave the theatre so the film could continue," recalled De Grasse. "They accepted his offer willingly. Since I had already given them $25 to attend, they went home very happily. From that day on he never used bad language or inappropriate lines during filming. He demanded everyone learn the dialogue and like the other actors he stuck to the script. I don't believe he ever found out that I had planted the lip-readers in the opening night audience, which is perhaps just as well or I might not be alive today!"

Meanwhile, Joe was getting along just fine. By 1914 he had cut his directing down to six films and his acting to ten more. Visualizing the potential of the industry and the impact it would have on the Los Angeles area in the years ahead, he decided to give high school students interested in the industry a chance to learn the basics of directing and acting. A *Los Angeles Times* story in 1914 told how he was teaching classes in film production at a number of high schools in the area. "He never took a cent in payment for what he believed was his way to return to the next generation the things the industry had given him," said Sam. "In addition, he often went back to the Grand Opera House, where he directed and played roles from Othello to Hamlet."

While Sam was using his dental training to promote his career, Joe was using his accountancy knowledge to help dozens of the film industry's personalities who were finding that handling large sums of money was not their cup of tea.

Just before her death in 1975, when she was eighty-two, silent star Miriam Cooper recalled her long association with Joe De Grasse. "We met in 1914 on the set of *The Gunman*, which he was directing. We fell head over heels in love, but were both so dedicated to our careers that we never did get married. But he handled all my financial affairs and contracts, for I had no head for such things. He continued doing this until he died in 1940. His advice on investments was impeccable. When the Wall Street crash came in 1929 he had already removed most of my investments to safe havens and I was relatively unscathed by the disaster.

"I know, too, that after the crash he used thousands of dollars of his own money helping those who had lost everything. He was a good man. Looking back, I wish we had been married back in 1914. But wishes don't make reality."

Joe De Grasse set up the industry's first real accounting system designed for motion picture producers. It was so successful that it was used to set up special accounting departments in four of the major studios of the time. Many years later Mack Sennett said had he listened to De Grasse he would never have wasted the millions he did. "When we started making films," he said, "it was very slap-dash, and there was little need for complicated accounting. I went bankrupt because I ignored the advice of Joe De Grasse."

At an office he rented in the Sennett Studios at Edendale, Joe had two men employed full time looking after the investments of his clients. A separate telephone number, answered by a secretary, kept track of his acting and directing assignments and his other outside interests in the theatre. A third telephone was never answered unless Joe was there to answer it personally.

"I alone knew that number," said Miriam Cooper. "Even when he married Ida Mae Park in 1917, Joe and I maintained contact by phone. When I had days of depression I would phone him. He would always be in his office each morning at 6 a.m., even Saturdays and Sundays. I knew I could count on that."

According to Sam De Grasse, Miriam Cooper was not the only one with the private telephone number. "Joe once told me he was the 'father confessor' to many people, important and unimportant, in the industry who, when they needed personal advice, called him at his private number."

In 1915, Joe either acted in or directed more than thirty films. His wife, Ida Mae Park, recalled in 1954 that "he was the most industrious man I ever knew. He was a director for the Universal Victor Company, acted in many of their films, still maintained an office for his financial clients, still spoke to the high school students, and consoled — by phone — a dozen or more of the industry's leading ladies who at that time in the industry's turmoil seemed to need an awful lot of consoling."

Somehow the De Grasse-Park marriage survived. "Joe was a dedicated man. I knew that before we married and I understood his needs," said Ida Mae. "He didn't leave me out of his life. When he signed new actresses to first contracts, like Louise Lovely or Dorothy Phillips, he asked me to keep their feet on the ground. So I officially became their manager and, as such, spent a lot of time at the studio with Joe. He also encouraged me to write and edit his script ideas and as film history records show, we collaborated on a lot of successful screenplays."

By 1915 Sam had purchased a beautiful home on twenty acres of wooded land high in the Hollywood Hills. He lived there in state and threw lavish parties for his friends in the industry. But he wasn't averse to making a little money from the property. "I rented out the house and grounds to film makers looking for a class setting in which to work. I imagine more than 100 films were made on the grounds or inside my home. Joe and I were both earning large amounts of money and probably as early as 1915 we were both independently wealthy enough to have quit work and rested on our laurels had we so wished."

In 1916 Sam played a major role in the D. W. Griffith film *Intolerance*. The part of Jenkins, in the modern story segment, only called for him to work for six days, but since he was under contract to Griffith, who enjoyed having him around, he was designated additionally as a "scenic adviser." "Really, I was the forerunner of today's script assistant," he recalled in 1943. "I had a keen eye for detail and Griffith knew I would correct things that would not match when shown alongside previously shot film. I believe I was the very first person who insisted on a still photograph of each set when a scene was finished, and when they went back days later to the same scene we could see for ourselves just what everyone was wearing and where each object was placed. Griffith took credit for that idea, but really it was mine!"

In 1916 he also acted in seven films under the Fairbanks banner, "and I always had my trusty tooth drill at the ready."

Sam entrusted his earnings, and the growing gold-mine profits, to Joe. The money was invested wisely and by the early 1920s he was a very wealthy man. Selling his property in the Hollywood Hills he moved into the growing downtown area of Hollywood, where he designed and constructed two apartment buildings. He set himself up in a penthouse apartment that had, at that time, the first high-rise rooftop lawn large enough for his guests to play miniature golf. He added a rooftop swimming pool for good measure. Among the frequent guests were Douglas Fairbanks, Sr., and Mary Pickford.

During 1916 Joe met actor Lon Chaney, Sr., who appeared in two of the films he directed. Joe took over Chaney's tangled business affairs and soon had him on a sound financial footing. Their association continued until Chaney's death in 1930.

Sam continued his association with Fairbanks, and — despite his wealth — was rarely to be found relaxing by his rooftop pool. In 1917 Joe directed

Sam in *Anything Once*, a Bluebird film starring Franklyn Farnum. It was the second, and last, time the two appeared together professionally.

Douglas Fairbanks kept his promise and gave Sam De Grasse superb roles in his company's productions. He appeared as King Philip II of Spain in *In the Palace of the King*, Talleyrand in *The Fighting Eagle*, The Pharisee in *King of Kings*, King James II in *The Man Who Laughed*, and Prince John (possibly his most evil role) in *Robin Hood*. Fairbanks was honest enough to admit, in a *New York Times* story following Robin Hood's premiere, that "Sam De Grasse steals the show. He is surely the meanest, slimiest, most evil villain in the motion picture industry."

Mary Pickford used to tell a story with great delight about the premiere of *Robin Hood* in New York. "Doug and Sam decided to do a stunt for one of the city newspapers. They both went to the top of one of the city's skyscrapers where the newspaper's cameraman took pictures of them showing their abilities as marksmen with a bow and arrow. The newspaper had set a target on another high-rise about 100 yards away. Unfortunately, no one won the contest, which had to be called off when one of Sam's arrows landed in the backside of an elderly tailor who was standing with his rear towards an open window close to the official target. Of course it made a great story, but it cost Doug $5,000 in damages to stop the injured tailor suing them both."

The *Chicago Herald Examiner* said, in 1919, of Sam De Grasse: "He has the unique ability of being able to excite an audience without indulging in the favourite custom of screen villains, face-making. Undoubtedly he is the villain to end all villains in the motion picture industry."

In 1920, Charles Ray, then an important actor at Universal Studios, signed Joe De Grasse to direct his first film there under a new contract. Ray's co-star was another Canadian, Marie Prevost. The result was so satisfying to Ray and the studio that Joe was given a two-year contract at a salary of $2,000 a week to direct all Ray's films.

Sam, successful and wealthy, was by now hob-nobbing with the elite of Hollywood. One of his best friends was the young actor, Jackie Coogan, who had shot to fame in *The Kid*, with Charlie Chaplin. Coogan spent many non-working days around the pool at Sam's apartment building. Many years later, when he was appearing in the popular television series, *The Addams Family*, Coogan talked about Sam De Grasse. "He was the best friend in the world to me and many more young people in the industry. He gave us the run of his lovely home and even though we were very young we were not too young to appreciate the beautiful young actresses who were always present. He gave us support when we were depressed by situations at home or at the studio. He loaned us money and never, ever, asked for it back."

Coogan could never be shaken from a statement he made to the *Los Angeles Times* in 1964. "I know you will find it difficult to believe," he said, "but Sam De Grasse was married for a while to Jean Harlow. Jean lived at the apartment. I think she was about sixteen at the time, and everyone referred to her as Mrs. De Grasse. Sam taught her how to act and although she never admitted it publicly, or even talked about their relationship, I saw them together so often that I have no doubt she was married to him."

Some film history books show that Harlow was married to a "Hollywood businessman" when she was sixteen but he is not named, nor is there any report of a subsequent divorce. Friends of Sam De Grasse, questioned in the 1960s, agreed with Jackie Coogan that Harlow did live in the De Grasse apartment for more than two years, but no one seems sure whether or not they were married.

Both Sam and Joe De Grasse worked less and less as the years went by. Money was of no importance to either of them and it was only on special occasions that they could be convinced that the industry was the same friendly, satisfying place it had been when they arrived in California.

In 1925 Sam convinced *Movie Weekly* to run a contest to give a young actress, Lucille Le Sueur, a new name. She had been a former Shubert chorus girl, but Sam felt looks alone wouldn't get her to the top in Hollywood. "She must have a new name," he told the editor of *Movie Weekly*. The editor agreed and launched a nation-wide contest. A mid-west housewife who suggested the name Joan Crawford won the prize. Actress Constance Bennett, who starred in *Sally, Irene, and Mary*, the first film Crawford made under her new name, later claimed she had originated the contest, but Crawford herself supported the De Grasse story. "I have no doubt that it was Sam who initiated the contest. The magazine was interviewing him when I walked into the office in search of some publicity. Sam, who had met me several weeks earlier on the set of *Lady of the Night*, introduced me to the editor and said, 'Is Le Sueur a name for a beautiful girl?' He pronounced it 'sewer.' The editor took the bait and I got my new name, and a film contract from all the publicity."

In 1926, while visiting New York, Sam became friendly with a young actress hoping to find success in Hollywood. Her name was Jane Peters. "You won't get anywhere with that name," said Sam. "You need to change it to something more glamourous." While they talked they passed a drugstore on

Sam De Grasse in the Douglas Fairbanks film *The Black Pirate* (1926).

Lexington Avenue. "There," said Sam. "That's the name you should use." She looked up and saw the store name, The Carrol Lombardi Pharmacy. She took Sam's advice and became Carole Lombard. Many years later she officially credited Sam with choosing the right name for her in a story written for *Picturegoer* magazine.

With sound films on the verge of being unveiled to an eagerly waiting world of moviegoers, Joe looked enthusiastically ahead anticipating that his stage experience would stand him in good stead for delivering dialogue. Sam was less optimistic. In 1929 he officially announced his retirement to concentrate on his business investments. "It was my evil manner that made me famous," he told the *Los Angeles Times*. "But my voice doesn't match my appearance." He was right. He had a low-pitched, strangely peaceful voice that contrasted dramatically with his tough appearance.

Sam made only one film in 1930, *Captain of the Guard*, before deciding it would be his final appearance before a camera. In a radio series, hosted by D. W. Griffith in 1933, the great director said he regretted the coming of sound for only one reason. "It brought an end to the film career of Sam De Grasse, whose soft and gentle voice belied his evil appearance. I used him so often over the years because he was the most reliable actor in the entire film industry. He never let anyone down. He knew what a director needed from the actor. He rarely needed to do two takes of even the most difficult scenes. I regret the retirement of this gentleman of our industry."

Joe still made a number of films with Douglas Fairbanks, Sr., and in March 1932 he sailed with Fairbanks and a film crew from San Francisco to Tahiti where he planned to make a film called *Mr. Robinson Crusoe*. Edward Sutherland directed, with Maria Alba playing Crusoe's girl Friday. Fairbanks hired a two-masted schooner for the adventure, which was also designed to be a two-month vacation. "Joe used to laugh about the voyage on many occasions," said Sam in 1943. "Fairbanks had taken with him two young girls, ostensibly listed as personal assistants, but they were there exclusively for Fairbanks' own use. You might have thought this would be enough for him, but Joe told of his time in Tahiti where the young and beautiful island girls were lining up on the dock waiting to be invited into Fairbanks' cabin. I'm sure there must have been a lot of Douglas Fairbanks juniors running around on the island nine months later."

The unspectacular film had little excitement, possibly because Fairbanks was so tired after all the action in his cabin. It was released in 1933, but was not a great success.

In 1934 Joe sailed with Fairbanks to London, England, where Alexander Korda directed Fairbanks in *The Private Life of Don Juan*. Also starring Merle Oberon and Binnie Barnes, it was Joe's last venture with Fairbanks, who became upset because of Joe's off-screen activities. In London Joe met Lady Diana Manners, to whom he had been introduced ten years earlier when she was appearing in Max Reinhardt's play, *The Miracle*, in New York. The two were seen dancing and dining every night in London clubs and stories of their "romance" were printed prominently in both Europe and the United States. Joe's wife put a stop to the stories by sailing to England where she confronted Lady Diana and Joe in a nightclub. The resultant brawl hit the headlines, and it put a halt to the flirtation. Five days later, the film completed, Joe and Ida Mae sailed for New York and, presumably, lived happily ever after.

In 1935, Joe and his wife decided to get out of Hollywood for good. They purchased a beautiful home in Eagle Rock, California, and settled down there to relax and ride one of the dozen horses on their 100-acre ranch. For a while Joe contributed a weekly humourous column to the local newspaper. But his enthusiasm waned fast and when his writing contract came up for renewal after six months he said goodbye to his journalistic career.

Although he always drove the latest model car, Joe preferred to walk or ride his horses wherever he could. On May 25, 1940, he saddled up and headed toward the town of Eagle Rock. At the edge of the town he hitched the horse to the exterior of a hardware store, as he had on many earlier occasions. He walked off briskly to the town centre, telling the storeowner he'd be back in an hour or so. It was not to be. Joe De Grasse, at sixty-seven, collapsed on a street corner in Eagle Rock with a heart attack. Taken to hospital, he was pronounced dead on arrival.

Joe De Grasse left all his considerable wealth to his wife of more than twenty years, with instructions that she must send monthly support payments to more than forty former film personalities of the silent era who had fallen on hard times. Sam, asked to wind up the estate, discovered Joe had been giving money to these same actors each month for more than a decade. "Ida Mae was aware of what he had been doing and she has continued the payments until today," said Sam in 1943. "She sent the children of these old actors through college and never let an old friend be in need."

"He was the best brother any man could hope for, an inspiration to me and many, many more people," said Sam at the funeral service. "He goes to join our parents, who gave us both the opportunity to live our lives in a manner that neither they or we can in any way regret."

Sam devoted three years of his life providing entertainment for the many service people who came into Hollywood between 1942 and 1945. He joined with former director Sidney Olcott in ensuring that servicemen and women be given the time of their lives while in the glamour capital. When the war ended he was seen less and less in public. Four long-time servants staffed his beautiful home, and he occasionally entertained former friends from the film industry.

While visiting Mary Pickford's showplace home on Summit Drive in 1943 with a group of servicemen and women, he mentioned to her that he and her late husband, Douglas Fairbanks, Sr., had once built a dentist's surgery in the basement of their house. He led an amazed Mary down to the saloon and unveiled the lock by sliding a board aside. Mary called for a locksmith, and in a short while the room was revealed to her for the first time. "I'll tell you a secret, Sam," she said. "I often wondered why you and

Doug used to lock yourselves away down here." She laughed! "Would you believe that I now and again let myself believe that perhaps you and he were a little peculiar. I am glad that thought is finally banished!"

Occasionally Sam gave interviews to historians researching the early days of Hollywood, but was not interested in returning to the bustling sound studios. His last recorded public appearance was at the funeral of Sidney Olcott, his friend of many years, in 1949. He told a reporter after the funeral, "I am now seventy-three, an old man. I'm sorry I can give you no exciting story, no exciting news, but I and many here today were part of a wonderful world I don't think the young people in the industry could ever visualize. I was quite important in the early days of motion pictures, but I am not important today, but thank you for speaking to me."

Four years later he died peacefully in his sleep at his home in Hollywood. He left a will dictating that there be no funeral; he was to be cremated immediately. "This is not a time to be sad," he wrote. "Let me go silently into the beyond, for I have had a wonderful life."

Half of his substantial wealth was left to be shared equally among the four servants who had been a part of his home and life for more than three decades. The rest was divided among theatrical charities.

The De Grasse brothers had vanished in the mists of time until 1990 when the new owners of Pickfair decided to pull the magnificent old structure down and rebuild a new home on the site. When dismantling the saloon bar in the basement, the wreckers came on the hidden room containing the dentist's chair and all the old dental equipment. A Hollywood paper reported that they had discovered what they believed was an old torture chamber that Pickford and Fairbanks must at one time have used for some unknown reason. A day later the story was retracted when it became clear the room was nothing more than an old-fashioned dental office. There was no one alive to tell them who built it or who used it. If they read this, they will know for the first time.

MARIE DRESSLER

"Marie Dressler was loved by everyone who knew her. She never had a bad word to say about anyone. She had time for everyone. She loved life. She would get out of her car at the studio gates at the end of a long day and talk for hours to the people who were always waiting there. She signed every autograph she was asked to give. She answered every letter she received personally. She was a guardian angel to me and to many others. It is time now for me to tell, for the first time, the story of how she once saved my life."

(Greta Garbo, New York, 1980)

M arie Dressler wrote her autobiography in 1924, before the sound films that were to make her fame everlasting had been invented. She called it *The Life Story of an Ugly Duckling*. Like the duckling enshrined in the fable with a similar title, Marie Dressler overcame the many handicaps she faced in her life and, though she never won any awards for her beauty, she became, as Louis B. Mayer said when he announced her death in 1934, "The most adored person ever to set foot in the Metro-Goldwyn-Mayer studio."

The road to the worldwide fame that Dressler travelled in the early years of the twentieth century was far from being an easy one. She struggled from dingy theatre to dingy theatre before Broadway discovered and acclaimed her immense talent.

Thanks to a young man she had helped on his way to becoming the greatest comedy producer in the history of motion pictures, she bettered even her Broadway successes with a stunning appearance in a silent film that is still considered one of the great classics of the 1920s.

She lost that fame when she had the courage to champion the cause of the underpaid chorus girls and boys in the New York theatre. When her brave stand helped create Actors Equity, the first theatre union, she was blacklisted by every major producer and most theatre managements across the nation.

Vaudeville, in which she had enjoyed considerable success, was on its way out and Marie Dressler was virtually cut off from the work she loved.

In the 1920s she was reported in *Variety*, the theatrical trade newspaper, to have applied, in desperation, for a job as housekeeper to a wealthy family in New Jersey.

Dressler wrote a second autobiography, *My Own Story*, in 1934, but died before it was published. In the 1930s the ugly duckling had been transformed into a magnificent swan because three men and one woman believed it was a disgrace that such a talent should be cut off from the audiences who loved her. The quartet, a writer and three studio heads, declared their intention to ignore the stage ban because they felt she had what the era of sound in motion pictures desperately needed. These four people believed in her and made her, by 1932, into the highest paid actress in the world.

"I was born homely," she said in her second autobiography. "And for fifty years it has been my lot to make my living on the stage, where the first requisite for a woman's success was supposed to be a face that's easy on the eyes. I was born serious, but I have earned my bread by making other people laugh."

Marie Dressler was born Leila von Koerber on November 9, 1869, in the small town of Cobourg, Ontario. Her father, Alexander von Koerber, was Austrian by birth, but travelled to Canada when he was too young to remember the voyage. He was a music teacher and, occasionally, a concert pianist.

Her mother, the former Anne Henderson, was the daughter of a wealthy Irish-Canadian family who owned trading stores, a small fleet of sailing ships that plied regular routes between Canada and the West Indies, and were proud possessors of what was, at the time, considered to be the finest racing stable in Canada. The marriage was not acceptable to the Henderson clan. Not one member attended Anne Henderson's wedding to von Koerber, and the once wealthy heiress was destined to spend a life that at times fringed on poverty.

When her father died at the ripe old age of eighty-seven, he attempted to make amends for his cruelty to his daughter. To the disgust of several members of the family, he left, in his will, his entire fleet of ships to his daughter. Unhappily, on the evening of the day the will was read, the entire fleet of eight ships was destroyed by fire, some reports say deliberately, while at anchor in Toronto harbour. The insurance companies involved refused to pay for the loss, so Anne von Koerber got nothing.

Despite the constant shortage of money, Leila and her sister, Bonita, five years her elder, lived in a home made warm and friendly by their mother, and always full of music from Strauss to Beethoven provided by their father. On numerous occasions Leila (soon to be Marie) is reported as saying, "I adored mother, but I can't say I ever liked my father. He really didn't make our house a happy home."

The von Koerber family moved from town to town, sometimes three or four times a year. "Father was an arrogant man," she said. "In each town my mother was able to drum up enough young piano students for him to teach. That usually brought in sufficient money with which we were able to eat and rent a house. But every time, in every town, his temper got the better of him and he screamed and shouted at the boys and girls he was supposed to be teaching. One by one they cancelled their lessons and as the numbers grew smaller I knew it was only a matter of time before we would have to move on to a new town where nobody had heard of his tantrums.

"In every community, when we first arrived, he checked out all the churches to see if any of them needed an organist. If they did he used that as his stepping stone to opening a music school. If there were no vacancies, he used to hire the town hall and announce himself as a great European pianist, just passing through, and able to stay one night to give a concert.

"Really, I suppose he was a very good concert pianist. If his concert drew a big crowd, as such concerts did in those days, he would announce his love for the community that had given him such a warm reception. 'I have been asked to stay awhile and teach the rudiments of the pianoforte to a number of fortunate young students,' he said. 'I shall be receiving applications from those desirous of benefiting from my knowledge in my hotel suite tomorrow morning.'

"We always stayed at a good hotel when we first arrived in a town. He felt it created a good impression. Next morning, there was usually a line-up of parents with willing, or unwilling, students ready to be enrolled in his music school."

Marie Dressler realized she was an "ugly duckling" when she was only three. "My sister, Bonita, was like a little Dresden doll, and when we walked to church on Sunday, dressed in all our finery, benevolent grown-ups would stop us between our house and the church to pat Bonita's head and coo, 'My isn't she lovely!' I don't remember one occasion when they ever patted my head."

Her earliest ambition was to join a circus, but she never did succeed, although for one week, while visiting a cousin, she rehearsed with a young bareback rider in a circus that was tenting in the town.

"There have been many stories told about my supposed circus life," she told a movie magazine in 1933. "I would like to say they are true, because I loved the circus, but, alas, I was always a heavy child and they didn't seem to build horses that could stand up, for any length of time, to my weight. So I must reluctantly deny the fascinating stories that I have read about my days in the circus."

When she was only fourteen, Leila von Koerber became Marie Dressler. "I announced my intention to become an actress," she recalled to the magazine. "My father bellowed at me that never would the name von Koerber be associated with a theatrical event, I guess he didn't call his piano concerts theatrical events, so I told my mother I would in future be called Marie Dressler. It was the name of an aunt living in Germany who I had never seen but who wrote me long and interesting letters."

In 1883, an actor-producer called Herbert Nevada, who owned a rather seedy theatrical stock company that travelled from town to town in eastern Canada and the northern United States, was announced as arriving in the town where the von Koerbers were living at the time. As the brother of a renowned prima donna of that era, Emma Nevada, he and his company got some quite undeserved adulation.

"To me he was a very famous person," said Dressler. "And since he was associated with the stage on which I was determined one day to be even more famous, he was not only very important but my exit door from the uninspiring life I was living at home. Somehow I convinced Bonita, who was then nineteen, to go with me to an audition that Nevada was holding.

"We arrived at the theatre to find the 'great man' in the middle of a rehearsal. He stopped when he saw us. 'How old are you?' he asked. I lied and said I was eighteen and Bonita was nineteen. 'Can you leave with us when we depart this town on Sunday?' he asked. Of course, we said together. We really had no idea if we could leave or not but we hoped father, who was out of town, would stay away until after Sunday. We knew we could convince mother to let us go, providing we were going together.

"Mr. Nevada told us to go and pack our bags and be ready to leave. I ventured to ask would there not be an audition. The 'great man' snorted and said, 'Audition? Absolutely not. I can tell an actress when I see one! Be here at two this afternoon for your first rehearsal.'

"What he didn't tell us at that time was that three female members of his company had walked out, and anyone who had two legs, two arms, some sort of a face, and a voice loud enough to be heard in the upper balcony, would have been accepted as an 'actress.'"

Marie Dressler and Bonita von Koerber left home with their mother's rather unenthusiastic blessing. "I was told years later by mother that all my father said when she told him we had joined a travelling dramatic company, 'Well, that will allow us to spend more money on food and clothes.' He wasn't even mad, or so she said.

"Nevada gave us each six dollars a week, paid our rail fares from town to town, and provided all costumes except modern day dress," said Dressler. "My very first role was Cigarette in *Under Two Flags*. I was absolutely petrified when I stepped out on the stage, but I didn't forget my lines and apparently he was quite satisfied. It was that sort of company.

"Bonita didn't have a part, so Nevada made her repair all the torn costumes, and there were many not only torn but quite tattered."

Dressler and her sister learned that being professionals was not an easy task. "If an audience didn't like the show we planned to stage, we would be called up with less than twenty-four hours notice to perform a different one on the second night. That Bonita and I hadn't got this large repertoire of plays into our heads seemed not to matter to Nevada. He would thrust a script in our hands, tell us which parts we were playing, and expect us to be ready, word perfect, in time for curtain rise next night.

"Nevada never seemed to remember that we would have no idea where we were to stand on stage or who or what we were to address our lines to. All that mattered to him was that the audience be happy and the box-office good.

"After six months on the road, mostly staying in towns one or two nights, occasionally full weeks in which we could really unpack our bags and imagine we were in heaven, I had learned my lines in seventeen different plays. But that didn't inspire Nevada. The turnover of actors and actresses was amazing. A lead player would be with us one night and gone the next. So instead of playing the part we had so carefully rehearsed we would be told, often on less than an hour's notice, that we had been assigned a totally different role."

Dressler credits her year with the Nevada Stock Company as being the greatest training in the world. "I learned to ad lib lines," she recalled in her first book. "If someone else forgot his lines I found myself jumping in with something totally unscripted until the other player had recovered his equilibrium.

"Years later I appreciated this ability more than ever when I played opposite some of the biggest names in the theatre, people who loved to rewrite the plays as they went along. I was able to hold my own with the best and found work easy to get because people knew they would have a lot of fun if they worked with me."

After about nine months of touring, Bonita decided she had more than enough of acting. "A young playwright came along with a couple of plays which we staged," recalled Dressler. "He and Bonita hit it off from the start and when he had seen his plays performed he announced that he and Bonita were leaving immediately to get married. It turned out that she chose well. Richard Ganthony later wrote the Broadway hit play,

Message from Mars and, apart from a few early years of hardships, they both lived happily ever after."

Of the $6 Dressler received each week she lived on $3 and sent $3 home to her mother. "We always kept in touch, it was very important to me," she said. "She would write me regularly and passed along any news that she had from Bonita. She never mentioned father, but I presumed he was still alive. This went on for several years until the Nevada Stock Company was booked into a theatre in a small town in Michigan where my mother, and father, were living.

"When I walked into the house they had rented mother threw her arms around me. I was pleasantly surprised to hear my father welcoming me with more than a little enthusiasm. Despite this change of attitude I never really liked him."

Nevada's road company ceased to exist in a small town in upstate New York. "We had put on a play written by Nevada that was so trite I was surprised we weren't railroaded out of town. By Tuesday night there were less than two dozen people in the audience. When we arrived at the theatre next morning we found all our hampers and costumes dumped in the hallway leading to the stage door. Our scenery was lying outside in an alley. The manager stood between us and the stage. 'Pack up and go before you get lynched,' he said. So we did what we were told. A local amateur operatic society was already rehearsing on stage.

"We checked out of our rooms and walked to the railroad station where Nevada gave us the bad news. 'This is where we part company,' he said. He gave us each a ticket to New York City and $2 in cash. Then, without a word of regret, or thanks for all the work we had done for him, he started loading the sets and costumes into the baggage van. We all went to New York, he sitting in state at one end of the coach, us at the other. He never spoke a word during the journey. One of our junior actors is said to have spat in his face as he left the train. I wish I had thought of that."

Dressler decided to use her vocal talents for her next job. "The only company casting at the time we arrived was the Grau Grand Opera Company, so I auditioned and landed a job in the chorus. The pay was eight dollars a week, so for several months I was able to send four dollars home each week to mother."

When Grau's company ran into financial difficulties he found a very clever way to rid himself of some of the cast. "He arranged with friends in different cities to send telegrams to those members of the cast he considered superfluous. Mine read: 'Need you in Philadelphia for costume fittings for opening here next month.' It was signed by someone I had never heard of.

"Grau assured me the telegram came from their costume designer who would meet me at the Philadelphia railroad station. 'We can do without you for a few days,' he said. I found out later, when I ran into one of the others he had let go, that she and others had also received telegrams, but we were all shunted off to different destinations. I learned many years later, when Grau was in court being sued for money by more than 100 different performers, that only half the company was on stage when the show opened the Monday night after I left the show."

Dressler arrived in Philadelphia, expecting to be met at the station by the costume designer. With less than two dollars in her pocket she was shocked to find that theatre people in the town had never heard of the mysterious "costume designer."

"I had nowhere to stay, but I had learned in my short life as a professional entertainer that honesty was always the best policy. A friendly policeman directed me to the Continental Hotel. There I told the elderly desk clerk that I needed a room but had no money, and then added, perhaps a little dishonestly, that I expected to have some by the weekend. He looked at me, smiled, pushed the registration slip over, and asked me to fill it out. He handed me the key and said, 'You'll be all right there until Saturday, miss.' Next morning I found an envelope pushed under my door. I opened it and found five dollars and a scrawled note that read, 'Good luck, I've got a kid of my own in the theatre.'"

Dressler never wasted time bemoaning her situation. "This is a credo I've stuck to all my life. Get on with it, I told myself. Somewhere work is waiting. If anyone tells me I've been unlucky in my life I always tell them the story of what happened next.

"Walking down the street from the hotel to the theatre where the Deshon Light Opera Company was completing the last week of a long run, I bumped into two old friends from my early days with the Grau Road Company. Both were appearing with the Deshon Company. One, May Montford, who later married John Golden who had a theatre named after him in New York, said she thought there would be a chance for me to join their show. 'Some of the company don't want to go on the road next week, they want to stay in Philadelphia.' One hour later I was a member of the company. The manager said I could walk on that week to get the feel of the company's approach to light opera, but he could only pay me $2 since I wouldn't really be working. With a promise of $10 for each week of the twenty-week run to follow, I accepted gladly."

With the $5 from the hotel clerk and the $2 already in her possession, Dressler survived the week until Thursday. "I checked out of the hotel, and figured I could sleep in one of the costume hampers at the theatre on Thursday, Friday, and Saturday. The Philadelphia theatre was one of the few which had showers for the performers so I didn't imagine I would fare too badly. Thursday I fasted. Friday I fasted, until late in the afternoon when I knew I had to eat something or I would surely pass out on stage.

"So I tried honesty again. I went to a small Jewish restaurant near the theatre and told the owner, who was waiter, cook, and everything else, that I had no money. 'Order from the menu,' he said. 'Anything your heart desires. You can pay me next time you come in.' I ate well, thanked him, and promised to be back. Unfortunately, I hadn't realized that this Jewish restaurant would be closed on Saturday for a special Jewish holiday. I banged and thudded on the door after I received my $2 pay, but couldn't make anyone hear. We left town next morning. I had a terribly guilty feeling that I had let this wonderful, trusting man down."

It was eight years later when Dressler returned to Philadelphia. "I was the name above the title on the theatre marquee for *Lady Slavey*, the play I had starred in on Broadway. We were into the first few weeks of a national tour that lasted almost two years. I was earning $800 a week, but I checked into the Continental Hotel, still as run-down as it had been when I was there before, courtesy of the night clerk. I had reserved a suite of rooms, which they made by opening an adjoining door to a second bedroom, and by adding in a table and two easy chairs.

"The little Jewish restaurant was still there, but had closed for the day when we arrived late on Sunday evening. Bright and early, next morning, I was waiting at the door when the proprietor opened the doors. I handed him $3, $1.50 for the meal he gave me, and $1.50 as a tip. 'I promised I would come back and pay,' I gushed. 'I'd just about written you off as a dead-beat,' he said. And he handed me $1.50 back. 'That's all you owe me,' he said."

Dressler enjoyed her breakfast in the restaurant. "I don't think I've ever enjoyed a meal more. Now I didn't owe the wonderful man anything. This time I left a tip and he accepted it without a word. As I was about to leave I asked if he was married. 'Fifty-five years,' he said, 'Forty-seven when you were last here.' 'Well, Mr. Gosswich,' I said, 'I'm playing at the Philadelphia Theatre and I would like to invite you and Mrs. Gosswich to be my guests there this evening.' 'Isn't that where Marie Dressler is playing?' he asked. I told him it was. 'Well, I've heard a lot about her,' he said. 'We accept your invitation.'

"The play was a riotous comedy, and the capacity audience stood and applauded for several curtains when the show ended. When I had changed and was in my street clothes ready to walk back to the hotel, I stepped outside the stage door, and who should be there but Mr. and Mrs. Gosswich.

"Mr. Gosswich greeted me with a big smile. 'You should have told us that Miss Dressler wouldn't be appearing tonight,' he said, 'but you did a wonderful job as her understudy. She's going to have to watch out or you'll be taking over the part permanently.' I was so stunned I couldn't do anything other than smile broadly. We shook hands, and as they walked away, Mr. Gosswich turned back and said, 'If you ever get to be a big star you'll still be welcome in my restaurant, don't you forget.'

"I didn't forget, and whenever I appeared in Philadelphia, and that was many times, I not only ate all my meals there but took some very important people along to dine with me. By the time I had finished my stage career and taken up residence in California, Mr. Gosswich's small restaurant had become the place for top theatricals in Philadelphia to dine and be seen. Their son took over when Mr. Gosswich died and his wife retired. Of course they had realized long ago who I really was, and we laughed about it many times. As far as I know, my autographed picture is still standing in their front window."

But a lot of water had to pass under the entertainment bridges before Marie Dressler became a Broadway star.

The Deshon Light Opera Company was a highly reputable touring road show. "Everyone got paid on time, the costumes were first-class and soft to the touch as I had found out when I slept in the costume hamper in Philadelphia, and the sets we travelled with us were quite opulent. We travelled enough for five different comic operas. The company did best with material by Gilbert and Sullivan and I longed to play the lead in one of their musicals. I adored *The Mikado* and desperately wanted to play the role of Katisha. I was still back in the chorus wishing that my musical father had only just had the compassion to teach me music the way he taught so many others. But he had heard me sing in the church choir and had told me that he 'only taught young people with talent and Leila you really do not have a voice that will get you anywhere.'

"I practiced everywhere, in the hotel bedrooms, on the streets if they were mercifully deserted as I walked home after the show, and on stage in the afternoons when there were no matinee performances. But it all seemed rather hopeless. Agnes Hallock, who played Katisha, must have been the healthiest singer in the business. When others went down with colds or sore throats, Agnes was out there bellowing 'my songs' every night.

"Often I convinced stagehands — who should have been cleaning up backstage — to read the part of Ko-Ko while I did Katisha. There must still be a lot of retired stagehands in the United States who think Marie Dressler is, and was, totally insane.

"But my hard work paid a final dividend. Agnes didn't get a cold, not even a sore throat, but she did step in a pothole on the streets of Washington and sprained her ankle so badly she was sidelined for three weeks. So my solo debut was in the nation's capital, Washington. I wish I could tell you the president was there, but he wasn't. I did, however get my first real critical review.

"It said: 'Miss Dressler, in the role of Katisha, totally dominated the company's opening night. Whether it was because her voice is very loud or whether she really has the talent that shone through like a lighthouse beacon, remains to be seen. She must learn to tone down the foghorn a little. If she was worried that she couldn't be heard at the back of the upper balcony I can assure her she was. I went up there for safety after the intermission. But Bravo, Miss Dressler. I, among many, will look forward to your return to Washington in perhaps a more subdued role.'

"Fourteen years later that same critic, then a well-known impresario, came to New York to ask me to appear for a week of seven performances in the same theatre. 'We hope to raise a lot of money for needy people,' he said. 'We couldn't hope to pay you more than $1,600 for the week, would that be acceptable?' It was obvious that this former critic had not recalled that I was the subject of his review of my debut performance, but I had not forgotten, and treasured the copy I always carried with me. 'No,' I told the impresario. 'Sixteen hundred dollars would not be acceptable.' His mouth dropped, so I continued, 'I will appear for $10 a week.' He couldn't believe his ears. 'Ten,' he said, 'why on earth ten?' I promised him I would reveal the secret at the final performance. He left shaking his head, and he hadn't a clue why I wanted $10. But, of course, that was what I received the week he gave me my first review. I read that review to the audience on the final night of my visit.

"There is a fascinating sequel to that story. He approached quite a lot of important performers to appear with me for that week. But I was his big attraction, and I discovered he had whispered to those he approached that he would guarantee them '$1 more than I am paying Marie Dressler.' He made a lot of performers feel very important, until they got their $11 cheques, but he must have raised a lot of money that week for Washington's needy people. And, by the way, President William Howard Taft did attend and became one in a long line of presidents I met over the years."

When her tour with Deshon ended, Dressler was invited by George Baker, who ran the George Baker Opera Company, to be one of the company's principals. "I was still singing loud but it must have been a little more under control for Baker actually put my name, along with his other principal singers, on the billboards. I conned a theatre manager out of one of the posters when we played in Chicago and I still have it as one of my most prized possessions."

Dressler learned from the George Baker Company a secret she always told young actors, in too much of a hurry to reach stardom, who asked for her advice. "Join a small stock company," she would tell them. "You'll play every kind of role, you'll iron the costumes, even repair them, you'll play a lead one week and a walk-on part next. But you'll become an actor who has humility, and all great actors have that."

And she gave a quotation in an interview with a Boston newspaper in 1890, when she was only twenty-one, that has, over the years, been claimed by many famous performers to be their creation. "Remember," she told the paper she would tell young actors, "there are no small parts, just small actors."

Dressler stayed several years with the George Baker Company. "George was a delight to work with, and I learned more from him than I have learned from anyone else in my entire career. By the second year of my tour with him, I had gained quite a lot of weight. I had always been pleasingly plump," she told the *New York Times* in 1906. "But now I was, hopefully, pleasingly fat. They say fat people are jolly, well that was Baker's attitude, so I was given all the comic parts. If they weren't intended to be comic, George ordered me to make them funny.

"Since all our regal costumes, both male and female, were made to fit junior elephants, and I was the only junior elephant in the cast, I played all the queens and duchesses, even occasionally some kings when the actor scheduled to appear was still sobering up in the dressing room. I still wore my queenly robes, but they added a false moustache and beard and I dropped my voice accordingly. I didn't need to act for that to be funny."

The great comic Eddie Foy caught one of her appearances in Chicago, and convinced her that acting the "foil" for him in his comedy skits would get her to the top faster than playing kings and queens in light opera.

"I joined him in Chicago where he, and his leading lady Adele Farrington, were to star in a new musical, *Little Robinson Crusoe*. The show was a big success and although I was just a second banana I was singled out for considerable praise in every city.

"I had reached the $100 a week plateau," she told the *New York Times* in a full-page article in 1916. "By now I was staying in the best hotels and eating in the best restaurants, except in Philadelphia, of course. We didn't play New York but we came near enough for the big city papers to write about us. Eddie Foy wasn't very happy when I was singled out by a New York paper for a special feature article. He warned me that if such a thing happened again I would be fired. It did, and I was!"

Dressler found another show almost immediately. She toured with Frankie Bailey, touted as the girl with the most beautiful legs in the world, in a play called *The Tar and the Tartar*. "I guess I was the obvious choice, with my legs, to play opposite Frankie," she told the *Times*. "It wasn't a bad show but it folded on the road and never did give me my Broadway debut, as I had hoped."

The long awaited New York engagement finally arrived on May 28, 1892, when she was twenty-three. The play, in which she was cast in the unlikely role of a thief, was written by Maurice Barrymore, father of Lionel, Ethel, and John. *The Robber of the Rhine* was panned by the critics, but Dressler was encouraged when Barrymore told her that the fault was his, as the playwright. "You were born to make people laugh, Marie, but this play never gave you a chance."

Dressler couldn't afford to be out of work. She was sending money home to her mother, was helping two aunts back in Toronto who had lost their husbands and were penniless, and was temporarily supporting Bonita and her husband who were struggling to make ends meet while the young author tried hard to write a hit play.

She took a job at the Atlantic Gardens, a beer hall, in the Bowery. Each night she sang half-a-dozen bawdy songs to an audience of rowdy drinkers who weren't the least bit interested in her or her vocal efforts. "I got $10 a week from the Gardens, and on Sundays sang the same sort of stuff at Koster and Bial's beer hall on 23rd Street. I was there for six hours and earned $15 more. I managed to honor my obligations and made ends meet by walking back to my cheap lodgings every night. That was about three miles, and I was amazed that I didn't lose any weight. That was when I first realised I was destined to be a plump lady forever."

The theatrical agents in the 1890s were nearly all based in a two-block area off 14th Street. "I walked up hundreds of flights of stairs each day, waiting in dreary outside offices. I got to hate the dust on the chairs, on the desks, and on me as the weeks went by. I found I could nod approvingly, without even listening, to old actors who wanted to recount their days of glory when they played Hamlet. I began to believe everyone must have played Hamlet, or was it just that I was chosen by God to meet all those who had. I heard the inner office doors open so many times that I was tempted to join in with the agent who always seemed to say the same thing: 'Sorry, my friends, I have nothing to offer you today.'"

Broadway audiences, agents, and managements had forgotten that Dressler's name had been in lights briefly for the Maurice Barrymore play. "Every agent in New York must have haunted the city's beer halls, for the only thing they remembered was hearing me sing songs to drunken customers there."

After two years of auditioning she won the part of the queen in the revival of the play, *1492*. The revival failed to interest the public, as it had on its first time around, and in less than a month Dressler was once more pounding the hard New York pavements and working in the city's dingy beer halls.

Eddie Foy, the man who had fired her for taking away the spotlight from him, was instrumental in getting Dressler her first big break at the Casino Theater. He told the reigning star of Broadway, Lillian Russell, that he knew the perfect person to play opposite her in her new musical comedy, *The Princess Nicotine*. "I learned a lot later that Foy had introduced me to Lillian Russell because he was fed up with reading about her in the newspapers and magazines."

"I figured Marie Dressler would take the limelight away from her. Russell needed taking down a peg or two," he told the *Los Angeles Examiner* in 1914 when both he and Dressler were working in the silent film studios of the time.

"The strategy worked and it didn't work," Dressler told a reporter. "I did get rave reviews, but no one was more delighted than Lillian. We became great friends and have remained so to this day."

Russell was so delighted with Dressler's work that after the play had been drawing packed houses to the Casino Theater every night for several weeks, she ordered Dressler's name to be put up in lights just under her own on the theatre marquee.

Marie Dressler never forgot the night she arrived at the Casino to see her name on the sign. "Not only was it flashing," she said, "but it was above the show title. Lillian is a generous and lovely person. Few stars would willingly share the headlines as she did. I never expected it and never would have dreamed of asking for such an honor. I loved every minute I worked with her.

"In the second act, where she, as the princess, and I as the haughty duchess, had a long scene together, we both used to try out new comedy bits without saying a word in advance. In less than a month we had basically rewritten the second act and it brought the house down every night. Neither of us knew what the other was going to do next and I learned from her how to perfect the art of instant thinking, which I had learned years earlier with the Nevada Stock Company, in any possible situation. She was, perhaps more than anyone, my greatest teacher, and still my friend."

New York newspapers loved the impromptu on-stage antics of the couple and the top show business columnists referred to them almost daily as "Beauty and the Beastie." The show never had to seek publicity, the newspaper writers sought the stars out and, of course, the show settled in for a long and successful run.

"Until I worked with Lillian," she told the *New York Times*, "I was always shaking before I went on stage. One night she noticed this and said to me quietly after the show that she knew the cure for stage fright. She took me to a really posh restaurant and ordered raw oysters for both of us. I warned her I had never eaten anything as exotic as raw oysters, but she just smiled and told me to try. I watched what she did, and how delicately she removed them from the shell and placed them in her mouth. I tried, but the darned things kept slipping all over the place. I was totally embarrassed as I watched people at nearby tables grinning at my efforts.

"When I finally got one of the oysters in my mouth, and gulped it down, an elderly gentleman at a nearby table shouted 'Bravo' and gently applauded. Others joined in and I could see they were not laughing at me, but with me. 'Anyone who can eat raw oysters in a posh restaurant should never again suffer from stage fright,' said Lillian Russell. 'All you have to do is think that the audience out there is waiting for you to eat a plate of oysters and they'll love you for trying.'

"Never again did I suffer from stage fright. In fact, at the end of the run of one play I took a plate of oysters on stage after the final curtain and ate them, still rather sloppily. I didn't say a word and they stood up and cheered me."

Dressler never forgot the people who helped her along the way. "As is usual, in a long-running show, people playing some of the smaller parts are often replaced. So once I was established in the show I waited for changes to offer some of my friends the roles. The two young actresses, May Duryea and May Montford, who had helped me out of a desperate situation in Philadelphia when they talked the Deshon Opera Company into hiring me, were both engaged for *The Princess Nicotine* after a few months and stayed with us to the end of the run. I was excited, because for both of them it was their Broadway debut."

Russell and Dressler appeared together in three more musical shows, each one enhancing Dressler's image. "There were almost as many people waiting at the stage door to see me as there were to see Lillian," she told the *Times*. "I used to kid her about it, as my fans used to stand on one side and hers on the other. I must say she did attract all the young and handsome men. My supporters were quite a motley group but they liked me and that's all that mattered.

"We used to have a little bet each night as we left the theatre together. We stood at the stage door and counted our fans while they applauded us. I counted hers, she counted mine. Every night she had more I gave her $10, and vice versa. Unhappily, I must report that she made nearly $800 from me during the run of *The Princess Nicotine*."

Dressler made her debut in New York society during the run of *The Princess Nicotine*. A story about her first visit to the home of Mrs. Orme Wilson, one of the city's most renowned hostesses, was told in the *Washington Post* the night before Dressler was to appear in the U.S. capital at a special performance for President Theodore Roosevelt. This is the story as she told it to the newspaper.

"I became very enamoured by the shining bannister that ran from the third floor of Mrs. Wilson's home to the great hall below," she said. "I told myself that I would die if I didn't slide down from top to bottom. So I walked upstairs to the third floor and straddled the bannister. Before I had time to think whether I should do it or not, I was off. It was a memorable run, and I landed on my you-know-what on the floor at the foot of Mrs. Wilson's rather haughty butler. He picked me up without a smile as several other guests watched my shame. Then he whispered to me, in a very English accent, 'Very good, miss, very good indeed. I've always wanted to have a go at it myself.' He bowed, and I went on my way as though nothing had happened. Not a soul mentioned the happening to me. I suppose in good circles things like that just didn't happen."

That evening, after the performance, the performers were lined up on stage to meet the president. "He proved to me that presidents do read papers," said Dressler. "I would like to invite you to lunch at the White House tomorrow, Miss Dressler," said the president, "but I must warn you, our bannister at the White House is only one floor in height, but it is shiny."

Next day Dressler examined the bannister from a distance. "But I didn't dare do my slide in the White House. When we left the president shook hands with me and said: 'I'm rather disappointed with you, Miss Dressler, I had the bannister specially polished for your visit.' And he winked at me and added: 'Perhaps next time, Miss Dressler?' I winked back but didn't dare say a word."

In 1896 Marie Dressler was given her first starring role on Broadway. The show, *Lady Slavey*, had a two-week try-out run in Washington before it opened in New York City. The elite of Washington turned out to see the lady who had become the toast of the town.

Grover Cleveland was another president Marie Dressler met. On opening night he was there in the president's box with his wife and his special guest, Lillian Russell, who wanted to see the show before it reached Broadway. She had asked the president if she might share their box.

Dressler's co-star was the dancing idol of Broadway, Dan Daly. Before the first rehearsal, Daly had never seen her work. He was shocked by the size of his new leading lady. "This could kill my career. I don't want to dance with an elephant," he told the director, George W. Lederer. Lederer calmed him down and urged that he watch Dressler at work. Before the rehearsals were halfway through, Daly apologized to Dressler and requested that they be given time away from rehearsals to work up a number of quick dance routines. Asked by Lederer why, he responded, "Because Marie and I are going to get so many encores we must be ready." He was right, they did get many curtain calls, and they showed they were ready by earning standing ovations for two-minute routines that soon became an accepted part of each performance.

In those days many big stars on Broadway were little known outside New York City. Newspapers in other centres rarely bothered to write about performers and shows their readers would never likely see. This policy was changed by an announcement Marie Dressler made after the show had run for three months.

"It looks like we will be in New York for a while yet," she said, "but I want everyone to know in Boston, Chicago, San Francisco, all the little places in between, that Mr. Daly and I have already agreed to take this complete show, at the end of its run, with its entire cast, scenery, and costumes, on the road for twelve solid months."

Newspapers across the nation started writing about Dressler, Daly, and anything else in the show they could think of to write about. It was probably one of the greatest publicity campaigns ever launched by a Broadway producer. It worked, for more than 200 theatre owners wrote to the producers, Canary and Lederer, asking that their theatre be one of those in which the show would be staged while on tour.

Dressler and Daly, asked for their choice of cities, agreed that two out of every three theatres must be smaller ones away from the regular route for major touring shows. Because of this, Mack Sennett, later to become the King of Comedy in Hollywood, was spotted by Dressler in the small town of Northampton, Massachusetts. Her story of their meeting differs somewhat from that told by Sennett. She recalled it this way: "I visited a small theatre where he was playing a very funny comedy role. Our own theatre in Northampton had been closed for the night because one of the boilers burst and we had no heating. I was very enamoured by his performance and suggested he take a few weeks off his regular work, he was not at that time a professional actor, to go to New York. I gave him the name of my friend, the impresario David Belasco, and later that night I wrote a letter to Mr. Belasco urging that he find Mr. Sennett some work. I understand he was able to get Sennett started in the professional theatre and that makes me very happy."

Once again, in *Lady Slavey*, Dressler found parts for her friends from her early days in the theatre. "You must remember," she told the *Times*, "I did this not only because they were friends but because they were very talented performers who needed an opportunity to be seen. I provided that opportunity, as other people had provided opportunities for me."

Lady Slavey's planned twelve-month national tour was extended to twenty-four months. Records show that there was not one single empty seat in the house during the entire run. When she and the company finally returned to New York, Dressler was concerned that they had been away too long. "I was afraid we would be forgotten," she said, "but I found out that stories of our travels had been keeping our names alive the entire twenty-four months. A newspaper [the *New York Daily Times*] printed the arrival time of our train, and we couldn't believe the cheering crowds who greeted us. The papers next day said there were at least 5,000 people waiting. The police department ushered us through the crowd or we might never have got to our hotel. It was a time of excitement I shall never forget."

Joe Weber, of Weber and Fields, the great comedy team of the late 1800s, had just split up with his partner when Dressler returned to town. Needing a strong comedy presence, he proposed to Dressler that she should co-star with him in a production at the New York Music Hall that he proposed to call *Higgledy-Piggledy*.

The show was also to feature the very popular Anna Held, who had won renown not only for her beauty and her vocal and acting talents, but through photographs of her bathing daily in goat's milk. After three weeks Held announced she was leaving. "I was horrified," said Dressler to the *Times*. "Now I'd be in trouble with Joe Weber. It was obvious to everyone why she was leaving. My press notices had far eclipsed hers. She was not an easy person to work with; if I say she was 'stuck up' that is an understatement."

But all turned out well. The great Anna Held called a press conference to announce her departure. "I cannot compete with Miss Dressler," she said. "She outclasses me in every way except beauty." A reporter called out, "and goat's milk, Miss Held." Held smiled. "We should need extra goats to cover Miss Dressler," she said. "And even more to immerse her immense talent."

Joe Weber was so delighted with the success of his first production that he tripled Dressler's salary for a second show, *Twiddle Twaddle*. This time only Dressler's name was in lights above the show title. Weber relegated himself to a spot further down the bill.

While she was working with Joe Weber, his former partner, Lew Fields, approached her with an offer that far eclipsed anything Weber could hope to pay if he was planning a third show.

"I read the script once and liked it," said Dressler to the *Times*. "I read it a second time and loved it. If Lew Fields had gone bankrupt and still wanted to do the musical comedy I would have paid him to hire me. I thought he was offering me far too much and I told him I'd work for the same money I was getting with Joe Weber."

"Hey, Marie," said Fields in his broad New York accent, "I'm the god-damned Jew in this deal, let me beat you down. OK, I'll offer you what Joe is paying you. Will you accept?"

"I couldn't resist getting the better of him, so I told him no," she said. "What do you mean no," said Fields. "Ain't we got a bargain?" "No," she told him, "I'll work for one dollar a week less than I'm getting for Joe." Fields threw up his arms in mock horror. "Marie," he said. "Tomorrow you and I are going to see the Rabbi. I'm gonna get him sign you on as an honorary Jew." "And he did," she told the *Times*, "but I didn't."

Tillie's Nightmare, which opened in 1910, was the biggest hit Broadway had ever seen. Before the show opened it was completely sold out for ten weeks, an unheard of happening on the Great White Way. On the opening night there were carriages lined up for two blocks from the theatre, their top-hatted occupants waving money at those about to enter the theatre. They offered, according to *Variety*, $300 for tickets that had cost from $5 to $12. But there were few takers. Everyone wanted to be there on Marie Dressler's opening night.

Programs for the opening night were specially printed with silk covers. Given free to every member of the audience, they were being sold outside the theatre after the show for $20 to disappointed would-be patrons who had hung around to hear what the people thought about the show. It is interesting to note that one of these programs, signed by Marie Dressler and Lew Fields, who merely produced but did not appear on stage, sold in 1992 at a memorabilia auction for $1,400.

Dressler was now the undisputed queen of Broadway. Important people vied for the honour of driving her in their carriages from the theatre to her hotel after the show. Included were James J. Jeffries, the champion prizefighter, Barney Oldfield, the fastest man alive who had just broken the world speed record by travelling at more than 131 miles-an-hour over a one-mile track, and, on one occasion, President Taft, who had travelled to New York just to see her show.

The show might have run more than thirty months if Dressler had not called a halt. "I have lots of friends outside New York who want to see me," said told a press conference. "I shall be travelling from coast-to-coast in a revue which I shall call *Marie Dressler's All-Star Gambol*."

Once again managements clamored for her to appear in their theatres. As before, she chose two small towns for every big city. She reported, on her return to New York ten months later, that not one single seat had been empty in any theatre at which the show had played. She announced yet another tour with a new show, *Marie Dressler's Mix Up*. She found forty more theatres that wanted her presence and the second tour triumphed like the first. Dressler added fifty more theatres and extended the road tour to almost two years.

She hired a publicity girl named Elizabeth Mayberry to travel with her on both tours. She was given the job of making sure photographs of Dressler with celebrities in the different towns the show visited were sent back to the New York papers. The theatre magazines and trade papers were kept informed of her every move.

"Elizabeth did an amazing job," Dressler told the *New York Times*. "When I saw the results of her work I began to feel homesick for Broadway."

But she was not destined to return to the big city for another three years. A call in 1914 from Mack Sennett in Hollywood, the man she had started on the road to success seventeen years earlier in Northampton, Massachusetts, took her to the Sennett Studios for her debut in silent motion pictures.

Sennett got her permission to write his own version of *Tilly's Nightmare* as a silent screen production. He promised her the most important supporting cast that any performer had ever been given in the youthful history of the movies.

Although Sennett's version of the Broadway hit in no way resembled the original production, Dressler, realizing the limitations of silent films, gave it her approval. "It was very, very, funny," she said to the *Los Angeles Times*.

Sennett kept his word about the supporting cast! With *Tilly's Punctured Romance*, the name finally given to the completed script, only one name was printed in huge letters above the title: Marie Dressler.

The supporting cast included Charlie Chaplin, Mabel Normand, Mack Swain, Chester Conklin, Charlie Chase, and just about every star on the Keystone lot who could be fit into the script or used in crowd scenes. Today, *Tillie's Punctured Romance* is available to film buffs on video, and is often seen, with background music added, on late night TV shows. The film made a lot of money for Sennett's studio. Dressler was paid $2,500 a week for the four-week shooting schedule.

"TILLIE'S PUNCTURED ROMANCE"

Charlie Chaplin, Marie Dressler, and Mabel Normand in
Tillie's Punctured Romance (1914).

In 1957, Charlie Chaplin was asked how he, a major star himself in 1915, felt about playing second fiddle to Dressler in the film. "It was my great delight," he said. "I had seen her on stage in New York in the play and considered her one of the great comediennes of all time. I seriously considered asking her to team up with me on some of my later pictures but I was too afraid she might steal every scene in which we played together. She walked away with honors from *Tillie* and I find it a very pleasant memory now to know that I worked with such an astonishing talent. Remember, she was around forty-five when she made the film, I was still only twenty-five and had a lot to learn, as I still have today, when I meet up with a performer so awesome."

Sennett made two follow-up films with Dressler, *Tillie's Tomato Surprise* and *Tillie Wakes Up*. Both were rushed out too fast and were pale imitations of the first *Tillie* feature. Although they made money for Sennett they did nothing to enhance Dressler's own motion picture career.

In between films Dressler joined with other performers in rallies to sell bonds to help the European war effort in which the United States had become involved. She became a favourite of President Woodrow Wilson.

In 1917 she returned to New York, not to appear in a play but to offer support to the New York chorus girls who had gone on strike for more pay. Even those appearing in the top Broadway shows were receiving no more than $12 a week.

Dressler called a press conference in Times Square early on a Sunday morning. Thousands of dancers and other theatre performers attended to see what she had to say. Traffic was brought to a standstill, but police officers, brought in to keep traffic moving, did nothing but watch Dressler as she made her speech.

"I was once a chorus girl," she said. "To look at me now with this barrel figure of mine you might find it hard to believe, but I was. And so I promise my financial and moral help to these stars of tomorrow who are being downtrodden by theatre managements who are too willing to line their pockets but not at all willing to line the stomachs of these important people, the dancers, with enough pay to keep them above the poverty line. I will not appear on Broadway again until this strike is ended with the creation of a theatrical union that will provide fair pay to everyone, not just the stars."

The applause went on for nearly ten minutes. The traffic police forgot their duties and were pictured in the *New York World* next day applauding with the rest of the huge crowd.

The strike resulted in the creation of Actors Equity, the theatre union still operating today. When it was over, and Dressler was ready to go back on stage, she discovered New York theatre managers and producers had long memories. They blacklisted her, and theatre owners refused to let her perform in their New York houses.

By the early 1920s she had no money left. A report in *Variety* said she had sold the house she had purchased in Long Island during the run of *Tillie's Nightmare*. A few weeks later *Variety* reported that an unnamed, but important, lady and gentleman in New Jersey, had said she had applied to them for a job as a housekeeper. Dressler later denied this story, but added: "It might have been a very good idea. When money goes, friends go. I moved into a small apartment with three of the chorus girls who I had been able to help a few years before, and waited patiently. I knew that eventually things would change."

Elizabeth Mayberry, who had toured as Dressler's publicist for nearly two years, had risen, by 1923, to the top of the publishing world. Respected as a literary agent, she had placed stories for a young writer, Frances Marion, who had, as a result, been given a job at Metro-Goldwyn-Mayer studios in Hollywood as a screenwriter.

Mayberry had not forgotten her enjoyable years with Dressler, and she contacted Marion in Hollywood and suggested she write a script to utilize Dressler's talents. Marion, who had loved Dressler's work, produced a script entitled *The Callahans and the Murphys*. She took it to the MGM studio head, Louis B. Mayer, and urged that he give one of the leads to Dressler and the other to a studio contract artist, Polly Moran.

Mayer weighed up the situation and asked to view a copy of *Tillie's Punctured Romance*. Next day he called Frances Marion and asked how much she thought they could get Dressler for. Marion suggested $2,000 a week. Mayer countered with $1,500. In days a contract was signed and Dressler was put on the fastest train to Hollywood, first class.

Everyone thought *The Callahans and the Murphys* was going to be a big hit. Special preview showings had the audiences "rolling in the aisles." A massive publicity campaign was set up to promote the film. Mayer was delighted with his "new find." Then the bomb burst.

Temperance societies from coast-to-coast started crusades to ban the film. The gin-guzzling characters Dressler and Moran portrayed had, they said, offended the principles of every anti-drinking organization in the United States. Mayer announced, very reluctantly, that the film would be shelved indefinitely. It never was released and the negative is believed to have eventually been destroyed.

Dressler's career once more seemed to have ended. But Frances Marion, with the support of Elizabeth Mayberry, wouldn't give up. She approached Charles and Al Christie whose Christie Comedies were at that time very big at the box office. She showed them a copy of *The Callahans* and they agreed the team of Dressler and Moran had potential.

The Christies had just purchased the former Metropolitan Studio on North Las Palmas, and decided to gamble on three comedy films, with no drinking, featuring the two actresses. The films were so successful that they extended the series to six films. The final one was the Christies' first sound film. Both Dressler and Moran made the transition with ease and it looked as though their careers were right on track.

But the Wall Street crash ended the Christie brothers' plans. "We just had no more money to pay for performers like Dressler and Moran, who were now getting top dollar, so reluctantly we had to say goodbye to them," recalled Al Christie in 1943.

Frances Marion refused to give up. "All of us at MGM had fallen in love with Marie, and it wasn't hard to get her a role in Corinne Griffith's *The Divine Lady* being made at First National," the author said in 1943. "I made sure Mr. Mayer saw the film, and, with a bit of urging, he offered her a chance to re-team with Polly Moran in a sound film, *The Patsy*. It was very popular with fans and made a lot of money for MGM. That same year we were planning *The Hollywood Revue of 1929*, in which all our stars were to play in comedy skits and sing or dance. I pushed Marie into the film although she wasn't under contract, and she was the hit of the show. Letters poured in for her, I believe the count was around 4,000 a week. None of our glamour girls or male stars drew anything like that quantity of fan support."

Frances Marion's greatest achievement was to convince Louis B. Mayer to give Dressler a non-comedy role in Eugene O'Neill's *Anna Christie*. It was to be Greta Garbo's first talkie and the pre-release publicity was all about Garbo. "When the film was shown all hell broke loose at MGM," said Marion. "Garbo was great, her voice registered well for sound, but it was Dressler who stole the show. Everyone finally knew we had a star on our hands."

Mayer was worried about Garbo. Already in a depressed state of mind, he feared that having the film stolen from her would make her suicidal. He needn't have worried. After the film premiere, Garbo is reported to have arrived at Dressler's home bearing a huge bunch of chrysanthemums. "For you," was all she said to Dressler, who answered the door. She fled to her chauffeur-driven car and went home.

In New York, in 1980, the reclusive Garbo, then seventy-five, who had for years refused to give interviews, agreed to talk about Marie Dressler. "I will talk about Marie," she said. "But the conversation will end if you ask anything about me. I did go to her house with the flowers, but they were red roses, not chrysanthemums. I wanted to say thanks to her for making it so easy for me to make my first sound film. I was absolutely terrified when I started, but like everyone else on the set I was entranced with Marie, who seemed to have no fears. So we all relaxed. Yes, she stole every scene in which we played together, but I have never been one to fear the better actress winning."

Garbo then talked of an incident that took place some eighteen months after the premiere of *Anna Christie*. "This has not been told before. Only Mr. Mayer knew. I had tried taking pills for suicide, but they didn't work. I was depressed and lonely. It was difficult for a star to have real friends. My only one was Marie. She was not, like all the others, seeking something from me. She was a giving person at all times.

"One night when I was very alone and longing for my own country so far away I decided to turn on the gas stove without lighting it. But when I had done it I knew I had to tell someone why, so at least one person would really understand the feelings inside me. So I called Marie. She was so calm, so reassuring that I told her I needed to see her before I died.

"Well, she was at my door in less than ten minutes. She had hired a taxi and, I discovered later, gave him a lot of money to ignore the rules of the road. When she arrived I was quite sick and reeling, you could smell gas all over the house. Fortunately we rarely locked our doors in those days and she rushed in and carried me out to the lawn behind my house. She opened every window and removed the gas. We sat and talked all the night long, sitting out on the lawn, right on the grass, no chairs.

"Next morning she helped me pack a few things and took me to her home. For three weeks I stayed there. Only Mr. Mayer knew, and work on both our films was stopped. Mr. Mayer just told the newspapers we were both sick with bad colds and sore throats.

"Marie gave me the will to live. I have never looked back from that moment. Something inside me said things could only get better and they did. I would like to show you something I have treasured through the years."

She produced an invitation from Louis B. Mayer to a special sixty-second birthday party for Marie Dressler. "I did not usually go to such things, but I went to this one. I owed so much to Marie it was a small way in which I could repay my huge debt. She knew how much I hated parties, and I think she realized it was for her alone that I would attend."

In 1930 Frances Marion wrote another script, especially for Dressler. *Min and Bill* also starred Wallace Beery. A massive box-office success, it earned Dressler an Oscar. When she received her award from Norma Shearer, she made a brief acceptance speech, proving that she never forgot those who helped her. "You can be the best actress in the world and have the best producer, director, and cameraman, but it won't matter a bit if you don't have the story. This is really for you, Frances Marion."

Dressler went from success to success. In 1932 another Frances Marion story, *Emma*, set new box-office records and earned her another Oscar nomination. The award went to Katharine Hepburn. Dressler sent her a note. In 1995 Hepburn said she still had the letter, which she treasured. It read: "Had anyone other than you received the award it would have been a terrible mistake. You were magnificent."

In 1933, when Dressler was sixty-four, she was loaned by Mayer to David Selznick for his all-star feature, *Dinner At Eight*. As the decaying theatrical grand dame, she stole the show and won acclaim from audiences and critics.

Marie Dressler, Wallace Beery, and Dorothy Jordan in
Min and Bill (1930).

Her final film, late in 1933, was *The Late Christopher Bean*. Considered by many to be her finest performance, she became very ill before it was shown in public.

Louis B. Mayer, who joined with everyone at MGM in offering their services to Dressler as she lay ill in bed, was so persistent in being at her bedside every waking hour for more than three months, that she finally had to tell him, "I love you, Louie, but there are times when I must go to the bathroom alone."

President Franklin Roosevelt and his wife Eleanor, who had hosted Dressler at the White House several times during the early 1930s, travelled by train across the United States to visit her bedside. The president offered the services of any doctor in the world she would like to attend to her, but she was reported by her long time black maid, Minnie Cox, to have told the president, "Only God can help me now, and I doubt if even you can get his services for me."

Marie Dressler died of cancer of the liver at the home in Montecito of her great friend, C. K. G. Billings, on July 28, 1934. Her estate totalled more than $300,000. She left $100,000 to be divided among a number of friends from her early days in show business, $150,000 to cancer research, and $50,000 to Minnie Cox, who she said "stayed with me for more than twenty-five years, including many times when I had no money to pay her wages. She has earned every penny of this bequest."

The funeral was private. Marie Dressler is buried in Forest Lawn Memorial Park, Glendale, near Los Angeles. Louis B. Mayer followed the casket into the church, tears streaming down his face. Frances Marion said, in 1943, that Garbo was there, heavily veiled, trying hard to stifle her sobs. "Token members of each department at MGM had been chosen to attend to limit the mourners at Marie's request."

She left behind an unsolved mystery. Neither of her biographies mentions her marriages. The first to George E. Huppert, supposedly in 1894, broke up after two years. Her second marriage is recorded in some biographies as being to James H. Dalton, her manager for many years, who died in 1921.

No one has been able to identify Mr. Huppert, nor has any marriage registration or divorce been located. The stories that talk of her marriage to Dalton never include a date and place of marriage. Again, no marriage record has been found.

Certainly, they lived together for a number of years, and historians wonder if perchance there was no second wedding because she never was able to get a divorce from the mysterious Mr. Huppert. It is unlikely now that anyone will ever find out.

The following is a radio tribute to Marie Dressler broadcast on July 28, 1934, by Will Rogers. Rogers knew at the time he spoke that Dressler was seriously ill, and unlikely to recover. He also knew that her boss at Metro-Goldwyn-Mayer, Louis B. Mayer, was at her bedside and had promised to turn on the radio at the broadcast hour. Mayer said later that Dressler was able to understand what Rogers was saying and smiled at the end, saying quietly, "That he should say such things about me, little Marie. Perhaps I'll have the chance to say how I feel about him when I get better." That chance never came. That same night, just before midnight, she died.

Marie Dressler is the real queen of our movies. And we can say that conscientiously, because she is. There's been nothing — nothing like her career has developed in our whole moving-picture industry; on the stage either, for that matter.

I've known her a good many years. She was a star with a theatre full of people applauding her before — when moving pictures — the only way you could move 'em was to turn the leaves of a family album. That's when she first was a star. She was a sensational musical-comedy star when your fathers and mothers had to get a marriage license to see Niagara Falls.

She could sing. She had a beautiful voice. In later life, she did the most wonderful burlesque opera. You know, singing with a kind of comedy voice. She could do it wonderfully because she had such a wonderful voice. And she could do that better than anyone . . . She could dance in her younger days. And, in addition, she could act; and she had a tremendous lot of human quality about her in those days.

But, of course, like everything else, as the years mowed her down, there was nothing in her line on the stage any more.

But she came out here . . . All they wanted in those days was — just give us beauty, and — you know — give us plenty of beauty — and they couldn't come too young or too dumb. And she's the first one to come out and kind of do away with that whole theory. She started the whole new thing: that you didn't have to be beautiful, and that you didn't have to be so young.

She got a part with Greta Garbo in *Anna Christie* and was a sensation almost overnight. She didn't say — I was a star, I was this, I was that. For a start she wanted to take anything, and did take anything, and really won her way up just as though she had never really amounted to anything before in her life — which she had . . . There never was a career — one time big and then clear down, and now up again — like hers.

We'd often talked about doing a picture together. Every time I'd meet her, she'd say — when are we going to do that picture together? I'd known her a good many years. And I'd say — well, I don't know. I'm going to as soon as I git a chance. Gee, I did want to do one with her. . . That would be the proudest moment of my life — my whole amusement career — to say that I'd worked with Marie. Oh, — she's — she's marvellous.

Marie Dressler has more friends among the real people of this country — I mean from the president on down. Why, she visited the White House — regardless of political faith, or anything of that kind, she has entrée into places where none of us connected with the movies — where we couldn't get our nose in . . . And that's all been done simply on a marvellous personality and a great heart" (Will Rogers).

ALLAN DWAN

"I have worked with many directors in my long career and it is difficult now to distinguish one from the other. The exception is Allan Dwan. He alone was responsible for the success of my career in the mid-1920s when I so badly needed an understanding director who could develop my talents the right way. If I am still remembered today, Allan Dwan is the man responsible."

(Gloria Swanson, 1962)

Film historians believe that Allan Dwan directed more than 1,000 films in a fifty-year career that stretched from 1908, when he was twenty-three, to 1958, when he was seventy-three. Hundreds of these were silent era one-reelers that ran only ten minutes. None of these had any distinguishing mark to identify the director or even the performers. Most, unfortunately, have long since been lost by the ravages of time.

But well in excess of 400 films, both silent and sound, 100 of which are still available in archives or on videotape, are recorded as giving screen credits to this amazing director. By his own estimate, approximately 200 of these he also produced and wrote.

At ninety, in 1975, he was sought out by the *Los Angeles Times* for his opinions on Hollywood in the 1970s. His response was pithy, as usual. "You fellas get me out of my box every few years, dust me off, and put me on display like King Tut," he said. "What the hell can I tell you now that I didn't tell you five years ago? Except to remind you that creative talent is slowly vanishing from the entertainment scene, and television is getting worse and worse each year."

Joseph Aloysius Dwan was born on April 3, 1885, in Toronto, Ontario. "I changed my name to Allan because nobody liked Joseph and even less could pronounce Aloysius, much less spell it," he said in 1943 on the set of the film he was then directing, *Abroad with Two Yanks*. Asked how it was spelled, he snorted. "Hell, I don't know. It was a stupid name anyway. You could ask my father, but he's dead."

His father was a merchant who sold exotic medical cures to gullible housewives in the province of Ontario. After the family moved to Chicago in 1893, he became a politician. "That was a natural progression," said Dwan. "At first he was a con man, then a crook. But I'll say this for him, when he wasn't out there trying to sell his customers or his constituents something they didn't want and needed even less, he was a good, kind, and very generous father.

"If today's youngsters had fathers like mine there would be no wars in the world. We would all be too busy trying to swindle each other that there'd be no time left to build tanks, planes, ships, and guns. We'd be having so much fun that there wouldn't be any desire left to fight anyone."

The Dwan family prospered in Chicago. "All politicians at that time prospered in Chicago. People actually used to believe them then, incredible as it sounds," he said. "We lived in a nice house, people used to bow and doff their top hats when mother and father passed by. I always walked behind, trying unsuccessfully to tread on the trailing hem of mother's dress. My life would have been complete if only once I had caused her to do a pratfall while she was walking with such dignity on a main street."

Dwan had no intention of entering the film industry when he arrived at Notre Dame University in 1904. "Frankly, I don't think I'd ever seen a film at that time in my life," he recalled. "Most of the nickelodeons, as they were called then, were nothing more than converted stores or garages, and the people who patronized them were not the elite of Chicago, as we thought, I repeat, thought, we were. I was fascinated by electricity, so what do you think I studied? Try electrical engineering on for size. If only I had known that Douglas Shearer was studying the same thing in Montreal, we might have set the world on fire with both our intelligent minds working together. More likely we would have blown up the world and you and I wouldn't have been here today. I'll think about that and let you know my feelings about that a little later."

Dwan was a star of Notre Dame college theatricals. "I wasn't really that good," he recalled. "It was simply that everyone else was so bad."

He also became a star of Notre Dame's football team. "I wasn't really that good," he repeated. "It was simply that everyone else was so bad. Those definitely were not the golden years of Notre Dame college football, or theatricals."

After graduation, in 1907, he stayed on to teach mathematics and physics, to coach the football team, and to teach drama. "I reasoned that having graduated in all these subjects and recreations who better than me to teach the newcomers to do things equally badly."

In 1908, "having battered my head against many a brick wall trying to teach people with even thicker heads the rudiments of life, I decided the world was ready for me. I answered an advertisement placed by the Peter Cooper Hewitt Company of Chicago. They were looking for an electrical engineering graduate to help with their experiments in lighting. They liked what I had to offer, so I got the job."

One of the company's experiments in which Dwan played a major role was the development of the world's first mercury vapour lamp. "It was like chalk and cheese, showing how much better our new lamp could light the local theatres," said Dwan. "Everyone was raving about our lighting, except, perhaps, the aging prima donnas whose facial lines and grey hair had suddenly became more noticeable. Now if only I could have instantly invented a beauty cream to remove those wrinkles I might today be sitting on the beach on some exotic island having palm leaves waved over me by beautiful grass-skirted girls, instead of being here hoping to knock sense into a bunch of incompetent actors."

George K. Spoor, one of the two owners of the Essanay-Spoor-Anderson Film Company, located on South Argyle Street in Chicago, heard about the new invention that was revolutionizing theatre lighting in the city and wondered if the same lights might also do wonders for the early emulsion film and primitive cameras.

"One day," said Dwan, "a little man came to the theatre where the company was experimenting with the mercury vapour lamps and said 'We need you, young man, in the moving picture industry.' For a moment I was thrilled. Could it possibly be my features were what the fledgling industry was looking for? And all this without them even knowing how brilliant my acting was. Then I sobered up quickly and figured he was maybe offering me a job with a furniture removing company, handling exclusively the moving of pictures on the walls.

"It turned out that it was neither. Mr. Spoor — I later discovered this was his name — wanted me to take some of the new lighting to his studio, together with all the wires and gadgets we would need if we were to avoid blowing up the entire city. It turned out he wasn't too concerned if we only blew up a building or two, perhaps even a block or two, but he assured me he would balk at the possibility of the entire city going 'poof.' At least, not until they had their cameras rolling.

"It was at that moment I became seriously interested in the 'moving picture' industry as a possible career. After all, hadn't I always wanted to blow up a city?"

Next day at the "moving picture" studio, Dwan demonstrated the effects of his new mercury vapour lamp. "They agreed to experiment with four of the lamps," Dwan recalled. "Until that time they had either gone on location to benefit from the sun or had waited for sunny days to light the interior of their studio through the glass roof that covered the entire floor area. That had one major drawback. When the sun was at its best for shooting, the studio was like a hothouse; in fact, I was told that one of the technicians did grow some excellent tomatoes in a corner of the studio. He sold them to the actors who were so poorly recompensed for their services at the time that they even considered being paid in cut-price tomatoes was an advantage."

When the four lights were set up, George Spoor looked horrified. "Everyone looked like walking zombies," said Dwan. "In the theatre we had coloured filters, here there was nothing but the blue light from the mercury lamps. Spoor was all for cancelling the experiment until I convinced him — conned him with shades of my father — into believing we had tried photographing scenes on stage and that photographically it was the greatest invention since the wheel."

Spoor decided to gamble a full day's shooting under the lights. "All he had to lose was a few thousand feet of film," said Dwan. "It was too cold and dark outside to shoot exteriors. Next morning when I went to the studio to see what had developed, figuratively and literally, I stuck my head carefully around the studio door and walked in, making sure there was no one between me and the exit in case I had to beat a hasty retreat.

"Spoor rushed over and I stepped back a few yards until I realized he was smiling like a Cheshire cat. If he'd had a tail he would have been wagging that like a dog. 'Allan,' he said. 'It's magnificent. Come and look.' We went into a little projection room and he rolled the film. Suddenly my tail was wagging, too! The clarity of the pictures was incredible. The entire studio staff and actors crowded in to see what was happening and everyone cheered. I looked around to see if the president had entered the studio, but, no, it was my lighting results they were cheering."

With the blessing of the Peter Cooper Hewitt Company, Dwan stayed at the studio for a week, adjusting the lamps for best effects. During that week he decided the movies had a definite place for him. "But it wasn't as a director," he recalled. "It was some time before I realized that the man in the chair, fast losing his already grey hair, was the director. He could have been the bailiff waiting to collect the rent, for all I knew about films. What I did discover was that the so-called stories they were filming had been bought from amateur writers who just dropped them off and came back a week later to see if any had been accepted.

"The so-called scripts were very primitive, but I discovered they brought their writers anywhere from $15 to $25. They wouldn't, at that time, have paid Peter, John, or Paul more than $25 for their entire contributions to the Bible.

"I had written quite a lot of short stories for Notre Dame's college newspaper, and still had all the originals. So I went home, picked out the twenty best stories, and trotted back to the studio like a mare in heat. I was more like a stallion when I went home. Spoor read the lot before lunch and came to me waving a fistful of dollars. 'I'll buy 'em all,' he said. 'Every one. How about $300 for the lot?' He seemed so eager I decided to play hardball. 'Five hundred,' I said. 'Four hundred,' he countered. 'Done,' I said, and he counted out $400 from the pile of notes in his hand. When he'd finished I realized he still had several hundred bucks in his fist. That was my first lesson in negotiating with producers. Never accept any offer without first walking away from the bargaining table to see if they follow you, still talking."

Dwan took some more stories into Spoor the next day. "Hold it," said Spoor. "Keep them till Monday. We've never paid anyone more than $300 in one week, but I'll tell you what, how about becoming our script editor and I'll pay you $305 a week plus $10 for every script you write that is acceptable. You'll have to read about fifty scripts a week that are sent in to you. How about that for an offer?"

"This was lesson two in negotiating," recalled Dwan. "'Four hundred plus fifteen for each script,' I countered. He shook his head, so I turned and walked away. He trotted along behind me. 'Three-fifty plus twelve,' he said. 'Three-seventy-five plus thirteen-fifty,' I said, still heading for the door. As I got my hand on the doorknob he said 'Done,' and I knew I was on my way to making a success of my career in 'moving pictures.'

"I hadn't been there more than a couple of months when something happened to my dreams of being mayor of Chicago. I'd worked out a good system of script buying by that time. I put all the scripts I wrote in one pile — and I was turning them out at home in colossal numbers — and all the scripts that came in from other writers in another pile. The system was easy. I bought two from my pile, one from the outside pile, two more from my pile and one more from the other writers. It didn't do anything for the company's bank balance but it certainly helped mine.

"The something that changed my life? Well, I was approached by three top executives of the Essanay-Spoor-Anderson Company, the men with the money. They had quietly formed a corporation called the American Film Company and wanted me to join them as script supervisor and writer. I think it was $600 a week they were offering, something like that, certainly enough to drag me, with little reluctance, away from Essanay-Spoor-Anderson.

"At that stage in the evolution of the movies, there were a lot of problems for independents like the new American Film Company. A group of the bigger companies like Kalem, Biograph, and, I think Vitagraph, certainly Essanay, had banded together under one umbrella they called The Patents Company. They owned exclusive rights to half a dozen patents, which made it very difficult for independents to operate because they needed to infringe on the rights The Patents Company owned just to get the film to work in the camera.

"A man called George Latham invented a loop that was necessary for any film to be threaded in the camera. The Patents Company bought his licensed invention and weren't about to let anyone not in the 'movie mafia' use it. The big companies tried, and succeeded in many cases, in stopping production on dozens of what they called 'illegal' sets. So little companies like ours moved out of the big cities to remote locations where they hoped the cartel wouldn't hear about their operations until the film was ready for showing.

"Thus I — and a band of actors and technicians — fled Chicago for the wilds of Arizona. And when I say 'wilds' I mean 'wilds.' My new mercury vapour lamp, by now making a fortune for the Peter Cooper Hewitt Company in every film studio in the nation, would have been no use down there unless you could plug it in to a cactus tree or the rear end of a pack mule. There was no electricity, and no indoor or outdoor plumbing, which taught us all some very unpleasant habits. Putting this in simple words, we all had to be toilet-trained again when we got back to civilization."

The Patents Company was not averse to using strong-arm tactics to ensure the "loop" or any of their other licensed inventions were not used by unauthorized film units. "They had a bunch of hoodlums who smashed up more than one outlaw studio in New York," recalled Dwan. "They would even go out into the wilds of New Jersey — yes, there were wilds there too just after the turn of the century — where some of the companies shot their western films that were all the rage. They infiltrated the company's extra ranks and when the cowboys chased the Indians there were real bullets flying. Thank God they only aimed at the camera. They had won the war if it, and the loop, were destroyed."

There are no records showing that any actor, director, or technician was ever hurt by the gunmen, "but a lot of good cameras bit the dust," said Dwan.

On arrival in Arizona the American Film Company found it had a major problem. "Our director, who shall be nameless, had been drunk all the way down on the train," said Dwan. "He was so soaked that even when he was sober, a few rays from the sun, and there were plenty in Arizona, had him reeling from side to side. And that was the only reeling he did. He couldn't have directed the cameraman to start the film reel turning if it was to save his life.

"I sent an urgent message back to Chicago. It read something like this: 'Director unable to direct due to sunstroke. Send new director. We are waiting, Dwan.' The reply came within hours. 'We have no new director. You are now director. Money increased by four hundred dollars provided you turn out minimum of three films a week,' and it was signed by the company president whose name I forget, as I would anyone who did such a gross trick on a poor scriptwriter.

"I gathered the actors and crew together and told them if they didn't accept me as their director they would all be returned to Chicago unpaid. Unanimously they agreed, even applauded, if I recall correctly. 'So what does a director do?' I asked. 'Direct,' came the intelligent answer in unison from all present. One actor with a bit more on the ball than the others told me to stand beside the camera and I would soon learn the rudiments of directing. He taught me to shout either 'OK, let's go' or 'Action' if I so preferred. He said that the actors will do what the script says. The only other thing you need to know is to shout 'OK, let's stop' or 'Cut' if I so preferred. 'That will save a lot of film,' he said. 'Most cameramen keep on cranking until they hear those words.'

"For the chase scenes, where the cowboys pursued the Indians or the Indians hunted the cowboys, where they couldn't hear my cries of 'Hit the trail' or 'Whoa,' I learned to hold a red flag high in the air where they could see it. When I dropped it they had to start riding, when I raised it, they had to quit the chase. That explains why, in all my early westerns, the cowboys and Indians always had their heads turned toward the camera, regardless of which way their horses were going. They had to be able to see the red flag to know when to quit the chase.

"Unfortunately, on many occasions they were over the hill and gone before I could raise the flag, and who knows how many miles they might have galloped if I hadn't decided that all chase scenes would, from then on, be directed from the top of the hill, with the action taking place in the valley.

"The cameraman, with his eye glued to the lens, was a problem until we hired a little Indian boy who kept his eyes on the flag and when it dropped he nudged the cameraman, which probably accounted for some rather shaky film at the beginning of my early films."

Dwan made quite a number of one-reel films in Arizona before the gunmen arrived. "They never did manage to hit the camera," recalled Dwan, "but they did hit the rear end of one of our pack mules and we never saw it, or the water supplies it carried, again. I was getting a little fed up with the hoodlum activities so I told my cowboys and Indians to load up with real bullets and sharp arrows and when the next raid came to ride full tilt for their shooting positions and fire.

"I don't believe our sharpshooters were so sharp, for we never heard of any of the hoodlums getting hit, but one of our Indians reported recording a direct hit on the posterior of one of the fleeing men. It was confirmed the next day that a doctor in the nearest town had removed such a spike from an unidentified male.

"I had all the cowboys and Indians lined up waiting the arrival of the gunmen and when the first bullet arrived I hollered out 'OK, boys, lets go.' Our cameraman, who had his head under the black cloth at the time of my call, started cranking the camera and since I never shouted 'stop' he would have gone on filming for ever if the film hadn't run out.

"That was the first film ever released that had a combined posse of Indians and cowboys fighting side-by-side against the bad men. Once we knew it was in the can I wrote a script to fit the occasion. One of the Indian chiefs, who had lent us part of his tribe for our films, presented me with a peace pipe for showing that Indians and the 'white men' could work together for the good of all mankind. Not that my early films could really have been called for the good of all, or any, mankind."

Never again did Dwan run into the 'movie mafia' hit men. After the battle in Arizona, Chicago ordered the unit to head for California. "I don't think we ever did discover Hollywood on that trip," said Dwan. "There were film units working like mad to produce westerns all around the city of Los Angeles, and after a bit of searching, during which time I developed saddle sores that have stayed with me throughout my career, we found San Juan Capistrano. That's why I have an air donut on my director's chair. I have my name on it in case there are any other saddle-sore directors still around.

"Unfortunately, no one told me that thousands of swallows come back to that delightful community in March of each year. They chose the day we started shooting to arrive. Now if you've never seen the swallows come back to Capistrano you won't know that they work themselves up to such a pitch of excitement at being home that they dive bomb every living creature for miles around. Our second and third days were spent waiting for the actors' clothes coming back from the wash. After a few rather futile attempts to film a western in this gorgeous little Spanish town, we gave up and moved south. Every time a gun was fired the entire swallow family rose up and attacked us."

The unit moved south to a small community near San Diego called La Mesa. "We checked out the possibility of any bird arrivals, but since none were scheduled we moved in. We were there from late September 1911 to just before Christmas 1912. In those fifteen months we must have made, at a guess, perhaps 200 one-reel films. I wrote about half of them, and if you like to call what I did at that time producing, I produced and directed every one.

"We got our ideas and scripts wherever we could. I recall buying one from a twelve-year-old Mexican boy that was just as good as anything else we were writing. For some reason he never did come back with another offering. Possibly because we were only paying twelve-year-olds at that time $5 a script!

"We got away from the western theme with about eighty percent of the films. Chicago had notified us that barring another masterpiece like the one in which the Indians and cowboys rode together, we should try to think of something different.

"Even the westerns we filmed had comedy in them, but in one-reel you can't hope to get more than a couple of real belly-laughs if you hope to get a bit of shooting and a chase in as well. We even tried producing documentaries, if you can call ten minutes of United States battleships sailing into San Diego harbour a documentary.

"They had dozens of parades in the small Californian villages and towns and we wrote scripts around these parades. I don't think we were ever asked to pay any one of the musicians or paraders one red cent. Often we had a cast of thousands with less than ten people getting paid."

By this time Allan Dwan was being touted as one of the nation's top ten directors. Invited by the University of California to speak to a class of students learning the secrets of filming, he was asked to explain his personal techniques as a director.

"I wasn't aware until that moment that there were any techniques to making a film. Certainly I had none. So I told them I decided where to put the camera, where to place the actors who, hopefully, knew what they were supposed to do, and what we were hoping to achieve. Then I told them to go ahead while I ate a sandwich. I don't think I was a great success because when I asked for questions I only got one. A student, obviously enthralled by my knowledge, asked: 'What kind of sandwich?' I was never invited back until this year [1943] when presumably the 1911 professors had all been put out to pasture and my initial class had long since left the area. I accepted, hoping that the new students wouldn't have any idea what an idiot I'd made of myself thirty years earlier."

In 1913 the American Film Company unit, which had changed very little since it left Chicago late in 1908, moved up the coast to Santa Barbara. "We had a bit of luck that we didn't expect in Santa Barbara. I had an idea to do a film called something like *Pouring Oil on Troubled Waters*. It was to be based on the oil drilling that was going on just off the coast. I had a rough idea what I wanted the story to be about and I was contemplating how to write it when a nationally-renowned author, Stewart Edward White, dropped by the hotel where we were staying. I showed him my rough notes, and asked if we paid him a few hundred dollars could we put his name on the film as the writer. He didn't seem too enthused about that, possibly because he wasn't too enthused about my writing. Then he came up with a gem of an idea. 'Why don't I write the story along the lines you suggest, I'll sell it to a national magazine, retaining the film rights, then I'll sell those to you for a thousand dollars, and you'll have my name on your film.'

"I wasn't too sure about the thousand bucks, but when he sold the story to *Saturday Evening Post*, and we were able to promote the picture as being the first national magazine story by a well-known author to be filmed, Chicago didn't quibble. White got paid twice for the same story and we had a film, eventually called *Oil on Troubled Waters*, that made the company a great deal of money."

Dwan had introduced three men to his company who went on to considerable fame in the years that led up to World War Two. J. Warren Kerrigan was the leading actor of the unit. Wallace Reid, a competent actor who became an international star until he died from using too many drugs, and Marshall Neilan, an actor who later became a successful director until drink and drugs made him such a liability to the companies that hired him, helped make Dwan's unit into one of the most successful then producing one-reelers.

In June 1913, Dwan was lured away from the American Film Company by the fast-growing Universal Picture Company. "Mickey [Marshall] Neilan, by then directing at Universal, set it all up. I was getting around $1,000 a week with American and considered I was doing rather well. But Mickey ballyhooed my abilities to Universal and told them I was making around $2,000. He said there was no way they could get me for less than $3,000. They swallowed the bait, and I accepted when I found I was leaving one-reelers behind and would be directing two-, perhaps three-reelers at the new studio that was just being completed.

"I was offered the use of a house on the lot if I wanted it, provided I didn't object to it being used as a set for occasional films, a car and, get this, a secretary to type my scripts. That is definitely what sold me. I had never had the luxury of a secretary before. This surely was heaven. I even got to choose my own girl from a pool — not a swimming pool, a typists' pool — although the former might have been more interesting. I chose one not so beautiful that it would interfere with my train of thought, and ugly enough that she must have some skills as a typist. It worked out well. I got a peach of a secretary who stayed with me for more than ten years until she got married and moved to San Francisco."

Dwan's first film at Universal, late in 1913, was *The Call to Arms*. "I gave Mickey Neilan a good part. He was dividing his time between acting and directing at this stage of his checkered career. I hired Pauline Bush to play the female lead and Wallace Reid to play the leading male role. I had conned Universal into hiring my lighting man, my cameraman, and two other technicians, I forget now what they did, but it must have been something useful. Perhaps they got me my cups of coffee. I don't recall. But we all stuck together and we made more than fifty films as a team."

In his early films at Universal, Dwan introduced Lon Chaney, Sr., who later became world-renowned as "the man with a thousand faces." "Chaney had an incredible ability to become the character he was portraying," said Dwan in 1943. "The first time I saw him on my set was in 1913. He was our property man, but not just an ordinary property man. He would come in day after day wearing different disguises and sometimes he was so good I spoke to him without realizing who he was.

"One day I said to him, 'Lon, what's the idea of all these get-ups? Do you want to get in front of the camera? Do you want to be an actor?' 'Gee, Mr. Dwan,' he said, 'I thought you'd never ask.' After that, what could I do but put him in my next picture?"

The picture was *Back to Life* with Warren Kerrigan in the lead and Pauline Bush as his wife. Lon Chaney played his evil rival and totally stole the show. So I convinced Universal to put him under contract. This marvellous man, marvellous actor, used to go back into the prop room to work when we didn't have a film for him. He was the most down-to-earth man I ever met. Although he was fast becoming a film favorite he saw no reason why he shouldn't revert to being a prop man now and then. He was so utterly unspoiled that everyone shook their heads in disbelief. I don't think I ever enjoyed working with anyone as I did with Chaney. I believe we did sixteen pictures together. Every one was a privilege for me. I knew I was working with one of the nicest people in the business, and also one of the most talented."

By late 1913 Pauline Bush was Dwan's favourite on-screen heroine, and off-screen they became a twosome seen together in all the right places. Magazines gossiped about their romance and tried to guess when, or if, they would get married.

"She had first worked for me in 1911 at La Mesa, California. She just came in off the street and told me she wanted to be an actress," he recalled. "She was absolutely beautiful, and a remarkably good amateur actress. Told us she had played in little theatres in Los Angeles but believed the movies were where she would have her greatest successes. She was right. I used her in more than fifty of the films we made at La Mesa and Santa Barbara, and when I went to Universal in 1913 she was part of the deal. I was able to get her a contract for a year, starting at $500 a week."

Between 1913 and 1915 Pauline Bush starred in more than twenty films with Dwan as her director. "Around March 1914, when both our contracts ended with Universal, we decided to move on together. Famous Players had been talking to me for several months and we both agreed their offer, which guaranteed I would make nothing shorter than three reels unless I requested it for some specific reason, was a step up the ladder for both of us. Famous was delighted to get Pauline, so we signed lucrative contracts for one year, with an option, on our side, for a second year."

"Both of us were excited to be going to New York for the first year of our contract. Believe it or not, neither of us had ever seen the big city. That first week we were there we played the part of tourists. If the Empire State Building had been built by then we probably would have visited it each day. But there were hundreds of other things to see and we saw them all. I learned to love New York and, of course, I was already in love with Pauline and she with me. We both knew it but didn't say it out loud.

"Famous Players studio in New York was the top story of a building on West 23rd Street. I was somewhat disillusioned after the splendour of Universal in California, but they had a very competent group of people working for them and it only took me a couple of weeks to realize that sometimes small is better than big. I could get at anyone I wanted in minutes. Sometimes that took days at Universal."

In his first film for Famous Players Dwan introduced world audiences to Marguerite Clark, the girl at one time expected to rival Mary Pickford in popularity. "She had the world at her feet. I don't know what happened.

Perhaps it was because Famous already had Pickford under contract and just signed Clark so no one else would get her. Perhaps it was that she didn't make her debut until she was thirty-one. The film I made with her, *Wildflower*, was a great success. It brought her lots of fan mail. Perhaps Mary stepped in, I don't know, but only once more was I allowed to use her in any of my films. She made quite a lot of films with other directors, competent men, but I believe to this day I was the only one who really understood her potential, and I was the only one who could have made her a really big star. Unhappily, it wasn't to be, and, tragically, she died just three years ago [1940] following a bout of pneumonia."

Wildflower also brought Dwan face to face with another potential star. Jack Pickford was at that time being pushed into important roles in anything Mary Pickford wanted him to be in. He was cast as the young male lead in the picture, but after two days of rehearsals Dwan went to Adolph Zukor, head of the studio, and told him he wanted Pickford off the set.

"He must have been around eighteen at the time," said Dwan. "He had a bottle of liquor with him all the time. He was arrogant and told me I didn't realize his great talents when I suggested he was creating a totally wrong image for his character. He disrupted the entire cast. There was no way I was going to let him play the lead in a film I believed would make Marguerite Clark into an international star.

"Zukor told me plainly that my request put him on the spot, but I reminded him I had total control, in my contract, over all casting for my films. He said the casting, in this case, was Mary's decision, and she had an even better contract than mine that gave her total control over casting of all Famous pictures.

"I told him I would see a lawyer as it appeared my contract had been broken. I shook hands with him, wished him goodbye, and went to join Pauline in the apartment we had rented. He shook his head as I left but said nothing.

"Later that afternoon, the doorbell to our apartment rang. I opened the door and there was Mary Pickford, standing with her face as long as a fiddle. I hardly knew her. I'd only met her when I was introduced to the bigwigs at Famous when I arrived in New York. 'Can I come in?' she asked. 'Sure, Pauline will make you a cup of coffee,' I said. 'I'd rather have a glass of whisky,' she said. 'I need something a little stronger than coffee.'

"Now I had never before that day had a drink of hard liquor and Pauline was a non-drinker too, but we sensed this was to be a moment to remember, so we poured Mary a double and ourselves enough to wet the bottom of the glasses.

"She started talking the second the whisky got down inside her and gave her the courage she needed. 'Mr. Dwan,' she said. 'I realize the problems with Jack, but mother and I are afraid he'll do something drastic if we take him off your film. I want you to help me, Mr. Dwan. I need you to help me.'

"I had to think pronto. This was only the biggest star in the industry I was talking to. Maybe my future, as well as brother Jack's, was on the line. I paced up and down a bit and I'm not a very good pacer; if I'd had a cocked hat I probably would have looked like little Napoleon. Then it came to me. Why couldn't I create a special part in the film for Jack? The bell rang! I would write in a comedy role of the leading man's valet for Jack. Was I thinking fast! I told Mary it would give him the chance to use some of the comedy abilities I'd heard he had. It wouldn't be the lead, but people would, I promise, remember him.

"Well, Mary broke down and cried. Pauline had to take her in the bedroom to repair the damage to her makeup. Eventually they both surfaced, smiling. 'You're a very bright man, Mr. Dwan,' said Mary. 'I think I'd like you to direct me in one of my films. Now what do you say about that?'

"I told her there were very few female valet parts available, but I was sure I could find something that would do. 'And you will find a part for Jack in our first film, won't you, Allan.' That was the first time she had called me by my first name.

"Really, she was quite a stodgy old prima donna of twenty-something at that time. But we became good friends from that moment on. I still talk to her on the phone now and then. If I visit her home, Pickfair, she still drinks a glass of hard liquor but there is always a cup of coffee for me."

As promised, Dwan created the valet role for Jack Pickford in *Wildflower*, and convinced him that his future lay in comedy and this special role would enhance his career in that direction. "Actually, I was right," he said. "He had all the makings of a fine comedy actor and his contribution to the film was singled out for praise by most of the critics. But the top critical acclaim was kept for Marguerite Clark.

"I only got to direct her once after that," recalled Dwan. "I know she went to Zukor requesting that I be assigned as her director, but through the grapevine I learned that Mary had vetoed the proposal."

Pauline Bush suddenly realized she enjoyed not working more than she enjoyed working. "She told me she felt it was time for her to retire," said Dwan. "That was the announcement that I had been waiting for. I had vowed that I would never marry an actress. But now, she was no longer an actress, so I popped the question. She said 'yes' and we were married three weeks later.

"She told me years later that she had heard me say so many times that no wife of mine would be an actress that she had been waiting patiently for her contract to expire, so she could quit work to see if anything happened.

"We lived happily, not ever after, but for six years, then things started to come apart. In the 1920s I was travelling all over the country for location shooting and she didn't like being left at home. But since she hated travelling, I was in a spot. I had to work, but if I did I knew I would lose her. Unhappily work won out and I lost Pauline."

After the divorce Dwan and Bush remained good friends. "I gave her, and still give her, a monthly allowance that helps her to live very comfortably in retirement. I bought her a waterfront home in Santa Monica and paid for a live-in maid to make sure she would never be alone. I still call her on the phone now and then to see if she is in need of anything."

In 1963, when she was living in retirement in San Diego, Pauline Bush Dwan (that was the name on her mailbox) recalled her years with Dwan. "I remember Allan with very pleasant and wonderful memories. I never made a film in which he wasn't my director. He had a philosophy that I, and other actors, loved. Unlike most directors, he didn't think all actors were dumb. He allowed us a great deal of freedom in our actions and movement. He wasn't constantly telling us how to move our hands, or how to walk. His only concern was seeing that we did our best to make a good film. And because he was not interfering with us, or nagging us to act the way he demanded, we were all relaxed and he got the results he wanted. It wasn't hard to fall in love with this man.

"I worked with him first in La Mesa, and later in Santa Barbara, but it wasn't until he got to Universal that he really came into his own. He never raised his voice to correct an error, however stupid it was. He made us perform well, because we loved working with him and hoped to continue working for him in the future. When our marriage broke up we did it in a civilized way, and we stayed good friends. He has looked after me very generously, and since I don't think I could ever find another man as wonderful as Allan, I've never even considered re-marriage. He calls me quite often, and I've had a Christmas and birthday card from him every year since we were divorced. There is always a note inside that makes me laugh. He's that kind of man.

"Do I ever regret not going on with my career? At times I like to wonder how famous I might have been if I'd let work take priority in my life. But, no, I must be truthful. I don't regret a thing. Except perhaps that Allan and I couldn't make a go of our marriage. It would have been wonderful if we could have grown old together.

"When his second wife, Marie Shelton, a former Ziegfeld Follies showgirl, died in 1954, I wondered whether I should go and see him. I did write him a long letter, but if I had any dreams of us getting together they ended at that time. I realized it was far too late to revive a marriage that had died more than three decades earlier."

Dwan remained with Famous Players for the duration of his contract, although he returned to California for the final six months to complete his assignments there. "I did get to direct Mary Pickford twice in 1915. *The Girl of Yesterday* was, though I say it myself, a real stinker. Of course Jack was in it, and that didn't help.

"It had a sterling cast, including Donald Crisp who went on to greater success and won an Oscar two years ago [1941] for his role in *How Green Was My Valley*. A great Scotsman who bought us all kilts to wear on the set on Robbie Burns Day. I still have that kilt. Wouldn't part with it for a million. Last year when he got home after receiving his Oscar I was waiting on his front lawn, decked out in the kilt he had given me. Mickey Neilan had the same idea, and there we were both standing there resplendent in our Scottish outfits, each flanked by a bagpiper we had hired. Fortunately there was one Scottish song they both knew so at least they were in harmony when he arrived home. If I had been a drinker that was the night I would have been stoned out of this world. Never did win any awards myself, and I don't think Mickey did either, so we were thrilled to the bone for Donald."

The second film Dwan directed for Mary Pickford, *The Foundling*, was, according to Mary Pickford in 1943, one of the best she had ever made. But it was never released. "It was given great reviews in the trade papers after a special studio showing, and we were optimistic for its chances. But before we could get prints made the negative was destroyed in a fire at the studio. The entire film was lost. We made it again about a year later, but Allan wasn't available and the second version, directed by a competent man, John O'Brien, just didn't have the Dwan touch and it was not a success."

As a reward for his work with Mary Pickford, and for his perseverance with Jack Pickford, Dwan was given Marguerite Clark as the star of his final contract film for Famous Players. "Needless to say I had Jack to contend with again. Apparently he had decided Marguerite was to be his plaything, and it made shooting very difficult. He was constantly telling her how to do this and that and I could see the spark going out of her performance day by day. She had a little weep at least once a day and I finally went to Mary and told her Jack was ruining the film. She must have spoken to him because he was a little better behaved after that.

"But what really did the trick was when the previously demure Marguerite slapped him twice across the face after he had pawed her too much, and she screamed at him using words I'm not sure he or I had heard before that day. It worked. Jack was a subdued actor long enough for us to finish the film. But it wasn't a success."

Late in 1915 Dwan accepted an offer to become a principal director with the Triangle Company. "I didn't get any more money, but I was to go back to New York and work in their Yonkers studio. It gave me a chance to work with D. W. Griffith, whose films I had admired for several years. Griffith was actually my supervisor and I was able to discuss with him his techniques. You see, by now, I'd realized there were techniques to film making.

"I was on the set when he made *Intolerance* and though I can't claim to have had anything to do with the direction of the film I did solve a technical problem for him. He built a gigantic set for the film, and it was all done in secret. Only the construction workers and Griffith were allowed to see it until it was ready for unveiling. There was no such thing as a boom to raise the camera in those days and Griffith was stymied because he desperately wanted to bring the camera in from a long-distance shot of the entire set to a close-up of one person's face. So I told him I had an idea. He listened and agreed to try it out. We put an elevator on top of a railroad track that was to carry the camera. This way the camera could go forward and upward at the same time, allowing him to come in very close to the principal players without having to cut the film. If you've seen *Intolerance* you know how effective it was. We had every director in the nation trying to figure out how we did it. Of course Griffith took the credit!"

It was at Triangle, after his return to California, that he first met the great screen lover, Douglas Fairbanks, Sr. "He was already well known, although he had only made three films since coming from the New York stage," said Dwan. "I'd watched him work and he was so natural that I asked to be given one of his films. Griffith assigned me to a light-hearted piece of froth called *The Habit of Happiness*. I always insisted on at least two days of rehearsals, during which we ran through the entire script with the actors and camera operator, before we actually started filming. Doug came up to me. 'Have you read this crap?' he asked. I told him I had. 'Then what are we going to do about it?' he demanded. 'We're going to make it the funniest bit of crap ever to stick to a movie screen,' I said. He laughed, gave me a slap on the shoulder that nearly dislocated the joint, and sat down. 'I'm going to enjoy this film,' he said."

The film was a great success. "Possibly this was the first time I realized that I loved comedy and I enjoyed even more having an actor as competent as Fairbanks to work with," said Dwan. "Triangle knew they were on to a good thing so they sat us down together and asked if we would like to work on a series of films. 'Yes,' we both said in unison. 'But I want to approve all scripts,' said Fairbanks. 'And I want to approve all casting,' I said. We shook hands!"

Over the next decade the great screen lover and Dwan combined on twelve films. Every one was a success. "But Triangle also gave me more of their top stars to work with," said Dwan. "People like Sam De Grasse, the evil genius who never missed a Fairbanks film, Norma Talmadge, Bessie Love, Wilfred Lucas, and Hedda Hopper. Hopper is the same one who is now a vicious, backbiting columnist who I blame for the break up of my first marriage. She's a real bitch and a hazard to the film industry. I had people like Erich Von Stroheim and Arthur Rosson as my assistant directors. Both of them went on to greater glory on their own. Those days at Triangle surely were the most satisfying of my career. The work was easy, the companionship wonderful. It was the right time of life for a man to be in the position I was in."

Late in 1917 Dwan moved over to the combined Artcraft-Famous Players-Lasky Company. "Fairbanks had gone to this unit and wanted me to go with him. By that time he was the hottest thing on the screens of the world. He would produce, he said, and I would write and direct. In 1917 I was earning half-a-million dollars a year. That was an incredible sum at that time."

Fairbanks only worked for about ten weeks out of every year, but maintained Dwan on a year-round contract. "He allowed me to accept any outside work I was offered and never took a cent of the fees I made.

"Perhaps my saddest experience in the film industry was working with William Randolph Hearst's paramour, Marion Davies. She is still alive but hasn't worked since 1937. I told her to her face that she didn't have any talent, none at all. Surprisingly, she accepted my comments with a laugh and we remain good friends to this day. She visited me on the set only yesterday and I enjoyed lunch with her. Marion told me once I was the only person she knew in Hollywood who would tell her the truth. If she hadn't been Hearst's girlfriend she wouldn't even have had work as an extra.

"Over the years I only knew one director who ever achieved a good film with her as the star. That was Sidney Olcott and I believe, in *Little Old New*

York, he actually hypnotized her into becoming a competent actress. I'm not the only one who believes Olcott has hypnotic powers and uses them on incompetent actors. When he refused to make any more movies with her, for personal reasons I believe, she never did make another good one."

Hearst had created Cosmopolitan Films especially for Davies. Louis B. Mayer, guaranteed by Hearst that his columnists would never write scathing or scandalous things about Metro-Goldwyn-Mayer or its stars, agreed to let him use the MGM studios as the company's base.

"I made two films with Marion at MGM," said Dwan. "That was the first time I had come face to face with Mayer. We had something in common, we were both 'little people.' I suddenly realized, when I went into his office block, that everyone was my height or less. When I met Mayer I knew why. I got on the right side of him from the start. He had a huge mirror in his office, so knowing I was hired by Hearst, not him, I beckoned him over to the mirror. We stood side by side. He didn't look too happy, until I said, 'Mr. Mayer, I believe you're half an inch taller than me.' I could see in the mirror that he was standing on his toes almost like a ballet dancer, but I didn't let on that I had noticed. He looked at me and gave me a broad grin. 'And don't you forget that, Mr. Dwan. Don't you forget that,' he said.

"From that day to this we have been Louie and Al to each other. I hardly ever worked for him directly, but I knew I was always welcome at MGM if I was assigned there by another company."

Dwan stayed with Fairbanks for almost a decade. In between films he set up his own production company and made several films that he produced, wrote, and directed. Two, *A Broken Doll* and *A Perfect Crime*, which starred actor Monte Blue, who had been blacklisted by Warner Brothers, made a lot of money. "The audiences wanted to see Blue," he recalled. "They weren't happy that he couldn't get work, and when the films were released they flocked to the theatres."

Other ventures with his own company were less successful, and by 1922 he had put the company in limbo. It was that same year that he made the first of a number of films that became collectors' items in the years that followed. By this time Mary Pickford, Douglas Fairbanks, Charlie Chaplin, and D. W. Griffith had founded United Artists to distribute their own films and others that they felt reached the quality they demanded from their own productions.

One of the company's first successes was *Robin Hood*, which Dwan directed for the Fairbanks Corporation. The story was written by Dwan and Elton Thomas (a pseudonym for Fairbanks) and transferred to a screenplay by Lotta Woods. "It had a terrific cast," said Dwan. "Fairbanks, of course, doing his own very risky stunts, Wally Beery as King Richard, Enid Bennett as Marian, Sam De Grasse, in his greatest role as the evil Prince John, and in there as an extra was Mary Pickford. I believe she sensed this was going to be a memorable film and wanted to have a part, however small, in its success. I forget how much it cost, but it was the most expensive film made to that time. Even Fairbanks cringed when the bills came in."

In 1923 Dwan made the first of six films for Paramount Pictures. The star was Gloria Swanson. "They were superbly written comedies," said Dwan. "Once again I realized how much I loved comedy and how lucky I was to get the best performers for my direction. Gloria Swanson had a delightfully wicked sense of humor, and it came through in every film. They were a roaring success, and made me a lot of money and millions for Paramount. *Manhandled*, which I made in 1924 with Gloria, has to be one of my favourites of all time. I even put my wife, Marie Shelton, into this one, and she and Swanson are still the greatest of friends."

In 1950, when Swanson was asked to make *Sunset Boulevard*, playing the role of an aging star of the silent era, she urged that Allan Dwan, still directing at the age of sixty-five, be hired to direct the film. "This was not to be," she said in 1965. "Billy Wilder, who wrote the script, wanted to direct, and, of course, no one could dispute his abilities to do a good job, so I acceded to his wishes. After all, I badly wanted to do the film, I needed the publicity.

"But I must tell you something that I don't believe anyone else but Allan and I know. When all the newsmen and photographers are waiting for me to leave the mansion at the end of the film after I have been charged with murder, one of the photographers, and you can see him very clearly, is Allan Dwan. I paid the extra hired to do the job to hand over his camera to Allan. He told me it was the only time in his entire career that he had been seen on camera."

Dwan had his first experience working with colour film in 1925. "There was little colour around at that time," he said. "Paramount wanted us to try it for *Stage Struck*, which was to star Gloria Swanson. Most of the film was on location in West Virginia. It is possible, but I can't swear to it, that this was the first time any studio tried the newly patented Technicolor. We used a real showboat on the Columbia River and got some magnificent scenes. The only problem was that we couldn't see rushes the next day of what we had shot. All the film had to go back to the Technicolor processing unit in Hollywood, and that sometimes took a week.

Allan Dwan (left) with Gloria Swanson on the set of
Stage Struck (1925).

"Our scenic designer, back in the studio in California, built us a few interior sets we needed for a dream sequence. Unfortunately, no one remembered to tell him we were using colour and they turned out to be the drab, black and white sets like most were at that time. I solved that by telling our lighting man to project some colour on the white walls. I suggested he might try changing the colours as the scene went along, and in Technicolor it was quite unearthly, perfect for a dream scene, and rather unexpectedly the big scene stealer of the film."

Dwan entered the world of sound much earlier than most directors of his repute. "I knew it was coming, and I'd heard that Fox were experimenting in recording sound for their Movietone newsreels that were shown in the theatres every week before the feature. I asked William Fox if he would let me direct just one reel of the news. He seemed fascinated that a feature film director, and I had quite a big reputation by that time, would want to do something like that, so he gave the OK. I spent a week at West Point and came up with a sound newsreel that really had audiences jumping in their seats. I had time to experiment with the microphones and the cadets marched around for us so many times in that week I'm surprised they could stand up. It prepared me for the sound revolution that was to come less than a year later."

William Fox was so impressed by Dwan's achievements with a simple newsreel that he signed him to a long-term contract early in 1928 and put him in charge of all sound film production at the Fox Studio. He was allowed out of his contract in 1929 to direct *The Iron Mask*, the last of the great swashbuckling films that starred Douglas Fairbanks, Sr.

"We shot half the film without sound. Doug wasn't sure how his voice would come over, despite his years as a stage actor before he came to the movies, and we had decided we would simply add a musical background after the film was completed. But halfway through he made a decision to add sound to the rest of the film. I should explain that Fairbanks, with his stage background, was one of the few actor-producers who insisted on his films being shot in the sequence they would be shown on the screen. This was shockingly extravagant, we had to keep moving everything back to a set we'd used days before, but he insisted and he was the boss. So halfway through we added sound. He needn't have worried, his voice came through with a richness that I was amazed we were able to capture with the primitive apparatus of that time.

"In the long run it was a great success. We didn't stress the sound aspect of the film in advertising and when audiences suddenly heard Fairbanks's voice after sitting through the first half with nothing but a musical background, they actually stood up and cheered and applauded. It was a result we never expected, but it packed the theatres and made Fairbanks a lot of money."

Dwan stayed at the Fox studio until 1941, occasionally being loaned out for films at other studios. One was at the request of Gloria Swanson, who wanted him to direct her first sound film, *What a Widow*. It was a big success and re-started Swanson's career.

In 1933 William Fox allowed Dwan to travel to England to make three films. *Her First Affair* introduced to the screen the beautiful Ida Lupino. A few years later Dwan brought her to Hollywood and introduced her to producers who made her into a star who survived well into the 1970s.

In *Human Cargo*, a 1936 film he made at Fox Studios, by then 20th-Century-Fox, he gave a role as a Mexican dancer to a young girl he had spotted in a dance line at a Hollywood nightclub. Her name, Rita Cansino, was later changed to Rita Hayworth.

In 1968 Hayworth spoke of Allan Dwan. "I had hit my head against a brick wall for two years when Allan gave me a chance to show I had some ability. He guided me through my part as if I were the star. In fact, both Claire Trevor and Brian Donlevy, who were the stars, protested to him that they should be getting the attention, not me. I was having some trouble at home at the time, and he drove me home to his wife after he had found me crying in a corner. I lived there for more than a month. It was Allan who introduced me to the producers and directors who later built up my career."

Hattie McDaniel, the African-American actress who later made her name immortal by her superb performance in *Gone with the Wind* in 1939, a role which won her an Academy Award, credited Allan Dwan in her acceptance speech "with giving me the will to continue in my chosen profession back in 1936 when he directed me in *High Tension*. It was the first time any director had treated me like a lady. He gave me acceptance by inviting me to join him in the studio commissary for lunch. For the first time I was an equal member of the company."

In 1932 Dwan was chosen to direct 20th-Century-Fox's biggest star, the inimitable Shirley Temple. "It was probably my greatest challenge," he recalled. "Surely this million-dollar miss couldn't be anything other than a spoiled brat. I prepared for the worst. And I got the best. She was, and is, a genuine angel. I loved her from day one. I have always loved kids, but can't have any of my own. If I'd been able to choose I would have chosen one just like Shirley."

On the set of *Heidi* and *Rebecca of Sunnybrook Farm*, two of Temple's biggest successes, Dwan created a police department. "Shirley was Chief of Police. I was only a captain. Dear old Jean Hersholt was a member of the force, as were Arthur Treacher, Randolph Scott, and Slim Summerville. We all had to wear our badges; in fact in *Heidi* there is one scene in which you can clearly see Arthur Treacher's badge. Since we figured no one would ever know what it was, we didn't reshoot the scene."

Dwan recalled an occasion when he was driving to the studio, wearing his captain's badge, when he was stopped for speeding. "The cop who pulled me over took one look at the badge, saluted, and apologized for stopping me. He waved me on. I always wore it after that when I was breaking the law but never got caught again. I still have the badge in my box of special souvenirs. I must ask Shirley one of these days if she still has hers."

After 1941 Dwan freelanced from studio to studio. "I can't see myself signing any long-term contracts," he said in 1942. "I don't have to worry about money any more, I'm living in comfort, so I can stay home with my wife if I wish, or work if I wish. In a year or two I expect I'll retire, perhaps teach at one of the universities that have made film production an important part of their programs."

Allan Dwan in 1943, with starlet Daun Kennedy.

But he didn't retire, and he didn't become a college teacher. Through the forties and fifties he made a number of first-class comedies, several starring his great friend, Dennis O'Keefe.

O'Keefe said of Dwan in 1957, "He is a kind, quiet, and dignified man. I was Bud Flanagan when I first worked for him in 1936. He told me if I wanted to be Irish I should be an O'Keefe. After weighing up a few first names he settled on Dennis. And that's who I've been ever since. I know of nobody who ever had a bad word to say about Allan. Even his ex-wife thinks he's a real gentleman. He is one of our industry's unsung heroes, the nice guy who never made the headlines but certainly didn't finish last."

In 1949 Dwan and John Wayne teamed up to make *Sands of Iwo Jima*. A few months after the film had become one of the biggest box office successes of the year, Dwan told the *New York Times* that "This is the one I'll be remembered for. If I never make another film this will be my epitaph. Wayne was the best kind of actor to work with. He didn't know too much and didn't pretend he did. You know something, Wayne actually told me that he had once had a small part in one of the Swanson pictures I made. Said he was sixteen and his name was Marion Morrison then. Hell, even with that name, surely I wouldn't have forgotten that big lug."

There were no more *Iwo Jimas* for Allan Dwan. He continued to make two or three films a year, but many of them were for smaller companies like Republic. "His wife was very ill for some months before she died in 1954," said Dennis O'Keefe. "My wife, who had acted under the name of Steffi Duna, had worked with him several times early in her career, and she spent many days at his home looking after Marie. We were thrown together a lot at that time and it was obvious to both of us that he was losing interest in the industry."

In 1955 Dwan agreed to direct a film for television's "Screen Director's Playhouse." He chose Dennis O'Keefe and Fay Wray, the girl who will always be remembered from the original King Kong film in 1933, as his stars. It was one of only two films he directed for the growing medium of television.

"I don't think television agrees with me," he told the *Hollywood Reporter* in 1956. "I felt like I was back in the one-reel days, except that the money men were tugging at my sleeve every minute warning me how much money I was wasting if I dared shoot a scene twice."

Thirty years before pay television came on the scene, Dwan predicted its arrival. "It may be the salvation of television," he said. "It will make possible the resurrection of the creative minds of the industry where bankers and investors won't be sitting around watching every penny spent. I may direct another film when pay television arrives."

In 1958, when he was seventy-three, Allan Dwan directed his final film, *Enchanted Island*, for producer Benedict (Ben) Bogeaus. He had worked on several Bogeaus films earlier but had not achieved real success with any of them. Offered a cast that included Dana Andrews and Jane Powell, he decided to try once more. The film made enough money to convince Bogeaus that Dwan, at seventy-three, was far from washed up.

Dwan worked on three more unfinished projects for Bogeaus. *Will You Marry Me* in 1959 was scripted by Dwan from a story he had purchased. It was shelved when the producer failed to find the necessary financing. *The Bridge of San Luis Rey*, a big hit for the producer in 1944, was rewritten by Dwan, but the remake never materialized owing to lack of backers. *The Glass Wall* came to the same disappointing ending.

Allan Dwan made an independent film in 1957, *Most Dangerous Man Alive*, but it was not released until 1961. In some biographies this film is erroneously listed as Dwan's final film. It did not get distribution until Columbia Pictures purchased it in 1960.

In 1967, when he was eighty-two, Dwan was asked to write a screenplay from the biography of General Puller, a hero of the Korean War. He was to direct the film for Warner Brothers. Jack Warner was enthusiastic about the plan, saying to *Variety* that "Allan Dwan, at eighty-two, has more know-how that ten directors half his age." But Warner, himself seventy-five, decided to sell his studio before the film could be started. The new owners pulled the plug on the project.

When he was ninety, a writer with Associated Press decided Dwan's career deserved remembering. Dwan told a story of his early days, and the stars he had worked with, that brought him thousands of letters.

The *Los Angeles Times* ran a photograph of the aging director surrounded by heaps of letters. On each of the arms of the settee in which he relaxed, sat a beautiful secretary complete with notepad and pencil. The caption read: "Allan Dwan, famed director of the silent film era, prepares to answer the mail which has poured into his home following a story printed about his career last month." It quoted him as saying: "These secretaries are far too beautiful to waste their time on answering letters. I must see if I can find them something more useful to do."

In 1976, when he was ninety-one, he received the first public tribute accorded him in his entire career. The Los Angeles Film Critics Association announced their intention to give him their highest honor, the much-coveted Career Achievement Award. He had little to say at the ceremony, but his brief remark brought the audience to its feet. "What took you so long?" he asked. The applause had continued for almost five minutes when he waved his arms at the audience. "Shut up, for heaven's sake," he said. "When you get to my age, if you get to my age, you'll understand why I need to sit down."

Dwan was interviewed again in 1980, when he was ninety-five. He told the reporter to go away and come back in five years. "By then I may have thought up something exciting to tell you. If I'm not here, I'll leave my forwarding address."

He was not around in 1985. On December 21, 1981, the man said to have directed more films than any other man, living or dead, said goodnight to his housekeeper of many years and fell asleep, never to awaken. He left a letter, undated, addressed to the reporter he had asked to interview him on his one hundredth birthday. "Sorry to disappoint you," he wrote. "I really had some important things to tell you. And, regrettably, I must tell you my future address is, as yet, unknown."

There was no funeral. He left a will requesting that his body be given to a medical school for research. "There must be something in there useful to somebody," he wrote. The remaining contents of his will were never divulged, nor was the amount of his estate published, but it is believed that he left all his considerable wealth to the same place as his last earthly remains.

FLORENCE LA BADIE

"I cannot recall, in my lengthy career, directing an actress so knowledgeable and yet so eager to learn as Florence La Badie. She was, at eight, a polished professional. At eighteen she was astounding directors and fellow performers with her instant memory of complicated lines and her ability to achieve near perfection at the first reading. And yet she at all times remained so down to earth and so completely approachable. Her death is a major blow to the world of theatre and motion pictures."

(Actor-Director Chauncey Olcott, 1917)

Florence La Badie was seen on the world's movie screens for less than nine years. But in that short period of time she became one of the most loved and respected actresses of the early days of motion pictures.

Giants of the early movie industry, like Mary Pickford and director D. W. Griffith, called her the most talented actress they had ever worked with. The silent movie serial, *The Million Dollar Mystery*, in which she starred, is believed to have been shown in more movie theatres around the world than any other weekly serial of that era.

But when Florence La Badie died mysteriously at the age of twenty-four, six months after a "car accident" from which everyone thought she had recovered, the movie industry closed ranks and had few, if any, comments to make about the incident. Newspapers — despite being provided with information that her death was worthy of investigation — never printed a word to dispute the official report that said her fatal car accident was just that, an accident.

A story printed in the *Boston Globe* in 1927, ten years after the "accident," questioned the accuracy of the police report of 1917. The writer wondered why no one had apparently been concerned when the car in which La Badie had the "accident" vanished mysteriously, only days after the incident, from the garage to which it had been towed. It was never recovered and thus never officially checked to discover if the "accident" might have been a deliberate attempt to silence Florence La Badie.

But the story brought no response from readers. If there was any interest aroused it was obviously not important enough for the story to be followed up in subsequent editions. Or, as one reporter believed, they had been told to drop the incident by people in high places. It was almost as though Florence La Badie had been totally forgotten in only ten years.

It was not until 1943 that actress Valentine Grant, wife of screen director Sidney Olcott and one of La Badie's best friends, spoke publicly of her belief that La Badie's death was no accident. But today, almost six decades later, the mystery is no nearer being solved than it was in 1917. Only speculation remains as to why her silence was perhaps very important to a person or persons unnamed.

Florence La Badie was born in Montreal, Quebec, on April 14, 1893. Her parents were among the upper class society in the city. Her father was a banker, her mother simply that, a woman dedicated to giving her daughter all the good things in life.

The good things included the finest education a girl could receive. The Convent of Notre Dame in Montreal was renowned for the quality of its graduates. Tuition was expensive but education standards were high. Along with her fellow students, Florence La Badie learned to speak English, French, and German fluently. Her future was expected to be the wife of a prominent Montrealer, her duties to raise a family to follow in her footsteps.

But Florence La Badie had other ideas. At the age of eight she gatecrashed an audition seeking a young lady to play a small part in *Ragged Robin,* a new play starring a distinguished actor-director of that era, Chauncey Olcott. There were more than 100 applicants for the part, but Olcott told the *New York Times* in 1917, the year of La Badie's death, that once he had heard La Badie there was no further question who would get the role. "She was so natural that I was convinced she must have rehearsed the role before arriving at the theatre. I was puzzled how she could have done that because I alone had control of the scripts and not one of the auditioners had early access to the dialogue," he said. "I learned later that she, along with the other auditioners, read the part only once, but that she had an uncanny ability to be able to memorize lines on sight."

Olcott was somewhat surprised to discover that the eight-year-old had come to the audition alone. "Where is your mother?" I asked. "At home," she replied. "Does she know you are here?" I enquired. "Of course not," replied La Badie. "She has no idea that I plan to become an actress when I leave school."

At that moment one of the mothers attending the audition with her daughter entered the conversation. "I know Florence," she said. "She attends school with my daughter. I doubt very much if the school, too, has any idea she is here." Florence unhesitatingly confirmed this suspicion.

"It was obvious that I had a problem," said Olcott to the *New York Times.* "She was the perfect girl for the part but I had no idea if her parents would permit her to be in the play. The solution was to request the mother who knew her from the convent to go with me, and Florence, in my carriage to the La Badie home."

The butler who answered the door at the La Badie mansion ushered them in to what Olcott later described as "a drawing room of such immense proportions that I could have staged even the largest scenes for any one of my productions there. It was truly magnificent. Mrs. Helene La Badie swept into the room with such grace that I knew immediately where Florence had learned her confidence and style. The lady who had accompanied us, a Mrs. Levesque, introduced us, and I told my story. I anticipated an uphill battle but had the shock of my life when Mrs. La Badie eliminated all further discussion after she had heard the basic details."

"Then if my daughter wishes to accept the role in your play," she said, "she has my complete approval."

Olcott said he was, for a moment, stunned. Recovering from his confusion, he asked Mrs. La Badie what terms of salary would be acceptable. "You must take that up with the Convent of Notre Dame," she said. "We would never think of accepting money for Florence's services, but I think a contribution to the convent from your company would be a very satisfactory solution."

Olcott never did say what sort of financial arrangement he made with the convent, only to comment, "I wish I had a manager capable of bargaining on my behalf as did the Sister at the convent."

The La Badie family agreed to Florence being used in publicity for the play, and the story of her participation was a major news item throughout the play's rehearsal period. "Florence was so good that I rewrote the script to make her role much larger than we originally intended," said Olcott. "She knew every line after one reading and on stage you would have sworn she was a veteran five times her age."

The play was a big success. La Badie's performance was a triumph. "She upstaged me at every turn," said Olcott, "and so totally stole the show that I took her hand in mine and walked with her in front of the final curtain after each performance. I am sure that ninety percent of the applause was for her, not for me." Since forty-one year old Chauncey Olcott was a renowned and popular performer of that era, his statement was unexpected, but generous, and probably true.

Despite her instant success on stage in Montreal, Florence La Badie's life appeared not to change. In a 1914 interview with *Motion Picture World*, when her fame as a film actress was at its peak, she said that "once the play's run was over, I went back to my normal life as an eight-year-old learning how to be an eighteen-year-old."

She produced for the magazine writer a scrapbook that covered her life from 1901 to 1908. Just a few months after her "professional" debut she was once more in the news. Her father, as a prominent banker in the city of Montreal, was chosen to host a delegation of German bankers scheduled to visit the area. La Badie, with her command of the German language, was named "official interpreter" for the party. At nine, she translated financial discussions with "total ease," said a Montreal newspaper. Asked by the 1914 interviewer how she managed to deal with the technical aspects of the translation, she said: "You must remember I lived in a home where banking was the major topic of conversation, and I was never afraid to ask questions if I didn't understand what they were talking about."

She topped her achievement as a translator by playing the piano and singing — in German — at a banquet given to honor the visitors. Those present gave her a standing ovation, said the Montreal newspaper.

Another Montreal paper quoted one of the German bankers, Herman Kreiner, a director of the Berlin Opera House, as saying: "In Europe this child would be a sensation in the musical theatre. Here, I understand, she simply goes to school. I was instantly rebuffed when I suggested to her parents that she be brought to Europe under the auspices of my bank to make special appearances. This is a unique talent being totally wasted."

Two days later, in the same newspaper, Kreiner apologized to the La Badie family for his unintentional and uncalled for intrusion in their private lives. But he added: "This must not be taken to retract my feelings about the remarkable talents of young Florence La Badie."

By the time she was ten, La Badie had appeared as a singer, or pianist, or both, at many concerts in Montreal that were organized for charitable reasons. One of these appearances was with the visiting Philadelphia Orchestra, formed only two years earlier. The German-born conductor, Fritz Scheel, is reported as saying: "This child is already a musical giant. She must be permitted to attend the Philadelphia Academy of Music, where I can personally supervise her musical growth." He also pointed out that her ability to converse with him in fluent German was "heart warming."

Florence La Badie was reunited with Chauncey Olcott on March 17, 1905, when he returned to Montreal for a St. Patrick's Day concert. Although he was renowned for his dramatic roles, Olcott had started his career with a "black-face" minstrel show in the 1880s, and for several years he was the leading tenor with the Duff Light Opera Company, singing the lilting melodies of Gilbert and Sullivan.

His love of Irish songs, inspired by his ancestry, led him to make many appearances singing ballads from the old country. The Irish musical play, *Mavourneen*, was written specially for him and St. Patrick's Day was always of special importance in his life.

"He wrote to me some weeks before his arrival asking if I would sing some Irish songs at the concert with him," La Badie told the interviewer. "I recall one was 'My Wild Irish Rose,' which he had made famous.

"During our morning rehearsal, a gentleman named Ernest Ball came to see Mr. Olcott and I could hear them discussing a song they had written together. They called me over and asked would I like to give the first performance of their latest song. I could accompany myself at the piano if I wished. I asked to hear it and Mr. Ball played it for me. I was enchanted and said 'yes, please,' I would love to sing it. So that night I introduced 'Mother Machree' to the world. The audience stood and applauded and I was asked to sing it twice more."

There was a sequel to the Montreal concert, she told the interviewer. "In 1911, six years after the Montreal concert, I attended a matinee performance in New York of *Barry of Ballymore*, in which Mr. Olcott was starring. I was a little surprised to hear him sing 'Mother Machree,' which the program said had been specially written for the show and was being introduced to the public for the first time.

"I went backstage after the show was over and Mr. Olcott greeted me with warmth," she recalled. "His wife, Margaret, whom I had met in Montreal, suggested that I join him on stage at the evening performance to sing 'Mother Machree.' They both remembered that I had introduced it in 1905 on St. Patrick's Day. It was a remarkable evening. Although, of course, my face was by then well-known to moviegoers, and for more than a year my name had been used in film credits, on posters, and in advertising, nobody had ever heard my voice.

"Mr. Olcott introduced me to the audience and said that despite what the program told them I really was the first person to sing 'Mother Machree' back in 1905. He explained that it had not been used from that time until it was written into *Barry of Ballymore*.

"The reception was amazing. I almost wished I had continued with my singing when I heard the applause. I suddenly regretted the coldness of a movie studio where no one cared about my voice and there was no applause when a scene was ended."

Florence La Badie had moved to New York early in 1908, one year after her father died from pneumonia in Montreal. "Mother and I had no financial problems," she said. "Father had provided for us well, but we both wanted to get away from the city that held so many memories of him.

"We settled in New York because mother had two sisters living in New Jersey and one of father's best friends was a Mr. Woodrow Wilson, who would become governor of New Jersey in 1910. They had first met at Princeton University where Mr. Wilson was the college president and my father was often a guest lecturer. And, of course, I felt that New York was where my future lay as an actress."

Within a month of arriving in New York La Badie was working in the professional theatre. In an interview with the *Motion Picture World* she said: "We happened to bump into one of the cast of my first play in Montreal, *Ragged Robin*, and she said she knew of a young girl's part in a play called *The Blue Bird* that would be perfect for me. Mother and I went to the New Theatre where auditions were being held and that same day I was hired for a six-week tour. Of course, mother travelled everywhere with me.

"My entry into the movies was really just as simple. Producer David Belasco, who saw *The Blue Bird*, asked if he could become my manager. Through Mr. Belasco I met Mary Pickford and her mother, and as Canadians we soon became firm friends. Mr. Belasco had sent her to the Biograph Studios, where she had soon made herself indispensable — that is Mary's way — and she invited me to see her making a film. Before I knew it I was playing a very small role and within a week I was on the payroll of Biograph. It all sounds so easy, doesn't it?"

Although, at first, movie-goers did not know the beautiful newcomer by name, since film companies were afraid to publicize individuals in case sudden popularity made them demand higher salaries, Florence La Badie soon became known to both movie-goers and avid readers of magazines and newspapers as the "Stanlaws Girl." She earned this title when she became the favorite model of Penrhyn Stanlaws, then considered the finest still photographer in New York.

Glamorous pictures of her were splashed across front pages of magazines and newspapers. When her first film was released theatre managers took it upon themselves, much to the annoyance of the Biograph Company, to have stickers printed to paste over the posters saying the film featured the Stanlaws Girl, sometimes in letters bigger than the film title.

In 1909, when she joined the Biograph Company at $30 a week, the two most important actresses at the studio were Mary Pickford and a beauty named Florence Lawrence. "It didn't take me long to realize that they were going to get all the best parts with the crumbs being thrown my way," she told *Picture Play* in 1916. "I knew I had to go somewhere else if I was to achieve success, so when David Thompson, a casting director at Biograph, told me he was leaving to join the Thanhouser Company, based at New Rochelle, New Jersey, I eagerly accepted his invitation to move with him. Especially when he told me the owner of the studio, Edwin Thanhouser, had personally selected me from all the actresses at Biograph."

When she arrived at the New Rochelle studio she found the company's first priority was selling to the growing markets in France, Germany, and England. La Badie made a unique suggestion to Ed Thanhouser that made the studio the first to produce silent films in three different languages.

"Although, of course, there was no sound from the screens, I persuaded them to make three separate films, at least as far as my role was concerned. In each one I spoke my lines clearly into the camera in English, French, and German. Lip-reading was very popular among the deaf in that era," she said, "so I wanted the watchers with that special ability to know exactly what I had said."

David Thompson, who had convinced her to join the Thanhouser Company, was given the opportunity to become a director shortly after they both arrived at the new studio, and La Badie worked with him frequently until the end of her career. He confirmed her comment that she filmed the silent pictures in three languages.

In 1915 he told the *Chicago Sunday Tribune* that the company agreed to an unusual request by La Badie "because she rarely needed to do more than one take of a scene. To do three with her, each in a different language, was often cheaper than the five or six times they had to shoot scenes for other less competent actresses. It may sound strange to do silent films in English, French, and German, but we know it was appreciated and helped our distributors in Europe. We got a lot of letters from individuals who were astounded to find, when they lip-read Miss La Badie's dialogue, that it was in their own language.

"Thanhouser's French distributor sent us a large story from a major Paris newspaper telling of the satisfaction of the National Association for the Deaf, who were delighted to find that an American actress could actually speak French."

Although La Badie had created a lot of attention in her short stay at Biograph, the studio had already given the title "The Biograph Girl" to another Canadian-born actress, Florence Lawrence. Many writers have suggested over the years that the first Biograph Girl was yet another

Canadian, Mary Pickford, but she denied on many occasions that she ever used that title. So it was as the Stanlaws Girl that La Badie moved from Biograph to Thanhouser in 1910.

Later that same year, when Florence Lawrence was lured away from Biograph by Carl Laemmle to his new Independent Motion Picture Company of America (IMP), he decided to use her name in advertising since he couldn't use the words Biograph Girl. That started the ball rolling. Biograph immediately put Mary Pickford's name on their posters. And Thanhouser announced his Stanlaws Girl was, in reality, Florence La Badie.

At this point in the youthful history of the motion picture industry, the three highest-rated and best-known actresses, Mary Pickford, Florence La Badie, and Florence Lawrence, were all Canadian-born.

La Badie's success story continued. In 1911 she made twenty films. In 1912 her total was no less than thirty-five. By 1912 her new contract with Thanhouser was for $160 a week. Mary Pickford, under contract to Majestic Films that same year, earned $275 a week. Pickford talked of those early days to *Film Weekly* in 1948. "These were incredible sums of money in those days," she said. "We got together often just to talk about our good fortune."

The occasional visits to the Thanhouser Studio by Governor Woodrow Wilson of New Jersey, which started in 1911 when La Badie arrived in New Rochelle, grew to be almost daily visits by 1912. Newspaper reporters who saw him there were told that movie making fascinated him. "But it was obvious to the film company employees that he was much more fascinated by eighteen-year-old Florence La Badie, the daughter of his old Canadian friend," said Valentine Grant in 1943.

Grant recalled that the fifty-year-old governor's visits became embarrassing to La Badie. "She told me it was a difficult situation to be in," said Grant. "She didn't want to offend such an important man who on many occasions gave approval for the studio to use government buildings for location shooting, buildings that were closed to other companies. And because he had been such a good friend to her father she accepted, with some misgivings, the gifts he frequently brought. They were never seen in public together but they often dined in private rooms down in the city. Florence was unhappy but was pressured by Ed Thanhouser to go along with the inconvenience for the good of the studio."

In 1913, when Governor Wilson became President Woodrow Wilson he continued to visit La Badie at the studio as often as work permitted. "He told us on one occasion," said Grant, "that as a former Governor of New Jersey

Florence La Badie

he felt he had an obligation to come back to the state as often as possible to ensure nothing was being lost to New Jersey by his move to the White House. But we all knew he was really coming to see Florence."

La Badie had her greatest success in 1914. Charles J. Hite, president of the Thanhouser Company, asked her to take the lead in a serial that would be issued worldwide to theatres in fifteen weekly episodes. It would, he pointed out, make her the first woman ever to be the star of her own weekly series.

She talked about the series in the *Dramatic Mirror* in 1914. "I really didn't want to do it. I was afraid of overexposure, but James Cruze, who was also to be in the series, convinced me," she said. "I valued his opinion and said 'yes' to Mr. Hite if the studio would make all the sets closed to all visitors so we could keep the endings of the unusual stories a closely guarded secret."

"This may have been her story to the newspapers but she told me quite clearly that this was the only way she could hope to keep the President of the United States from constantly slobbering over her and pawing her," said Grant.

The series, *The Million Dollar Mystery*, was proudly announced in trade magazines and news releases as Thanhouser's most important production of the year. Hite signed the best supporting cast possible. In addition to James Cruze he hired Lila Chester, Frank Farrington, Marguerite Snow, and Sidney Bracy. "Florence read some of the stories and began to be enthusiastic about the series," said Grant, "and the freedom from the president for three months was like a ton of bricks lifted from her shoulders."

Each of the segments of the *Million Dollar Mystery* was a complete ten-minute movie with a continuing theme that was not resolved until the final episode. La Badie was the heroine of each episode with Cruze, Snow, and Bracy playing the same characters each week. Different actors of repute were added in each episode to play her rescuer or the villain.

At the start of the fourth week of shooting Ed Thanhouser surprised La Badie by bringing to the set a youthful but distinguished looking gentleman. "I would like you to meet your leading man for this week's episode," he told La Badie. "May I introduce His Grace, the Duke of Manchester, an important member of the British peerage. I must stress that at all times he must be referred to as 'Your Grace.'" "Then you had better get me a new leading man," said La Badie. Turning to the duke she said, "Don't you have a first name?" "Of course," he said, "it's Robert." "Then welcome, Robert, to the Thanhouser Studio," said La Badie. "Let's start rehearsing."

La Badie told *Picture Play* in 1916 that the duke was a delight to have on the set. "Although he was not a great actor he was willing to learn and I spent hours with him going over the range of expressions he would need for the camera," she said. "As far as I know it was the only film he ever made and it brought us a lot of publicity in the world's newspapers. I should mention that he spoke French fluently and we were able to add his role in French to our releases for that country."

But the duke and La Badie did not confine their get-togethers to the studio. Night after night they were seen in fashionable restaurants sitting, as the gossip columnists reported, "as closely as was allowable while preserving the correct decorum." The "romance" blossomed for about four weeks before the duke sailed for home.

"Did you have any communication from him after his return to England?" asked the *Picture Play* reporter. "No," said La Badie. "But I did have a letter from his wife telling me she had no intention of divorcing her husband. Good heavens, I had no idea he was married!"

Grant said she always believed La Badie's public display of affection for the duke was intended to be "a message for the president." But when President Wilson's wife, Ellen, died in August 1914, Grant said La Badie told her that her days as an actress were very nearly at an end. "I know the president will not allow me to continue working in the public eye," she said. "I believe he wants to marry me!"

"Closing the *Million Dollar Mystery* sets to visitors displeased the president," recalled Grant. "The studio suddenly found its requests to use government buildings for location shooting were refused and police officers constantly harassed Thanhouser film units working in public parks or on streets where traffic was disrupted. Ed Thanhouser finally had to plead with Florence to make an exception to the closed set rules and admit the president so they could get the permits they needed. Florence relented, reluctantly, and her problems began again."

In early 1914 La Badie had two books of poetry published, one of which, *Thoughts of a Young Girl*, became a bestseller. "People would bring copies to the studio and wait outside for her to leave so she would autograph them," said Grant. "She would talk to them for an hour if the president was anywhere around. She discovered that by having lots of people around she could drive the president away from the studio. Even though his wife was no longer alive, he was reluctant, so soon after the funeral, to risk gossip that might defeat his chances of re-election in 1916.

"Quite by accident, she found another very effective way of keeping the president at arm's length. Helen Badgley, a four-year-old from New Rochelle who was appearing in a number of Thanhouser films, took a liking to Florence who, in turn, delighted in keeping Helen fascinated with some of the ghost stories that came easily to her creative mind. Helen told her friends, and it was arranged that up to ten could visit the studio each day at noon and four in the afternoon so they could listen to Florence. It was great publicity, and also a perfect screen to keep the president away. Parents came along with the young children and — presumably — the president feared that parents might talk. She kept this up until the end of 1914."

In June 1914 she is reported by the *New York World* to have spearheaded a drive to raise funds for the illumination of the Statue of Liberty. The newspaper said: "Miss Florence La Badie, 'The *Million Dollar Mystery* girl,' led a cavalcade of cars from Broadway and Sixty-third Street to the United States sub-treasury on Wall Street. She drove in her new ivory white Pullman coupe presented to her by the Thanhouser Company in recognition of her services to the company and the motion picture industry."

At the treasury she was met by hundreds of bankers and brokers who had agreed to promote the illumination fund among their employees and customers. La Badie gave a speech from the steps outside the treasury. "It is of great importance to our nation, in this time of war in Europe, that we display our willingness to accept the world's refugees by lighting up the Statue of Liberty as a signal of welcome."

The report said that thousands of school children, given a day's vacation to join the demonstration, joined her in singing the United States national anthem. But if the drive to raise the illumination money succeeded, no subsequent stories in the *World* announced the fact.

During the early summer of 1914, a major story in the nation's newspapers told of the search for a missing four-year-old boy, Jimmy Glass. The child had vanished from the garden of his parents' home in New Jersey. The hunt to locate the missing boy came close to home for La Badie when someone reported to the child's mother that a person resembling the boy had been seen at the Thanhouser Studios.

It was October when New Jersey Police Lieutenant James P. Rooney, accompanied by the boy's mother, arrived at the studio with a warrant to check the company's files for the home addresses of every young person used in a Thanhouser film during the previous six months. La Badie heard of Mrs. Glass's visit and invited her to her dressing room while the police did their routine work. So fascinated did she become with the story that she asked to speak to the police officer about the case.

Next day, the following comment, made by Lieutenant Rooney, was printed in the *New York Telegraph*: "The actress lady [La Badie] just took me off my feet," he said. "Ideas just seemed to pop out of her head like gun flashes, every one of them a peach. She certainly is going to help us in a mighty big way."

One of La Badie's ideas was to send a sketch of the missing boy, done by a studio artist, along with every reply to the mounds of fan mail that came into the studio daily. With the sketch was a small poster offering $1,000, which La Badie guaranteed, to the person giving information that led to the recovery of Jimmy Glass.

La Badie's two friends, Mary Pickford and Florence Lawrence, asked that they too be allowed to send out the information in their mail. Each added an additional $1,000 to the reward offered. In October 1914, *The Moving Picture World* estimated that more than 2,000 pieces of mail containing the missing boy's description left the three studios every day.

Hundreds of leads arrived at the studios and police departments in more than twenty states and four Canadian provinces followed these up. Unhappily, the boy was never found.

"Early in December, Florence and her mother, Helene, received invitations to spend Christmas in Washington at the White House," said Grant. "Of course, the studio was delighted, they visualized great publicity possibilities, but Florence was terribly upset. She, and her mother, discussed the situation with Ed Thanhouser, who told them the invitation could not be turned down. He said it was an honour they couldn't refuse. Florence was so upset that she begged time off from the studio until the new year. It was obvious to all of us that she didn't want to go to Washington, and she came to our home on several occasions and did nothing but cry all evening. She told us she was afraid of the president."

But there was no way out. La Badie and her mother were chauffeured to Washington in a limousine sent by the president. Much to their disgust, the studio had been refused permission to use the story in any publicity plans.

"When she came back to the studio, in January 1915, we were all shocked to see that she was a changed person," recalled Grant. "She refused to say a word about her visit to the White House, and even a mention of Washington sent her into crying spells. She spent hours alone in her dressing room and didn't seem very interested in any of the films she was making. She only made four films in the first three months of the year before requesting a six-month leave of absence, which Thanhouser approved and announced to the newspapers.

"She didn't say goodbye to any of us and when we tried to reach her by phone at her home on Claremont Avenue, overlooking Riverside Drive, in New York City, we were always told she was not well and wished to be left alone. My husband [Sidney Olcott] and I were away for several months around that time on location shooting in Florida so we knew little of what was going on until we returned in late June."

Newspaper writers who enquired were told she had been given time off as she was suffering from a nervous breakdown. Even writers who had known her well received the cold shoulder when they tried to contact her at home.

Early in 1916, while the Olcotts were once again in Florida filming, La Badie returned to the Thanhouser Studio as though nothing had been wrong. James Cruze, who joined the Kalem unit in Florida, said she apologized to all the crew and cast for her unfriendliness earlier in the previous year. She explained that she had been working too hard and that the breakdown and her behaviour were a direct result of that overwork.

Thanhouser officials were glad to see her back. They took out full-page advertisements in the trade papers to detail her film schedule for the year ahead. Within a few days she was hard at work again. She made five films in the first three months of 1916 before once more complaining that the workload was too heavy and she once again needed a rest.

In April, Thanhouser officially announced La Badie's retirement. "She will spend a few years travelling to other countries," said the official news release.

Nothing more was heard from her until April 1917, when the New York newspapers printed details of a car accident in which she had been involved. The *New York World* reported that "Miss La Badie was driving down a hill on the outskirts of Ossining, a small community near Westchester, New York, when the brakes apparently failed on the vehicle and she was thrown out of the car when it overturned at the bottom of the hill." The story continued: "A male person in the car with Miss La Badie was seen to jump out during the car's wild run and was apparently unhurt. He has not yet been located or identified."

According to the story La Badie was taken to the nearby Ossining Hospital but was not considered to be in serious condition. "She is expected to leave the hospital within a few weeks," the report concluded.

The Olcotts immediately phoned the hospital and asked for information on La Badie's condition. "She is doing very well," said the nurse who was attending her, "but it will be some time before she can have visitors."

"Since we couldn't see her, Sid and I wrote her a long letter and took it, along with a large bouquet of flowers, to the hospital," said Grant. "We hoped perhaps the doctors might relent and let us see her, but we got no further than the reception desk.

"We were puzzled as to why her mother hadn't contacted us, and try as we may we failed to reach her. Ed Thanhouser seemed reluctant to talk about Florence. When the subject got around to her accident he always excused himself from the discussion."

The flowers the Olcotts delivered were never acknowledged by La Badie, and two weeks after the accident enquirers were told she was no longer a patient. Calls to her home by the Olcotts and others brought no response. The phone was never answered. A personal call at the house by the Olcotts found the doorbell also unanswered. "There were no lights, and the house looked as if it was no longer occupied," said Grant.

"A few weeks later a 'For Sale' sign went up on the house and, we later discovered, the house and all the contents that they had gathered so lovingly over the years, were sold to a George Smith of Washington, D.C. Neighbors told us the furniture was moved out during the night and for a long while the house remained empty. We tried to locate Mr. Smith but ran into a dead end wherever we tried.

"We were not the only ones concerned. Florence and her mother had many friends who were puzzled about their seeming disappearance, but for some reason that seems incredible today, no one was seriously concerned enough to do anything about it.

"Two weeks later Sid and I left for California where he was to work with Famous Players," said Grant. "We made one final check at the studio for information about Florence but Ed Thanhouser told us not to worry, although he wasn't sure where she was travelling, we would no doubt hear from her in due course. We left our new address in Los Angeles with Ed and several other people, asking that it be given to Florence when they heard from her."

Less than a month after reaching California, the Olcotts were shocked to read in the West Coast movie trade papers that La Badie had died on October 13 in the Ossining Hospital "from the after-effects of a car accident two months earlier" (the "accident" had in fact happened in April, six months earlier). Funeral arrangements were announced for October 28 from the Campbell Funeral Home, 66th Street, in New York.

"We immediately telegraphed a floral wreath and telephoned the Campbell Funeral Home asking that Mrs. La Badie please call us as soon as possible. We requested that she be told that we would welcome her in our home once she felt able to travel, but we never had an answer.

"Newspaper friends in New York told us later that the funeral was a quiet one, with only a few studio heads present, and with none of her contemporaries like Pickford or Lawrence attending. 'Florence's mother was not there,' said one reporter who had known La Badie well. 'When I asked the funeral director where I could reach her, I was rather rudely told it was of no concern to me or my paper!'"

Valentine Grant's memories of Florence La Badie ended at this point. "The story doesn't have any ending, I know," she said. "To add anything more would be to speculate on things about which we have no real knowledge."

Sidney Olcott also seemed reluctant to delve any deeper into the strange happenings of 1917. "It all happened twenty-six years ago," he said. "Perhaps it might be better to leave it as one mystery without an ending."

Mary Pickford, when asked about the mystery a few days later, said: "I think Sid and Val should not discuss those happenings of so long ago. There are things I could tell you, but you would say they were impossible to believe, so if you will allow me I would like to change the subject. These things happened so many years ago and there is no point now in trying to find out the truth. There are some things that are better left unresolved."

Asked if she remembered Governor, then President, Woodrow Wilson visiting the studio, she became quite agitated and said: "I don't wish to talk about or remember that man." She walked out of the room without another word.

James Baird, a junior reporter for the *New York Telegraph*, aged seventeen at the time of La Badie's death and still living at the age of ninety-three in 1993, claimed that he had discovered shortly after the "accident" that the brake line on La Badie's car had been cut through with a knife.

"I reported it to my editor and he seemed quite excited when he read the story. But next morning, when I asked why it wasn't printed, he told me the story had been killed and that I was to do no more digging about the car or Florence La Badie's accident.

"The police handling the case knew the brake had been deliberately damaged because they admitted that to me after I had talked to the mechanic who checked the car in the garage where it was towed.

"Despite what my editor told me, I went back to the garage a few days later and discovered the car had vanished. The garage owner said 'officials' had taken the car. The mechanic who had told me about the brake damage had gone, too. 'He got a better job,' said the owner. Asked where, he said, 'I have no idea.' I reported these latest facts to my editor, but again he told me, angrily, to let the matter drop. Twenty-four hours later I was fired. Somebody up there with considerable power obviously told the paper to print nothing.

"Two days later, when I went back to the police office in Ossining to ask for their help in writing my story, which I felt I could sell somewhere, I discovered someone had blacklisted me. No one would talk to me. I was no longer welcome at the police office.

"With the war still on, good reporters were at a premium, and I figured I'd have no trouble getting a new job. But once I sent my name in to the editors I got no further than the front door. Finally, to get work I had to go to a small paper in upstate New York. Even up there I was contacted by two tough looking men who pinned me to the wall one night outside the house where I was staying. 'Not got any more ideas about La Badie's car, have you,' said one. I told him that incident was closed as far as I was concerned. 'Good,' said the other man. 'You'll find it healthier to keep thinking that way.' They then walked away.

"Quite by accident I met the maid who had been employed at the La Badie home on Claremont Avenue when Florence retired for the first time in March 1915. It took some time to gain her confidence but one day she told me something I had suspected for a long time. Florence had a baby in September [1915].

"I spent every spare moment I had over the next ten years searching the registers of births in New York and New Jersey and Washington, D.C. The baby was not registered in New York but in Washington, and the father was listed as George Smith. His address in the files was that of an office block that no longer existed. I have tried for many years but have failed to discover what happened to George Woodrow Smith, for that was the name the baby was registered under. I advertised for him in daily and weekly newspapers across the country. Spent all my money doing that but got no replies.

"And that is the end of my story," he said. "I think it is obvious who needed to shut Florence's mouth. But I can't prove it. I don't think it ever will be proved after all these years."

Florence La Badie is buried in Greenwood Cemetery in New York. The grave is well tended by the cemetery, and the grave marker can still be clearly read. Occasionally some red roses are placed on the grave. But no one can say where they come from. Perhaps James Baird? Or perhaps George Woodrow Smith, if he was ever told the truth about his parents!

Of Mrs. Helene La Badie's fate there appears to be no record. New York city and state files, which go back well beyond the year 1917, have no listing of her death. So, presumably, whatever happened to her must have occurred beyond the state line. The plot in Greenwood Cemetery was purchased jointly for Florence La Badie and her mother. Why her mother never joined her there is anyone's guess.

And who was the unknown man who leaped to safety from La Badie's car just before it crashed? That is one more mystery in the life of Florence La Badie that will likely now never be solved. Even James Baird was unable to suggest an answer to that riddle!

One more unanswered puzzle is why Florence La Badie, well enough to be discharged from the Ossining hospital before the end of April, contacted none of her friends after that date. James Baird added a final enigma. "Why would it take six months, until October, for her to die 'from the after-effects of an April accident' from which she had officially fully recovered?" he asked. "And how did she die? The death certificate said natural causes. At twenty-four?"

FLORENCE LAWRENCE

"She was by far the best actress in the early days of Biograph. Many of us learned from her the craft that has given us so much over the years. That she should need to end her life in this way is very sad. But there is only so much pain one can endure. I have lost an old friend, a very dear friend. The industry has lost a great talent."
(Mary Pickford, 1938)

When Florence Lawrence died in Hollywood in 1938, at the age of forty-eight, she had little left to live for. Her fame from the silent era of motion pictures was long gone. The ravages of a painful and progressive bone disease showed clearly in her slow movements, and the constant pain from the illness could be seen in her lined face.

Few people she passed on the street recognized her. Those to whom she was pointed out were shocked to see this former star, who had earned $1,000 a week when most people were delighted to earn $20, looking so pathetic.

Happily, Lawrence never went short of money for food and other necessities of life. At no time did she have to live in the misery that was the fate of many of her contemporaries. Louis B. Mayer, head of Metro-Goldwyn-Mayer Studios, had made sure of that. She, and more than a dozen others who had fallen from silent film fame to near poverty, were under lifetime contracts with his studio.

Detractors, and there were many, called Mayer's generosity nothing more than "charity." But records show the former stars were able to maintain their dignity by appearing regularly in MGM's major films, even though the parts were small. Mayer instructed all his producers to give the old-timers as many parts as they could handle. He sent memos to every director that the former stars were to be put in prominent places in crowd scenes. He told friends he was determined none of them would ever lose faith in the industry that had once made them stars.

In her last two years, Lawrence lived with two young employees from the costume department at MGM in a comfortable, well-furnished, three-bedroom apartment on Cahuenga Boulevard, on the fringes of affluent Beverly Hills.

When there was work for her at the studio Mayer, remembering her days of glory, always sent along his own car to drive her to and from the set. Douglas Shearer, the MGM sound genius, said there were many occasions when Mayer's car was not available to him because it was occupied by Lawrence and other former stars. "He would hail anyone leaving the studio, from stagehand to producer, seeking a drive home to his Bel Air mansion. As a last resort he would take a taxi," said Shearer. "Mayer was quietly a very generous man, but he never broadcast his generosity. And he was also thrifty. He didn't believe anyone should own two cars at the same time."

Although her days as a big star were long gone, Lawrence still had a fan club. Newspaper reports at the time of her death said it still boasted more than 5,000 members. Letters from her fans arrived at the apartment daily, and despite the growing pain from her illness that made her depressed and often unwilling to get out of bed, she carefully answered each letter by hand.

A stack of autographed photographs, from her days of stardom, could always be seen on her dressing table waiting to be sent out to those who wrote to her. One, which was found after her death, waiting to be mailed to a devoted fan, read, "If only the studios would remember me as you have done through the years, my life would be very, very different."

Florence Lawrence was born in Hamilton, Ontario, in 1890. A resume she sent in 1907 to the Biograph Studio gives the date as September 23. Other biographies name January 2 as the important day, but records at the Hollywood Memorial Park Cemetery, where she is buried, give her birth date as January 1. There was no birth certificate around to give cemetery officials an accurate date, so they took the word of Louis B. Mayer, who paid for her funeral.

Lawrence was just five years old when she made her debut on the Toronto stage. Her mother, born Charlotte Bridgewood, was known by her stage name, Lotte Lawrence. She and her husband, Herbert Lawrence, were owners, producers, and stars of a touring theatrical repertory company known as the Lawrence Dramatic Company.

To all accounts, it was a small-time company that played mainly around the Ontario theatre circuit in Canada. Many printed stories say Lawrence lost her father when she was only seven. "He didn't die," said Mary Pickford in 1958, "he ran away with a seventeen-year-old actress in the company and neither of them was ever heard from again."

Lawrence was not heartbroken over her father's departure, said Pickford. "From what she told me he had not been the best of fathers, beating both Florence and her mother on a number of occasions, so both rejoiced when he finally went his own way."

To get out of the theatre circuit where she feared her husband might be appearing with his new "wife," Lotte Lawrence moved young Florence and her company to a new base in Buffalo, New York. The company must have become quite successful on its new theatrical circuit because Lotte was able to employ a tutor for Florence who was, by the age of eight, appearing in almost every one of the company's plays. When there wasn't a part suitable for her, she appeared between the scenes as a vaudeville act. Billed as Baby Flo, the Wonder Whistler and Singer, she was accompanied by her mother on piano and more often than not stopped the show with her talents.

Lawrence recalled, many years later in an interview with *Motion Picture World*, that her tutor doubled as an actor in the evenings. "I owe him a great deal," she said. "He gave me a much better education than I could ever have got in any school. And, to his credit, he spent as much time teaching me to act as he did teaching me how to add two and two together."

In 1905 Lawrence, although only fifteen, was fast becoming a stunningly beautiful young lady. She had been a competent actress for some years, and from the age of thirteen had been playing adult lead roles. It was 1905 when her mother decided it was time to show off her talented daughter to more important places than the small towns around Buffalo. So the Lawrences moved, complete with the tutor, to New York City. "I thought it would be easy for Florence to get work in the big theatres," Lotte Lawrence said in 1910 to the *New York Telegraph*. "But it didn't turn out that way. Her tutor ran away with a young actress in a company that was touring the United States, and for a while I had to take work in the kitchen of a large restaurant."

Lawrence recalled that the motion picture industry was very young when she and her mother arrived in New York. "I had no thoughts of becoming an actress in an industry that really had no reputation at all. But we needed money so badly that in December 1906 I went out to the small Edison Studio on East 21st Street and auditioned for a part in a film about Daniel Boone.

"The first person to give me a chance was Edwin Porter, a studio supervisor for the company. I thought the part was going to another girl when he asked one final question, 'How many of you can ride a horse?' Mother, who was with me more as a chaperon than an actress, and I were the only two to raise our hands. 'Are you sure?' asked Porter. 'Yes,' I replied, 'both of us have been riding for years.' This was completely true, as we had lived in Buffalo in a house built next door to a riding stable. 'Then I'll be able to use both of you,' said Porter."

The film turned out to be a surprise success. *Daniel Boone: Or Pioneer Days in America* was a one-reel film, lasting about ten minutes, but it made people talk about the young, unknown newcomer to the industry.

"I played another small role in a film at Vitagraph Studio in April 1907, before mother and I decided to audition for important roles in the touring stage version of Melville Raymond's stage play, *Seminary Girls*. We got the parts and Mr. Raymond gave us six-month contracts. He paid me $18 a week, and mother $10," she said to the *Telegraph*. "It was a happy time for both of us. We saw the United States as far west as St. Louis and Chicago playing in some quality theatres."

When the play returned to New York, in January 1908, Florence decided to take another look at the potential of the motion picture industry.

"Vitagraph's general manager at the studio in Brooklyn, Albert Smith, heard from someone that I was back in New York. He remembered me from the small part I had played there in April 1907, and asked if I would like to play a part in a new film he was planning."

J. Stuart Blackton, Vitagraph's vice-president, told *Film Weekly* twenty-five years later a different story. "Florence came to our studio looking for work. Albert Smith said she was too young for a part we had in mind, and I said she was too pretty for the role, but she convinced us in an unusual way that we were wrong. When we told her the role was that of a young Irish girl, she immediately started talking to us in a genuine Irish brogue. Imagine, we hired a girl because of her accent to take part in a silent film!"

"*The Shaughran* wasn't a very important film, but once again I was noticed and people started making nice comments to me around the studio," said Lawrence to the *Telegraph*. "It was a fun film to make, mostly on location in Central Park, and for the first time I began to look seriously at motion pictures for my future."

In 1908 Lawrence became a full-time employee at the Vitagraph Studio. "I was given a twelve-week contract, at $20 a week, to take part in every film they wanted to put me in. The $20 was very important to mother and I, so I did what I was told. I only remember the names of two of the films, *A Game of Hearts* and *Love Laughs at Locksmiths*. There were several others; in one I was dressed up as an Egyptian dancer, I think its title was *Salome*, and in another I was a slave girl captured by Vikings. None were of any consequence."

Lawrence later credited Smith and Blackton as being the two men who did the most to get her career off the ground. They, in turn, credited her with creating the motion picture industry's first "daily rushes." "Rushes," today commonplace in the film industry, are prints made overnight of the previous day's shooting to give the director and actors a chance to see how well — or how badly — they carried out their work. "Florence came to me one afternoon," said Smith, "and said she felt she was not improving in her work. 'How can I improve if I am not able to see myself act,' she said. So I arranged that on all her films the first order of business in the morning would be a brief showing of the previous day's work. It was remarkably successful. We spotted flaws in the acting or direction and were able to re-shoot some of the scenes before the sets were dismantled. It took us a little longer, but the results provided a much higher quality production than ever before, so we made it a rule with all our directors. Within months all the other companies were copying us."

Lawrence did enough good work at Vitagraph to catch the eye of a young director, D. W. Griffith, who was just beginning his illustrious career at the Biograph Studio, located at 11 East 14th Street in New York.

"Lots of stories have been printed that suggest I went to Biograph looking for work," she told the *Telegraph*. "That just isn't true. I was approached by Mr. Griffith while I was sitting in a small restaurant opposite the Vitagraph Studio. At first I told him to go away. I had never heard of him and I thought it was just some man trying to get fresh with me. But a friend from Vitagraph came over and silenced my protests by telling me to listen to Mr. Griffith as he really was a good director."

Griffith, in one of the many books written about him, said, "I knew I had a real actress on my hands. Suddenly I had a person I could really direct. She was a natural performer. Fortunately, her stage work had not given her a tendency to overact and she seemed to realize the subtle changes of expression that had to be made for the camera. And she had the most expressive face I had ever been fortunate enough to see."

He also admitted in an interview with *Film Weekly* in 1928 that he had actually gone to the Vitagraph Studio to see if he could lure another actress, Florence Turner, into the Biograph fold. "I heard someone call the beautiful girl sitting at a table Florence, and thought I had found Florence Turner. When she arrived at Biograph the following week I discovered my mistake, but decided to give her a try as we were ready to shoot a film. That error was the most lucky mistake of my life."

Florence Turner? She stayed at Vitagraph for many years and became renowned as the Vitagraph Girl. "When I told Florence [Lawrence] six months later that I had really been hoping to sign Florence Turner, she laughed and said, 'All right, Mr. Griffin!' And she insisted on calling me 'Griffin' from that day on."

In 1908, Florence Lawrence made thirty-four films at the Biograph studio. None was longer than one reel, and Griffith directed every one. "My first day at Biograph was a memorable one for me," she told the *Telegraph*. "My leading man was a young, but experienced, actor called Harry Solter. The film,

The Bandit's Waterloo, was quite a forgettable film, but I found Harry Solter was far from forgettable. We started going out together from that first day. We dined together almost every evening. Mother wasn't too happy, after all, I was only eighteen, but she liked Harry and decided to trust me with him alone."

Solter appeared in fifteen of Lawrence's thirty-four films in 1908. "Mr. Griffith said we were the perfect team to work with. But by the end of the year we knew our futures would be much more than just on screen," she told the *Telegraph*. "Mother wouldn't hear of us getting officially engaged, she felt I was far too young, but Harry gave me a ring and I wore it around my neck on a chain, night and day. Harry had ambitions to be a director but knew he would get nowhere at Biograph where Mr. Griffith was directing just about everything they made."

By the end of 1908, Florence had obviously convinced her mother that Harry Solter would be a good son-in-law. He and Florence Lawrence were married on December 23 at a quiet ceremony attended by only a few friends.

Lawrence is credited by *Film Weekly* as being the originator of the first stock company at a film studio. D. W. Griffith said, "She came to me one day and told me how well stock companies in the live theatre worked. A group of performers of all ages banded together and appeared in many different plays. One week an actor would be playing the lead role, next week a small walk-on part. So we decided to try the idea at Biograph. It worked remarkably well until some of the actors, having tasted star roles, became very upset when they were given minor roles in the next film. We solved this by putting them all under contract at the same, above average, wage and after that no one complained."

It was D. W. Griffith who officially called Florence Lawrence the Biograph Girl. "We were still not willing to give publicity to the performers under their real names, but so many people wrote to ask about Florence so we gave her the title we felt would help sell our films," he said.

Griffith also told *Film Weekly* that another idea that came from Lawrence saved the Biograph Company many thousands of dollars. "Often when we went on location the filming drew quite large crowds who were becoming fascinated by the ever-growing motion picture industry. Often the crowds got so large we had to hire several policemen at $5 a day to keep the crowds out of camera range. Florence suggested that we buy a number of police uniforms and dress up some of the extras, being paid $2 a day, but not needed in a particular scene, and let them control the onlookers. It worked beautifully. Since we already had to pay the extras anyway it didn't cost us a cent. I don't believe any other company ever found out about our little trick."

In his autobiography, Griffith said when he started making films for Biograph, in 1908, he was given a budget that ranged from $300 to $400 per film. "As the quality of films improved, and we needed extra actors, and often had location expenses, I was permitted to spend as much as $600 on one film. That is why we often had to make as many as three films in one week so we could divide the costs of our higher paid actresses like Florence Lawrence — then earning $45 a week — among the different productions."

Lawrence recalled in an interview she gave to the *Los Angeles Times* in 1936 that "Mr. Griffith and I, often helped by people like Harry Solter, used to sweep up the studio at night after the non-contract players had left. We didn't have to be told to do so, we just felt this was a natural part of our duties. I clearly recall Mary Pickford, who had only just arrived at Biograph when I was getting ready to leave, brushing the studio floor along with us."

After the article was printed, Mary Pickford, in a letter to the *Times* denied that she ever swept the Biograph Studio floor. "It was never asked of me or expected of me," she said. "I think my good friend Miss Lawrence has had a memory lapse."

Among the stock company members at Biograph in 1909 were such important members of the industry as Flora Finch, Mack Sennett (later to become the King of Comedy), and two actors named John Compson and Arthur Johnson, both later to play important roles in Lawrence's life.

Compson teamed with her in the first comedy series every filmed. As *Mr. and Mrs. Jones* they found themselves in riotous situations. After the first two films of the series were released the studio was deluged with letters asking when they could expect more of the same kind. The films had such titles as *Mrs. Jones Entertains*, *Mr. Jones at the Ball*, *The Joneses and Their New Neighbours*, *Mrs. Jones's Burglar*, and *Mr. Jones and the Lady Book Agent*.

With Harry Solter becoming very unhappy at Biograph with the lack of directing opportunities, he and Lawrence decided it was time to make a move. But when they approached the Essanay Film Company about the possibility of them being hired as a team, she to act, he to direct, the plan backfired. Essanay reported the approach to Biograph, who promptly fired them both. Worse, they were blacklisted with the ten major production companies that had joined distribution forces as the Motion Picture Patents Company. The ten companies controlled sixteen patents, including those for film, camera, and projectors. Called the "trust," they effectively stifled much of the work of the new companies that were being formed almost daily.

Fortunately for Lawrence and her husband, a courageous film exchange owner named Carl Laemmle refused to be dictated to by what writers a decade later often called the "New York film mafia." He teamed with the wealthy industrialist Robert Cochrane to form Independent Motion Pictures, better known as IMP.

When no more films starring the Biograph Girl were left to release, the Biograph Company instructed that all queries about her be answered with the comment, "The Biograph Girl is dead." This rather stupid comment, which D. W. Griffith many years later said was one of the worst blunders of his life, spread rapidly and the *New York Times* finally printed a large story that said the Biograph Girl had been killed in a street car accident in New York. One of their reporters had decided to believe the rumors and, apparently, added his own version of her demise to add a little zing to the tale.

Meanwhile, IMP had lost an injunction for infringement of copyright of several patents owned by the Motion Picture Patents Company members. Although he was unable to release any of his IMP films, Laemmle decided to continue with production of as many films as possible with Lawrence as the star and Solter as her director, a role that he very quickly proved he was capable of carrying out.

Laemmle had a good friend, Fred Talbot, in St. Louis, Missouri, who controlled film distribution to more than 200 theatres, many of which he owned. With his own exchange serving more than 400 more theatres, Laemmle decided to risk the "trust's" threat to cut him off from all their films if he released any of his own IMP product. Laemmle guaranteed the St. Louis exchange that if they lost the "trust's" product he would be able to supply enough film from his own studio and other independents to satisfy the St. Louis moviegoers.

The *Times* story about Lawrence's death was the spur to his decision. Determined to make the most out of Biograph's stupidity, Laemmle took full-page advertisements in all nine film trade papers then being published, and large advertisements in all the New York daily newspapers. They read as follows:

Yes
THE BIOGRAPH GIRL IS DEAD
but she is very much alive as
THE IMP GIRL

and is making pictures every day
at the studios of
INTERNATIONAL MOTION PICTURES (IMP)
Her real name is
FLORENCE LAWRENCE
and her first film for IMP
will be in your theatres next week.

Known until then only as the Biograph Girl, Lawrence suddenly found every paper was writing stories about the only person in the industry they knew by name. Suddenly she had shot from being the Biograph Girl to the first real star of the film world.

Moviegoers, who had adored the Biograph Girl, besieged their local theatre box offices asking when films of the IMP Girl, Florence Lawrence, would be seen. The theatres, in turn, pressured the "trust" into getting the IMP films. After two weeks, during which some theatres were boycotted by audiences for refusing to deal with Laemmle's film exchange, the "trust" gave way and settled their dispute with Laemmle. He was guaranteed their product for distribution if he would guarantee the IMP films would be available to their exchanges.

Laemmle was triumphant. Although he still had a few injunctions to settle he felt sure this could be done out of court. He was right. Everything was settled with a handshake.

Laemmle was a very honest dealer. As a way of saying thanks to Fred Talbot, the film exchange owner in St. Louis, he placed advertisements in every newspaper within 100 miles of the City of St. Louis. The ads were basically the same as those in the New York trade papers and dailies, with one big difference. Tagged on the end of every ad was the following message:

MISS FLORENCE LAWRENCE
The first and greatest star of motion pictures
will appear
IN PERSON
at
the following theatres in St. Louis
[names and appearance times were listed]
on
April 11 and 12, 1909

and will
introduce her new leading man
well-known to St. Louis stage audiences
MR. KING BAGGOTT

Laemmle made sure that every newspaper in which he had placed an advertisement was aware of the date and train number on which the "first star" would be arriving in St. Louis.

In New York, Laemmle, who had hired a special private Pullman coach for his party on the westbound express, climbed aboard with Lawrence, Baggott — a great favourite of stage audiences in St. Louis — and Harry Solter. He had also made sure the New York papers knew when the "star" and her entourage were leaving, and next day Lawrence became the first film personality to be pictured, and named, on the front pages of New York's major daily newspapers.

When Lawrence joined Carl Laemmle at IMP she took with her the comedian John Compson, and actor Owen Moore, soon to become Mary Pickford's first husband.

Laemmle offered Lawrence a contract at $600 a week, with an extra $300 for Harry Solter to exclusively direct all her films. "I just couldn't believe my ears when he told me," she recalled years later. "It seemed such an impossible amount of money for anyone to make. Harry [Solter] investigated Laemmle thoroughly and was convinced IMP was financially sound and could pay me what the contract said they would. It was all settled when Carl offered to put ten weeks' salary in an escrow account at my bank."

When Compson died from pneumonia, at the age of twenty-six, Lawrence was quoted in the *New York Times* as saying, "He was one of the industry's greatest comedy geniuses. I made more than a dozen films with him and found him so easy to work with. He was becoming a great personality in our industry when he was taken away by this tragic illness."

Florence Lawrence's reception in St. Louis was probably the highlight of her career. It was the first time the public had been given the privilege of meeting, in person, a motion picture personality. The *St. Louis Post Dispatch* gave her the entire front page the day after her arrival. Included were pictures of the huge crowd at the rail terminal, estimated to be from four to five thousand. Many had, said the story, been waiting at the train depot for hours. The story featured seven close-ups provided by Laemmle, and one full-length picture of her standing on a soapbox at the railroad station trying to quieten the cheering crowd. The headline said simply: "She's Alive and Don't We Know It!"

Lawrence made twelve appearances in two days at four different theatres. The St. Louis exchange had given each theatre owned by Talbot a preview of different and as yet unreleased IMP films in which she starred with King Baggott. He is reported as being "the local boy who made good." He was cheered at every entrance he made in the films.

Laemmle was not the kind of man to do things by halves. He had commissioned, in New York, one of that city's top composers and arrangers to write musical scores to accompany each of the films. Talbot increased his small regular musical group to twenty in each movie house, and the sound was, said the *Post Dispatch*, as though the St. Louis Symphony was in each theatre.

The first show started at 1 p.m., the last at 8 p.m. Lawrence was joined on stage by King Baggott and Harry Solter. They, too, were overwhelmed by the standing ovations they received. Solter told the *Post Dispatch* that "it was impossible to think that a mere director could receive such adoration."

Lawrence and her cohorts answered questions from the audience for at least an hour at each session in each theatre. "They asked questions about everything from how to get into the movies to the color of my underwear," she told the *New York Telegraph* on her triumphant return to New York. "Did you tell them?" asked the reporter. "Yes and no," answered Lawrence. "But yes to which and no to which?" persisted the reporter. "Well, I certainly didn't tell them how to get into motion pictures," she answered. "Blushing prettily," wrote the reporter.

Lawrence made forty-three films in 1909. As her fame grew, and the clamor for more and more of her films increased, Laemmle raised her salary to $1,000 a week with $500 more a week for Solter, who directed every one of the films.

All of the films were one-reelers, running approximately ten minutes, and both Lawrence and Solter were anxious to attempt to make two- and three-reelers, which Griffith had started to turn out at Biograph. Laemmle perhaps made the biggest mistake of his life when he rejected this suggestion. "You are getting a share of the profits," he said. "They are immense from the one-reelers. Why should we change and risk failure with the longer films?"

In October, with only three months left in the contracts they held with Laemmle, Lawrence and Solter asked for three months leave of absence. "We are both exhausted," said Lawrence. "We want to take a long vacation in Europe." Laemmle, with enough Lawrence-Solter films in the can still unreleased, agreed. "We have enough to keep the audiences going until you return," he said.

The duo sailed for England with a royal send-off in New York. The word had been spread and thousands appeared at the dockside to wave goodbye and wish them well. It was reported in the *New York Telegraph* that they had to take an extra luxury cabin next to their own to hold all the flowers that had been sent to the boat. The report also said they received more than 200 bottles of champagne as going away gifts. Later stories told how they handed over the champagne to the captain and the bubbly was distributed free of charge to all dining tables in the first-class section of the boat.

In London they hired a limousine and chauffeur. A maid and valet followed behind in a second rented car with all the baggage. After taking in all the sights of England, they — reportedly — renewed their marriage vows in front of Gretna Green's famous blacksmith, who had become renowned for legally marrying runaway couples who had eloped across the border from England into Scotland. Lawrence told the Glasgow newspapers that she intended to make a film about "romantic Gretna Green" when she returned to the United States. There is no record that she ever did keep this promise.

A newspaperman hired by Lawrence and Solter went ahead of the two cars to every city in which the couple planned to stay. He made all the hotel reservations and made certain that everyone knew who they were and how important they were to the film industry.

Another member of the entourage travelled a few days behind the touring parties in yet another rented vehicle. She was charged with locating every newspaper in which something had been printed about the vacation. It is said they brought back with them to the United States three huge scrapbooks filled with stories and photographs.

The happy couple crossed the English Channel by boat to Europe and continued their travels to more than half a dozen countries. On her return to New York, Lawrence told the *New York Telegraph* that "we were treated like royalty everywhere we went and, in fact, were received by the crowned heads of several of the countries we visited." She didn't specify which countries honored them by royal commands, and in view of the stuffiness of most of Europe's crowned heads of that period, her comment may well have been exaggerated a little, if not entirely.

Carl Laemmle, who had been concerned that he had not heard a word from Lawrence or Solter while they were away, was waiting at the dock when the liner arrived. He was first on board to greet them. "I asked when they would be ready to start work again," he said in a press release to all the trade papers, "and was shocked to hear that their contract with me had expired and they planned to look for another company that would allow them to make the kind of films they wanted to make. Then they dismissed me from their presence as if I was the bell-boy awaiting a tip."

Two days later announcements in all the trade papers said Lawrence and Solter would be signing one-year contracts with Siegmund (Pop) Lubin, whose Lubin Studio had grown rapidly in strength during 1909. "Florence Lawrence will be appearing in many more two-reel films while she is working at my studio," said Lubin. Rumors, never confirmed, said she was to get $2,500 a week, plus a share of profits in the films she made, and Solter was to get $1,000 a week with a guarantee that he alone would direct every one of her films.

Lubin was ecstatic about his signings. "This will make Lubin Studio a name to be reckoned with in our industry," he said. "Miss Lawrence will have total control over the choice of all stories and wherever possible I will attempt to obtain the supporting actors she feels will enhance her immense talents."

Lubin, one of the original members of the "trust," had apparently been willing to forget that Lawrence had been fired from Biograph, and had defected to the "outsider" IMP. His studio was not in New York or New Jersey as were all the others then in operation. "I'm from Philadelphia," he said, "and that's where I like to work. I know Miss Lawrence and Mr. Solter will enjoy living there." Apparently they did, showing their enthusiasm by buying what is described in a newspaper story as "a beautiful home just outside the city, standing in five-acres of well-treed and landscaped grounds where they act as hosts to the elite of Philadelphia society."

At Lawrence's request, Lubin signed actor Arthur Johnson to a year's contract. "I had loved working with him at Biograph," she told *Motion Picture World*, "and when I heard he was at liberty I asked Mr. Lubin if we could not get him to come to Philadelphia. He was delighted to accept and we renewed our partnership on the screen."

Lawrence made forty-seven films for Lubin before her contract expired in February 1912. Thirty-seven of these featured Arthur Johnson as her co-star. "There is a magic between us that comes over so well on the screens," she said to *Picture Show* in September 1911. "He is now a very important star and has enhanced every film we have made together." By this time, every actor and actress with any talent at all was being exploited by his or her real name. Mary Pickford was fast becoming Lawrence's great rival.

Occasionally, Lawrence and Johnson were seen dining together in the best restaurants around Philadelphia. Sporadically, there were rumors that all was not well in her marriage to Solter, and that Johnson was moving in for the kill.

But nothing happened, and when she and Solter left Lubin to form their own company early in 1912 Johnson stayed behind. He remained with Lubin five more years, until 1916, when he died, at only thirty-eight, from tuberculosis.

Laemmle obviously decided that Lawrence's importance in the industry outweighed any grudge he may have felt for her defection from IMP in 1911 and in May 1912, when Lawrence and Solter returned from yet another two-month vacation in Europe, a joint announcement was made that Laemmle, Solter, and Lawrence were joining forces as equal partners in a new company to be named the Victor Film Company.

There were no details of financial arrangements for Lawrence and Solter, the stories simply saying that all three partners would share equally in the company's profits. The trio set up a studio in Fort Lee, New Jersey, and signed Owen Moore as Lawrence's leading man. He stayed until the end of 1912 and they made eighteen films together. Solter was still her exclusive director.

Owen Moore was a first-class actor, but had a rather unfortunate reputation for playing around with his leading ladies. Late in 1912 this led to fisticuffs on the set of a film appropriately called *Tangled Relations*. Although Moore was the stronger and tougher of the two, Solter won handily and filming had to stop for a few days while Moore got a new set of teeth and was willing to apologize to both Solter and Lawrence for his actions.

Even with the abject apology, it brought an end to Moore's contract. Lawrence refused to work with him any more. But she apparently remembered that Owen Moore had a younger brother, Matt, also a competent actor, with the ability also to keep his hands to himself. So, as Owen went out the door, Matt moved in.

Lawrence purchased a 100-acre estate in Westwood, only sixteen miles away from the Fort Lee studio, and made it into one of the showplaces of the area. "The grounds are ablaze with roses of every hue," said the local newspaper. "The lawns are immaculately maintained and contain a miniature golf course for the benefit of guests." Lawrence added tennis courts and an outdoor swimming pool, and her home soon became a home-away-from-home for every actor and actress working at any one of the New Jersey studios.

Sidney Olcott, who often used the facilities of the Victor Studio, remembered Lawrence, and her beautiful home, well. "Val and I were often invited for weekends. Always pleasant breaks from shooting, they were totally relaxing, and Florence was a marvellous host," he said. "She had a permanent house staff of nine, although she was always in the kitchen supervising the delicious meals that were served. There were also four full-time gardeners, and although she was always charming to everyone, I often worried for their jobs if I saw a single blade of grass out of place."

"Florence shipped many fine antiques back from her trips to Europe," said Valentine Grant. "Everything in the house was in impeccable taste. But she would rarely talk about the pieces or tell of their history, and I often wondered if she had just hired an expert to fill an empty house and really knew very little about the expensive objects on display."

Towards the end of 1912, invitations to the Lawrence-Solter home grew scarce. "We had noticed a distinct coolness between the two lovebirds, and odd shouting bouts at the studio confirmed what we feared, that the marriage was coming to an end," said Grant.

In November, Lawrence announced in the trade papers that she had decided to retire. "I have ample money on which to live in comfort for the rest of my life and feel it is time I gave something back to the people who have made this possible." She didn't expand on this theme, and no one at the studio was surprised when she left — alone — for another two-month tour of Europe. Most appropriately, the last film she made in 1913 was a very successful two-reeler entitled *A Girl and Her Money*.

When she returned from London she refused overtures from Laemmle that she return to the studio. Solter was reported as still living in their lovely home, and — occasionally — they were seen in public together. He continued directing other actors and actresses at the Victor studio, but Lawrence decided to stay home and make her beautiful house and grounds even more beautiful.

In 1914 she announced that she would return to the Victor Company. A big party was held on the set when she arrived for the first day of shooting of *The Coryphee*. Large stories in both trade papers and daily newspapers proved she was far from forgotten.

Apparently she still believed in Harry Solter's abilities as a director, announcing that he would, once again, direct all her films. For a while it looked as if the couple had managed to patch up their differences. They were friendly on the set, and went home together at night as though nothing had ever been wrong.

Laemmle, one-third owner of the Victor Company, was by this time also sole owner of a fledgling company he had named Universal Films. His plans to move the new enterprise to Hollywood, the new West Coast location of many companies, were daunted a little when Lawrence refused to sign with Universal and move out to California.

What would have happened if she had said "yes" to the proposal is anyone's guess, but the ending of her career, and life, would likely have been very different to the tragic happenings that were soon to unfold.

In those early days of the industry, even highly paid stars like Lawrence were expected to do most of the stunts that today are the exclusive domain of qualified and experienced stuntmen and women. While making a three-reeler, *The Pawns of Destiny*, she was asked by Solter to take part in a dangerous stunt that called for her to escape down a fiery staircase to safety. The stunt was tried several times without fire and everything seemed timed to perfection. Unhappily for Lawrence, during the real take, the fire got out of hand and she was seriously burned, and in trying to escape the flames she slipped on the stairs and badly bruised her spine.

Lawrence attempted to return to the studio following two months intensive treatment by a group of the best doctors the studio could find, but permanent burn scars under her chin and on the back of her hand were difficult to hide, even with heavy make-up. She was obviously in pain when she arrived on the set, and it was apparent to everyone that her back was still troubling her. Somehow, she managed to complete ten more films by the end of 1914 before once again announcing her retirement.

From home, she instructed Laemmle to buy Solter out of his contract and get him out of the studio. She had twenty-four-hour guards placed around her house to ensure he never returned there for any reason. In November Lawrence and Solter were quietly divorced. Trade papers said Solter got a $300,000 settlement from Lawrence. He is also reported to have received $100,000 from the Victor Company in settlement of his studio contract.

Lawrence's retirement lasted until May 1916, when it was announced she would star in a film, *Elusive Isabel*, to be made by the Bluebird Company. It was to be released by Laemmle's Universal films from Hollywood. Planned as a six-reeler, it was to be her first long feature, and was touted as a major comeback for what the trades described as "the first really great star of our industry." The cast included a number of competent veteran actors, including Sydney Bracy, Harry Millarde, and Paul Panzer.

Making the film, which was well received by reviewers and moviegoers, proved to be a much greater effort than Lawrence had estimated, and often she was ill while working at the studio. When the film was released, and exhibitors asked for her presence at special trade showings, they were told she was "not well enough to attend." A month later she was reported by one trade paper to be "living alone in her lovely New Jersey home, constantly under round-the-clock care of doctors and nurses."

Harry Solter was reported to be "keeping in touch with Lawrence" and news of his unexpected collapse on the set of a film he was making was said, by friends, to have "made her very upset." Solter never did recover from what is now thought to have been cancer, and he was never able to work again before his death in January 1918.

A clipping from a New York daily paper in 1919, apparently one of a series of stories of successful people who started with nothing but an idea, tells how Lawrence's mother, Lotte, had invested all the money she had received every week from her daughter in the purchase of land and apartment buildings in New York City.

But in 1931, Florence Lawrence told a sad tale to the *Los Angeles Times*. Her mother, she said, had sold all her holdings in 1923, purchasing with the proceeds stocks and bonds that she believed would bring her a substantial income for life. Unhappily, added Lawrence, all the money was lost in the Wall Street crash of 1929 and her mother had died "broken-hearted" only a few months later.

On May 12, 1921, Lawrence married a cosmetic salesman, Charles Woodring, at her home in New Jersey. The trades reported the wedding briefly and added her comment that she had no intention of ever returning to make any more films.

But a year later, a small item in a Hollywood trade paper told how this "first star of the motion picture industry" had sold her estate in New Jersey and had arrived in Hollywood for her first visit. She would star in *The Unfolded*, said the report, a film to be made by a small company, Producers Pictures. "I have decided I have stayed away too long," she said. She told another trade paper that her husband, Charles, had convinced her that she is still remembered in the industry. "I sold my home in New Jersey, and until I find the right property to buy, I have rented a beautiful home in Beverly Hills."

She wasted no time in making contact with some of her old friends now in Hollywood. Mary Pickford welcomed her and threw a party in her honour. In 1943 Pickford recalled the party. "It was not a very successful evening," she said. "I invited many of the elite of the industry who I felt would remember her, but only a few accepted the invitation. I was embarrassed, although Florence seemed delighted to meet those who did attend."

The Unfolded had a good cast. In addition to Lawrence, who got top billing, it featured Barbara Bedford, Charles French, William Conklin, and

Murdock MacQuarrie. "I was told later that Florence didn't receive a salary, and may actually have invested money in the film, in order to get the lead role," said Pickford. "It really was quite a good film, but the producing company was not important enough to get the film the distribution it deserved. Sadly, her return did not create the interest she had hoped."

"She told me that her husband had convinced her to sell her New Jersey home and use the money to make yet one more comeback as an actress," said Valentine Grant. "He also persuaded her to invest in a project of his own that he told her couldn't fail. With the money Florence gave him he created a cosmetic line with her name and picture on every box. She made a few personal appearances to launch the cosmetic, but few attended the receptions. It was clearly too late in her career for such a venture. I believe she lost most of her money in this cosmetic dream and in the failure of the film which she hoped would bring her back to the attention of the big producers. It was a very sad story."

After the failure of *The Unfolded*, Lawrence decided to make a return to the live theatre. "She got quite a number of bookings in vaudeville," said Grant. "Actually, she was a very good entertainer, and a lot of people went to see her because of her success in films, but vaudeville was ending, being beaten at the box-office by the very films she was turning her back on. But she was able to work almost every week for a year, and she added to her theatre salary by demonstrating and selling her cosmetic line in each city she played."

In 1923 she made another attempt to regain film fame in Hollywood. She made contact with producer Ben Wilson, who had known her years before in New York and now had his own company in Hollywood. "With a little pushing from a number of us, he agreed to give her a role in *The Satin Girl*. But she wasn't the star. She had fourth billing below Norman Kerry, Mabel Forrest, and Marc MacDermott," said Mary Pickford. "For old times sake Ben gave her a lot more money than the role deserved."

In 1924 Wilson gave her one more chance. "He put her in his film *Gambling Wives*, but it was even smaller than the part she had the year before," said Pickford. "Hedda Hopper, long before she became a columnist, was the star. It was a good cast including Marjorie Daw, Dorothy Brock, Edward Earle, Lee Moran, and Ward Crane. But the part was not big enough to get her any good notices."

Lawrence's last hope at regaining the stardom she had once known came in 1925. Paramount announced it was looking for an actress to play Peter Pan. She applied, was tested, and was one of five finalists from which the choice was to be made. She was stunned when she was advised that the part had been given to Betty Bronson, who used it as a stepping stone to a forty-five-year career that ended only with her death in 1971.

But Lawrence wouldn't give up. Money was now in short supply. Despite this precarious situation, her husband refused to go out and get a job. "She told friends that he told her he only married her for her money and she had better get out and earn some," said Grant. "She got small parts in two films in 1926. Janet Gaynor, who had met Lawrence at the Pickford welcoming party, was the star of *The Johnstown Flood*. Lawrence appealed to her for help, and the film's producer, Irving Cummings, agreed to find her a small role." Gaynor discussed the film in 1980. "It was a very sad case. I tried to help but it was obvious she could never be a major star again. Irving paid her ten times what the part deserved. I only hope, in retrospect, that we did help a little."

Writer June Mathis, who had known Lawrence in New York, got her two different roles in First National's *The Greater Glory*. She played in a dramatic scene with Anna Q. Nilsson, and in a comedy scene with Jean Hersholt and Boris Karloff.

At the end of 1926 she divorced the husband she told the court had "spent and wasted all her money, and given back nothing to the marriage." Woodring's attempt to get the court to pay him alimony was laughed at by the judge. "Your days of getting are over," he said. "You should start thinking about giving something to those who trusted you. If I could, I would give you something, but it would be six months in jail." As they left the court, friends reported that Woodring approached Lawrence and begged for ten dollars so he could eat. "She kicked him you know where," said Lila Reeves, another silent film actress who had attended the court hearings. "It was just what he deserved."

In a letter she wrote to Valentine Grant in 1927, then in New York, Lawrence told of the excitement she felt when she received a personal call from Louis B. Mayer, then fast becoming the most important figure in Hollywood. "I hoped it might be for a big fat part," she said. "But dear old Louis, he just wanted to put me on a lifetime contract at MGM for old times sake. But I wasn't ungrateful when he offered me $75 a week for life, with a five per cent increase every year. He had done the same to lots more people I knew, like King Baggott, down on his luck, like me. And he hasn't just ignored us, he is actually giving us parts, not big parts, but we are working, and are able to keep our self-respect and dignity. I know by now I will never be a big star again, but every day I go to the studio I feel like I am one.

Would you believe that dear Louis sends his car and driver for me every time, and when I have finished work and am ready to go home the car is waiting by the side of the set. Mr. Mayer's driver always opens the door and helps me into the limousine. I really feel like I am someone again."

In the next ten years, MGM records show that she appeared in more than fifty different films. But not one role was important enough to get her any newspaper reviews. Many years later, in 1943, Hedda Hopper, then a famed newspaper columnist, said, "How wrong we were. We felt we were doing these former stars a favour by not mentioning them in our columns or reviews. When just a line or two would have made the day for them. I feel guilty, but just didn't understand their inner feelings."

In November 1927 Lawrence married a Los Angeles businessman, Henry Bolton. Once again her choice of a husband was unfortunate. Five months later she was in court seeking a divorce and protection from a man she said had "beaten me severely on several occasions; once I was taken to hospital and was only semi-conscious for two days." The elderly judge, who perhaps remembered when Lawrence was famous, threatened Bolton with imprisonment if he ever went near the former star again. "Divorce granted," said the judge.

Louis B. Mayer, who had quietly attended the hearings, sitting at the back of the court, took her to his home where he and his wife looked after her for several weeks. Mayer then found a nice apartment with three bedrooms at 3171 Cahuenga Boulevard and installed her there with two workers from his costume department. Mayer paid the rent.

In 1929, the *Los Angeles Times* published a large story about the former stars that Mayer had put under contract. It was syndicated across the United States and suddenly Lawrence found herself once more receiving lots of mail from former fans that had not forgotten her days of glory. A few months later the *Times* printed a story that told how her former fan club president had restarted the club and had recruited more than 5,000 members. "I get mail every day," she said. "How wonderful it is to be remembered. I am constantly sending out photographs to all parts of the United States." The story quoted the club president as saying, "When she was very important in the industry she always had time to see us and talk to us. Many of us were invited to visit her lovely home in New Jersey. So now it is our turn to repay that graciousness."

Lawrence continued to play small parts at MGM, but early in 1937 she began to suffer from severe pains in her arms, legs, and back. Doctors, hired by Mayer, gave her the bad news that it was a progressive bone disease that was unlikely to get any better.

Florence Lawrence in *The Old-Fashioned Way* (1934).

On December 28, 1938, she decided the ever-increasing pain was too much to bear. Her apartment had been having problems with ants, and in the kitchen cupboard were two tins of ant paste. She opened one and managed to eat almost all the contents, arsenic-based paste, before collapsing. When her roommates arrived home from work she was unconscious but still alive. Rushed to hospital, she died within an hour. Her last comment to the doctor, when she recovered consciousness briefly just before the end, was "I didn't think it was that strong. It didn't kill the ants, why is it killing me?" At the inquest the doctor said he didn't believe she was really trying to kill herself. "Her statement to me suggests that she thought the ant paste would kill her pain and not be strong enough to kill her. I think she was really making a cry for help."

She was buried in Hollywood Memorial Park Cemetery. Louis B. Mayer paid for the private service and interment. With all his generosity Mayer forgot one thing. No one ordered a marker for the grave! This was an omission that wasn't rectified until 1992, when a simple plaque was placed on the gravesite. Who ordered it? Cemetery officials say they are not permitted to tell.

For many years Florence Lawrence's name wasn't even printed on the map to celebrities' graves that is given to those who visit each day, looking for the tombs of the more recent stars. But it was written in by hand on some of the maps in the 1980s by a conscientious member of the cemetery staff. Recently, on the latest cemetery maps, the location of her grave is shown alongside such people as Cecil B. DeMille, Tyrone Power, and Paul Muni.

Not one of the silent films Lawrence made has been transferred to video. The only way now to see the beauty and talent of Florence Lawrence is to join one of the many silent film clubs in the United States and Canada. Showings of films made, for example, by D. W. Griffith, are often listed in the newsletter that links the clubs together, and in this way the real film buffs can see why this long-departed actress was considered not only the first star of the movies, but perhaps the best and most beautiful.

Ironically, the "first star" of the motion picture industry does not have a star of her own on Hollywood's Walk of Fame. Bill Welsh, president of the Hollywood Chamber of Commerce which approves and installs all the Walk of Fame stars, had this to say about the omission: "It is perhaps unfortunate, but really, her fame was not in Hollywood but on the East Coast. However, if any person wishes to nominate Miss Lawrence we will consider adding her name to the Walk of Fame. The nominator will, of course, have to pay the cost of the star and the installation ceremony (approximately $5,000)."

DEL LORD

"Del Lord has a flair for comedy like no other man I ever met. He can sense in a minute why a comedy effect is not working. The Three Stooges owe their continuing fame to his inventiveness. I don't believe there is any one of their most hilarious bits of 'business,' that are their trademarks today, that he didn't invent."

(Mack Sennett, 1950)

It is doubtful if one in a thousand of the men and women working in Hollywood's entertainment business today could identify Del Lord's role in the growth of the motion picture industry. Even when he died, three decades ago, his passing from this world rated no more than a dozen lines in the industry's trade papers, and no space at all in the national daily newspapers.

But if people like the King of Comedy, Mack Sennett, and Moe Howard, one of the original Three Stooges, are to be believed, he was one of the most talented creators of comedy of all time and an even more talented director of comedy films.

Ben Turpin, the cross-eyed comic, and one of the funniest men from the silent film era, said in a 1939 movie magazine article that Del Lord was the originator of almost every one of the routines that made him famous. "Sennett got most of the credit, but frankly Sennett didn't know what to do with me until Del Lord showed him. Sennett fired me when he was with Keystone, but Lord convinced him to take me back when he went on his own. Ask Buster Keaton and Charley Chase, even Charlie Chaplin, and they will tell you how highly they regard Del Lord."

Lord never became wealthy, never directed a major motion picture, never lived in a big house in Beverly Hills, and never was nominated for an Academy Award, or indeed any award, so far as film historical records show, but he left his mark on the motion picture industry when it was in its infancy, a mark that can never be erased.

He probably directed more pictures, mostly short one- or two-reelers, silent and sound, that were classed as "B," or second feature, films than any other Hollywood director. A tribute to his comedic talents is shown in the number of films which he directed four, five, and even six decades ago, that have been revived and are selling, on video, in their thousands to movie buffs who want to know what it was all about in those early days.

Moe Howard, one of the Three Stooges, in a 1970 interview, said Del Lord was the only director the Three Stooges really enjoyed working with.

"He wouldn't be on the set five minutes before he had everyone laughing. He was totally in control, calm yet bursting with enthusiasm. We didn't get much money in the 1930s and 1940s, but we sure had a wonderful time making the short features that seem as fresh today as the day we made them. We were the stars, but Del Lord deserved equal billing. He knew what we were capable of doing and he dragged every ounce of it out of us."

Del Lord was born Delbert Edward Lord in Grimsby, Ontario, on October 7, 1894. His father died when he was only nine, and at ten he was working in the vineyards of the Niagara peninsula, alongside his mother.

At fourteen he became enchanted by the circus that tented in the summer of 1908 in Niagara Falls. His mother had taken a job there in a large nursing home and young Del had plenty of time on his hands to make friends with the performers.

During the summer the ringmaster allowed him to attend every performance provided he would agree to be dragged out of the audience by one of the clowns and thrown around the ring. In a *Film Weekly* story published in 1941, Lord told how the acrobats taught him to tumble without getting hurt so the clown antics, while looking dangerous, were really quite harmless.

"It was a world I had never dreamed of being part of," he told the 1941 interviewer. "It was not a big circus, but it was that, just a circus, plain and simple. Not like they are today, surrounded by raucous carnival sideshows. The performers were the kindest people I had ever met. I knew long before September came around that I would be moving on with them when they headed south for the winter."

Unlike most circus-struck boys, Lord got permission from his mother to move on with the lions, tigers, aerialists, and clowns as they headed south toward the circus winter quarters near Jacksonville, Florida. "She knew there was little for me in Niagara and she wished me well, gave me a hug and a kiss, and sent me on my way. It was the start of a life for me that has been enjoyable every step along the way."

During his first winter in Florida, Lord became part of an acrobatic act that he had watched in amazement every night from the sidelines. "I couldn't believe it when they asked me to join the troupe," he said in the story. "And for some reason I was never afraid, even doing the flying stunts."

His delight was tempered in the early spring of 1909 by the contents of a letter he received from the minister of a church in Niagara. "I am sorry to tell you that your mother passed away following a bout of pneumonia," wrote the minister. "She was proud of you and asked me to make sure you knew what had happened. She is buried in the churchyard and if you ever come this way again you will see the stone which I and the parishioners have erected to her memory."

It was in Florida that Lord got his first glimpse of the motion picture industry at work. "They had built a small studio near Jacksonville and when our circus arrived they asked if we would agree to work with them on two films they planned to make with circus themes. They made both films in two weeks. I got a small part in one, throwing a bucket of water over one of the actors. I have wondered many times since who he was, and who the director was who controlled everything. I think it was the absolute control the director had that fascinated me most. Perhaps I knew it even then that one day I would be doing that same thing."

For three years Lord travelled with the circus. It went from town to town, from Florida to Seattle, by way of Chicago and Denver and dozens of small towns in between. In 1912 it arrived in California, where it tented for six months.

Lord loved California from day one. "I remember picking my first orange directly off the tree," he said in 1960. "We would have been arrested for doing that in Florida. And when we were asked to set up our tent for a week near one of the film studios, which were just beginning to open up in the Los Angeles area, so that they could use us in a story they were filming, I knew I would never leave California again."

Lord made sure he had a job to go to before saying goodbye to his circus friends. "It was late in 1912 and Mack Sennett, who I had never heard of until that time, had taken over an old studio on Edendale Boulevard, and was putting up a huge sign that said Keystone Studio. I applied for work and was hired to help with the construction of several new buildings that were going up. I was able to find a place to stay near the studio and although I only earned $6 a week I was able to save money right from the start. I kept my early savings in an old sock I tucked away in my suitcase under the bed.

"Sennett and his actors didn't wait for the construction to finish. Of course, a little hammering and banging didn't affect silent film production. Whenever they wanted people to stand around in the background of the scenes they were shooting they yelled at those of us working on the buildings to come down and become extras."

Lord remembered clearly the arrival of Charlie Chaplin just before Christmas 1912. "He was the talk of the studio. He had a shrill voice and it carried quite a distance. Most of us had never heard a London accent before and when Sennett told him to look around the studio I started joking with him, trying to mimic his voice. We had quite a little comedy scene going that stopped the construction work until Sennett came over and put a stop to the fun. Later in the afternoon Chaplin came over to me and asked if I knew a place where he could stay. I told him there was an empty room in the boarding house where I lived. 'That will be jolly excellent,' he said. I told him I would be through in about half an hour and he said he would meet me by the studio gate. All he had was two battered suitcases, so I carried one and we walked the quarter mile to my rooms where Mrs. Maruzzi, the lady who owned the boarding house, welcomed him in."

"So you're an actor, eh," she said. "I'll need a week's money in advance." Chaplin dug in his pocket and came up with the $3 requested. "You'll get a hot breakfast at six," she said. "Eight on Sundays. All other meals you can make yourself if you know how without destroying my kitchen. I shall charge you for whatever food you use."

That night Chaplin showed off, probably for the first time in the United States, some of the culinary skills he had picked up while travelling around England and the United States. "I enjoyed the best meal I'd had since I left home," Lord recalled in 1943. "Charlie kept me up half the night telling stories that had me laughing so loud the landlady came downstairs to see what was happening. After she had heard a few of the stories she stayed with us and laughed just as much as I did."

Chaplin stayed for several weeks at the small house close to the Edendale Studio. "When he left he told Mrs. Maruzzi that one day, when he became famous, he would hire her to look after his home. She laughed, but only two years later, when Chaplin was earning $500 a week, he bought his first house and moved Mrs. Maruzzi in as his housekeeper. She stayed with him more than ten years until she died."

Interviewed in London, England, in 1956, where he was making *A King in New York*, his first film after his exile from the United States, Chaplin was asked about Del Lord and his story of the comedian's first night in California. "Oh, yes," he said. "That is absolutely right. Del and I became great friends. In fact, until the day I left the United States, we had a standing arrangement to play a game of tennis on my court every day, but I haven't heard from him since I moved to Europe."

Chaplin went on to describe his feelings that first day at Edendale. "You know, I was a very scared person. I knew nothing about making films and when I saw the chaos in the studio I felt sure I would be on my way back to

Fred Karno's vaudeville show within a few weeks," he said. "The second day
was different. I had a friend."

Chaplin recounted how he got Del Lord his first bit part in a Sennett
film. "They had me working on my third day in the studio, but neither I
nor the director, Henry Lehrman, had any idea what sort of character
they wanted me to create. It was a frustrating time and I needed a friend I
could talk with, so I convinced Mack Sennett to put Del Lord under
contract as an actor. There were no plans for him specifically other than
my request that he be given a small part in each of my films. I think they
paid him about $15 a week, which was probably much more than he was
earning as a carpenter."

Del Lord did not let Chaplin down. "Within a few weeks it was obvious
that he was a born comedian. He and I used to get together every evening," said
Chaplin. "We would work out little routines, often in the street outside either
his house or the little hotel where I was then staying. If the neighborhood
youngsters who came out to watch laughed, we knew we were heading in the
right direction. He was a perfect trainer for me. I learned a lot from him, and I
believe he did from me."

Asked if there was any one specific thing in his career that he could
credit Del Lord with creating, Chaplin laughed. "Yes, indeed," he said. He
left the room. When he returned he was wearing the "tramp" moustache,
which had been for many years one of his movie trade marks. "Watch," he
said. And he twiddled the moustache right, and then left. Everyone started
laughing. "That," said Chaplin, "was Del Lord's idea."

It wasn't long before Sennett also realized that Del Lord had the potential
to be a first-class comedian. Sennett recalled in 1943 that Lord "constantly
came up with ideas to make a scene much funnier than we had planned. I put
him in the Keystone Kops and Keystone Fire Brigade and because of his circus
training we gave him a lot of the toughest stunts to do."

Over the years, different writers have listed the actors they believe
formed the original Keystone Kops. Del Lord's memory in 1943 adds to the
confusion. His list includes two names not mentioned today by historians. "I
believe the first group included Sennett himself," said Lord. "The rest were
contract actors including Edgar Kennedy, Walt Parsons, Bev Griffith, Charles
Avery, Ford Sterling, and Hank Mann. Mann was the first Police Chief but he
was soon replaced as he was wanted for bigger roles. That was when Ford
Sterling took over. I came in very soon after the group was created and played
in quite a number of Kops films. What people today don't realize is that there

were only a few films with nothing else in them but the Kops. More often than not they came in for comedy relief in films starring other people."

In 1943 Lord had a large store of memories from those early days in the motion picture industry that he loved to share with his friends. "I don't think anyone today would say we were sane if we did some of the things now that we did thirty years ago," he said. "But there were no unions then to demand extra pay for dangerous stunts, and our jobs seemed at times more important than our lives."

Lord never tired of telling one story from his early days as a Keystone Kop. "I remember once being told to sit in a car that had been deliberately stalled, straddled across the streetcar lines. My job was to leap out at the last possible moment before the oncoming streetcar hit it. I presumed they had hired the streetcar and the driver and people in it were all actors. Anyway, I hoped so. The first time I tried the stunt I miscalculated and landed on the front of the streetcar instead of the road. I had to cling on to save my life.

"Ford Sterling was waving his hands and shouting with glee. 'Wonderful,' he said, 'what a stunt, but we didn't get it all first time. You should have told us what you were going to do, and then we would have had the camera in the right place. O.K., let's do it again.' 'No way,' I told him, 'that was no stunt, that was an accident.' 'If you can do it once you can do it again,' he said. So I tried and came nearer to death than I'd ever been in my life. This time I couldn't hold on to the streetcar and fell down in front of it. Fortunately for me they had a cowcatcher attached to the front of the streetcar so it swept me aside. Without even helping me up or asking about my health, Sterling told everyone to pack up and head back to the studio. 'We got a good shot there,' he said."

How close he came to death no one now will ever know, but his acrobatics won him a regular place in the Keystone Kops. "My salary went up to $20 a week," he said. "Today [in 1943] they ask $2,000 to do a stunt much less dangerous."

The early days at Keystone were the days of the "custard pie" comedies. "I was on the receiving end of dozens of 'custard' pies," he said. "They were a special mixture devised by Mack Sennett that wouldn't damage the eyes of the victim. One day I suggested to Sennett that all this was getting rather boring. I explained that far too often the arrival of the pie, thrown from only two or three feet away, was telegraphed by the intended target who closed his eyes long before the pie arrived. What you want, I told Sennett, is someone who can throw pies accurately from, maybe, ten or twelve feet away, out of sight of the victim. Then, if you don't tell the target in advance, it will really look as though the whole thing was a big surprise."

"So where do we find someone who can throw pies accurately from that distance?" asked Sennett. "Try me on for size," I said. "In the circus I threw pails of water that distance so accurately that a person sitting next to the victim didn't even get wet." "Let's try it," said Sennett. "Sterling never gets a pie. Throw one at him in the next scene. If you miss and hit someone else you're in trouble."

Del Lord didn't miss, and the entire set was convulsed with laughter as Ford Sterling showed in no uncertain terms how annoyed he was. "The camera kept rolling and as usual it was written into the script," said Lord. "All pies to be thrown in future will be thrown by Del Lord," said Sennett. But throwing pies wasn't enough for Lord. He constantly pestered Sennett with ideas for comedy films and eventually Sennett gave way and let him direct.

Sennett in 1950 talked about Del Lord. "Had I been intelligent in those early years I would have joined forces with him and formed a company called Lord Sennett. How about that for a title! I put him off so many times when he wanted to direct and only because I badly needed another director one day did I give him a chance. That's when I realized what I had been missing.

"I look at old footage today and without being told I know which film was directed by Lord and if there are custard pies flying I can tell instantly if they were thrown by him. Putting a pie in Del Lord's hand was like handing Rubens a brush and palette. He was an artist to his fingertips."

At Keystone Studio between 1914 and 1917 some of the greatest stars in the industry, like Harold Lloyd, Wallace Beery, and Gloria Swanson, began their careers. But far too often they went elsewhere after Sennett had developed their talents but couldn't afford to give them the money that they were offered from other studios. Del Lord stayed.

"I felt I still had a lot to learn and at Keystone there were more opportunities than at any other studio. I worked as gag writer, stunt man, then finally director of many of the giants of the industry at that time. I never did direct Charlie Chaplin because soon after he arrived at Keystone he convinced Sennett to let him direct his own films, but I began a friendship that has never ended," he said in 1943. "To this day we are in contact several times a week. He loved my idea of subtle slapstick because it contrasted with the rough and rather crude humour of that era. Right from the beginning he liked intelligent gags and we cooked up hundreds between us."

Among the greatest of Sennett's successes was the formation of the Sennett Bathing Beauties, who were seen singly or as a group in hundreds of different films. Their main purpose at the studio was to be photographed with the comedians under contract. Sennett reasoned that the magazines and newspapers, to which they sent hundreds of press releases and still photographs, would be much more likely to print a picture containing a pretty, scantily dressed girl than one of a comedian alone.

Sennett always claimed he selected each one personally, but Bev Griffith, one-time driver of the Keystone Kops patrol wagon, who died in Butler, Georgia, in 1972, at the age of eighty-two, told a different story in an interview in 1970. "Del Lord, the gag writer and director, and I chose ninety percent of the girls," he said. "We used to watch for likely candidates standing at the gates of the studio and invite them in. We checked out their vital statistics very thoroughly in the bathing suits that were always available in wardrobe. If we thought they were good enough we took them to Mack Sennett and let him announce that he had discovered another Bathing Beauty.

"Despite all the things you might have read to the contrary, Sennett wasn't too interested in girls, so he didn't object when Del and I put the pick of the crop on his doorstep. He had one favourite, Mabel Normand, but every time they got close to getting married he backed away. Lots of us wondered why! He tried to prove his masculinity by chasing after some of the girls, but I don't think he knew what to do with them when he caught them.

"There were always dozens of girls waiting at the studio gates hoping to get into the movies," he said. "Word got around fast that Del and I were the selection committee and we were never short of female company. Of all the questions we asked the girls you would have expected the first would have been "can you swim?" But since only one or two of the Bathing Beauties ever got wet that was the last thing Sennett wanted to know."

Lord had many stories to tell about the stunts the Sennett comedians devised. One of his favourites was this: "As the firemen, we were all inside a blazing building, and I mean blazing, none of the phony controlled fires used today. We had to run outside, panic-stricken, knocking down walls, falling over things, you know, the usual pratfalls, but I decided to add a finale to the scene on my own. I was the last fireman out and I stood in the house doorway, with the flames blazing so close that I was getting singed. The cameras always kept rolling until the last person was out in all dangerous stunts, so I reached in my pocket and pulled out a box of matches and some cigarettes. I pretended to try to strike three matches, but made quite sure they wouldn't light. Then I looked around casually, put the cigarette in my mouth, and leaned over to light it from the flames of the house fire. Then I strolled casually out from the burning building as it collapsed on the spot where I had been standing seconds before. Everyone applauded on the set; they appreciated good bits of business. When the film was released it brought the house down, this time not literally!"

By 1917 it was obvious that the Keystone Studio was reaching the end of the road. "Chaplin had left for Essanay, and then on to Mutual. By then he was earning thousands of dollars a week," said Lord. "People were getting tired of the same old stunts. A pie in the face was no longer very funny. Other studios, like Universal, were producing five- or six-reel films that had more drama than comedy and audiences loved them."

At the end of the year Sennett decided to sever all connection with Keystone. He relinquished all rights to the name Keystone and formed his own company, Mack Sennett Comedies, for release by the Paramount Picture Corporation. Del Lord was one of the few Keystone regulars who went along with him. "I had found Mack to be an honourable man who was willing to listen to new ideas," he said. "He offered me a lot of money to devise and direct my own films under his banner, so I never hesitated, even though I had been constantly badgered by Chaplin to join him at an even higher salary. I couldn't see myself getting anywhere with Chaplin. He was a one-man show with everyone working with him just being an employee. I decided I would rather know him as a friend than an employer.

"Ben Turpin, the cross-eyed comedian, who had been fired by Sennett in 1916 had remained friendly with me. I told Sennett I had a few ideas that would develop his character and since he had no other people in mind he agreed to bring him back, and try him out in his new company. Turpin became a big star and more than justified my faith," said Lord.

As Sennett's star declined, and there was not enough work to keep Lord going full time, he accepted offers from Monogram, Fox, First National, and United Artists. When Sennett joined Educational Pictures in 1929, he asked Lord to rejoin him for a series of sound comedies. "But I'm afraid the style of comedy he wanted was no longer what the public wanted," said Lord.

"In 1929 I was working at Universal, directing the *Vitaphone Follies*, a series of musical films, actually little more than a string of performers put together into one big musical show. I had managed to make the transition from silents to sound thanks to the belief Carl Laemmle, the Universal boss, had in me, and I was still making comedy short features, but now with sound. I made one full-length feature film, *Barnum Was Right*, at Universal in 1930 but it wasn't a success, and suddenly I was finding it tough getting people interested in putting money up for the sort of films I wanted to make."

In January 1931 Lord decided to say goodbye to motion pictures. Jobs the previous few months had been few and far between and the early signs in 1931 were not promising. Although he had managed to save and invest a sizeable amount of money from his Keystone years he couldn't see himself sitting around with nothing coming in and everything going out. He had been married to a former secretary in Sennett's office, Edith Howard, for seven years, and they both agreed that it was time to look elsewhere for a new career.

In the summer of 1931 Lord bumped into Kenneth Warren, an old friend from his early days at Keystone. The man looked prosperous so Lord asked what he was doing now. "I have a car dealership," he replied. "Everyone wants cars. Business is booming. So what are you doing now, Del?" "Nothing," said Lord. "I'm getting out of the movie business and into something more secure." "Then join me," said Warren, "I need a good salesman. You were a great salesman at selling us ideas at Keystone. Why not try that technique on selling cars?"

So Del Lord ended 1931 as a car salesman. Within weeks he was the talk of the town. "I did all kinds of stunts to bring in the customers, and most of them paid off. I walked on my hands across the tops of cars. I swung over the heads of prospective customers on a trapeze."

But his best stunt was one that made Kenneth Warren many thousands of dollars and put Lord back into the movie industry. "The dealership offered anyone who bought a new car their money back if I couldn't hit them in the face with a custard pie from twelve feet. The cars were going like wildfire, but I never missed and not once did Warren have to give the car away free. Secretly, he had increased the price of every car by ten percent so if I missed once in every ten throws we wouldn't have lost money. We put bibs on the customers and covers over their hair, and no one got hurt. There were laughs all around and we sold more cars in a month than we had done in the previous six months. When the promotion was over, Warren gave me half the extra ten percent he had charged and four days before Christmas I went home with more money in my pocket than I ever dreamed possible.

"Mack Sennett, still well known to the public, although his star had faded, came along and joined in the fun, even bringing a few Keystone Kops to add to the photographic opportunities. I'll always be grateful to Mack for coming along to give our promotion a boost. He wouldn't take a cent for being there."

Sennett remembered the occasion clearly. "If I was there every day for a year with all the Kops in the world," he said, "I couldn't repay Del for what he did for me and the industry when we desperately needed to know where we were going."

The automobile dealership publicity caught the eye of a former Keystone director, Jules White, who remembered Lord's work in the 1920s, when both of them had worked on some of the best Sennett comedies. Just appointed by Harry Cohn, president of the fast-growing Columbia Studios, as head of the company's short-subject division, he decided Lord was the man to give the department new lustre.

In an article printed in the *Los Angeles Times* in 1940, White talked about Lord and his return to the movie industry. "I heard about his antics at the Ford dealership and needed a new car so decided to go along and see what it was all about. Lord didn't recognize me in my new $100 suit so I waited near the car lot until the end of the day before approaching him. His eyes popped out when he realized who this prosperous-looking individual talking to him was. 'How would you like to come back into the movie business?' I asked. 'I wouldn't,' said Lord. 'Do you know how much money I'm making here, and I get a new car to drive home every night.' I told him I'd double whatever he was making, and the studio would give him a new car, if he would come to work at Columbia. 'Columbia,' said Lord. 'That's a pretty small studio to be offering that sort of money. I don't think so.'"

But Jules White persisted. He was authorized by Cohn to take a signed contract to Lord with even better terms than those he had originally offered. "When I put the contract, with Cohn's signature on it, on the hood of a car in the lot, Del Lord was finally impressed. After thinking about it for an hour, during which time he called everyone he knew in the industry to ask their opinion of Cohn and Columbia, he signed his half of the contract. He insisted on giving a month's notice to the dealership and that a clause be added to the contract permitting him, when he wasn't needed at Columbia, to go back to the car lot to help his friend sell cars."

Many years later Lord talked about his doubts of re-entering the film industry. "I'd heard a few things about Harry Cohn that didn't make me too enthused about his studio, so I didn't want to lose contact with my friend at the car dealership in case I was out on my neck, contract or no contract, and needed a job to go back to. I was back on the lot selling cars whenever I had any spare time over the next four years. But when Warren decided to sell the franchise I felt I didn't owe any allegiance to the new owner."

Lord spent the next fifteen years at Columbia Studios. He often told the story of his first — and last — run-in with Harry Cohn. "He had treated a friend of mine, Harry Burgess, rather shabbily by firing him for no good reason, and on the set, so everyone could hear. So I called him 'a no good son of a bitch.' Half an hour later I was called to his office, and I imagined I was on my way back to the car lot."

"Lord," he said, "I understand you were very impolite about me on the set today." "I was, Mr. Cohn," I answered. "And if you treat any more of my friends the way you treated Harry Burgess I'll think of worse things to say next time." Cohn roared with laughter. He got up from behind his desk, walked around, and put his hand out. "Let's shake hands," he said. "I like a man with courage to say what he feels. Call me Harry, Del. And tell your friend he is rehired."

Many years later Cohn, in an interview, said, "I despised the studio employees who said 'yes, yes, yes' to everything I suggested. I wanted people with guts who knew I couldn't be right all the time and weren't afraid to tell me so. When I found one, from a studio gatekeeper to a director or producer, I tried not to let him get away. One I remember particularly was Del Lord, a comedy genius who helped build this studio with the Three Stooges shorts he directed. He would, and did, tell me to my face if I interfered in what he was doing. But I didn't interfere often, he was far cleverer than I was at comedy."

"From that moment on I never had a bad deal from Harry Cohn," said Lord. "Even Jules White and stars like Harry Langdon and Buster Keaton called him Mr. Cohn, and there was I calling him Harry every time he came on the set. Film historians have suggested that it was White who gave me the chance to direct the Three Stooges, but it wasn't, it was Cohn. I protested to him that the different directors on the Stooge short films were providing no continuity of gags and just weren't getting the most out of their unique comedic talents. I told him a few ideas I had and next day Jules White came to me and said he had decided I would be the person to direct the Stooges from then on."

Del Lord directed his first Three Stooges short in March 1935, and before he decided to leave Columbia in 1948 his name was listed on the credits of forty-one of the comedy two-reelers. In 1995 more than 200,000 copies on the Three Stooges films were sold on videotape to today's new wave of Stooge buffs.

By 1970, the Stooges comedies were being run and rerun all over the world on television. In 1968 Lord instigated a court fight to try to get some of the millions of dollars the films were now bringing in to owners who likely hadn't been born when the films were made. "I am not doing this because I need the money," Lord told the *Los Angeles Examiner*. "I was never a big spender and am not without enough money to last me for the rest of my life, but the families of the Three Stooges could do with a share of the money their films are making."

The courts threw the case out. The judge said everyone had been fully paid the money their contracts called for, and the films and any income from them belonged to the present owners. It is interesting to note that the children of the Three Stooges reopened their case for residual rights several years later, after the death of Lord, and won a substantial sum plus a share of the income from all future use of the films.

But Lord shouldn't be remembered alone for his achievements with Larry, Curly, and Moe, despite the longevity of the series that was made non-stop between 1934 and 1952. One of the best films he directed was *The Pest from the West*, made in 1939 with Buster Keaton as its star.

Director Del Lord with Joan Davis on the set of
Kansas City Kitty (1944).

Writer Clyde Bruckman talked about the film in 1943. "With Lord all you needed to do was write a basic outline for a story. Then he, especially when given a comedy genius like Keaton, would do the rest. I don't think they ever knew in the morning what they would be filming for the rest of the day. They would work as many as sixteen hours a day to get the results they wanted. Everyone on the set would be howling with laughter. I remember one lighting man had to have a handkerchief shoved in his mouth before each take to stop him ruining the sound track with his howling.

"It is a great pity that Lord and Keaton never teamed up for a series. But Del Lord was so occupied with his Stooges films that it would have been asking too much of him. Often he worked seven days a week, sleeping over on a cot in his studio office so he could start work at six o'clock next morning."

Buster Keaton, in 1959, in the twilight of his career, remembered Del Lord. "I am supposed to have a deadpan face and never laugh, but some of his ideas were so original and hilarious that I often fell out of character and joined in the fun. With Del you could never know what was going to happen next. Although the custard pie era, which I loved, was long past, Del never forgot the fun of those days. He used to commission a restaurant across the street from Columbia to make him a dozen custard pies each week. Well, they weren't custard, you know, but he had the recipe and got what he wanted. He kept them in a small box beside his director's chair and suddenly, from out of the blue, one of the pies was flying across the studio and never missed its mark. I'll swear he threw some of them twenty or thirty feet. If there had been any tension on the set it vanished when the pie landed."

Keaton listed a few of the people who were recipients of Lord's pies. "I didn't see it, but it was the talk of the studio when he hit Harry Cohn right in the face. Spoiled his new suit they said. Everyone waited for the explosion from Cohn, but it never came. Apparently he laughed as loud as anyone else before walking over to Del's little cupboard of pies and, taking one out, he splattered it in the face of Del. I would have given anything to have been there that day. Cohn was a bastard, and that moment would have made my life worthwhile.

"But he did hit a few rather important people. W. C. Fields got one, and all he did was demand all the pretty girls on the set lick it off his face. Fred Astaire, who idolized Del, used to visit the set regularly. The crew had to wait more than six months before Del hit him in the face. He didn't say a word, just walked out and never came back again. Upset his dignity, I suppose.

"Huey Long, the governor of Louisiana, got one too. He came out with a mouthful of obscene language at first then started laughing like everyone else. This was just a month before Long was shot to death in September 1935 in Baton Rouge. Irving Berlin got one when he was visiting the set. But he hadn't much sense of humour and he didn't take it too well. We used to take friends on the set hoping Del would give them one of his pies. Often he did.

"But his most memorable throw was one that hit a rather stuffy visitor who had been on the set watching the Stooges go through their paces. His whole body shook when he saw something funny but he just didn't seem to know how to laugh out loud. So Del aimed his pie and hit the British Prince of Wales right between the eyes. Everyone thought he had gone too far this time, and a hush settled over the studio. Then the Prince started to laugh and everyone joined in. Wiping the goo off his face he walked over to Del and said, 'Thank you, Mr. Lord, I've won $100 from Mr. Cohn. He said you would never dare throw a pie at me.' He stayed another day and was a different person after the pie incident. We were all sad to see him go, a real down-to-earth gentleman."

Del Lord recalled in 1959 that he came up with a unique way of tightening up one-reel comedies. "We took a recording machine with us to a theatre where we had decided to try out one of the Stooges comedies. Synchronized with the movie it recorded all the laughs from the audience. Next day we ran it through at the studio, again synchronized with the film, and were able to get maximum laughs by re-cutting the film. If laughs came too close together and overlapped, we added a bit of film and evened things out. If they didn't come at all we cut the scene. Most people don't think of our two-reel comedies as being made to perfection, but that is exactly what we sought and by using the laugh track we got as close as possible. Once in a while, if a scene really fell flat, we would re-shoot it and add in some more business."

Looking back in 1963, Lord said, "I think I was able to sustain the high level of comedy better in the short features. Thinking now about some of the full-length features I made, perhaps it was not my forte to keep the pace going for as long as sixty minutes. I quickly lost interest and the films suffered as a result."

Among the full-length features he made was *Kansas City Kitty* with Bob Crosby, Joan Davis, and Jane Frazee. "I directed Bob's brother Bing in his first film with Sennett just after sound arrived," he recalled, "and now here I was introducing his brother in his first film. Bob was much easier to work with. It's a pity he was always in the shadow of Bing."

Mel Tormé, who made *Let's Go Steady* with June Preisser at Columbia in 1945, recalled Del Lord as being a man "totally in command, always calm, always delightful to work with. A fine director who would have been perfect for today's situation comedies on television. He had so many ideas for funny bits we couldn't keep up with him."

Bandleader Phil Harris, who was directed by Lord in two films at Columbia, *Memory For Two* and *I Love a Bandleader*, recalled Del Lord from his home in Beverly Hills in 1991. "He was a honey to work with," said Harris. "A real charmer. Even when we did things wrong he didn't ever rub it in. I tried to get in touch with him in the 1970s when I was doing a lot of television but was told he had died. He had more going for him than the pipsqueaks directing today. They don't make 'em like Del Lord any more."

At the end of World War Two, Lord and his wife Edith decided to see the world. They set sail for Hong Kong, then took another boat from there to Australia. They sailed on to Singapore, India, and Egypt before landing in England, where they stayed for several months before returning to the United States.

"I don't think I will ever direct any more films," he told the *Hollywood Reporter* on his return. "Edith and I have seen so many more important things that need doing in the world. We have no children to take care of so we hope to take care of some of the world's children who have no one."

Between 1950 and 1960, Del and Edith Lord opened the home they purchased in Calabasas, California, to refugees from a variety of nations. "At times we had six or seven young people speaking as many different languages," he said in 1962. "We had to hire two people to help us look after the children. Unfortunately, in 1960, I had a heart attack, which made continuing with our project impossible. I am not able to do very much these days, but Edith is a wonderful help, and we have a nice home in which we enjoy our lives."

Many of the young people he and his wife had adopted over the years were constant visitors at their home until Lord died on March 23, 1970, at the age of seventy-six. They have continued to be companions of Mrs. Lord since her husband's death. In 1973 she said, "All the love and care we gave these youngsters was repaid many times over as we watched them grow and go out in the world. Thanks to Del's many friends, a number of them are working in the television and film studios. One boy we adopted from Hong Kong is following in Del's footsteps, writing and directing many of the top comedy shows on television."

There were no famous people at Del Lord's funeral. "But the twenty-one young people who had found a better life through his generosity and love were there, and that must have made him very happy," said Mrs. Lord. "They meant much more to him than any of the stars he helped create through the years."

LOUIS B. MAYER

"Though he never lost his love for Canada, which had given him, and his family, refuge and the freedom of opportunity, that found fulfilment in the United States, it was his love for America that made him an authority on our country, and his counsel was sought by men in high places. Yet he never lost the common touch."

(Spencer Tracy, 1957)

He never knew the real name of his parents. They anglicized their name to Mayer when they arrived in Canada in 1893. Some early records in Saint John, the hometown he adopted, give the family name as Meyerinski, but Louis B. Mayer would never accept this as fact.

He never owned a birth certificate, and despite his wealth and power he was unable to convince authorities in Russia, Canada, or the United States to give him one.

The "B" in Louis B. Mayer was his own creation. He felt it gave him more dignity. It was not until newspaper columnist Hedda Hopper demanded to know what it stood for that he chose Burton. It was, he said years later, the name of the writer whose script he had been reading when he was asked the question.

He didn't know his real age, or the actual date of his birth. When he became an American citizen in 1923 he chose 1885 as being close to the truth and July 4 because it seemed appropriate for a new American to be born on Independence Day.

He rose from scavenging scrap metal at the age of eight to become the most powerful mogul in the history of motion pictures.

Louis Burton Mayer was born in Minsk, Russia, on July 4, 1885, if we are to accept his own guess as being accurate. When he was eighteen months of age, or thereabouts, his parents fled from their homeland and found safety in Saint John, New Brunswick.

It is difficult now to say how much of his life story is fact and how much fiction. He hired the top publicity men in America to polish his image. For example, the scrapyard that he and his father ran in Saint John had become a ship salvaging business employing 100 people in later studio biographies of his life.

One thing is sure, before he died, Louis B. Mayer accomplished more than any other man in the history of motion pictures did, and he left behind a legacy of achievements that seem, in retrospect, difficult to accept as coming from the brain of just one man.

When he was eight he started work for his father, Jacob Mayer. He pulled his toy red wagon around the dock area of Saint John, picking up pieces of scrap metal that ship repair companies had thrown away. These he hauled more than a mile to his father's scrapyard.

"I missed a lot of formal schooling when I got the word that they were dumping metal at the docks," he said in 1943. "But I was learning more important informal knowledge, a knowledge of people, that made it possible for me to be where I am today."

He left school when he was only fourteen, and immediately became a junior partner in Jacob Mayer and Company, which became from that day Jacob Mayer and Son. "Don't let anybody tell you I was not clever," he said. "I was top of my class in just about everything that I felt was important. That is why, today, I can spot errors in Canadian history, made by my writers, just as easily as I can pick up blunders in American history. To me the two countries are one. One day perhaps they will be. I hate people who spell Saint John in New Brunswick with an 'St'. That is an insult to a fine city. St. John's is in Newfoundland. You see, I know these things."

It was a long climb from the Saint John scrapyard to being the most powerful man in Hollywood. But Mayer never faltered along the way. "I never doubted for one moment that I would make it to the top in some industry," he said. "I have found there is no room in this world of success for doubters."

When he was about eighteen he convinced his father to expand the family business to Boston. "Wherever there was a shipyard there was scrap metal," he recalled. "And I felt it was time for me to see a big city. I was wise enough to know that whatever my future was going to be it was not going to be achieved in Saint John."

It was in Boston that Mayer became interested in the "moving picture" industry, as it was then called. "I saw lines of people waiting to get inside one of the nickelodeons that were sprouting up everywhere," he said. "So I joined the line and went inside. The films that flickered on a makeshift screen were crude and really not very entertaining. But I felt inside me, that first time I saw a movie, that this was the industry I wanted to join and, eventually, lead."

Mayer spent every spare moment visiting the different nickelodeons in Boston. "I had a girl friend, Margaret Shenberg, who went with me," he recalled. "We were both eighteen and Margaret had ambitions like me. We both wanted me to become important, and we both knew that collecting scrap iron wouldn't be the answer."

When they were nineteen, Margaret Shenberg and Louis Mayer (there was no "B" then) were married. Neither her parents nor his were enthused about two people so young getting married, but they all attended the wedding at a small synagogue in Boston, where a compassionate rabbi had decided to overlook the fact that Mayer had no birth certificate to prove who he really was, or what his real age might be.

Years later Mayer returned the favour. He built a synagogue for the rabbi, who had by then been transferred to an impoverished town in New Jersey. "I went there and helped put the bricks and mortar together," he said. "Anyone can give money, but it must be accompanied by the sweat and tears of its donor if it is to be from the heart."

Mayer was to follow that credo throughout his life, and his greatest giving came after he had reached the top of the tree in Hollywood. Rarely did he announce his good deeds. In fact, he was often described as "the meanest man in Hollywood." He was proud of the fact that not once in his entire life did he claim a donation to a worthy cause on his annual tax returns. "I don't give for that reason," he said. "Mr. Mayer," said his accountant, "will never have to fear a government audit. They wouldn't dare make one because they know they would discover they owed him millions."

Three years after he married, Mayer spotted an advertisement in a Boston paper offering a small theatre in Haverhill, Massachusetts, for sale. "We went to look at it and for a few minutes were more than a little concerned at finding it looking so run-down. The Gem Theatre was an old burlesque house seating around 1,000," he said. "It was so dilapidated the locals called it the Germ Theatre.

"But what I saw in front of me wasn't that dingy theatre," he said. "I saw what it could become and I convinced Margaret that I knew what I was doing. I got the owner down to about half what he was asking, and gave him a hundred dollar bill as a binding down payment.

"We had bought a small home in Boston, and I had some savings from the scrap metal operation. On the way back to Boston I had all the finances figured out. I would hand over management of the scrapyard to a young man who had been my senior assistant and I knew my father wouldn't lose with him in charge. If I could sell our home and use every last cent of what money I had in my savings account, I knew we could meet the cost of the theatre."

The Mayers moved to Haverhill, converted the manager's office at the theatre into a small apartment, and started work on the badly needed restoration work. A small newspaper editor in town openly scoffed at their efforts. "This place is a loser," he said. "You're wasting your money. I shall need cash for all your advertisements, when, and if, you ever get this flea pit open." Mayer didn't forget the editor. After two years in Haverhill he bought the paper and physically threw the editor out on his neck.

"It took us about three months before we were ready to show it to the people of Haverhill," he said. "We did most of the work ourselves because we had no money to pay for outside help. Our only assistant was a lumberyard foreman, a skilled carpenter, who volunteered his services for nothing. He had already given us all the wood we needed with no more security than our word that we would pay the bill when the theatre was a success.

"The Gem had quite good seating and the stage floor was solid and just needed scrubbing and polishing. The dressing rooms had running water and only needed a coat of paint, new mirrors, and a bit of carpet on the floor. Even the stage curtains were in good condition, but very dirty. We took them down and scrubbed them by hand."

One month after the theatre, renamed the Orpheum, opened its doors Mayer paid the lumber bill. He added to that repayment a decade later when he opened his first film studio in Hollywood. "I wrote to the man who had believed in us and offered him a job in the Californian sunshine. When he said 'yes' I sent him the money for a rail ticket to Los Angeles. I put him in charge of all my lumber purchasing and set building and today, twenty years later, he is the senior buyer of all wood and other materials we need here at MGM."

There were four other theatres in Haverhill at the time, and Mayer knew he had to do something special to draw attention to the Orpheum.

"I installed an organ, mainly because I couldn't afford even a small orchestra like some of the other theatres, but it was such a novelty that it attracted almost as many people as the movies. I found out later that it was the first organ to be installed in any motion picture theatre in the United States. Ten years later hundreds, perhaps thousands, of theatres had installed organs.

"I hired boys and girls to deliver printed flyers to every house in the community inviting the people of Haverhill to come and look at the new Orpheum. Margaret and I, and three girls who were to became ushers at the theatre, served tea and cookies to each one of the thousands who came in the three days we held the open house. We had the organist playing lively music, and everyone was excited. To every person who visited the theatre we gave a free ticket to see our first film.

"We chose *From the Manger to the Cross,* a movie that was well ahead of its time. It was directed by Sidney Olcott, and had received tremendous publicity in New York where it was still running after three months. Olcott sent me a copy of the music that had been specially written to accompany the film. Our organist, Wilbert Greenway, made it sound like we had a full orchestra."

Before the opening show, Mayer and his wife went on stage to announce that the Orpheum's policy would at all times be to offer clean, wholesome, family entertainment.

"That first week we sold less than a thousand tickets, but we didn't have an empty seat. More than 3,000 used the free tickets we had issued. The film was expensive, but it ran for six weeks; imagine that, six weeks in a town of around 30,000 people. Even Sid Olcott was so astounded that he came up to Haverhill to see what we were doing right.

"Olcott arranged with Kalem, the company who owned the film, to give us exclusive rights to show *From the Manger to the Cross* in the entire state of Massachusetts. In the second week they sent the film's star, Robert Henderson Bland, who had arrived in New York from England, to appear on stage to answer questions after each show.

"Normally we just showed the film once a day, but when Bland was with us we had to add an extra early show and we still turned crowds away from each performance. When they couldn't get in to the first show they stayed outside the theatre to wait for the second performance. Wednesday and Saturday we added a third show and still turned people away. We had made sure the papers in the towns around, including Boston, of course, knew that Bland was to appear, and a big percentage of our audience came from out of town.

"I'll never forget Bland. He was an incredible man. He walked around the streets of Haverhill every day, wearing long white robes. He visited every church, chapel, and synagogue in the area and invited the clergy to visit the show as his guests. We had to block off a section of seats each night for these good church people.

"At the end of six weeks ours was the only theatre in town that people talked about. While the film was on I went into Boston and convinced the director of the Boston Light Opera Company to bring his entire company to the Orpheum. He agreed to come for one week, but the show, which opened when *From the Manger to the Cross* closed, had to stay two weeks because so many people were clamouring at the box office for seats that we didn't have."

Mayer and his wife added up their profits at the end of the first eight weeks of operation and decided they had made enough to take an even bigger gamble.

"We knew we had to spend money to make money, so I went to Boston and New York asking managers to give us their best touring live shows for the Orpheum. Some scoffed at first, but a letter I got from the Boston Light Opera Company, saying how delightful their two weeks in Haverhill had been, convinced the doubters. I persuaded Maude Adams to appear on stage with her New York company of *Peter Pan*. She liked the way we treated her so much that she convinced her good friend, the great William Farnum, to play the Orpheum in one of his biggest Broadway successes, *The Littlest Rebel*.

"I even got the big stars like Marie Dressler and Lillian Russell. I made sure they had the red carpet rolled out for them and their comments, when they got back to New York, made our little theatre famous."

In the first four years they operated the Orpheum the Mayers never lost money on any show they presented on stage or on the screen. They constantly worked to improve the theatre, and made the dressing rooms luxurious for even the smallest performers on the bill.

Mayer also quietly purchased a local hotel and turned it into the first "all suites" hotel in North America. "I had to be sure the stars who visited us were pampered in every way," he said.

"This was around the time when film makers were letting the world know the names of their stars, so I persuaded Griffith at Biograph, Olcott, and Kalem and others to send along the stars of their films for personal appearances. I even had Mary Pickford and her brother Jack, but we won't talk about Jack. Mary was a darling. Everything we asked, she did.

"But the most co-operative star of all was Florence Lawrence, the former Biograph Girl who was now known by her own name. She sat in the lobby of the theatre for several hours each day for a week signing autographs. Thousands lined up to meet her. She shook hands with everyone, kissed every baby, and even a few men who dared ask, including me. I was able to repay her many years later right here in Hollywood. A beautiful lady. She, and the Pickfords, and several others didn't cost us a penny. The film companies were delighted with the publicity their stars and films received. I believe we started a trend. Nobody else had thought of stars making personal appearances at that time."

Mayer had special weeks at his theatre. "There were thousands of Irish people in the area so I talked Sidney Olcott into sending us all the films he made while he was in Ireland. We ran three shows a day for two weeks."

Within a few years, Mayer owned all six theatres in Haverhill. He spruced them up and gave each one a specific type of film to show. "One played only westerns, another cops and robbers, a third nothing but love stories. At the Orpheum we maintained a policy of playing the biggest and best films available, with stage shows every second week."

After Mayer had been in Haverhill for three years he was asked to run for mayor of the town. "I declined," he said, "because I recalled that the previous two mayors had been run out of town."

By 1911 Mayer owned other Massachusetts theatres in nearby Lowell and Lawrence. "I now had a chain of theatres that made people sit up and pay attention," he said. "I formed the American Feature Film Company, as a distribution house. It was easy for me to convince more than thirty other theatre owners in six New England states to let me be their booker. I guaranteed quality, wholesome films. And I gave them what I promised."

Mayer persuaded D. W. Griffith, whose greatest film, *The Birth of a Nation,* was about to be released, to give him sole rights to show the film in all the New England states. This so annoyed his chief competitor, Nathan Gordon, owner of the huge Olympic Theatres circuit, that in frustration at being deprived of the Griffith masterpiece, he suggested he and Mayer should combine their two companies.

Mayer considered this proposal for less than a week before agreeing. But how he achieved his first show business miracle has never been fully explained, for Mayer, with the smaller group of theatres, came out as chief shareholder in the two companies when they merged. Louis Mayer was on his way!

He told the *Los Angeles Examiner* in 1932 that he paid Griffith $30,000 for the rights to his film. Doubters proclaimed such extravagance would bankrupt the huge chain of theatres. But Mayer knew what he was doing. The instinct that later made him the movie industry titan he became in Hollywood told him he was right. When the books were tallied up on *The Birth of a Nation,* Mayer's American Feature Film Company had made more than $300,000 profit.

His flair for showmanship, which put him ahead of the average theatre owner, was never demonstrated more than when he persuaded Griffith to "loan" him all the stars from the film. They included some of the biggest names in the fast-growing industry. Lillian Gish, Mae Marsh, Henry Walthall, Miriam Cooper, Wallace Reid, Sam De Grasse, Donald Crisp, Raoul Walsh (later to become one of Hollywood's great directors), and Bessie Love made the trek from New York to Haverhill.

Miriam Cooper, who wrote a book of her memories in 1973, recalled that all the stars were given cars and drivers. "The cars had our names in large letters on canvas covers along both sides of the car. We couldn't open the doors because of the posters so the drivers had to lift the women in and out of the cars. Mayer was showing the film three times a day at all his theatres, and in one week I appeared on stage to talk to the audiences at eighteen different theatres.

"He kept the best for his flagship, the Orpheum. All of us, I believe there were twelve, appeared together at the same time on the stage of this one theatre. The audience stood up and cheered and wouldn't let us go. They filed past us on stage where we sat at a long table signing autographs. I recall it was almost two on Sunday morning when the last person left. Mayer was sweating profusely because in those days no one was allowed to keep a theatre open after midnight on Saturday. In those days nothing but churches were open on the Sabbath and the Sabbath started at the stroke of twelve. I think a lot of police palms were greased that night, for I never did hear of him being taken to court for breaking the law."

Mayer became more and more frustrated with the quality of product some of the movie companies were offering his theatres. In 1915 he formed the Metro Company, with himself and his wife as the company's directors. "I knew I had to produce my own, superior films, if I was to satisfy the audiences I had built for my theatre chain, by then more than sixty strong.

"I set up a studio in Brooklyn and for two years we produced what I still believe were the best films made in that era. I got together my own resident studio company but became very concerned with the short summers and long winters that limited our production scope.

"Things were happening in Hollywood by 1917 and Margaret and I decided to sell our theatres and move out west." Before they moved they had a signed contract from the new theatre owners guaranteeing to take films from Mayer's production company for twenty weeks out of every year.

When the Mayers arrived in California, they found a small unused studio on Mission Road in Los Angeles. The story of the first sign Mayer put up on the studio is legendary, and is believed to be where his reputation for meanness began. The sign on the old studio read:

LOIS WEBER PRODUCTIONS INC.

He is said to have found the original craftsman who carved the letters for the Weber sign. "All I shall need are an 'A' a 'U' and a 'Y,'" he is reported to have told the carpenter. Then if you will turn the 'W' upside down, change the letters around a bit, and add the new letters you will be able to create:

LOUIS MAYER PRODUCTIONS INC.

The story continued that he insisted the woodcarver leave the letters "E" and "B" in the studio because he would find some use for them later on.

The story may, or may not, be true, but Mayer never lived down his reputation for saving every penny he could. The truth, as it came out many years after his death, showed that Mayer was probably the most generous studio head ever to grace Hollywood.

The Mayers started life in California with a sizeable bank balance. "We were able to buy ourselves a nice home close to the studio," he said in 1943. "I still wasn't too sure whether I liked automobiles so I walked back and forth from home to the Mission Road studio every day, and when I mean every day, I mean seven days a week, fifty-two weeks a year. My days sometimes started at five in the morning and ended at midnight.

"Margaret was so concerned about my health that she built a kitchen at the studio and cooked nearly all my meals there. After a while it became a business on its own. The actors and technicians kept asking her to make them snacks, so she hired a cook and two girls and we set up a small restaurant where everyone who wanted to eat without going outside could dine in comfort. It was, I now believe, the very first studio commissary to exist. And it made a profit, which Margaret put in a separate account of her own."

Backing his faith in the star system, which he later pushed to great heights at Metro-Goldwyn-Mayer, he signed personalities like Anita Stewart, Renée Adorée, Mildred Harris (then Charlie Chaplin's wife), and directors Fred Niblo, John Stahl, and Reginald Barker.

His first feature, *Satan Sanderson,* was released four weeks after the studio opened its doors, and he was soon turning out four or five features a week. "Make no mistake, they were all quality films," said Mayer. "Not only the sixty theatres we contracted with in the east were showing them, but within a month of producing our first feature we had over 500 theatres clamouring for our product."

Before he left New York, Mayer withdrew from Metro Productions in favour of using his own Mayer Productions name in California. Metro was purchased by Loew's, Inc., soon to open the famed Loew's State Theatre on Broadway as the flagship of their chain of more than 100 smaller theatres that stretched to the Midwest as far as Chicago.

In California he also formed another company, Anita Stewart Productions, Inc. He used this strategy to lure Stewart away from his competitors.

In 1923 Mayer made first contact with producer Irving Thalberg, then at Universal Pictures. He convinced Thalberg that the Mayer company was going to be the biggest studio in Hollywood in a few years. The duo began a relationship that produced some of the greatest films ever made in Hollywood and ended only with Thalberg's untimely death in 1936 at the age of thirty-seven.

In 1924 Loew's, Inc., purchased Goldwyn Pictures Corporation. It had been founded several years earlier by two brothers, Archie and Edgar Selwyn, and Samuel Goldfish, who changed his name to Goldwyn to fit in with the company's name. By the time Loew's stepped in, Goldwyn had run into financial problems and had been pushed out of the company by the Selwyn brothers.

Samuel Goldwyn later formed another company, Samuel Goldwyn Productions, but, contrary to many stories, neither it, nor he, had at any time any connection with the mammoth organization that was soon to become Metro-Goldwyn-Mayer. Many film histories claim Goldwyn was one of the founding partners of MGM with Mayer, but Goldwyn himself denied this.

With Metro and Goldwyn combined, Marcus Loew decided he needed a competent overseer of all production at his new studio in Culver City. He invited Mayer to be that person. Mayer accepted his offer provided the name "Mayer" be added to Metro and Goldwyn, and that he had complete control over every film to be produced by the new company.   Loew, who had seen the quality of films Mayer was producing at his growing Mission Road studio, was happy to put Mayer in charge.

Sadly it should be recorded that Mayer's claim, made many times over the years, that he had personally selected the magnificent lion that graced the opening of every MGM film, was totally erroneous. The lion and the loop of film that surrounded it, together with the emblazoned Ars Gratia Artis ("Art Is Beholden to the Artist") was the idea of Archie Selwyn at the first Goldwyn studio.

Mayer did, however, select the lion that was used when MGM made its first sound film. For more than two years after the lion was filmed with its roar, Mayer kept the friendly beast on the MGM lot. It lived in luxurious quarters, had a staff of six to see to its every need, and was trotted out to greet any distinguished visitor to the Culver City lot. Mayer loved to greet important visitors with the lion standing beside him.

Howard Dietz, the original publicist with the Goldwyn Company that merged with Metro, later claimed that he, not Selwyn, invented the roaring lion symbol. He translated its Ars Gratia Artis to be "Art for Art's Sake." Dietz later became one of MGM's greatest lyricists of the 1930s and 1940s, writing such hits as "You and the Night and the Music" and many of Fred Astaire's most popular songs. Whether he, or Selwyn, created the lion symbol we will likely never know.

Most people, including many of MGM's greatest stars, believed Louis B. Mayer was either president of Metro-Goldwyn-Mayer or of its parent company, Loew's Inc. "It was a misconception I corrected many times," he told the *Los Angeles Examiner* in 1952. "I was vice-president in charge of production, and that was the title I retained until the day I retired from MGM.

"I was president of the Academy of Motion Picture Arts and Sciences from 1931 to 1935 and president of the Association of Motion Picture Producers of America from 1932 to 1938. Those were quite enough presidencies for me. I have never had any desire to be president of MGM. After all, where do you go from president? Only one way, down."

The Culver City lot that had at one time belonged to producer Thomas Ince, then to Sam Goldwyn, was one of the largest in California when Mayer took over in 1924. Sound had yet to arrive, but the six stages on a sixteen-acre lot, which contained the first permanent outside street scenes, were well equipped with the latest in lighting and technical equipment.

When Mayer retired in 1951, MGM spread over 187 acres and had thirty sound stages. An additional 195 buildings included a complete industrial centre, where just about anything a producer called for could be made, and the huge administration block dedicated to and named after Irving Thalberg.

When Metro-Goldwyn-Mayer started production in 1924, the stars from Mayer's own studio were combined with such notables as Ramon Navarro, Buster Keaton, Lon Chaney, Sr., Marion Davies, John Gilbert, Conrad Nagel, and directors like Frank Borzage, Rex Ingram, and Erich von Stroheim. It was a formidable array of talent that faced the opposition studios.

Mayer, who made all final decisions regarding scripts, talent, and money disbursements, left Thalberg in charge of day-to-day production of all major features. Harry Rapf, who was lured away from Warner Brothers by Mayer, was in charge of all "B" or second features and short films.

"Irving Thalberg was to me like the son I never had," said Mayer. "He had immense talents and impeccable taste. We often worked twelve or fourteen hours a day at that time and never once did I hear him complain. Despite his fragile health he worked as long or even longer than I did. I often wonder if perhaps I pushed him too hard. But that was what the industry was about in those days, hard work."

In 1953 Mayer told the *Los Angeles Examiner* what he claimed was the true story of his discovery of Greta Garbo while he was in Europe to supervise MGM's first major production there, *Ben Hur*.

"In 1925 every European actor and director wanted to come to Hollywood, the land of plenty. My manager in Berlin sifted through all possible people and showed me a film made by a director named Mauritz Stiller. I didn't care much for Stiller's work but there was a girl in the film who had the most beautiful face I had ever seen. I asked her name and was told Greta Gustafson.

"That night he arranged for us to meet at a club, and Stiller arrived with this girl on his arm. I couldn't believe it. She was the biggest girl I ever saw in my life. She must have weighed 200 pounds, she had arms like hams, and her legs were even fatter. I almost walked out, but that face, that beautiful face, it was her.

"I signed her on the spot for around $400 a week. That was a lot of money and I had to give Stiller a contract, too, because that was the only way I could get her to come to America.

"I whispered to Greta Gustafson as tactfully as I knew how that in America we don't like fat ladies, but I said not to worry because we had doctors and other people at the studio who would help her lose weight. 'Ya,' she said, 'I know dot you Americans like scrawny wimin. I lose for you.'

"When I got back to Hollywood, Thalberg and everyone else I showed the pictures of her to said I was crazy. But when she arrived, almost a year later, she had lost nearly seventy pounds and had learned to speak English very well. We named her Greta Garbo and you don't need to be told I was right."

In January 1926 the nation's theatre owners listed the top ten productions they had booked during the previous twelve months. "All ten of those were MGM films," Mayer recalled proudly in 1943. "And I bet if they had gone down to the twentieth picture we would have had most of those, too."

Mayer never wavered from his policy of giving youth a chance in all aspects of the motion picture industry. "I knew what youth was all about in 1924," he told the *New York Herald Tribune* in 1950. "I know what it is all about today now that I am sixty-five. I started young and stayed young; I hired young people around me and taught them to think, as I did, that the sky was the limit if they weren't afraid of hard work."

But he always blended youthful talents with veteran performers and directors. He probably created more stars at MGM than all the other studios did, combined. Asked what makes a great star, Mayer told *The American Weekly* in 1948 that the question was a tough one to answer. "So many people think they know the answer and have spouted off with erroneous answers that the general public has an entire misconception about stars and how they are made.

"I hope you made a note that I said 'made' not 'born,'" he said. "The idea of a star being born is bush-wah. A star is made, created, carefully and cold-bloodedly built up from nothing, from nobody.

"The raw material is what counts. That is what I look for. I have standards that I expect to be met. I know in here (he patted his heart), I can tell by instinct, after years of looking, not for great stars, but for interesting faces. When sound arrived, I added, as stage directors had done for generations, interesting voices.

"But real greatness only comes from persistence. The great stars at MGM would do anything for a chance at fame. That's how they often came to our attention. They did something to make themselves stand out from the crowd.

"But in the final count, it was we, at MGM, who made them stars. We made them with our brains, our know-how, and our enthusiasm. Without us, the trainers, most of today's stars would be out there selling shoes or waiting on tables. Because of us they are millionaires, idolized the world over. They are stars because they were made into stars by people like me, not because they were born stars."

It is interesting to note that Mayer, in an article printed in *Festival Magazine* in 1939, under his by-line, said just the opposite. "Actors are born, not taught," he wrote. "The inner spark must be there, but if this exists, training helps bring the quality in the actor out."

When sound arrived at MGM in 1928, the studio had on its payroll one of the greatest electronic wizards ever to grace a film studio. "Douglas Shearer arrived at MGM in 1925," said Mayer. "We let him tinker with his toys and he gave us better cameras, he gave us better lighting, he gave us real sound on film when other studios were still experimenting with records synchronized to the action. He won more Academy Awards than any other man for his technical brilliance, and yet Shearer was never once seen on the nation's screens. Douglas Shearer is one of the secrets that we nurtured from raw material. He is one of the unseen heroes who made MGM great."

At a time when people in the entertainment world were reluctant to identify themselves as belonging to any political party, Mayer was the odd man out. In both 1928 and 1932 he was a delegate to the Republican National Convention. A close friend of Herbert Hoover, he is said to have spent as much as a million dollars of his own money trying to get Hoover elected president.

But he refused to allow any contract artists at MGM to support any specific candidate. "We can't afford to alienate fifty percent of our audience," he told Jean Harlow, even though she too wanted to speak out for Hoover.

Mayer claimed he continued learning every day of his life. He kept a huge dictionary on his desk, and first thing each morning he would open it at random. Everything else had to wait while he found his "word of the day." He ran his finger down every column until he discovered a word he had not heard before. After writing the word and its definition on a piece of paper, he would glance at it several times during the day until it, and its meaning, was fixed in his brain. If a visitor to his office used a word he didn't understand, he would hold up his hand for the speaker to stop talking. "Now what was that word you just used?" he would say. Sometimes he would ask for it to be spelled out. Then he checked it in his dictionary. Then he nodded, and added, "Carry on, I understand now what you are saying."

Asked by a reporter why he needed to learn words that likely he would never use, he replied: "Use them, I would never use them. I hate big words. But I want to be intelligent enough to know what they mean if someone else uses them."

When Winston Churchill visited Metro-Goldwyn-Mayer studio, Mayer was thrilled to discover that this political giant, visiting from England, was no taller than himself. He mentioned to Churchill that size did not correspond to greatness, and Churchill is said to have replied, "We know that Mr. Mayer, but do our people?"

Churchill was told of Mayer's morning habit of reading his dictionary, and in the brief speech he gave at the banquet at which he was honoured, he spoke as was his habit, using only a basic vocabulary, getting his points across by his superb delivery and appealing personality. Toward the end of his speech he referred to some peoples' thinking as "antediluvian." Mayer held up his hand. Churchill bowed gracefully to him, and said, "Mr. Mayer, 'antediluvian' is my Uncle Robert's wife." As they left the head table, Mayer smiled at Churchill. "You are a bastard, Winston," he said. "And you are still antediluvian," the great man replied. As soon as he had seen Churchill away from MGM, Mayer is said to have rushed back to his office to look up the word "antediluvian." When he found it meant old-fashioned, or antiquated, he is said to have written Churchill using every big word he could find. There is no record that Churchill replied.

It would take several pages to list the great stars Mayer helped create at MGM. Included are Clark Gable, Judy Garland, Lana Turner, Jeanette MacDonald, Spencer Tracy, Mickey Rooney, Greer Garson, Walter Pidgeon, Jimmy Stewart, Joan Crawford, Nelson Eddy, Gene Kelly, Hedy Lamarr, Red Skelton, Ava Gardner, Elizabeth Taylor, and the greatest screen dog of all time, Lassie.

Joan Crawford had this to say about Mayer in 1964. "He is the sweetest, kindest man who ever lived. He called me his daughter and treated me like one. He put me and other MGM stars on pedestals. He created a make-believe world around all of us. It was fun, while it lasted."

Spencer Tracy, who was regarded by Mayer as one of the studio's greatest actors, said: "I won't dispute his assessment, but I think he knows that I act by instinct, just the way he ran his studio. He knew how to pick faces and mould them into stars. The man was a genius, nothing less than a great and loveable man."

Mickey Rooney, Judy Garland, and Louis B. Mayer.

Actor Van Johnson said, in 1975, "Mr. Mayer was like a father to me. If I had troubles I took them to him and he solved them. He told me from the start to trust him and I did. He was the guiding light in my career. Mr. Mayer knew what was right for me, that's why I've been around so long."

Spangler Arlington Brugh, who was renamed Robert Taylor by Mayer, recalled in 1960 how he once went to Mayer's office seeking a raise. "I was a star, making the studio millions, and all I got was $100 a week. I wanted an extra fifty, but before I had finished Mayer had convinced me that I ought to be asking for a reduction in salary. He told me of the studio's financial situation. He told me he had accepted a cut that year (I learned years later that it was from a million to $900,000) and how things were so bad that he might have to cut some people off the payroll. He never specifically mentioned me, but I fell for the tears he shed for all the out of work people in the world.

"I thought I was an actor until that day. That was when I saw the world's greatest actor give a performance I later learned he had given to dozens of others who dared ask for a raise. He ended by putting his arms around me and telling me if I stuck with him one day I'd be earning a million dollars a year. He was right. I did stick with MGM and I did earn a million, for several years. What can I say about a man who taught me how to act, have humility, and make many millions. He was a great man."

In 1927 Mayer called all the heads of the major studios to a meeting in his office. He proposed that an organization to be called the Academy of Motion Picture Arts and Sciences be created to honour each year the highest standards from every production department of the motion picture industry.

The response was unanimously favourable. Six months later the Academy came into being. Mayer insisted that it should be independent of every studio, and those eligible to vote in any section would only be the peers of those who earned the right to be nominated.

The first awards were presented at a banquet held at the Hollywood Roosevelt Hotel on May 16, 1929. Mayer, sitting at the head table, awaiting the auditors' tallies of votes to be announced, was beaming with delight. His "baby" had been born and he was convinced MGM would win at least half of the twelve statuettes (not named Oscars for two more years) to be presented.

When it was all over, he left the room in despair. Paramount, Fox, United Artists, and Warner Brothers had taken eleven of the twelve awards. Joseph Farnham was MGM's only winner for his writing achievements.

Next year, at the insistence of Mayer, who had specifically demanded when the Academy was formed that no studio head must be allowed to dictate policies, only seven awards were handed out. Jack Warner, head of Warner Brothers, announced to the public following the ceremony that Mayer's manipulations had allowed MGM to take home three of the seven statuettes.

At the 1931 ceremony Warner once more blasted MGM and Mayer when MGM's Douglas Shearer won the newly added category of sound recording excellence. "How can that be," said Warner, "when we invented sound?" From that moment on, Mayer and Warner conducted all business through an intermediary. Not until 1943, when they both sat down at a luncheon at MGM, did they get together and make peace by shaking hands.

Walter Pidgeon, the Broadway actor who arrived in Hollywood in 1926 after a career in musical comedy, loved to tell the story of his first meeting with Mayer in his office at MGM. "Mayer greeted me cordially, shook my hand, and asked where I was born," said Pidgeon. "I told him my home town was Saint John, New Brunswick. He leaped to his feet, shaking with rage. 'Who told you to say that?' he yelled. 'How dare you claim to come from my home town. Get out of my office. We don't want frauds at MGM.'

"I stood my ground, after all my career was likely at stake. When he calmed down, I told him I really was from Saint John. 'Then tell me two of the principal streets,' he demanded. I named Queen Street and Duke Street. 'That's no proof,' he said, somewhat abashed, 'every town has one of those.' Then, triumphantly, he yelled, 'Spell it, spell Saint John, you phoney.' I spelled it out, as all Saint Johnners would, not 'St.' but 'S-a-i-n-t.' He stopped me, suddenly he was smiling. 'You really do come from Saint John, don't you. I was just testing you. Tell me about Saint John. For two hours we talked about Saint John.

"Suddenly he looked at his watch. 'Tell me, what did you want to see me about?' I told him I was waiting his approval for a contract with MGM. Without another word he called his secretary, Ida Koverman. 'Ida,' he said, 'prepare a contract for this man from Saint John, he will tell you his name, and Ida, add another fifty dollars a week on the contract for a good Canadian.' We shook hands and just like that I was under contract to MGM. 'You do act, don't you?' he asked. I nodded and left the room."

On September 4, 1932, MGM director Paul Bern was found dead in the home at 9820 Easton Drive in Beverly Hills that he shared with his wife, actress Jean Harlow. He had died from a single gunshot wound to his head. Married only a few months to Harlow, one of MGM's most important stars of the early 1930s, he was considered to have a brilliant future in the film industry.

The house maid who arrived at the Bern-Harlow home around seven a.m., according to neighbours, told police that she found Bern dead on the floor of the main bedroom shortly after ten a.m. and had immediately called Mayer at his home in Bel Air, who told her to call the police.

After this the story gets a little confused. The police department records show they were not called until eleven a.m. No explanation was ever made for the delay in notifying them.

Mayer was first at the house. He claimed he was let in by the maid, but neighbours across the street told newspaper reporters they saw Harlow let him in at around seven-thirty a.m. He later publicly denied arriving before ten-thirty a.m., a time his chauffeur confirmed.

The second arrival, at eight-thirty a.m. according to neighbours, who must have been rather nosy, was Howard Strickling, with another man never identified. Strickling was listed as head of publicity at MGM, but he told writers many times that his principal job was to make sure no hint of scandal ever touched MGM stars. Strickling told police he arrived just after ten-thirty a.m.

Mayer and Strickling said they found a note on the bed beside the body. If it was genuine it absolved Harlow of any possible involvement. The note ended: "… this is the only way, I am terribly sorry." It was signed "Paul."

When police were finally called, remarkably by the maid, despite the presence of Mayer and Strickling, neighbours told newspaper reporters that cars had been coming and going from the house since seven-thirty a.m. They mentioned, in particular, a white limousine with dark windows that took someone away around ten a.m.

The maid, or whoever called Mayer, must have been in the house at seven a.m. because phone company logs registered a call to his home at 7:02 a.m.

The maid stuck by her story that she called Mayer after ten a.m. and then called the police immediately. No call was logged to Mayer at that time and police records and telephone company logs showed the police call was not made until eleven a.m. "Sometimes they make mistakes," said the maid, and that was apparently accepted as a reasonable explanation. Apparently no one thought to ask the maid how she came to be in possession of Mayer's private telephone number. Surely it is much more likely that Harlow, who had the telephone number, made the call just after the maid arrived to discover the tragedy.

That Mayer and Strickling were there when the police arrived is not in question, but no one seemed to ask why — if Mayer was really called only minutes before the police were notified, as the maid suggested — they had arrived first when both Mayer and Strickling lived in homes much further away from the Bern-Harlow house than the police station.

The unknown man, seen by neighbours to arrive with Strickling, was never identified, and the investigation police team apparently accepted the statements of Mayer and Strickling that he never existed.

Harlow was said to have spent the night at the home of her parents because she was worried about her mother's health. Nobody admitted phoning from the Bern-Harlow home to her parents' home despite telephone company records that logged a ten-thirty a.m. call. Was this made by Mayer or Strickling to make sure Harlow had arrived safely in her white limousine before the police were notified?

Mayer perhaps unwittingly let the cat out of the bag in 1943 when he briefly mentioned the tragedy. "We could do anything in those days, there was always a way to avert scandal," he said. "We had the best lawyers, and the police officers who investigated were often far too captivated by the glamour of MGM to investigate too carefully. But we were sometimes quite stupid. Bern's suicide note was written in green ink, and no one, not even me, noticed. But that's not a story I want to talk about."

In 1973 Howard Strickling revealed, without realising it, what Mayer was trying to hide thirty years earlier. In a television interview he talked about MGM's fan-mail department. "The stars couldn't possibly answer all the thousands of letters they received," he said, "so we solved that problem by hiring a number of handwriting experts; let's be honest, they were forgers, some of whom had served time for their handiwork. We offered them legitimate work using their talents. They could imitate the writing and signature of every important person on the lot. They signed almost every photograph that left the studio in the 1930s and 1940s.

"We had, at first, a little problem with this system. We had to be sure which were real signatures and which were the forgeries. So we arranged that everything the forgers wrote must be in green ink. They had fountain pens full of green ink, and ink pots to refill them. Everything they wrote that went out of the studio was in green ink. It worked as a safeguard and I never recall any problems from our hiring former convicts. They lived, as far as I know, exemplary lives."

But did they? Could it be that the unidentified man who accompanied Strickling to the Harlow house was one of these forgers? Isn't it reasonable, knowing of Mayer's statement about green ink, that the studio forger wrote the "suicide" note, with a fountain pen he carried in his pocket, at the urging of Mayer and Strickling? If Harlow was at the house when the fatal shot was fired, that could account for the seven a.m. early call to Mayer.

Harlow was put under a doctor's care at her mother's house, and police who wanted to interview her were held at bay for a full week before he permitted her to be questioned. Police, who kept a car outside the house for the entire week, reported that Strickling and Mayer visited Harlow on several occasions and were permitted by the doctor to talk to her.

Was she kept on ice until her story for the police was perfected? Possibly. But all this does not make Harlow a murderer, as a number of newspapers hinted. But it does suggest she was present when the fatal shot was fired and was spirited away by Mayer or Strickling to make sure she was in no way involved in the tragedy. Harlow was never called to testify at the inquest and a finding of "suicide while of unsound mind" was announced.

An interesting footnote to the story is that several newspapers, not satisfied with the verdict, reported that the house maid vanished immediately after she had testified at the inquest. She was found two years later by a reporter who received a tip that she, and her husband, were living in a beautiful home in, of all places, Haverhill, Massachusetts. Neither worked but appeared to have a generous income from a source they refused to divulge. Only days after the story of her discovery was printed she and her husband again disappeared and there was never any further report of her location.

In 1933 Mayer faced another crisis. One of his most competent actors, Lee Tracy, had been sent with director Howard Hawks to Mexico to film *Viva Villa*. Tracy was fast becoming a big box-office name, despite the fact that he had one major problem. He drank too much. Hawks told Mayer he could control the difficult star, and Mayer agreed to the casting decision.

Mayer was to regret his decision when the telephone rang beside his bedside at three a.m. Hawks announced that "Tracy is in jail. Send someone with money to get him out." Not waiting for any explanation, Mayer slammed down the phone, redialed, and yelled orders to his "action team."

A plane containing lawyers and money men arrived in Mexico within two hours. An hour later Tracy was out of jail, and returned to Los Angeles in the same plane.

Hawks told the full story publicly to news reporters in 1970 when he was returning to Mexico, for the first time in thirty-seven years, with John Wayne to film *Rio Lobo.*

"Tracy had been drinking heavily after we had finished filming and he went to his room in the hotel we had taken over, to rest. When he woke up he needed to go to the bathroom, and in his confused state he went out on the balcony and urinated down on the street below. This might have been forgiven, except for the fact that he wasn't aware the Chapultepec Military Cadets were marching below. The Mexican authorities took it as an intentional insult and Tracy was hauled off to jail.

"Mayer's 'hit squad' arrived before morning and Tracy was released. I was told it cost more than $100,000 to grease the palms of police officers and government officials. But it worked, and Tracy was whisked away before they could lay charges.

"Mayer called me at nine o'clock and said he was sending a replacement for Tracy. I told him I refused to accept a substitute, that we had done all but a few scenes and could finish without Tracy. I told him if he insisted on a substitute I wouldn't direct the film.

"He answered simply that if I didn't I would never work for him again. And I didn't. He said he would blacklist Lee Tracy and he could do it in those days, he was a very powerful man. Tracy never worked at MGM again. He had a big hit on Broadway with *Front Page,* and was expected to repeat that success when a film of the play was made in Hollywood. But Mayer blocked him by buying the film rights and hiring Pat O'Brien to make the film.

"Mayer told every studio head that he would never lend them any of his stars if they used Tracy. And he told the actors at MGM that if any of them appeared anywhere with Tracy he would throw them out of Hollywood. No one dared go against Louis B. Mayer in those days."

Joseph Mankiewicz, the renowned writer, producer and director, told a humorous story about Mayer in 1953. "Warner Brothers had just had a massive hit with the musical *42nd Street*," he told the trade paper, *Variety.* "I was called into his office. Mayer banged his finger on the front page of the trade paper that headlined Warners' success. 'Joseph,' he said, 'we've got to beat them at their own game. I want a script on my desk next week.' 'What's the theme?' I asked him. 'Theme,' he said. 'You decide the theme. I'll give you the title. We'll call it *43rd Street.*'"

Mayer never forgot Florence Lawrence and her co-operation with him when she visited his Orpheum Theatre in Haverhill, Massachusetts, in his early days in the film industry. When he heard that she was in financial trouble he sent his car to bring her to MGM. There, he presented her with a proposal. "I will put you under a lifetime contract at MGM and will promise you not extra roles, but the best parts we can find for you."

Lawrence was overwhelmed. She is said to have wept in his office. But she didn't forget other former silent era stars who, like her, were down on their luck. When she told Mayer of their plight he immediately ordered two of his top aides to locate and bring to the studio any of the silent stars who were found to be living in poverty.

The list reached twenty before Mayer felt he had tracked down everyone who needed help. He put people like King Baggott, Flora Finch, Lillian Rich, Barbara Bedford, Naomi Childers, and Mahlon Hamilton on lifetime contracts. As with Florence Lawrence, he promised them roles in MGM films. He kept his promise.

It was two years before news of his generosity leaked out. The news stunned the industry, which had never seen this generous side of Mayer's makeup before. Some writers brushed the generosity aside by saying it was nothing more than a distasteful publicity stunt. But most newspapers ran stories congratulating him, and more than 5,000 letters were said to have reached him at MGM from fans applauding his move. Asked for a comment, he said, "If we can't look after our own, who will? They were once stars, and at MGM they will always remain stars."

Some of the former actors asked to be given chances to shine in new fields as camera operators, make-up artists, or directors. Several made the transition very successfully and became productive members of the MGM family. One became a gateman at MGM, at his own request. "I can meet the fans here," he said. "I'll bet I'm the only gateman in Hollywood who signs dozens of autographs every day."

Mayer made visits to Canada in 1936 and 1939. On the first trip he was the guest of honour at a luncheon given by the City of Saint John and presented with a "Freedom of the City" scroll. He is reported to have visited the grave of his mother, and talked with a hotel porter who was one of his friends in his schooldays.

In 1939 he visited Fredericton, and was given an honorary degree of Doctor of Laws by the University of New Brunswick, and another "Freedom of the City" scroll from the mayor.

That same year he was listed by the Securities and Exchange Commission as the highest salaried executive in the United States. He received $1,296,503, seven times as much as the president. He held this title for six straight years.

In the late 1930s Mayer started to build one of the finest racing stables ever assembled in California. Over a ten-year period, his horses won more than $10 million in purse money. His breeding showplace, at Perris, in Riverside County, produced some of the finest thoroughbred horses ever to race in the United States.

In 1950 he decided to sell his vast turf holdings. The *Los Angeles Examiner* reported that he disposed of his prized stables "like it was the greatest production of his film studio, and with the dignity which had been the trade mark of his entire career."

In 1943 he broke the colour barrier that had, until that time, given coloured (as they were then called) actors only supporting and secondary roles in the major studios. Often segregated in the studio commissaries and kept apart from white actors in dressing rooms and make-up rooms, they were made equal at MGM with one stroke of Mayer's pen.

Announcing his intention to film *Cabin in the Sky,* he signed a document that stated no one would, in future, be employed at Metro-Goldwyn-Mayer if they in any way discriminated against coloured performers. He wrote a memo to every department head that said, "All coloured performers and other employees of MGM will, in future, have the same access as white performers and employees to all the facilities of this studio." He kept his word, showing others the way, by dining in the studio commissary every day for a week with the star of *Cabin in the Sky,* Ethel Waters. They are reported to have "walked arm in arm back to the sound stage each day following lunch."

In 1944 Mayer shocked the industry by announcing that he and his wife Margaret would separate on a trial basis. Instead of a fortieth wedding anniversary the studio was planning for Mayer and his wife, they had to handle a morose Mayer who for several months seemed too preoccupied to carry out his daily routine.

In 1947 Margaret and Louis Mayer were divorced. Mrs. Mayer received $3.2 million in a settlement that was made before the case reached the courts. The couple were friendly in court and the proceedings were over in less than fifteen minutes. "I simply feel I must get on with my own life," said Margaret Mayer. "His work is now his wife and his life. There is no room for me any more."

In 1948 he eloped to Yuma, Arizona, with Lorena Danker, the forty-two-year-old widow of a popular radio announcer, Danny Danker. When the press

Louis B. Mayer, with June Allyson and James Stewart, celebrating
MGM's silver anniversary in 1949.

heard of his visit to Yuma they headed there in droves, only to find that every
move they made was controlled by the Yuma police, directed by Mayer's
"publicity man" Howard Strickling, who was, apparently, still manipulating
police departments.

During his career as the "Hollywood Rajah," as Bosley Crowther's book
about Mayer was called, the mogul received many honours. He was cited for
outstanding American activities by the California Department of the American
Legion, and received the Gold Citizenship Medal, the highest award given by
the Veterans of Foreign Wars.

France made him an officer of the French Legion of Honour.
Czechoslovakia gave him the Cross of the Order of the White Lion. Mexico
presented him with the Order of the Aztec Eagle. Jewish War Veterans of the
United States voted unanimously to give him their Gold Medal of Merit.

But the honour he most revered was the special Oscar he received in
1950 for his twenty-seven years of achievement in the film industry. The

Academy of Motion Picture Arts and Sciences had finally recognized the man who was their founder. When he reached the podium to receive his award he was so overcome with emotion that he wasn't able to speak. He merely bowed to the audience, which was standing applauding, and ran off the stage.

On June 1, 1951, Mayer left MGM for the last time. Dore Schary, the man he brought in to replace Irving Thalberg, had gradually fallen out of favour with Mayer. Schary took his beef to MGM's parent company in New York, and won the support of the board of directors. Mayer resigned and left the studio he had built from nothing to greatness. He never again passed through the studio gates.

The following year he was named chairman of the board and technical advisor to the Cinerama Corporation. The floundering company obviously hoped his name would bring them the extra capital they needed, but it didn't happen, and a few years later the company ceased operations.

That same year he received the Lewis Milestone Award from the Screen Producers Guild for his contributions to the motion picture industry. "It is ironic," said Mayer when he received the award, "that I am getting an award named for a director and producer who I gave his start in our industry. But I am honoured, very honoured, to be with all my friends today."

Sy Weintraub, then head of Sol Lesser Productions in Hollywood, picked up on what he considered an omission by the film industry, and proposed to George Stevens, then president of the Academy of Motion Picture Arts and Sciences, that an award be given annually to the person in the film industry who does most to recognize and encourage new talent. "This should be named the Louis B. Mayer Award, to perpetuate the memory of the man who did more than any other man to recognize and nurture new talent." The Academy board promised to study the matter, but nothing more was heard of the proposal.

In January of 1957 Mayer made his last bid to make a comeback in the industry he loved. He and Jack Cummings, his nephew from Saint John, New Brunswick, who had produced many of MGM's greatest musicals, including *Kiss Me Kate, Lovely to Look At, Three Little Words,* and *The Broadway Melodies of 1937* and *1940,* announced their intention to film the Lerner and Loewe musical from Broadway, *Paint Your Wagon.* "We expect," said Mayer, "that filming will start in October at a studio to be named." Mayer added "that neither Mr. Cummings or I will consider using MGM's facilities."

In August newspapers ran front page stories to say Mayer had entered Stanford Hospital in San Francisco for treatment of a "moderately severe" blood disorder. On September 15 he returned to his home in Bel Air, saying that he "felt much better and expected to be personally involved in the October start of *Paint Your Wagon*."

On September 25 he was rushed to the University of California Medical Centre in Los Angeles, suffering from "severe anemia." A hospital spokesman said on the following day that "Mr. Mayer is progressing satisfactorily." No further bulletins were issued at Mayer's request, and callers were simply told "he is doing well."

On Tuesday, October 29, 1957, newspapers and radios around the world announced that Louis B. Mayer had died from leukemia. Most papers, including the *New York Times*, made the story front-page news.

The *Los Angeles Examiner* ran a headline that said, "A Giant Has Left the American Scene." Tributes came from all parts of the world. Vice-president Richard Nixon said: "The motion picture industry has lost one of its really great geniuses, and I have lost a friend." David O. Selznick, who had at one time been married to Mayer's daughter Irene, said: "Louis B. Mayer was the greatest single figure in the history of motion pictures." Samuel Goldwyn, who never before professed anything but hatred for Mayer, changed his tune. "Louis B. Mayer has made an immense contribution to the motion picture industry." Jack Warner, his enemy for many years, said: "The industry that owes him so much will sorely miss one of its greatest creative minds."

More than 2,000 people jammed Wilshire Boulevard Temple for the funeral service. Almost every big star of motion pictures attended. Spencer Tracy delivered the eulogy. Tracy said: "He stands head and shoulders above the mystic memory of Hollywood's past."

Jeanette MacDonald sang "Ah Sweet Mystery of Life." She said later: "I promised him to do this a few years ago, but neither of us expected the sad day would come so soon."

The pallbearers included Howard Strickling, the trouble-shooter who had stood by Mayer throughout his life.

Rabbi Edgar Magnin, a friend of Mayer for more than fifty years, officiated at the service. Some months after the service, when it was revealed that Mayer's estate was less than $7 million, Magnin said he felt it should now be told that during the thirty years before his death he had given away in excess of $15 million to people in need. "If he heard of a family being burned out of their home, he arranged for the house to be rebuilt at his expense without anyone knowing the donor's name. And he and I would travel to the site of the rebuilding and work side by side hammering in nails and doing anything else that had to be done. It was easy for us; outside Hollywood few knew him by sight, and he always felt that giving money was not enough. 'You must give your person, too,' he told me. Over the years we went where there were fires, tragedies, floods, you name it, and Louis B. Mayer, the 'meanest man in Hollywood' paid the bill."

Mayer was buried quietly, with only his widow, Lorena, his two daughters, Irene [the former Mrs. David O. Selznick], and Edith [Mrs. William Goetz], and their four children attending the interment at the Jewish Home of Peace Cemetery.

Much of the $7 million that remained after taxes had been paid went to the Louis B. Mayer Foundation, set up some years before his death to provide money for medical research. His second wife and two daughters had been provided for prior to his death. The Foundation's money was wisely invested, and figures released in 1993 showed that it had disbursed, in the thirty-six years since Mayer's death, many more millions than the original bequest in grants to medical researchers and hospitals.

But, like Mayer's generosity in his lifetime, the money had been given away quietly to the deserving researchers still seeking to find a cure for the leukemia that ended his life in 1957.

In 1986, the last chapter in the history of Metro-Goldwyn-Mayer was written when Ted Turner, the communications and sports mogul, bought the rights to all MGM films, and the Sony Corporation bought the biggest studio in the world and converted it into television production studios. On April 18, 1986, the MGM lion logo, eighteen feet in height, that had dominated the administration building at the Culver City studio since 1926, was dismantled and lowered to the ground before being carted away, perhaps appropriately, to a nearby metal scrapyard.

SIDNEY OLCOTT

"I doubt if the motion picture industry will ever again see the likes of Sidney Olcott. He gave our industry a dimension and respectability that only he, in those early days, could envision. His role in the acceptance of motion pictures as a legitimate art form must never be forgotten. Sid Olcott must never be forgotten."

(Will Rogers, 1928)

Eulogies of such magnitude are usually heard as final tributes at funerals and memorial services. But, on February 11, 1928, when Will Rogers and more than 200 other celebrities from the era of silent films gathered at a testimonial dinner, Sidney Olcott had never been in better health. He sat in the place of honour at the head table in the crowded ballroom of Hollywood's Roosevelt Hotel, listening with obvious pleasure to the praise bestowed lavishly on his achievements.

Four months earlier, Olcott, at the age of fifty-five, had announced his immediate retirement. With the first sound films in production, Olcott, one of the most imaginative and innovative directors of the silent era, had been hailed as one of the few capable of making the transition. His unexplained retirement had stunned the industry.

Will Rogers was not alone in his praise. Star after star who owed their fame to Olcott's skilled direction rose to add their tributes. Norma Shearer, Richard Barthelmess, Pola Negri, and Warner Baxter pleaded with Olcott to continue to direct their films.

Marion Davies, the beautiful actress-protege of multi-millionaire William Randolph Hearst, said, "I have made only one film of which I am truly proud. That film was *Little Old New York*, which Sid Olcott directed."

Hearst, who had not even rated a head-table seat, rose from his place in the ballroom. "I have no words in which to express, adequately, my admiration for the artistry of Sid Olcott. If he changes his mind, these words of mine can be used as a binding contract. I will personally finance all the talking pictures he wishes to direct over the next ten years."

Telegrams lauding Olcott came from the great director, D. W. Griffith, Olcott's major rival, and such giants as English actor George Arliss. Their pleas were in vain. Olcott did not change his mind. Never again did he set foot in a film studio.

Twenty-one years later, when he died at the age of seventy-six, he was a forgotten man. Will Rogers had been dead for fourteen years. Many of his friends from the silent era who had failed to make the transition to sound were also dead or living in quiet retirement many miles from Hollywood. Those who had found a place on the sound stages had rolled back their ages and were trying hard to make people forget that they had been part of the early days of the industry. Sid Olcott was long erased from their memories.

Olcott was born on September 20, 1873, only three months after his parents had arrived in Toronto, Ontario, from their native Ireland. Christened John Sidney Alcott, he did not adopt the name "Olcott" until he was, at fourteen, a seasoned actor with credits in more than thirty plays.

His childhood was happy. Although the row house in which the Alcotts lived was far from luxurious, the family was never short of food and good clothing. Sidney's father worked on a road repair gang. His mother augmented this income by using her considerable talents as a seamstress for a theatrical costume maker and repairer. Sidney himself contributed to the family income by delivering newspapers to nearby homes when he was only five.

When he started school at the age of six, Olcott continued selling papers before starting classes. In the evening he earned small tips by delivering costumes from his mother's employer to nearby theatres.

His main friends came from a boy's orphanage that stood across the road from the Alcott family home.

His enthusiasm for the theatre grew. "It had an aura of excitement that thrilled me," he told the *New York Times* in 1927. "The day I received a twenty-five cent tip I decided my future lay in the world of entertainment. Anyone who could give a twenty-five cent tip had to be very rich and since I wanted to be very rich what better profession could I find."

From that day on, Olcott hung around the city's many live theatres every night. Friendly performers allowed him to stand backstage to get a close-up of the costumes he had delivered.

At nine he won his first role in a play. "They were rehearsing one Monday when I dropped by the theatre," he told the *Times*. "I was already skipping school two or three days a week because I was convinced the only education I would ever need would come from the theatre. The director spotted me and asked if I would be interested in playing a small part."

The director walked Olcott home, convinced his parents that the $1.50 salary he would earn each week the play ran would be useful to him in the years ahead, and four days later he made his stage debut.

Olcott's one line didn't make him a star, but it made him more stage-struck than ever. Despite his excitement he did not forget his friends at the orphanage. "The theatre manager let a few of the boys in every night to fill the empty seats," he told the *Times*.

In the next year he obtained six more roles. "Some were quite substantial," he recalled, "but I seemed able to remember lines instantly, however complicated, so I was very popular." At eleven, he was advising set painters how to make their scenery more realistic. "It may sound incredible," he said, "but they listened and did what I suggested." At twelve he was named in the program as assistant set designer!

By the age of fourteen he had appeared in thirty plays. He had also managed to graduate top of his class at school despite missing many classes.

Since Alcott was pronounced "Olcott" he officially adopted the name. "More often than not the program printers spelled it Olcott. Besides, there was a famous actor of that time called Chauncey Olcott. I hoped someone might think we were related," he recalled years later.

His first newspaper review came from a play critic in Peterborough, Ontario. It read: "The young boy, Sidney Olcott, as William, adds warmth and what little believability there is in a play so unbelievable. Young Olcott will go far. This play will not!" After his death, a yellowed and tattered copy of the review was found in his wallet.

In 1898, when he was, at twenty-five, a veteran of regional theatre in Canada, he decided his future lay not in Canada but on Broadway in New York City. Actors on the way down the ladder when they appeared in Canada with touring companies started him dreaming with their tales of life in the "big city."

The luck of the Irish was with him from the moment he stepped off the train in New York. A sudden gust of wind swept the top hat from the head of a dignified gentleman walking a few yards in front of Olcott. Dropping his suitcases, he chased after the hat and returned it to its owner. "He thanked me, and seeing my suitcases, asked if I was in the city for the first time," Olcott told the *Motion Picture Herald* in 1914. "When he learned I had just arrived from Toronto he handed me his calling card and suggested I visit his office if I found any difficulty getting a job. 'You'll find a small map on the back of the card showing where my office is located.'"

Half-an-hour later, sitting in a small room that a friendly police officer had pointed out as 'clean and Godly,' Olcott looked at the card for the first time. His jaw dropped when he read the name:

Mr. John Ince
Theatrical Producer and Manager
1620 Broadway, New York City

"I couldn't believe my luck," he told the film magazine. "In New York only thirty minutes and I had in my hand an introduction to one of the most reputable men in the theatre. Ince was one of the people actors in Canada told me to make an effort to meet."

In less than an hour Olcott was sitting in the waiting room outside Ince's office. A friendly receptionist heard his story and suggested he wait. Minutes later the inner door opened and Ince came out accompanied by a man Olcott recognized as one of Broadway's most renowned actors. "Ince looked around and saw me," recalled Olcott. "For a second he looked puzzled, then he smiled and invited me into his office."

"Young man," said Ince, "I like your style. We haven't been off the train two hours and here you are. Right now I need a messenger to deliver scripts and contracts to theatres and managements. Are you interested?"

Deciding this was not the time to tell Ince he was, at twenty-five, a veteran actor, Olcott accepted. The job paid $2.50 a week. Olcott decided it was a great opportunity to introduce himself to everything Broadway had to offer.

His climb to the top started only two weeks later. Olcott was busy dusting the outer office when Ince arrived. "Sidney," he said sternly, "I am very disappointed in you. Please come into my office." He pointed to a chair. "Sit down," he said. "I have spent the past two weeks trying to find a young actor capable of playing the second lead in a new play I am about to produce on Broadway. Now I find I have that young man right here in my own office. Why did you hide your acting experience from me?"

Olcott stuttered his apologies and explained that he didn't think he had the experience to deserve consideration for a Broadway show.

"Well," said Ince, now smiling, "I was talking to one of my friends in the lobby of this building when you rushed in, as usual, in a hurry. You didn't see me, or my friend, or you would have recognized a well-known actor who starred last year in a Toronto play in which you had a small, but, my friend tells me, a very well-acted role."

Within hours Olcott read for the part and a contract for the run of the play was signed. On cloud nine, he was not even fazed when he discovered the star of *When Harvest Days Are Over* was only eleven years old. Like Olcott, Joseph Santley was already a veteran of the theatre. He and Olcott became friends from the first day of rehearsals and Olcott acted as his mathematics and English teacher during the play's two-year run on Broadway and in theatres across the United States. "I was give a salary boost of $2 a week for the tuition," he told the *Telegraph* in 1917.

Olcott and Santley followed their first success with two more Broadway hit plays, *Rags to Riches* and *Billy the Kid*. Their friendship lasted until Olcott died. Santley, by then a renowned film director, was one of the mourners at the funeral.

Santley, who died in 1971, moved from stage to film acting in the silent era, then to directing both silent and sound films. He was one of the first major film directors to move into television, where he pioneered many of the early live TV dramas.

In a 1970 interview with a writer from the Academy of Motion Picture Arts and Sciences, Santley said of Olcott: "I knew from the day we met in 'Pop' Ince's office that we would be friends for life. He had a quiet air of confidence that I liked. I tried many times to talk him out of retirement and believe the medium of sound films would have been enhanced and enriched by his original and inspiring ideas."

During breaks between plays, Olcott returned to Ince's office where he ran errands and cleaned the floors. "Why not," he told the *Motion Picture Herald*. "I owed my career to him."

Olcott was soon to be even deeper in debt to Ince, though neither knew it at the time. Film production companies in and near New York were, by then, turning out hundreds of one-reel films that were fast growing in popularity. Few established actors would condescend to appear before the cameras. But John Ince believed that the new entertainment craze had a big future. One day he suggested that Olcott might investigate the work possibilities at the Biograph Studio, where the demand for competent actors was increasing.

"The industry already intrigued me," Olcott told the *Motion Picture World* in 1921. "So when 'Pop' Ince gave his blessing I had no hesitation."

Thanks to his lengthy list of stage credits, Olcott was hired immediately. As a member of the Biograph stock company he played several different characters each day. "I recall playing in as many as ten different films in one week," he said. But Olcott still found time to investigate the studio lighting, the crude set building methods and, most nights, he said, "I stayed behind and swept the studio floor."

Frank J. Marion, Biograph's sales manager, soon noticed Olcott's enthusiasm and creative talents. He, and Samuel Long, manager of the company's laboratory, had been discussing the possibility of forming their own independent film company. Olcott's arrival gave their idea impetus.

Long raised $600 from relatives. Marion, who had the use of a loft in a 21st Street warehouse, had $300 which he used to buy wood and other materials for set building. The two convinced George Kleine, owner of the largest film distribution centre in Chicago, to guarantee their bank account so they could purchase a camera, film, and lighting equipment.

Olcott, when offered a year's contract at $20 a week, was easily convinced to become the first employee of the new company. So Kalem (a name created from the initials of Kleine, Long, and Marion) came into being.

Kalem's first contract, with Olcott, was signed on a Friday in June 1907. The following Monday Olcott arrived at the 21st Street warehouse to find a carpenter, a lighting man borrowed from a New York theatre, and a cameraman with very little experience.

"Frank Marion handed me the studio keys and told me he expected the company's first film by Friday, at the latest," Olcott told the *Motion Picture World* fourteen years later. "That was the first time I realized I was expected to direct for the company. I gave the carpenter a rough sketch of what I wanted him to build, sent the camera operator out to borrow furniture from some of my friends, and told the lighting man to rig up the best he could from the few lights Kalem had been able to afford."

Marion and Long set to work creating a primitive laboratory while Olcott headed for 'Pop' Ince's office to recruit whatever competent actors were available.

Sketching out in his mind a possible story, Olcott found Joseph Santley, Santley's brother Fred, and another actor, Robert Vignola, who had worked with Olcott in *Billy the Kid*, waiting to see Ince.

The trio never did see the producer that day. "Sid was so enthusiastic," recalled Joseph Santley years later, "that we left the office, grabbed a streetcar, and headed for the Kalem studio. By the time we got there Sid had a story line for us. The set wasn't quite ready so he sat down and scribbled out on pieces of paper what I now believe must have been the very first film script. He rehearsed us as though we were preparing a stage production and by the end of the day we had completed Kalem's first film."

Sleigh Bells was a big success. George Kleine offered it through his distribution house as an "exclusive masterpiece from a company that will revolutionize the motion picture industry."

The film didn't set the world on fire, but it did nothing to diminish the stature of its principal actors. It is historic in that it used spotlights for the first time to emphasize individuals and objects essential to the continuity of the film. And it introduced Sidney Olcott to the industry as a highly competent director.

While Olcott was acting in some of the scenes, he deputized Robert Vignola as his assistant. As a result, Vignola too became a permanent member of the Kalem company. Within weeks, guided by Olcott, he was directing in his own right. Vignola went on to become one of the silent era's finest directors. He moved into the sound era with considerable success, and when he retired in 1937 he owned a large home in Beverly Hills and a solid bank balance.

Olcott stayed with Kalem for seven years. The company prospered under his guidance. His hand-written paper on the use of backlighting for special effects, prepared in 1909, was mentioned by Alfred Hitchcock in a 1942 interview with the *Los Angeles Examiner*. "It is quite remarkable," said Hitchcock. "What he suggested thirty-three years ago I still use today to create some of my most effective scenes. What a genius he must have been."

One of the first rules laid down at Kalem by Olcott was a firm directive that no film be started until a complete "written synopsis" was prepared by the director and approved by himself. Many of the "scripts" he wrote himself. Others came from writers he trained in the new medium.

Kalem records show that weekly profits averaged $5,000 only three months after the company's formation. The money was used wisely. Kalem purchased a four-storey building in Fort Lee, New Jersey, and converted it into a well-equipped studio complete with the most modern laboratory in the industry. Olcott said in 1943 that the New Jersey location was chosen because "it had many beautiful outdoor and waterside settings within walking distance," a far cry from today's decaying industrial areas near the location of the old studios.

Olcott recruited his actors in many different ways. One of his favorites was to find an actor with a wardrobe suitable for the film being planned. In need of an actor for a "society" film, Olcott encountered actor George Melford strolling down Broadway immaculately dressed in a "morning suit." "You're in," said Olcott. "In where?" asked Melford. "My next picture," said Olcott. After sitting down to a five cent drink, which Olcott entered in his weekly expense account, Melford joined the Kalem stock company. Like Vignola, Melford soon became a camera assistant and within weeks was a director in his own right.

Records show that Melford directed more than 200 films in a career that lasted until 1937, when he again became an actor in many major films including *A Tree Grows in Brooklyn*, *The Robe*, *The Ten Commandments*, and *The Miracle of Morgan's Creek*. In a 1953 interview, while filming *The Robe*, he told a *Picturegoer* reporter: "My entire career is due to Sid Olcott. He is dead now, and few people remember him. But he had a strange ability to make many people, like me, get the most out of everything we did. While people like me are still alive Sid Olcott's genius is still alive." *Picturegoer* printed a terse explanatory note: "Sidney Olcott was a silent picture director who is often recalled more for the performances he got from his actors than for his directing abilities. He died in 1949."

Actress Gene Gauntier made so many intelligent story suggestions to Olcott that he hired her to write on a full-time basis, the first writer to be hired by a film company exclusively to write scripts. Two other actors converted to directors by Olcott, Kenean Buel and James Vincent, became recognized as two of the industry's best. Gauntier told an historical writer from the Academy of Motion Picture Arts and Sciences in 1949 that "Olcott's greatest asset was his willingness to let people try things they had never done before. And he was never concerned that those he promoted might equal him in ability. He knew he was a genius but never flaunted it. If he created other geniuses he was delighted."

In the early days of the industry, directors stole many of their stories from books and magazines, rarely — if ever — crediting the original writer. Certainly, none received fees for their work. All that changed when Olcott used not only the story but also the title of Lew Wallace's *Ben Hur* for a one-reel epic. The estate of Wallace sued, and in the first court case of its kind, Kalem had to pay $25,000 to the late writer's family.

Olcott's film of *Ben Hur* was rather undistinguished, but because of the legal publicity it did record business and more than recouped the $25,000 court judgement. The film is still maintained in archives in the United States. From that day, most companies made sure they paid authors for their stories.

Olcott's self-proclaimed policy, "If in doubt, do it," got him into difficulties throughout his career. *The Scarlet Letter*, which he scripted and directed, was the first film to be banned by the National Board of Censors, the industry's watchdog of the time. To get the one-reeler on the nation's screens, Olcott had to shoot a new ending so that the "wronged" Hester married the minister who had "wronged" her. He wrote his own publicity material for *The Scarlet Letter*. "Is this the banned version, or the revised version? See for yourself." Needless to say, it was the revised version, but it drew many thousands of bonus paying customers.

Just before his retirement in 1928, Olcott told the *Motion Picture Herald* that on many later occasions he deliberately made films with scenes or endings that he knew would be unacceptable to the Board of Censors. "I filmed, at the same time, the alternate scenes I knew they would demand," he said. "When they banned the film I had to make simple changes. The banning drew crowds to the theatres and Kalem's profits continued to rise."

In 1908, when Olcott was thirty-five, he convinced the three Kalem owners to move out of New Jersey for the winter months. "The primitive cameras of the time froze easily in cold weather and outdoor shooting became impossible," he told the *New York Times* in 1927. "Since we had discovered that audiences loved outdoor scenery I suggested a move to Florida for five months, where the scenery was not only different but available all winter long."

A Jacksonville theatre owner, A. S. Hoyt, agreed to pay the cost of the unit's move to Florida if Kalem would guarantee that he would get first showing rights for his theatre. Olcott and Hoyt decided to make each opening a gala occasion with the actors and director attending. The studio loaned its lighting equipment to floodlight the theatre front and thousands of people gathered to see the "stars." The ten films made in Florida are on record as being the first "official opening nights" of the growing film industry.

Olcott's company took over a boarding house named Roseland in Fairfield, on the outskirts of Jacksonville. The rooms used as bedrooms at night were converted to indoor sets during daylight hours when the weather outside was too rainy for location work.

Hoyt told Olcott at the end of the season that he had made a small fortune from the Kalem films. During the next summer he built three new theatres and founded the Hoyt chain, which at one time owned more than eighty movie palaces.

Kalem used hundreds of local people in the Florida films. Rarely did Olcott need to pay for their services, and the huge nightly audiences at the Hoyt theatre were often these same "extras" with their families. They cheered every time they recognized a scene or person on screen.

The Florida venture almost came to an end after the showing of the first film. *A Florida Feud* told the story of murder and revenge among the sharecroppers (tenant farmers who paid a portion of their crops as rent) of the area. Olcott must have come a little too close to the truth, and the sharecroppers didn't like the way they were portrayed on screen.

Shortly after midnight on the night of the film's premiere, a group of hooded men raided the boarding house and dragged Olcott into the street. Next day's newspapers reported him as "badly beaten and left in a pool of blood." Rushed to hospital in Jacksonville, he was diagnosed with broken ribs and many cuts and bruises. The *New York Telegraph* ran the story on its front page, reporting that "only intervention by Kalem actors and technicians saved Olcott's life."

Olcott loved the publicity. He ordered the Fort Lee laboratory to issue the film nation-wide together with a lurid account of his beating. Kalem records show that the company made enough money from this one film to cover all the Florida winter expenses. The nine additional films were a bonus.

Was the sharecroppers' attack a hoax designed to create large audiences for the film? Olcott, many years later, admitted that he perhaps exaggerated his injuries a little. Kalem files show that he was back on the set, ready to direct, only twenty-four hours after the beating, suggesting that he may have exaggerated a lot!

Olcott and the other Kalem directors were still the only ones using a "scene and story" sequence, as the early scripts were known. Most directors not influenced by Olcott had only a rough idea of what they planned to film, improvising as thoughts occurred to them during the shooting. The few films made by Olcott that remain in archives contrast sharply with their intelligent continuity when compared to those of most other directors whose material had no pre-set pattern.

Success in Florida gave Olcott more ambitious ideas. Kalem quickly agreed to his suggestion that some of the winter profits be used to send a few actors and small crew to Ireland.

With many of the stories of "old Ireland" his father had told him as a boy deeply etched in his mind, Olcott, Gene Gauntier, Robert Vignola, and cameraman George Hollister sailed from New York to Queenston, Ireland. Hollister, one of the best cameramen in the industry, told the *New York Telegraph* that "the opportunity to work with Olcott would have taken me to the ends of the earth."

Ireland was all Olcott had hoped for. "I fell in love the moment the ship docked," he told the *Telegraph* on his return to New York. "I had the scene and story sequences written for several films and we were ready to shoot." The company found a local boy with a natural flair for acting and two hours after they set foot on land they were filming *The Lad from Old Ireland*.

Gene Gauntier took over the writing. Vignola directed two of the films. The entire group, including Olcott, played parts in the films. Vignola recalled years later that he played four different parts in one of the films.

The unit completed five films in two weeks. Olcott then cabled Kalem for more money so the company could travel on to Germany. Records show that Frank Marion wired him an additional $300. It was enough to permit three more films to be made in Germany before the unit headed for home.

Only absent from the United States for a little over eight weeks, the unit arrived home to a blaze of publicity. As head of the first film unit to travel overseas for location shooting, Olcott found himself in demand as a speaker. "The Irish clubs all wanted to hear me," he recalled. "I addressed eleven groups ranging in number from 50 to 1,000 in less than two weeks. As a result, all the films made in Ireland were profitable. It seemed everyone with Irish ancestry wanted to see the old country again." The German films didn't do too well, but Kalem still showed a handsome profit from the trip.

Profits were so good that Frank Marion urged Olcott to make another trans-Atlantic crossing in 1910. Remarkably, the success of the location shooting didn't inspire other companies to follow suit and Kalem's stock rose as their real scenery was compared to the cardboard sets and New York scenes which were getting to be a bore with moviegoers.

Gauntier, Vignola, and Hollister eagerly accepted Olcott's offer of employment on the second European trip. He added actress Alice Hollister, wife of the cameraman, three more actors, Jack J. Clark, Jack P. McGowan, and Helen Lindroth, plus a scenic artist, Allen Farnham.

Olcott wasn't a man to waste money. On the first day out at sea on the SS *Adriatic*, he called his group together and presented them with two scripts he planned to shoot on board. When the captain announced the unit's plans there was a long line of people waiting to be chosen as unpaid extras. "The captain insisted on first-class passengers being given priority," recalled Olcott.

Making his first film on board the Adriatic nearly cost Olcott his life. (Or was this another of his successful publicity stunts?) The script called for an actor to climb down a rope on the outside of the ship's hull. No one volunteered, so Olcott once more became an actor. Unfortunately for Olcott, a porthole opened just above the spot where he was clinging to the rope and a cook dumped a can of garbage on his head. His hands slipped and he only regained control two feet before the end of the rope. He climbed, as the script demanded, into an open porthole two decks down. The camera filmed the action and it is still available to be seen in film archives in Washington.

Since the scene inside the cabin had already been shot, it had to be re-done so that Olcott would have the garbage on his face as he climbed into the room to face the jewel robber. "I had to decide which of the two evils was the lesser," he told the *Motion Picture Herald*. "Whether I would go down the rope again or have a pail of garbage thrown over me. I decided the garbage was preferable."

The completed film is today viewed as a comedy. When filmed it was intended as a drama. And, if Olcott is to be believed, it was almost the end of his career.

In Ireland, a film written by Gene Gauntier about Rory O'More, an eighteenth century revolutionary hero, upset the British authorities. With threats of expulsion from Ireland hanging over their heads, Olcott put the unit back in favour by producing two high-quality three-reelers, *The Colleen Bawn* and *Arrah-na-Pogue*. The two films were adapted by Gauntier from plays by the Irish-American dramatist Dion Boucicault. A poem by Thomas Moore provided the story line for *You Remember Ellen*. In eight weeks the unit made seven films, most of them two- or three-reelers.

Olcott made sure he paid for the screen rights and his meticulous accounting for every penny showed receipts from the authors or their agents. Thomas Moore received three pounds ($12) for the rights to his poem.

"I always accounted for every penny I spent," said Olcott in 1942 to the *Motion Picture Herald*. The extent of his accountability is reflected in a couple of lines repeated on several occasions during the trip:

"Three shillings for service of extra girl after hours for personal pleasure."
"One shilling for Irish Whiskey to encourage extra girl to become friendly."

With huge profits coming in from virtually every film Olcott made, Kalem was not inclined to argue about this extra-curricular activity.

Even when Olcott and Kalem announced a third trip to Europe, in 1911, no competitors followed in the unit's footsteps. Kalem films were eagerly awaited and the company moved to the top of the production ladder.

Because of adverse British reaction to the New York success of the film glorifying Rory O'More, Olcott — at Marion's urging — decided to bypass England and Ireland. The 1911 unit, now eleven strong, including most of those who had made the two earlier pioneering trips, landed in France. They made five films there before heading to Spain and Morocco.

In Morocco, Olcott convinced two enemy Bedouin tribes to "hold a battle" for the camera. All went well until cameraman George Hollister got a bullet in his arm and had to be taken to hospital.

"This was the first time I realized they were using real bullets," Olcott told an interviewer from the Academy of Motion Picture Arts and Sciences in 1929. "I tried to stop the battle but the Moroccans were just getting in the spirit of things and wouldn't listen. So I shrugged my shoulders, took over the camera, and shot some scenes which I am sure, if shown today, would be quite horrifying."

Next day the battle ended and the two chiefs arrived arm in arm for their pay. "I gave them twice what I had promised and was never more happy to see anyone go away," he said.

Shooting additional scenes with less warlike locals, Olcott came up with enough ideas to make four different films in just over two weeks.

With his Irish-Catholic background, Olcott had long been fascinated with the idea of making a movie based on the life of Christ. He sent his unit to the Holy Land while he headed for London in search of an actor to play Christ. The announcement that he planned a five-reel epic called *From the Manger to the Cross* drew storms of protest from church organizations and those who remembered Rory O'More as a rather unsavory character.

Olcott sensed he had a box-office winner. In a *New York Times* article in 1913, he said, "I knew then I had to make the film. With all that free publicity the film would obviously be a big profit-maker."

In London he was shocked to find that actors and their agents were not interested in the role of Christ. Swayed by the bad press the idea was getting, actors feared association with Olcott would destroy their careers. On the verge of giving up, Olcott was approached by Thomas Blackmore, principal of Blackmore's Theatrical Agency. He said he had the perfect actor for Christ, and the actor was willing to take the role. When Olcott met Robert Henderson Bland, a gifted Shakespearean actor who had already achieved some fame on the London stage, he agreed. Bland walked into Olcott's hotel room wearing a long golden wig, dressed in a white flowing robe. "I am Jesus Christ," said Bland. "I will portray myself in your film."

Bland told them he had received a vision during the night and that God had told him he was His chosen son. "Frankly, we thought he was mad," said Olcott. "But we didn't argue, he was obviously what we wanted." Two days later Olcott and Bland sailed for Egypt where they found all pre-shooting preparations were complete.

Gauntier and the unit had built an outdoor stage that was large enough to hold sets for all the interior scenes. They had also obtained permission to shoot on the Sea of Galilee and along the procession route to Calvary. Local authorities, in exchange for generous handouts, guaranteed the company would have no troubles and as many extras as they needed, at no charge.

From the Manger to the Cross was the first five-reel film to be shot. Back in Fort Lee, Marion and Long rubbed their hands nervously as Olcott took five weeks to complete the film. The bills mounted as production time lengthened, but Kalem decided Olcott knew what he was doing and they offered no interference.

By the time for shooting came, Bland had grown his own golden hair to shoulder length and the wig was discarded. Olcott reported to Kalem that Bland was acting as though possessed. On his return to New York, Olcott told reporters that for the first time in his career he had allowed an actor to be in total command of every scene. "Bland needed no direction, he was superb," said Olcott.

Bland told Olcott that he was totally unaware of the camera and what he did came naturally "through some strange and compelling force."

Olcott, who played fourteen roles as well as directing the film, was a nervous wreck when the shooting ended. Gauntier took the negatives directly to New York while Olcott and the rest of the unit sailed to London where they had heard that Dean Inge, the "gloomy dean" of St. Paul's Cathedral, had issued a statement praising Olcott for his determination to show the "true story of Christianity." Olcott was received by the dean, an audience that prompted hundreds of letters for and against the movie in London newspapers.

A revived Olcott took his crew to Ireland, where they made four films in one week before sailing to the United States. Their return to New York was greeted with considerable press coverage and letters for and against the film filled the newspapers. Olcott admitted to a *Films in Review* writer some twenty years later that everyone from Kalem sent at least two letters to the papers. Some were designated to write in support, others asked that the film be banned. "Of the hundreds of letters the papers printed, we sent perhaps forty," he recalled, "but I must admit we set the ball rolling."

Robert Henderson Bland was brought by Kalem to New York for the special opening of the film in October 1912. Olcott had taken several months editing the hundreds of reels the unit had filmed.

Although Bland was not paid to travel first class, the captain of the liner, awestruck at the sight of the blonde giant strolling around in the robes he had used in the film, moved him into the best suite on board.

Bland was a sensation in New York. He refused to use any vehicle for his travels, walking everywhere. Crowds followed him every day and hundreds more waited outside his hotel for his daily appearance. Many knelt down or bowed when he left the hotel.

From the Manager to the Cross was screened publicly for the first time at John Wanamaker's Auditorium in New York City on October 14, 1912. An orchestra of forty musicians played a specially written overture and accompanied the picture with an impressive score. Everyone of importance in the religious life of New York was invited. Most attended, as did civic leaders and important people in the film industry.

Reviews in the New York papers called the film "entrancing," "spellbinding," "inspiring," and "the most wonderful use of the new medium of film." Most of the earlier criticism was now over, and the few letters denouncing Olcott and Kalem for daring to put the story on film as entertainment were drowned out by the hundreds in favour.

Olcott was triumphant. The industry he loved acclaimed him as its greatest director. Bland, too, was basking in the film's success. He stayed in New York for almost three months with Kalem willingly footing the bill. He received invitations to the homes of the city's elite. The widow of John Jacob Astor IV (lost on the *Titanic*) threw a special alcohol-free reception for Bland, during which she asked him to "bless" her son, born after her rescue from the *Titanic*!

Offers came in to Bland's hotel for him to appear on the New York stage and in other films. He turned every request down. At the urging of Olcott he made one personal appearance at the small theatre owned by Louis B. Mayer in Haverhill, Massachusetts. Just before he was scheduled to sail back to England, this time first-class, Frank Marion offered him a large cheque to say thanks for the publicity he had given the film. Olcott, who took the cheque to his hotel, talked for many years about an unusual happening when he met with Bland.

"I offered him the cheque, but he waved it away," said Olcott. "He then grabbed the cheque and pressed it to my forehead and then his own. "There are others who need it more than I," he said. He paused, then added: "There is a boys' home in Toronto, Ontario, to which this money must be sent."

Olcott emphatically denied suggesting the orphanage to Bland. "Why he said that I will only know after my death," he said.

But the money did go to the orphanage that still stood across the street from Olcott's first Canadian home. The *New York Telegraph* obtained a copy of an entry in the orphanage records that read: "Received from the Kalem Film Company, of New Jersey, U.S.A., at the express request of Jesus Christ, the sum of seven hundred and fifty dollars."

Bland returned to England, but from that time on would only act in religious plays. He made only one other film, *General Post*, in 1920.

During World War One Bland became an officer in the British Army, winning medals for his apparent disregard for his own safety. He is said to have saved many lives with his heroism. After the war he wrote a book entitled *From the Manger to the Cross*, in which he declared that Christ had entered his soul during the filming and he was unaware of what he had achieved until he saw the film in New York. He said Christ stayed with him during World War One and made him invincible.

Asked years later what he thought of Bland and his book, Olcott would only say: "I believe he was one of the greatest actors of all time, but that he was an actor, nothing more."

Kalem made millions of dollars profit from *From the Manger to the Cross*. It is still shown today to film societies and scholars studying early film making techniques. Even when compared with today's advanced technology, it contains striking and beautifully composed scenes that have rarely been equaled. When sound arrived in the industry in 1928, historians searched for the original orchestral score in vain. They had hoped to record the music to play with the film. "Despite its silence, it is still a very moving picture," said renowned director William Wyler in 1988.

Despite the obvious advantages of having a director of Olcott's stature on the Kalem payroll, Marion, Long, and Kleine declined to increase his salary beyond $150 a week. Angry with their attitude, he resigned and joined forces with Gene Gauntier to produce films independently. Planning to shoot all year, they set up business in Jacksonville, Florida.

In 1914, after completing a series of successful and profitable films, Olcott and Gauntier once again set sail for Ireland. Most of his old unit went with him, leaving New York on June 11. Scripts were already prepared before the unit left and Olcott rehearsed his actors on board ship.

Although the trip had to be cut short when World War One erupted, it was a journey that had an immense effect on Olcott's life. Before the boat reached Ireland, Olcott had fallen in love with actress Valentine Grant, who had been added to the unit at the last moment. In September they were married in a quiet ceremony in New York. It was a marriage that lasted, in harmony, until her death in 1948.

A number of articles over the years suggest that Olcott achieved "miracles with actors and actresses considered just average" by hypnotism. Actress Alice Hollister and her cameraman husband George, who worked with Olcott on many occasions, were convinced that hypnotism was the secret of his success. "He could calm the most erratic actor in seconds, simply by looking him directly in the eyes," said Mrs. Hollister. "We believe he used hypnotism. Just look at those piercing blue eyes and you'll see what I mean."

Other reports suggested he used hypnotism to obtain financial backing for his independent productions, but his inability to convince the extra girl in Ireland to be friendly without the use of whiskey, and his failure to convince Kalem to increase his $150 salary, suggest that hypnotism was a fancy of the Hollisters' imaginations.

But there can be no doubt that Olcott did have some form of thought transference powers that enabled him to tell actors what to do without speaking a word. Mary Pickford told actor Sam De Grasse that it was this method that made her bow to his suggestions during the making of *Madame Butterfly*. "He spoke very little," she said, "but I was never in doubt of his intentions. This is perhaps why I disliked him. I felt he controlled my mind." (Could this be the method by which Robert Henderson Bland knew about the boys' home in Toronto?)

Valentine Grant told the *New York Telegraph* that she said "yes" to Olcott's proposal of marriage before he spoke a word. "I knew he was going to ask me and I blurted out the 'yes'. Come to think of it, I don't believe he ever did ask me."

Mrs. Olcott told the *Telegraph* writer that on many occasions, while he was away on location shooting, she heard him telling her of happenings on the set. A day or two later, she said, a letter would arrive saying exactly the same words.

The *Telegraph* decided to test her statements. In 1916, Olcott, while in Boston, was told to write a series of words, given to him by the mayor of Boston, on a piece of paper. The words were revealed to no one else in the room. In New York, seconds later, Mrs. Olcott wrote down the same words on a piece of blank paper she was given. An open telephone line between the two cities confirmed that the words she wrote were the words given Olcott in Boston.

The experiment continued with words, numbers, and names for more than thirty minutes. Valentine Olcott was able to achieve ninety percent correct answers. When the experiment was tried in reverse, with Mrs. Olcott trying to send messages to her husband, the tests were a total failure.

Olcott had a sixth sense for impending disaster. He once called a friend, hundreds of miles away, urging that the friend take his wife and family away for the weekend. He said he sensed danger in their home. The friend did send his family to visit his mother, but he stayed home. Twenty-four hours later he was burned to death in a fire that was never satisfactorily explained.

Numerous other things are documented. Once, while on location in Florida, he halted shooting and moved his crew and actors to the shelter of a nearby barn. Only ten minutes later an unexpected twister swept through the area, killing several people and causing widespread damage. The twister swept through the location site but veered ninety degrees just before it reached the barn and the unit remained safe as the wooden structure was untouched.

The Olcott-Gauntier partnership lasted less than two years. The split was amicable. Gauntier was offered a lucrative writing contract with Universal films in Hollywood, and in the summer of 1916 she boarded a train west with Olcott's blessing.

Olcott perhaps sensed that his own future also lay in California. Six months after Gauntier's departure he and Valentine Grant were on a train heading for Los Angeles. Famous Players had offered him $1,000 a week to do nothing else but direct. Directing, he now knew, was to be his forte in life.

Before he left Florida, Olcott and his wife founded the Motion Picture Actors' Welfare League for Prisoners. Olcott and other production companies took their films to jails, often giving the prisoners a look at films not yet released. The stars and director accompanied each film, encouraging prisoners to think positively about their eventual release. Olcott himself donated a dozen projectors to the jails and other producers proved to be equally generous.

Olcott encouraged newly released prisoners to visit him in Hollywood. Often he was able to find them work in the studios. A few years before his death, he told the *Los Angeles Times* that one of the industry's top actors and a well-respected director were former prisoners who had "gone straight" on release. "I helped train them," he said. "Neither has given me cause to regret my actions."

The Welfare League remained in existence for more than fifteen years until prison entertainment became an official part of the rehabilitation system throughout jails in the United States.

Olcott received a hero's welcome to Hollywood. "I was offered my choice of scripts, my choice of stars, and the right to amend the scripts any way I wished," he told the *Los Angeles Examiner* in 1926.

His first choice was to direct another Canadian, Mary Pickford, then at the height of her popularity. The two feuded from day one on the set of *Madame Butterfly*. Pickford told the *Los Angeles Times* that Olcott "even tried to tell me, Mary Pickford, how to act. Even made me, no forced me, to do close-ups that I had never done before and didn't like."

Despite Mary Pickford's displeasure, *Madame Butterfly*, a five-reeler, was a great success. The close-ups Olcott demanded showed a remarkable range of expression that Pickford had never been able to achieve before. One year later she requested Olcott to direct her in *Poor Little Peppina*. Again they feuded, but once more they produced a very successful film, both financially and artistically.

It is interesting to note that when Pickford made a financial settlement with Famous Players that gave her the right to total ownership of ten of her films, she selected *Madame Butterfly* and *Poor Little Peppina* as numbers one and two. Years later she told an interviewer from the Academy of Motion Picture Arts and Sciences research department that despite their "artistic differences" she acknowledged Olcott to be one of the greatest directors of the silent era.

Stars like Will Rogers demanded Olcott as director of their films. The 1918 film, *The Innocent Lie*, which teamed Rogers with Olcott's wife, Valentine Grant, is looked on today as an example of film making that was technically and artistically years ahead of its time.

Seven Sisters, starring Marguerite Clark, *Diplomacy*, with Marie Doro, *The Smugglers*, with Donald Brian (the Broadway actor who was born in Newfoundland) and *Scratch My Back*, with T. Roy Barnes and Helene Chadwick, all enhanced Olcott's reputation in Hollywood.

In 1921 he directed *The Right Way*, a prison story that starred Edwards Davis and Helen Lindroth. Although Olcott refused to identify the actor he brought from jail to stardom, there is evidence to believe it was Davis. The story, written by Olcott, told of a prisoner's determination to make good. Davis went on to make fifty more films and a reputation as a "gentleman." He remained successful into the sound era, making movies until a year before his death in 1936. The identity of the former convict who became a director was also never revealed and his name is still a mystery.

Olcott was on top of the world in 1922 when he suddenly refused all new assignments offered him. Fellow workers said he had become depressed and was drinking on the set. Without any explanation he left his wife and home in Beverly Hills and bought a coach-class ticket to New York City. There he vanished.

Friends were puzzled. He left all his financial affairs in order. There was plenty of money for his wife and no debt. If Valentine Olcott knew the reason for his absence she told no one.

A year passed, and neither his wife nor his friends heard a word from him. Attempts to trace him in New York failed. It was a mystery that might never have been solved had it not been for the determination of publisher William Randolph Hearst, then king of the fabulous Hearst Castle on the "enchanted hill" in San Simeon, California.

Hearst, in need of a capable director to revive the flagging career of his beautiful actress-mistress, Marion Davies, viewed hundreds of films seeking the right person. The Will Rogers film, *The Innocent Lie*, intrigued him. He asked to see more Olcott films. Four films later Hearst was convinced. "Sidney Olcott must direct the next Marion Davies film," he said.

Frustrated because he was unable to locate Olcott, Hearst used the columns of his New York paper to find him. Within hours of the publication of a story offering a substantial reward to any person able to provide Olcott's present address, a New York tenement resident called the editor to say Olcott was living in a $3-a-week room in a run-down building. He was, said the caller, constantly drinking cheap whiskey and eating very little. "He is quite ill, and needs help," she said. When Hearst received the message he sent a telegram to the tenant asking that she tell Olcott to call him immediately.

When no call came, Hearst boarded a train from Los Angeles to New York. Met there by his driver, he was taken directly to Olcott's seedy address. He said later he was shocked by what he found. "But we carried him down to the car and took him to my New York apartment where a doctor was waiting."

Valentine Olcott was notified that she should join her husband as quickly as possible. Hearst provided one of his private rail coaches to bring her to New York. Nurses and doctors were at his bedside twenty-four hours a day, and within weeks he had gained twenty pounds and no longer demanded alcohol.

Three months later Olcott walked on the set of *Little Old New York* with Marion Davies on his arm. Hearst had gathered together dozens of the industry's major stars and they, together with hundreds of extras and technicians who had worked with Olcott in the past, stood and applauded his arrival. Olcott is said to have "cried like a baby." But an hour later he was directing Marion Davies in her first scene.

Little Old New York is the only one of the fifty films made by Marion Davies that was acclaimed by critics in papers not controlled by Hearst. Olcott's direction was applauded. Davies, who had been coached for each scene by Olcott, received rave reviews for her performance. It is interesting to note that *Little Old New York* is the only one of the films in which Davies starred that is remembered by photographs and a large theatre poster in the Hearst Museum at San Simeon in California.

Olcott was back! He never explained his absence to anyone, unless privately to his wife. And he never again directed Marion Davies. "There is a simple explanation for that," said Robert Vignola. "Sid was an honorable man. He found the advances by Marion Davies quite unacceptable. He could not betray his wife or Mr. Hearst so he declined to work with her again."

Olcott did, however, direct a number of films financed by Hearst. "I believe Hearst understood the situation without being told," said Vignola, "and he was showing that understanding by giving Sid some fine films to direct."

Stars were clamouring for Olcott to be their director. He was reported receiving $5,000 a week in the middle 1920s, a huge amount for that era.

George Arliss, the renowned English actor, gave the performance of his life in *The Green Goddess*. "I stood in amazement as Sid Olcott created a character for me in front of my eyes," he said. "He gave me a power of expression I was not, until that time, aware I possessed. He was a brilliant, firm, yet never abrasive, director."

Gloria Swanson worked with Olcott in *The Humming Bird*. "Sid was," she said, "tough, yes very tough, but a magnificent director who taught me a great deal about true acting. The simple truth is that he was a better actor himself than any he ever directed."

Norma Talmadge, directed by Olcott in *The Only Woman*, said, "I love him. I worship at the shrine of his brilliance."

Pola Negri, star of *The Charmer*, said Olcott was "unique, totally dedicated to getting the best out of every performer. He paid the same dedicated attention to the small-part actor or actress as he did to the star. It made filming very easy for all of us."

Warner Baxter, directed by Olcott in *The Best People*, said, "A genius. So patient, kind but firm in his determination to accept nothing but excellence from an actor."

Richard Barthelmess signed Olcott to a three-picture deal in 1926. He was to be paid $8,000 a week for each week of shooting and $5,000 a week for each of three weeks for preparation and rehearsal. "Olcott was a man of great integrity," said Barthelmess. He finished all three films a week early, thus losing $24,000. He could have stretched them out but he didn't."

Ransom's Folly, *The Amateur Gentleman*, and *The White Black Sheep* were all big successes for Olcott and Barthelmess. The actor had a long and lucrative career, retiring to a beautiful Long Island estate. One year before his death in

1963 he spoke of Olcott. "I owe him my career and my success. That I was able to retire to this magnificent estate is a tribute to his remarkable work. In 1926 he taught me more about acting than I had learned in my entire career. Sadly, I was not aware of his death in 1949 to pay my proper respects. Perhaps what I say now may in a small way make amends."

Shortly after *Little Old New York* was released, Olcott was pressured, against his better judgement, into directing Rudolph Valentino in *Monsieur Beaucaire*. He and Valentino's wife, Natasha Rambova, were at loggerheads from the first day of shooting. "The woman is a total idiot," Olcott told producer Adolph Zukor. "She knows nothing yet tells Valentino how to act and me how to direct. I want her off the set."

In a biography of Valentino, Zukor tells how he used dozens of pretexts to keep Rambova away from Olcott. The result was a film in which Olcott obtained, said the *New York Times*, the best acting of Valentino's career. The movie opened in New York, where it was filmed, and broke box office records across the country.

Olcott refused to work with Valentino again despite pleas from the great screen lover. "I told him bluntly," said Olcott, "that I objected to his uncalled for advances and that since I was not permitted to damage his pretty face I would kick him you-know-where if he didn't cease pestering me. Can you believe this poof came and sang love songs outside my hotel window in New York!"

In 1927 Olcott made just one film, *The Claw*, starring Norman Kerry. He then announced his intention of sailing for England "to spend twelve months making films in London for the British Lion Company." George Arliss, who had arranged the contract for Olcott, met Olcott and his wife when they arrived in London. At a press conference at the Savoy Hotel, Olcott described the coming twelve months as "the opportunity of my life. I shall be working with many of England's greatest actors."

But Olcott was to be disillusioned. Shown the town by Arliss and his wife Florence, he wrote to Robert Vignola that "I wonder every night why I waited so long to film the enchanting scenery that startles and astounds me at every bend in the road." Before the letter was even delivered, the film industry papers in Los Angeles headlined a story from London. "I will not be directing in England," said Olcott. "I will not be part of films which glorify crime and criminals. I am suing British Lion Films."

The Olcotts stayed long enough to win their lawsuit. The British court agreed Olcott had been falsely advised as to the nature of his work, and awarded him £10,000 (approximately $40,000 at that time) in damages.

When the Olcotts arrived home in October 1927, a pile of requests for his services was waiting on his desk. Shunning them all, he called a press conference and announced his total retirement.

"I am officially retired as from this date," he said. "I have no plans to direct any more films or to be further associated with the industry with which I have been involved for more than twenty years. This is my irrevocable decision." Declining to answer any questions from the reporters, he left the room. And, as one story ends, "leaving Mrs. Olcott and two maids to serve tea and sandwiches."

Never again did Olcott pass through the gates of any Hollywood studio. He welcomed show business friends to his home, but would never discuss the industry. His closest friend, Robert Vignola, said, "Even I am not permitted to talk about the films I am directing."

Years later it was revealed by George Arliss that he had convinced Olcott, in 1929, to give him personal coaching for his roles in the sound remakes of *The Green Goddess* and *Disraeli*. "We went through both scripts many times," said Arliss. "Valentine or Sid took the roles opposite me. We worked together for more than three months before I felt I was ready to face the cameras."

When the Oscar nominations were announced, Arliss received a unique honor. He was nominated for the Best Actor award for both films. His role as *Disraeli* won the award. In London, where he was filming on awards night, Arliss told the *Daily Express* that "I owe everything to Sidney Olcott. His was a remarkable feat. He directed this actor without entering the studio and without any official credit."

In the 1930s Olcott and his wife spent several summers in Ireland. In a small community just outside Cork he designed and paid for the construction costs of a chapel in memory of his parents. Some clippings in the British Film Institute suggest he did direct at least one film in Ireland, but no available records show his name as director.

During World War Two he opened the doors of his Beverly Hills mansion to servicemen and women. Every service club in the area was asked to notify him of visits by members of the forces visiting from Canada.

With the doors of Pickfair, where Mary Pickford reigned supreme, also open to Canadians, most servicemen and women headed there and ignored the Olcott invitation. His fame from the silent era was forgotten. Pickford and others still in the limelight were the magnets for service personnel. Those who did call Olcott and his wife were picked up by car from wherever they called and entertained royally.

Those who became Olcott's guests found a call from him to giants of the industry like Pickford, Mayer, or Warner opened doors that were closed to most people. Those who stayed a few days were occasionally shown some of the silent films Olcott had directed. Often accompanying the films on piano was the classical pianist Jose Iturbi, a neighbor and friend of the Olcotts. "My first job as a pianist was playing for silent films," Iturbi would tell the guests. "I loved it then, I love it now."

Sidney and Valentine Olcott lived in comfort. They had a gardener, a chauffeur, two maids, and a butler who came in each evening to serve dinner. Among their friends were stars like Cary Grant, Katherine Hepburn, Humphrey Bogart, Alan and Sue Carol Ladd, and Charlie Chaplin. The latter brought over his own films for Olcott's fascinated guests.

But Olcott never boasted of his own important role in the growth of the film industry. He took a back seat to the stars who were constantly in and out of his doors.

After the war, Olcott and his wife lived quietly. Their visits to restaurants ceased. Dining out with friends became more and more infrequent.

On March 12, 1948, Valentine Olcott died peacefully in her sleep. Olcott's last public appearance, at seventy-five, was to attend her funeral. Within a month he had sold his Bedford Drive home and moved to the home of Robert Vignola, his friend from the beginnings of the film industry. Vignola's wife had died on February 15, 1948, and he, like Olcott, was alone.

Olcott and Vignola remained in seclusion, with a house staff of five, until Sidney Olcott died on December 16, 1949.

"He had little to live for when Val died," Robert Vignola told the *New York Times*. "He just went to bed and died during the night. A great man whose fame is of yesterday. Sid Olcott showed hundreds of people the way to fame and success. I, and many others, will not forget."

Unhappily, most had. Less than 100 people attended the funeral service. In addition to Vignola, friends like Joseph and Fred Santley, George Melford, Herbert Brenon, and George and Alice Hollister were there to pay their last tributes. Only Jean Hersholt and Pat O'Brien were there to represent those still active in the industry.

This time the eulogy was brief. Robert Vignola said of his friend: "A friendship with Sid Olcott was a friendship for life. A friendship with Sid Olcott was something to be cherished. A friendship with Sid Olcott is something many of us hope to renew in the life hereafter. For eternity!"

Despite his long years of inactivity, Olcott died a wealthy man. His estate,

Sidney Olcott

in excess of $250,000, was divided among a few friends, with provisions for life annuities for many of his house staff including some who had retired years earlier. The American Cancer Society, the Salvation Army, the Motion Picture Relief Fund, and the Institute for Medical Research at Cedars of Lebanon Hospital all benefited from his generosity. In his will, made just one month before he died, he requested that one bequest be paid before all others. The sum of $5,000 was to go to the Boys' Home in Toronto.

A codicil to his will, added only days before his death, asked that his body be sent back to Toronto for burial in the cemetery where his parents lay. "I love Canada," he had added at the bottom.

JACK PICKFORD

"His life was one long story of wasted talents and opportunities thrown away. He saw life as one never-ending joke, but finally the joke was on him. He found life too easy because of his family connections. Perhaps if he had changed his name and chosen to find a career for himself, independent of his family, he would have been a big star today."
(Louella Parsons, 1933)

J ack Pickford, brother of one of Hollywood's most loved and admired stars, Mary Pickford, was only thirty-six when he died, alone and friendless, in a hospital in Paris, France.

The world had been at his feet since he was in his early teens, but instead of picking it up and running with it to the finish line, he chose to kick it around and not bother to reach the goals others had set for him. One day the world kicked back at him.

His mother, Charlotte Pickford, once said in a magazine article that "Jack was born with a smile on his face, and he smiled through the successes and failures of his life. We tried hard, but it seemed impossible to make him take anything in life seriously."

Mary Pickford had much heartache in her life, but she said in 1943 that none was greater than the heartache Jack gave her. "But I am totally, utterly, and completely responsible for what happened to him," she said. "I saw disaster coming but did nothing to prevent it."

Harrison Carroll, a noted Hollywood columnist, said this of Jack Pickford after his death in 1933: "He could have been a big star and an important figure in Hollywood. No door was ever closed to him, yet he chose to slam too many in the faces of those who tried to help him. He wasted more chances in his short lifetime than any one person has a right to expect in a hundred years."

Jack Pickford was born John Carl Smith in Toronto, Ontario, on August 18, 1896. His father, John Smith, was the purser on a Lake Ontario steamboat making daily runs between Toronto and Lewiston, New York. His mother's only work was her determined drive to see her children, Jack, Mary, and Lottie succeed in life. Her idea of success was fame on the stage, together with the wealth that would come with that fame.

After John Smith died, when Jack was only four, the entire Smith family joined a travelling theatrical road company. Popular actor Chauncey Olcott was responsible for changing the family name to Pickford, which he said "sounded more professional."

At the age of eight, when his sister Mary had already become well known as an accomplished juvenile actress in Canada and the bordering northern United States, Jack made his debut with a stock company in Buffalo, New York.

"This was mother's biggest mistake," said Mary many years later. "He adored the applause and the adulation of his elders and from that moment on his only wish in life was to earn the gratitude of those around him. I remember the play well, because all of us were in it, Jack, Lottie, mother, and myself. Hal Reid, whose son, Wallace, was also in the play, directed *The Little Red Schoolhouse*. Wallace and Jack became firm friends, something we were to regret years later in Hollywood."

Pickford recalled that all four members of the family appeared in the play for one week at a combined salary of $20. "I would give ten thousand times that $20 now to anyone who could wipe out of our lives that play which was to haunt mother, and Lottie, for the rest of their lives and probably will haunt me for the rest of mine."

Jack Pickford often boasted to his friends that he had his first drink of hard liquor during the play's run in Buffalo. Marshall Neilan was a brilliant film director, whose major career in the silent era of the motion picture industry ended after only ten years when he became too unreliable to hire due to his addition to drink and drugs. In an interview at the Woodland Hills Motion Picture Home, where he lived for many years until his death in 1958, Neilan said: "Many of us lived to rue the day we ever met Jack Pickford. He was the most happy-go-lucky man I ever met, but that was a facade he created in his early teens and probably maintained, strengthened by drugs and booze, until his dying day."

Neilan claimed that the murdered film director William Desmond Taylor was the supplier of most of the drugs that he, Pickford, and others used. "I know who killed Taylor," he said. "But it was good riddance. Why should I condemn somebody now for something I would have liked to do myself? He fed the drug craving we had tried to control for years before he arrived on the scene.

"Jack was one of those who secretly visited Taylor either early in the morning or late at night. We had an exchange system. Dozens of the books in his library were hollowed out in the middle. We took to his home our books, now empty of cocaine, in which we hid the money and he gave us a new one full of cocaine. That's why he had so much money on him when he was killed. He destroyed me. He destroyed Wallace Reid, and Pickford, and Mabel Normand, and many others who never made the headlines.

"There were hundreds of actors, actresses, directors, writers, you name it, who hated him enough to kill him. But it didn't come out about the drugs; too many careers were on the line. People were scared to talk. We all knew there was somebody higher up selling the 'coke' to Bill Taylor. We never found out whom.

"I'm sixty-seven now, and totally useless to this world. I wish I'd had the guts to kill Taylor myself years before he was murdered. Yes, I know who did it, and why, but I'll never tell now. I suspect most of those who knew what I know are dead and buried. The person who removed him from this earth is still alive."

When the Pickford family moved to New York in 1908, Charlotte Pickford began an assault on every agent and manager in the city seeking work for her children. Mary was easy to place. She had a record of stage successes and soon work began pouring in. Jack was different. Impresario David Belasco, who had taken Mary under his wing, told the *New York Times* after Jack Pickford's death that "he was only twelve when his mother brought him in to see me. Even then he was quite obnoxious. He was quite arrogant and told me I would regret it when I declined to represent him. Told me one day he'd buy the theatre which bore my name and put his own up there in lights."

But Charlotte didn't give up. Somehow she controlled Jack's arrogance long enough for him to be given an audition for a major role in a play, *Ragged Robin*, starring Chauncey Olcott, the man who had changed their name to Pickford. He remembered the family and after a brief audition Jack was given the role.

Olcott told the theatrical papers in New York that Jack Pickford was "the most natural actor anyone could hope to discover." His mother accompanied Pickford on the play's three-month tour, leaving Mary and Lottie in charge of a governess. At twelve, Jack walked away with most of the applause every night. Apparently he was well behaved on tour because he was chosen, when the company returned to New York, to co-star with Olcott in a second play, *The Three of Us*, to be staged on Broadway.

"Once he was chosen for the second play he dropped his pretended niceness to everyone," recalled Mary in 1943. "All the old arrogance came out again, so mother and I and Lottie decided he could only accept the part if he would agree to attend, during the day, St. Francis Military Academy in New York City. He was to be permitted to appear nightly in the play and Chauncey Olcott agreed to drive him back to the academy every night to sleep."

Olcott retired from the stage in 1927 and that year published his memoirs. He had this to say about Jack Pickford: "He was such a wonderful, natural actor, and on stage, with his ever-smiling face, he came over the footlights like an angel from heaven. I anticipated he would become a renowned actor in later years, but, sad to say, with a few exceptional performances in a few movies, he has not lived up to my expectations.

"Off stage he was a different person. He played disgusting tricks on members of the cast and on one occasion was caught by our wardrobe mistress in a very indelicate position with her sixteen-year-old daughter. Remember, he was only thirteen at this time. I was able to pacify the good lady and her daughter and, fortunately for Pickford, no charges were laid. I never hired him again, despite his acting abilities. His behaviour off stage more than outweighed his value to my company."

Mary Pickford never forgot the year 1909. She told friends who visited her home, Pickfair, on Summit Drive in Beverly Hills, that "neither mother nor I knew how to control him. At thirteen, he was a monster, but a monster wearing a constant angelic smile. He had far too much money, so his friends, who he bought with the money, stuck around to help him spend it."

Sending him to the military academy apparently didn't help at all. "Once the play was over he ran away on two occasions and we had to employ a boxer we knew to help watch over his dormitory at night," said Mary. "Although the academy had a wonderful reputation for instilling discipline in the young men who attended, he ran into the wrong kind at the academy. These were the kind who admired him for being an actor and helped make his big ego bigger. He used to take them backstage in the theatre where Chauncey Olcott was playing and they played some very dirty tricks, which I won't elaborate, on the actors and stage hands. Finally, when Mr. Olcott had him barred from going back stage, he and the other academy boys painted disgusting words all over the outside of the theatre. It really was terribly embarrassing and since everyone knew he was my brother it didn't help my career.

"Three other boys from the academy were expelled for their part in the escapade at the theatre, but mother could be very persuasive and Jack was allowed to stay on. Mr. Olcott was very generous and while he allowed the police to interview Jack, to scare him, he wouldn't press any criminal charges. I had to pay for the cost of removing the vile language off the theatre walls."

Jack Pickford had successfully destroyed his stage-acting career before it really began. At thirteen the New York theatrical managers and producers association blacklisted him. Despite his mother's determination, he was never again permitted to attend any professional auditions in New York City.

Jack went wild when he found out that his stage career was over. Sidney Olcott, to whom the Pickfords had appealed for help in controlling him, took him to the film studio where he was working. "I can't say it did any good at all," he said. "He brought a bottle with him to the studio and if we didn't keep him busy he would be drunk by lunch time. I must have given him fifty roles to play and when he was acting he was a different person.

"He never gave a bad performance, but I was heading to Florida with my unit and just couldn't see myself trying to control him down there, so, reluctantly, I severed my connection with him."

At the end of the 1910 school year, the Pickfords decided to take Jack out of the military academy. "I was making good money by then," recalled Mary Pickford, "but neither mother nor I could see any point in paying the substantial school fees if he was not attending classes and was, we were told, often out half the night with some of the older boys and some rather unsavory young girls. We made the mistake of giving him an allowance far too large, and he had access to some of the money he had earned with Chauncey Olcott's two plays. He threatened to go to the newspapers with stories that we were beating and abusing him if he didn't get the money. Since we couldn't afford such exposure we, regrettably, gave in to him."

With no school to attend, Jack started tagging along with Mary every day she went to the Biograph film studio in Brooklyn. "I got the studio to give him as many small parts as they could to keep him out of trouble," she recalled. "The sad part of this strategy was the fact that he kept turning in some excellent performances and soon I didn't need to ask people to give him work, they offered him all he could handle."

The parts were not large, but he was working and earning money at sixteen, money that he insisted on keeping for his own use. The two Gish sisters, Dorothy and Lillian, became friendly with the Pickfords and remained so until Dorothy's death in 1968, when a major dispute between the two families destroyed the relationship. After 1968, Lillian Gish, who lived to be ninety-three before dying in 1991, never again visited the Pickford mansion in Beverly Hills.

Some years before her death she told the *Hollywood Citizen-News* that the breakup of the Pickford-Gish friendship came when she told Mary of an incident that took place at the Biograph studio in Brooklyn. "I told her that when Jack was only sixteen I caught him doing things to Dorothy that neither of us understood at the time. When we told mother she reported the incident to Mrs. Pickford. She promised that such a thing would never happen again, and it didn't. Mary apparently was unaware of the incident and refused to believe me. She said Jack was no angel but never would he have touched Dorothy or me. And she never spoke to me again after that."

In 1911 the Pickfords moved to California. Mary was offered a contract with Carl Laemmle at $275 a week. But she refused to sign the papers until Laemmle also provided contracts that would give each of Jack, Charlotte, and Lottie $50 a week for the duration of her own contract.

In Hollywood Mary soon zoomed to the top and within a year was earning $2,500 a week, an astronomical amount at that time. Jack, Charlotte, and Lottie each had their pay packets upped to $200 a week.

Jack, Charlotte, and Lottie were given parts, often very small, in every film Mary made. Jack soon began being noticed by producers who had not heard of his antics off screen, and in 1912 he was given a lead role in *A Dash through the Clouds*. Reviewers loved his performance and touted him to be as big a star as Mary in a few years.

For several years all the news stories about Jack Pickford were good. He apparently behaved himself on the set, and in the evenings studied acting with the best drama coach Mary's money could buy.

In 1912 he made five films, each of which added to the stock of good reviews he had collected in 1911. Then the bubble burst.

Pickford became reacquainted with Wallace Reid, the young actor who had appeared with him on stage in Buffalo seven years earlier. Reid introduced him to actors Lew Cody, Norman Kerry, and Roscoe "Fatty" Arbuckle. They added director Marshall Neilan to the pack, and the escapades they were involved in found regular space in the gossip columns of the trade papers and dailies. Long before Frank Sinatra's much better-behaved "Rat Pack" came on the entertainment scene, Pickford's "gang," as they were called, also gained the title the "rat pack."

The Vernon Country Club, just outside Los Angeles, was the group's headquarters. They were reported to have literally destroyed the club, of which Arbuckle was a part owner, by their antics. Writers Louella Parsons and Harrison Carroll reported that their "fun" included "throwing elderly people who had done them no harm, fully clothed, into the swimming pool; throwing bottles of beer at people in the pool; smashing tables and chairs and uprooting carefully planted floral displays." The club tried barring them, but they answered this by driving a car through the club entrance doors. Once again, said Louella Parsons, "charges were stayed by the intervention of Mary Pickford, who paid for all the damages and donated a large sum to the club's coffers."

The pack next moved to the Sunset Inn, on Sunset Boulevard, where drugs were openly dispensed. "The tragedy is," said Harrison Carroll in his syndicated column, "that these are nice people if you can keep them apart." He added, "The exception is Jack Pickford, who is a blight to the lives of those who love him for himself, and those who love him for what he can do for them or give them."

One of the pack's least harmful ventures was to hire Paul Whiteman and his entire orchestra, quietly locating them on the lawn of Charlie Chaplin's Summit Drive home on the first night of one of his marriages. The band played Sousa marches as loudly as possible and refused pleas from an irate Chaplin and his bride to shut up and go home. An irate neighbor called the police and the pack and entire orchestra, including a protesting Whiteman, who said Pickford had assured him everything would be all right, were carted off to jail.

Mary Pickford, who lived one house higher up the hill from Chaplin, sent a servant out to see what was happening. When she learned that Jack was involved and was being arrested she dressed and had her chauffeur drive her to the police station where she is said to "have screamed her head off in a most unladylike manner at her brother." Once again she bailed him, and everyone else, out of the jail.

There is a rather funny sequel to the story. Police officials next day asked all the newspapers to print a story saying they were searching for two convicted felons who had escaped from the jail when the pack and orchestra were released. "There was little to distinguish these rowdies from the two prisoners waiting to go to the county jail," said the sergeant in charge. "They all looked alike to me so they got out at the same time." The convicts were at large for seventeen days before they were caught.

In 1915 Pickford co-starred with Louise Huff in *Great Expectations*. The reviews of both the stars were raves. "This is Pickford's finest film to date, and Miss Huff complements his every move with skill and charm," said one newspaper writer.

Louise Huff, who lived in retirement for many years at the Motion Picture Home and Hospital, talked about Pickford in 1970. "Jack and I had a showdown on our first day at the studio," she recalled. "He walked into my dressing room and slammed the door shut, locking it. 'Get your dress off, woman,' he said. And he started taking off his trousers. I yelled at him, 'What on earth are you doing?' 'Time for our first love session,' he replied. 'Didn't they tell you, all my leading ladies make love to me!' I learned later that he tried this with everyone he worked with, and with most he succeeded. But I thought quickly, and said, 'Jack, did nobody tell you, I prefer women!'

"He went white as a sheet, pulled up his trousers, unlocked the door, and ran across the studio to his own dressing room. I never had any trouble with him after that, and I spread the word. It is amazing how many of the leading ladies who played opposite him after that seemed to prefer women. Which, of course, we didn't!"

Marshall Neilan said "Only drugs kept Jack on his feet at the studio, as they did most of the rest of the gang, including me. I never ceased to be amazed at the excellent performances Jack gave, even after nights when he didn't even go to bed, at least not to sleep."

In 1916 Pickford played the lead in *Little Shepherd of Kingdom Come*. One critic called it "a masterpiece of realism borne to great heights by Jack Pickford's magnificent acting, though naturalness would better describe his superb performance." Another critic said the film contained "the finest performance to date from a young actor surely destined for major stardom." A third said "Pickford's angelic appearance filled the need in the industry for a young actor with charm and obvious humility in his accomplishments. His innocent portrayal was not acting, it is obvious that he is a good person and was intelligently chosen by the director." The last review was from a Chicago writer who obviously had never seen or heard of one of Pickford's off-screen performances.

That same year he made three more films, all successful, all profitable at the box office. *Brown of Harvard*, *The Bat*, and, perhaps appropriately *The Man Who Had Everything*, were all made by the Jesse L. Lasky Film Company. Lasky had put him under contract at the request of his sister Mary. His salary was reported to be more than $1,000 a week. Lasky admitted years later that Mary had paid half the salary out of her own pocket.

In 1917 Lasky told the *Los Angeles Times* that he considered he had made an excellent deal. "Pickford is now a calm and accomplished actor," he said. "His performances show that he has put aside his troubles and is now determined to become one of our industry's most prolific and successful actors. Every one of his films has made my company a big profit."

After reading the *Times* story, Pickford showed that Lasky was a little premature in assessing his troubles as ended. Lasky told Sidney Olcott that an enraged Pickford threw open the door to his office and screamed: "Bastard,

bastard. What is this crap? You make profits, I want part of those profits." He then threw his contract on the floor and stamped up and down on it for what Lasky thought was an eternity. He then pushed over two vases of flowers, smashing them on the floor, pulled down a picture of himself from the wall and smashed it on Lasky's desk. "The next film I make will be for my own Jack Pickford Film Company. And you, Lasky, won't get a penny of the profits."

Lasky announced a few days later in the trade papers that he had agreed to let Jack Pickford out of the balance of his contract as Pickford wished to produce his own films from then on.

A month later he accepted a role in *Poor Little Peppina*, which Sidney Olcott was directing, with Mary Pickford as its star. Olcott remembered the film well. "I was having a little trouble with Mary, she was very dictatorial, and I was urging her to let me use more close-ups, when Jack came over and started shouting at me. 'How dare you presume to tell my sister, the world's greatest actress, the world's most important actress, what she must do and what she must not do.' Then he turned to Mary, who had gone white as a sheet, and told her that 'Olcott must be fired immediately or I will take no more part in this picture.'

"That was the only time I remember Mary standing up to him. She was trembling when she moved close to him and said, 'Then you will be the one to play no further part in this picture.' And she slapped him hard across the face. To our astonishment, Jack cringed and burst out crying. 'I'll tell mother about you,' he said as he slunk away. We never did see him on the set again and Mary never mentioned the incident from that day on."

In 1917 Pickford, after a very brief courtship, unexpectedly married a beautiful former Ziegfeld girl, Olive Thomas, in New York. She was building a successful career as an actress and was touted as a potential star of the future. Pickford announced that Thomas was the girl he had been searching for and added, "From now on I will never look at another woman."

The happy couple returned to Hollywood, where Mary bought them a beautiful new house on Cienega Drive. They were seen at nightspots, holding hands, but Pickford drank very little and was polite to everyone.

"We thought a miracle had happened," said Mary Pickford in 1943. "Olive was a beautiful and talented girl. Somehow she had tamed him, something we had failed to do."

When Mary signed a three-picture contract with Adolph Zukor, which was to pay her just over $1 million, she asked Zukor to include her now reformed brother in the deal. The trade papers announced that Jack was to

Jack Pickford in *Tom Sawyer* (1917).

receive $50,000 a picture from Zukor, for a minimum of five pictures. There were also bonus payments to her mother and sister in the deal.

Pickford made three films for Zukor before shocking the film industry by suddenly announcing that he had enlisted in the U.S. Navy and would be making no more films for the duration of the war. Sidney Olcott recalled in 1943 that Mary had confided in him that "Jack feared his marriage was on the rocks and wanted to impress Olive with his enlistment. Also, he was afraid that he would soon be drafted and wanted to choose his own service where he could quickly become a commissioned officer."

A large contingent of stars saw Pickford off at the Los Angeles railroad terminus. Newspaper reporters, photographers, and thousands of fans waved him goodbye. The stars included, of course, his sister Mary, by then the most important person in the film industry, his mother Charlotte, and sister Lottie. Actress Blanche Sweet and her husband Marshall Neilan were on hand, along with director William Desmond Taylor, soon to be murdered, Owen Moore, at that time husband of Mary, and, of course, Pickford's teary-eyed wife, Olive Thomas.

The *Los Angeles Times*, in its story of the departure, asked those stars present who were not named to accept the paper's apology. There were just so many it was impossible to keep count, said the writer. Pickford's enlistment hit the front pages of almost every daily newspaper across North America.

Marshall Neilan remembered the day very clearly. "It was the biggest bunch of ballyhoo you have ever seen, but one thing sticks in my memory and will stay there forever. Just as the train was about to leave, Bill [William Desmond] Taylor walked up to the compartment door and handed Jack one of his famous books. 'This one is on me, Jack,' he said."

Magazines printed stories of "beautiful and lonely Olive Thomas waiting at home for her man who is bravely fighting the enemy." There were pictures of her at her writing desk, "penning long love letters to her beloved Jack serving in the navy." One story, printed on January 3, 1919, told how Olive Thomas was "thrilled to receive long letters from Pickford telling of his contribution toward ending the war."

On January 5, 1919, a *New York Times* front-page story told a very different story, and Jack Pickford's second bubble burst. "Scandal in the Navy" was the headline. "Jack Pickford Accused of Supplying Girls to Senior Navy Officers" said the sub-headline. The story went on say he procured the services of young actresses for the use of senior officers who had promised to give his friends, already in the navy, safe postings away from the war's danger zones.

"Mary was horrified," said Marshall Neilan. "For days she would see no one. Later we found out she was busy pulling every string she could pull to stop the navy court martialling Jack," he said.

"She told me months later that she had even gone as high as the White House to help get him off the hook. Obviously she succeeded, because Pickford was simply discharged from the navy as 'medically unfit to serve.' He didn't come back to California for several months, and none of us heard a word from him."

Stories published later in national newspapers told the whole story of Pickford's disgrace. He had allowed senior officers to use his luxury apartment in New York as the meeting place with the girls he provided. There was apparently unlimited liquor and, as one paper said, "other things much worse to demoralize the officers."

In return he got many favours for himself, including an office job in New York where all he did was talk to newspapermen about the great United States Navy. Other friends benefited from the orgies. Some, said the *Chicago Tribune*, never did get drafted, and those who did were classified in such a manner as to ensure they never saw any combat.

In March 1920, Mary Pickford and Douglas Fairbanks were married. "For a while," said Neilan, "Jack was banned from Pickfair, the house they had built. Fairbanks was a tough cookie and he is said to have turfed Jack out on one occasion using the toe of his boot.

"But Mary was still protecting her younger brother. She financed a film called *Through the Back Door* and named Jack as the director. Mary wrote the script and Jack, if he had used his brain at all, would have realized it was about him and his wayward life.

"The story told how a businessman with no talent — although that wasn't Jack a few years earlier — had got to the top, a place he didn't deserve, by being let in through the back door on deals cooked up by his sister."

The trade papers were kind to Pickford. "Probably," said Neilan, "because of the large advertisements Mary took out to promote the film. But they did mention, much to Mary's disgust, that she had found it necessary to bring in veteran director Alfred E. Green to assist Jack in the task of making something out of a nothing film."

The film was a financial failure, but *Little Lord Fauntleroy*, in which he next acted, and once again shared directing chores with Alfred Green, was a big hit. Mary herself took a part in the film and allowed her billing to be in smaller print that her brother's name.

A small item in the gossip columns early in 1920 said that Olive Thomas had moved out of Pickford's home and had announced her retirement from both the marriage and the film industry.

In August 1920 Thomas and Pickford announced they had settled their differences and would sail at the end of the month for a second honeymoon in Paris. The couple arrived in Paris early in the morning of September 9 and that same evening began a whirlwind tour of all the nightspots in the city. The apparently happy couple arrived back at their hotel around 3 a.m. on the morning of September 10 and two hours later Pickford called down to the hotel desk urgently requesting a doctor. "My wife has taken an overdose of drugs and needs help," he said.

The doctor arrived at the Pickfords' suite within ten minutes to find Olive Thomas writhing in pain on the bed. "She took some of my medicine," said Pickford, "but she obviously took too much." Within half-an-hour she was dead.

French newspapers, not showing the decency of the North American press, which classed the death as accidental, said Thomas had drunk a large quantity of mercury. It had been prescribed to Jack Pickford to help combat the venereal disease from which he had suffered for several years, and which Thomas discovered he had passed on to her.

Mercury was, according to Dr. Edmund Gros, of Los Angeles, Pickford's physician, the treatment for syphilis, and at the inquest he confirmed prescribing it to Pickford since 1917. "There is no cure," he said at the inquest. "But this sometimes holds the disease in check."

Friends of Thomas spread the word around after Pickford returned home from France, that Thomas told them before she left the United States that she had only gone back to Pickford because she needed help from Mary Pickford to boost her flagging career.

Blanche Sweet told Marshall Neilan that Olive knew she had contracted the disease before she left New York, but hoped the mercury treatment would help her beat it. "Blanche told me she didn't believe the death was accidental," said Neilan. "She mailed a letter to Blanche on the afternoon of September 9, which arrived several weeks after her death, saying that she would 'get her own back tonight on the bastard who gave me this terrible thing.' I believe that suggests suicide. And she had added, 'I got my hands on half of his money and it's safely tucked away in a friend's account.'"

Who the friend was who got what must have been a sizeable sum was never revealed. Man or woman, the now wealthy person obviously decided to keep the money and say nothing.

By now Pickford was being shunned by most of his Hollywood friends. "Women wouldn't go near him," said Neilan. "Frankly, I wasn't too friendly to him either. Olive Thomas was a wonderful, totally unspoiled person, until he destroyed her."

Pickford made one film in 1921, *Just Out of College*. "Mary financed this one, too," said Neilan. "They had a hell of a job getting a girl to play opposite him, and finally one agreed provided there was no physical contact with him during the filming."

At the end of July 1921 Pickford took off to New York, where his reputation was not as bad as in Hollywood. Vacationing on Long Island, he met a young actress named Marilyn Miller. She was another Ziegfeld girl, and when Pickford and Miller announced they planned to marry, Flo Ziegfeld publicly announced that such a marriage was a disgrace. He did everything in his power to break up the relationship. He offered Miller a huge contract, provided she broke off all contact with Pickford. He even told one newspaper that he would "murder the man" if he married Miller, but all his efforts were to no avail.

On July 31, 1922, Jack Pickford and Marilyn Miller were married on the Beverly Hills estate of Mary Pickford and Douglas Fairbanks. A truce had obviously been declared between Fairbanks and Pickford.

Jack Pickford and his wife Marilyn Miller.

Declared by the newspaper columnists to be the "social event of the year," invitations went out to the studio heads and the film world's most important actors and actresses. Even Ziegfeld attended, perhaps with a little pressure from Mary, who was reported to have invested heavily in the Broadway impresario's floundering empire. In 1943 Mary Pickford laughed about the "social event." "I put the word around that anyone refusing to attend would be finished in the industry," she said. "You know, in those days I had that power."

Private detectives and a group of professional wrestlers were stationed all round the estate to keep uninvited guests at bay. Only selected members of the news media were allowed in. Thousands of fans swarmed up Summit Drive trying to catch a glimpse of the ceremony.

"I was there," said Mack Sennett in 1943. "Wouldn't have missed it for the world. Jack arranged for two planes to fly over the house at the moment of the wedding vows. They emitted some sort of smoke and made a perfect heart in the sky. That would have been fine but the asshole had hired a third plane to dive through the centre of the heart and drop fifty bouquets of roses and lilies into the middle of the guests. Fortunately for all of us the first one hit the house and completely sheared off one of the gable windows. It must have weighed 50 pounds. When we realized that the 'bombs' being dropped were so heavy we all ran for cover as the remaining forty-nine crash landed where we had been sitting minutes before. A number went into the swimming pool where, I must admit, they looked very pretty. Now if Mary had only let me bring the Keystone Kops to the party we could have made a film that would have made us all millions."

Pickford made one more film after the wedding with his own Jack Pickford Film Company. *Valley of the Wolf* recouped its cost at the box-office.

Somehow Marilyn Miller managed to keep Pickford out of the gossip columns, and they were reported to be living very happily in their Cienega Drive home.

In 1923 and 1924 Pickford once again appeared to have reformed his ways. "He didn't return our phone calls," said Neilan. "Bill Taylor was dead and none of us were mixed up in the scandal, so perhaps Mary had finally got through to him that he couldn't just continue laughing at life."

Before the middle of 1926 he had made eight more films, some with his own company, some with other studios who had apparently forgotten his bad behavior of earlier years. "His own company would have flourished," said Sennett, "but he forgot that some of the profits had to be left in the business for a rainy day. He bought lavish things for Marilyn and himself. Even had solid gold taps put in both the bathrooms in their home. So, by the middle of 1926 he was not only broke, but deep in debt."

The day news of his impending bankruptcy was announced, Marilyn Miller told the newspapers that she was returning to New York to rejoin a Ziegfeld show on Broadway. "The marriage is over," she said. Next day she climbed aboard the transcontinental train to New York. "One of the rumours that spread around at the time was that she had taken the gold fittings from the two bathrooms with her," said Sennett. "We don't really know if the tale was true, but the story was enjoyed by everyone who disliked Jack, and Ziegfeld took to calling her his 'golden girl' in New York."

Pickford made his last film one month after Miller left for New York. Perhaps appropriately for the man who was said to have smiled through all his adversities, it was called *Exit Smiling*.

His co-star was the Canadian-born star of the English and New York stages, Lady Peel, better known as Beatrice Lillie. When the film was completed, Harrison Carroll interviewed her. "Jack Pickford was a perfect gentleman at all times. I found him charming and one of the best actors I had been given to play opposite in my career." She added, "It is difficult to believe Jack is thirty years old, he still looks like a sixteen-year-old schoolboy. I hope to work with him again." It was never to happen.

Early in 1927 Miller announced that she was seeking a divorce from Pickford, and would file suit in France. Pickford then made his own statement. "Marilyn and I will be sailing together in the royal suite on the *Berengaria* for Paris, where I will assist her in obtaining the divorce." Asked if sharing the royal suite could suggest a change of heart, Pickford said, "No, absolutely not, but since we are still married there is nothing wrong in us sharing the same bedroom."

Why they chose France for the divorce is not clear. Marshall Neilan suggested that the courts in the United States would have tried to uncover things the couple didn't want aired in public. In Paris the divorce was granted on the grounds of "incompatibility" and the session with the judge was over in less than twenty minutes. Pickford and Miller celebrated their divorce in the only way they knew how, a night on the town together, followed by a champagne breakfast in the still-joint bedroom.

When he arrived back in New York, members of the press flourishing copies of Chauncey Olcott's memoirs greeted Pickford. Pickford is reported to have stood quietly, reading the comments. Then he declared, in no uncertain terms, "Tell the bastard I'll sue him." No one knows who stopped the suit going to court. Perhaps the best guess is Mary Pickford, who once again was asked to bail her brother out of bankruptcy.

Jack's mother, Mrs. Charlotte Pickford, died on March 21, 1928, and suddenly, Pickford was once again a wealthy man. The contents of her will were for some reason released to the press. She left in excess of $2 million, an immense amount in those days. Jack and Lottie each received $250,000. Mary got the rest.

Gossip columnists made a point of querying how Mrs. Pickford could have amassed such a huge bank account in the few years Mary had been earning big money in Hollywood. One columnist suggested Mary had been giving her mother fifty percent of everything she earned from day one in recognition of her devotion to the family in the lean years. If that was true, she got most of it back after the funeral.

In 1929 little was heard of Pickford other than a small news item that said he had been rushed to hospital on February 5, suffering from a heart attack. The Pickford family announced that no further news bulletins would be issued, but that the press would be advised when he was able to leave hospital. Marshall Neilan believes it was a flare-up of the syphilis. "It must have been eating into him by this time," he said. "He hadn't talked to any of his old friends in a long time so we did nothing about contacting him."

Pickford remained in hospital for nearly two months before a brief news item said he had returned to his home at 1144 La Cienega Drive to find it had been ransacked by burglars during his absence and many of his valuables had been stolen. Asked by a newspaper writer how it was that none of his friends, presumably looking after the house, had noticed the state of disarray, he answered: "What friends?"

In 1930 he was reported to be in New York, where he was going to marry yet another Ziegfeld girl, twenty-four year old Marilyn Mulhern, who was ten years his junior. The couple travelled to Los Angeles by train, hoping, said Mack Sennett, to get Mary's blessing for the union. "Where the money left by Charlotte went we'll never know, and obviously he wanted Mary to bail him out once more. But she wouldn't even see him. The maid who answered the door at Pickfair told Jack that Mary had gone away and wouldn't be back for several weeks. But I'll bet she was peeping out of the corner of one of the upstairs bedrooms making sure he had left," he said.

"So the wedding at a small chapel in Del Monte was just that, very small." Newspapers reported that during the actual ceremony, which only lasted fifteen minutes, two process servers arrived with summonses seeking several thousand dollars said to be owed by Pickford to Hollywood tradesmen for work done eighteen months earlier. James Kirkwood, who was the best man, told Sennett some weeks later that he had paid the bills to keep Pickford from being arrested.

That same year, Prince George, the Duke of Kent, sailed into Santa Barbara aboard a British destroyer, and was asked what he wanted to see while in California. "What else," said the duke, "but Pickfair!" Mary Pickford was notified and she immediately sent her car to Santa Barbara to pick up the duke and his equerry.

Jack must have heard through the grapevine that this important member of the British Royal Family was at Pickfair, because he put his new wife in their car and drove up Summit Drive to Mary's house. Once more he was refused admission. Whereupon he started screaming obscenities at Mary and the Royal Family and finally had to be restrained by a police officer sent to the scene. "Once again there were no charges, Mary saw to that," said Sennett.

In 1931 Pickford was once more taken to hospital with, the papers were told, a suspected heart attack. "It was then that his wife found out for the first time that he had syphilis," said Sennett. "She ran crying out of the hospital and had a friend drive her home. Within hours she had moved out of the Pickford home to my home. I had met her in New York before their marriage and she considered me her best friend, even though I wasn't invited to the wedding. I called one of the wardrobe ladies at the studio and had her come over to stay as chaperone. I didn't want to tangle with Pickford. She vowed never to go back to him and I arranged for a doctor in a private clinic to examine her to see if she too had caught the disease. Happily, the answer was no."

A week after he came out of hospital Pickford drove to Palm Springs to visit one of his last remaining friends. "It was a tragic mistake," said Mary, in 1943. "The friend refused to see him and he got back in the car and, according to witnesses, drove back toward Hollywood at such a ridiculously high speed that he failed to take a corner and crashed.

"At three in the morning my phone rang by my bed. 'Miss Pickford,' said a voice, 'this is Dr. Matthews. I'm afraid your brother is in hospital again.' I was rather curt, and said if you are worrying about the bills I'll pay them as I always have. Then he said, 'No, Miss Pickford, I must tell you he has had a serious car accident. He is still unconscious and we found your number in his wallet.' Of course, I was horrified and called my chauffeur to take me to the hospital, some small place just this side Palm Springs. When I saw him I knew this small hospital could not handle his injuries. I spent the next few hours arranging for him to be moved to a private clinic nearer home. Of course I had to feel sorry for him, and once more we were reunited."

Marilyn Mulhern learned about the accident in a newspaper story. "She rushed right over to the clinic and stayed with him, almost day and night, until he was well enough to go home," said Sennett. "Then she moved back in with him."

The reconciliation didn't last long. Early in 1932 Marilyn Mulhern sued for divorce. "She told me he behaved like a madman at times and that she had to hire, with her own money, a bodyguard to restrain him," said Sennett. "He refused to eat and often spent the nights singing lewd songs, before falling asleep around dawn, sleeping through the day."

Pickford was removed to a private hospital in June 1932 and most of the time he was there he had to be restrained as, quite often, he became violent. While he was in hospital the divorce was granted with little evidence after a doctor declared that Pickford was at times insane.

"He is suffering from multiple neuritis which, because of a related illness, is attacking his brain," said Dr. Gros. Pickford, through his lawyer, agreed to a simple fifty-fifty financial settlement. "But she got almost nothing," said Sennett. "His house was mortgaged and he owed thousands. Mary paid off the debts and offered to pay for Marilyn's return to New York, where she was to have the use of Mary's own apartment until she got back on her feet. I believe she settled a sum of money on Marilyn, too."

In October 1932, Dr. Gros announced with, he said, full approval of Mary Pickford, that he had arranged for the transfer of Jack Pickford to the American Hospital in Neuilly, Paris. "It is," said the doctor, "the only hope that Mr. Pickford will be able to make a complete recovery."

There was no further news until the morning of January 3, 1933, when Dr. Gros announced from Paris that Pickford had died early that day. His diagnosis was that Pickford had finally succumbed to an illness that had plagued him for years. "The multiple neurosis has finally eaten away and destroyed his brain," he said.

Mary was advised on January 1 that Jack's situation was critical. She told the newspapers after his death was announced that she had made every attempt possible to get to Paris in time to see her brother before he died. "But I was told," she said, "that it would be impossible for me to get there in time."

The body was returned to the United States and a private funeral service, with only a few invited guests attending, was held on January 20 in the Wee Kirk of the Heath Chapel in Forest Lawn Memorial Park in Glendale, California.

Apart from the immediate family, the few invited mourners included Charlie Chaplin, cowboy star Hoot Gibson, Sam Goldwyn, Dr. and Mrs. Harry Martin (Louella Parsons), and actors Donald Crisp and Johnny Mack Brown. No member of the "rat pack" was invited. Marshall Neilan said he attempted to attend for old times sake, "But I was turned away, not too politely, at the chapel door."

The service lasted only ten minutes before the gun metal casket with a silver plate reading John Charles Pickford, was carried away to be interred in the Pickford crypt in Forest Lawn Memorial Park.

Jack Pickford left many unanswered questions in his wasted lifetime. Marshall Neilan said in 1959 that it was just like Jack to add one more piece to the puzzle as he left this earth. "Why on earth," he said, "was his casket labelled John Charles Pickford when the name on his birth and death certificates very clearly read John Carl (Smith) Pickford?"

MARY PICKFORD

"Mary Pickford was probably the most important woman in the world in the days when people believed in fairy tales. Her golden curls and perpetual look of innocence made her the girl every family wanted as their own daughter. But when life became harsh and moviegoers sought reality she never managed to make the transition. But her fame will outlive her. Mary Pickford was, and is, everything that is good about Hollywood."

(Sidney Olcott, 1943)

Pickfair, the most famous house ever to be built in Beverly Hills, home of Hollywood's elite, no longer stands in state at the top of Summit Drive. In 1990 it was pulled down to make way for a new, more modern mansion to house a young singer-actress, Pia Zadora, and her husband, a multi-millionaire Las Vegas hotel owner.

Decades after Zadora and her husband are gone and forgotten, the memory of Pickfair and its long-time resident, America's Sweetheart, will likely live on.

The beautiful estate at 1143 Summit Drive was once the home of Mary Pickford and her husband, Douglas Fairbanks, Sr. When their "dream" marriage disintegrated in 1935, Pickford remained on in the house until her death at the age of eighty-six in 1979.

Even when she took a new husband, Charles "Buddy" Rogers, into Pickfair in 1937, the glamour of the house never faded. Just about everyone who visited Hollywood sought an invitation to Pickfair, and until the late 1960s, when she was in her seventies, Mary Pickford obliged.

Winston Churchill requested an invitation, and got one. So did the British Dukes of Windsor and Kent. Albert Einstein was reported to be "entranced with Pickfair and Mary" when he visited. The King of Siam did not stoop so low as to talk with mere newspaper writers, but they reported that he kissed Mary at the door on his departure and that his face "wore a wide smile of happiness" as he was driven away in his limousine.

Parties held at Pickfair were legendary. Mary herself said that the only person who ever managed to gate-crash one of her parties was her next door neighbour, Charlie Chaplin who, when out of favour with Pickford, found the only way in was to climb over the six-foot ivy-covered fence between their two homes.

In 1962 Pickford laughed about Chaplin's unique way of arriving at her home. "I had got very tired of him dictating this, that, and everything," she said. "At times he was quite an obnoxious little man and for a long time after one of his divorces he used to sit on my front doorstep every morning waiting for the breakfast gong to sound. We always cooked a few extra eggs and some ham or bacon if we knew he was in town."

Pickford said she couldn't understand why Chaplin never became an American citizen. "This country made him famous and gave him his fortune," she said. "He owed it to us to become an American."

Two years later, Pickford, who had also made her millions in America, reversed her attitude. Born in Canada, she had taken out American citizenship in the 1920s, but in 1964 she sought, and regained, her Canadian citizenship and passport. "One should never abandon the country of one's birth," she said.

Gladys Mary Smith was born in Toronto, Ontario, on April 8, 1893. The home in which she lived on University Avenue has long gone and is now the site of the Toronto Hospital for Sick Children. When she was only two the family moved to 81 Walton Street, and in this house her sister Lottie and brother Jack were born.

Mary's mother, Charlotte, had been a small-time actress until she married the children's father, John Smith, a purser on a steamboat that sailed daily across Lake Ontario between Toronto and Lewiston, New York.

John Smith died following an accident on board the steamboat when Mary was only seven, and her mother, who had worked part-time in the theatre, was forced into full-time work to keep her children fed. Mary used to haunt the small theatres where her mother appeared in the melodramas of the late 1890s. When she was only six months old, Mary was carried on stage in one play, and when she was seven years old was given her first speaking part in a play entitled *Bootle's Baby.*

Mary was an instant hit. The golden curls that adorned her head until she was in her thirties, and made her America's Sweetheart, made her the still unborn Shirley Temple of Ontario in 1900.

Charlotte Smith told different writers over the years that Mary asked for the role in *Bootle's Baby.* "I did not push her into the theatre," she said. "Mary walked up to the director, who was auditioning several young girls for the role, and told him he needn't look any further, that she was perfect for the part. After she had recited a few lines of the script, he agreed. Then, and only then, did he come to me and ask for my permission to let her become the Valentine Stock Company's youngest and newest actress."

Mary never forgot her early days in the theatre. "Mother was in most of the plays so she took Jack, Lottie, and me to all the rehearsals. There was no money to hire someone to look after us, so we looked after ourselves, playing around back stage and trying on some of the company's costumes that were far too big for us. It was a carefree life, and I loved watching the actors create characters in front of my eyes."

By the time she was ten, in 1903, Mary was a stage veteran. "Most of the parts I got were very small, but the director, who also authored some of the company's plays, wrote me into as many of the company's productions as possible. At ten I was sufficiently well known to audiences as 'Little Mary' that I received applause when I went on stage for the first time in each play.

"Jack and Lottie were also getting parts now and then but Jack often upset the other actors by ad-libbing lines that weren't in the script. One night I remember one of the older actors taking him across his knee and giving him a good walloping right there on stage. The audience thought it was part of the play and applauded, so they had to keep it in every night. Mother padded his trousers with wads of paper so he wouldn't get hurt."

When she was ten, a wealthy Toronto doctor, realising the poor conditions in which the Smith family members were living, approached Charlotte Smith and offered her a large sum of money if she would allow him to adopt the obviously talented Mary.

Charlotte remembered the occasion in an interview with the *New York Daily News* in 1920. "He was a dignified gentleman with a charming wife. They had their own carriage and when it was parked outside our small home on Walton Street it drew crowds of onlookers. We listened to what he had to say and asked for a few days to think over the offer. I decided that Mary should make the decision, and happily she chose to stay with us."

The "Smith Family" became well known to the theatre-going public. That is the way they were billed in Buffalo, New York, when they were stars of two plays, *The Little Red Schoolhouse* and *The Fatal Wedding*.

"I was still known as Gladys Smith," said Pickford. "I played Little Eva in *Uncle Tom's Cabin* and Willie Carlyle in the pot-boiler that every company presented at one time or another, *East Lynne.*"

Chauncey Olcott, the singer-actor-director who was at the height of his fame in the early 1900s, spotted the Smiths when he visited a theatre where they were appearing in Lewiston, New York. "I fell in love with all four of the Smiths," he told the *New York World* in 1920. "I offered them a package contract. Mrs. Smith received the entire $30, and it was up to her how she disbursed the money amongst her children."

Olcott, who had given actress Florence La Badie her first stage role a year earlier in Montreal, now added four more Canadians to his discovery list. "I told them that Smith was not a suitable name for the stage. We had thrown a few names around when Mary suggested Pickford, the name of her favourite aunt. Charlotte, Jack, and Lottie said it sounded good, and so they became the Pickford family. Mary came to me when I was preparing posters for the printer and said she wanted to use her other name, Mary, and abandon the use of Gladys. I checked with her mother and she had no objections, so from that day Gladys Smith became Mary Pickford."

For several years the Pickford family toured the small theatre circuits in Ontario and the northern United States. In 1906 they joined a road company that took them as far south as Washington and Baltimore. While en route from New Jersey to Boston, they had a short stopover in New York.

"I loved New York at first sight," said Mary. "The theatres were lined up along the streets off Broadway and I saw names on theatre posters that I had only heard about from older actors who had once played there but had been forced into the smaller theatres, often by their inability to stay sober.

"I knew at once that New York was where we should be. I was fourteen, in 1907, when mother decided it was time for us to take a gamble with our lives. We found a small apartment near the theatre district and set out to tramp round the agents' offices to see what work we could find.

"The pickings were lean for more than three months. Mother and I earned a few dollars by posing for clothing advertisements and we were getting low on cash when I decided to be very cheeky and crash a rehearsal.

"I heard through the grapevine that David Belasco was holding first rehearsals for *The Warrens of Virginia*. I presented myself at the stage door of the Belasco Theatre and asked to see the great man. Somehow I must have impressed the stage doorkeeper because he went inside and asked Mr. Belasco if he had time to talk with me."

Belasco told the rest of the story to the *New York Sunday News* in 1920. "I was having serious problems with the young girl I had hired to play the part of Betty Warren. She was far too precocious for my liking, and when her mother started telling me how to direct, I stopped rehearsals and told everyone to take a break until the afternoon. As I was walking back to my office, the doorkeeper came and asked if I would see a young girl from Canada.

"I almost said 'no' because I had already taken too much nonsense from the actress I had hired. But something told me to say 'yes' and she was brought into my office. I was totally charmed by her look of innocence. Unlike most of the children appearing on Broadway she had no affectation. I asked her to read a few lines from the play, and within ten minutes I knew I had the Betty Warren I was looking for.

"She had just turned fourteen when we opened on December 3, 1907, with *The Warrens of Virginia*. Every notice she received was good. I had offered her $25 a week before the play opened, but I increased that to $50 when she turned out to be so very good. Despite her youth she was completely at home and showed none of the self-consciousness I had learned to expect with performers so young."

Mary Pickford continued the story. "Mr. Belasco was not only a brilliant man with so much knowledge of the theatre to impart, but he was also a very fine person to work with. For the first few weeks of the play's run he would coach me in the mornings for things he had picked up while watching the show in the theatre the night before.

"When he increased my salary to $50 I couldn't believe my ears. He was the only theatre or film studio owner I met in my entire career who offered me a raise before I asked for it. Mother, Jack, and Lottie were thrilled. For the first time in our lives we weren't having to buy only the cheapest food and clothes. Fifty dollars went a long way in those days."

Pickford spent two years with Belasco in New York and on tour. "We played only the big theatres outside New York and we were able to stay in good hotels and eat in good restaurants. When we got back to New York, when I was sixteen, we had managed to save more than $400. It is difficult now to explain how much that $400 meant to us. In our wildest dreams we had never thought we could have savings so huge."

When the Pickfords arrived back in New York it was summer, and the majority of the large theatres, without air-conditioning in those days, had closed their doors waiting for the fall season that started in late September.

But the motion picture studios remained open to satisfy the growing demand for their product from the hundreds of nickelodeons that were springing up across the country. Most of their exteriors were shot in the heat of summer, since the primitive cameras often froze in the bitter winters of New York.

"The old Biograph Motion Picture Company had its studios on 14th Street in New York, so I decided I would see if I could get work there," said Pickford. "Mr. Belasco said he had already sent a few actors to Biograph and encouraged all of us to try what the industry had to offer.

"Mother and I, together with Jack and Lottie, arrived at the studio at nine a.m. and less than half-an-hour later we were all working. I had no idea what the films were about. We were told to do this or that and we figured that somehow our strange actions would enhance whatever film they were making at the time. I was told years later by D. W. Griffith, the incomparable silent era director, that we actually appeared in scenes from three different movies that first day.

"We took home $20 between us, they paid in cash at the end of each day, and we were asked to come back the following morning at seven a.m. They started so early in the morning before the heat of the day made the studios rather like ovens.

"On my second day at Biograph I made friends with another Canadian, Florence Lawrence, who went on to become very famous. She found time to teach me the basics of film acting and I learned very fast what it was all about. Florence and I remained friends until the day she died, tragically so young.

"D. W. Griffith was, at that time, directing just about every film Biograph turned out. He seemed to like what I was doing and eventually singled me out for more important parts."

Pickford disputed film historians who have insisted that her first leading role was in *Her First Biscuits*. "I actually had the principal role in *The Violin Maker of Cremona* right at the beginning of June. I made three other films, I forget their names, before I made *Her First Biscuits*. I had been a principal player for at least two weeks before that. I remember *Biscuits* so well because Florence Lawrence co-starred with William Courtwright and me.

"You must remember that although we knew the names of the people we worked with, theatre audiences didn't. Only the director was named along with the title of the film. The companies wanted to keep our real names hidden in case we became too popular and started demanding extra money."

In two years Pickford played the lead in seventy-three films at Biograph. "We made at least one a week," she recalled. "There was no set time for shooting the one-reelers, we just started and finished when Mr. Griffith had what he wanted. Some days we worked from seven in the morning to ten at night.

"We took sandwiches for lunch and often ate them while we were filming. Breaks were few and far between. After I'd been there about a year, a little Italian with a cart used to bring hot food to the studio for those who wanted more than the sandwiches. In a few years he had carts at every studio in New York and New Jersey and went on to become a famous restaurateur in the city. I won't tell you his name, because he has got a lot too big for his boots these days and doesn't like people to think he once pushed a food cart through the streets. Today he denies ever having been at Biograph, or even that he met me there, so I refuse all invitations to his restaurant.

"I don't recall ever seeing a written script in the two years I worked at Biograph. Sometimes I used to think that Mr. Griffith himself didn't know what story we were filming. I know he improvised on the spot, and he had one policy for his cameraman, Billy Bitzer: 'After I call action you keep cranking the camera until I tell you to stop.' This way we often got a lot of unrehearsed and unexpected action, and if Mr. Griffith could find some justification it was in the finished film when the public saw it."

"Billy Bitzer has never been given his fair share of the credit for Mr. Griffith's success in those early days. It was Billy who first thought of doing close-ups; he invented those when he made a film with Sid Olcott. And it was Billy who devised a lot of lighting ideas that enhanced the sets." In the spring of 1910 Pickford paid her first visit to California. Biograph had decided to test the waters in this new paradise for filmmakers. Pickford loved the fresh air and beautiful scenery from the day she and a company of ten, led by Griffith, arrived. Included in the unit was Mack Sennett, actor and part-time director.

The unit departed from Jersey City. "It was a disastrous departure," Pickford recalled in 1960. "Owen Moore, who had been my leading man in about a dozen films, was almost in tears because Griffith had refused him the $20 a week increase he had demanded to be part of the group heading west. He was on his knees pleading with Griffith, and I was doing my best to convince him, too. It was then I first realised that Owen was becoming more to me than just a leading man. But Griffith refused to take him with us. I have often wondered if he knew then the attraction Owen and I had for each other and wasn't too keen on the idea since Owen was almost ten years older than my young eighteen.

"My brother Jack was crying because Biograph had refused to include him on the trip, and he yelled so much that Mr. Griffith finally relented and said he could come if I paid for his rail ticket. Mother was wheeling and dealing to get me an extra $50 a week to give to Jack, but she didn't win and I had him on my hands all the time we were out west. I financed a number of his wild escapades from my own pocket and wished we had left him at home.

"We finally boarded the express to Chicago and picked up the California Limited there for the rest of the journey. We travelled first class and if it hadn't been for Jack's never-ending bad behaviour, it would have been a memorable trip. I saw scenery that I never dreamed existed. And those Rocky Mountains!

I've never forgotten the first time I saw them." The Biograph unit registered at the Alexandria Hotel, one of Los Angeles' newest hostelries. "Jack and I and two of the company's young actresses rented ourselves a three-bedroom suite at the hotel," she said. "It was modern enough to have a bathroom, and only cost all four of us $25 a week. We found a cheap restaurant where we could eat and went back and forth to the studio on a streetcar. The studio was an empty lot on Grand Avenue that Griffith had rented.

"He had a carpenter construct a revolving platform on which we built our sets. To avoid shadows, we could turn the platform so it was always facing the blazing sun. When the breezes got strong we had to nail curtains and table cloths to the windows and tables; even then they flapped in the breeze and movie audiences must have often wondered why we had a gale rushing through what was supposed to be the closed interior of a house.

"But our biggest problem, until Mr. Griffith built a six-foot fence around the lot, were the hundreds of youngsters who watched us film every day. It is a good job there was no sound in those days, or every film would have been punctuated with hisses at the villain and cheers when he got conked on the head.

"We made about twenty films away from the lot using very little that wasn't natural scenery. The old churches and monasteries made excellent backgrounds and the priests were very co-operative if Mr. Griffith put a few dollars in the kitty.

"Just as I had been awed by New York when I first set foot on Broadway, I was enchanted by California. I had never seen palm trees and never believed I would ever see an orange actually growing on a tree. We made about a dozen films before Mr. Griffith decided to return to New York. I knew then that I'd be back in California just as soon as I could possibly arrange it.

"Mack Sennett was both acting in and directing the company's second unit. But he wanted to get in on something else. Mack desperately wanted to be a writer. Knowing that I had sold a few stories to Biograph he pitched me a wild comedy tale about a bunch of wacky police officers who constantly got in the way of everybody but never caught a criminal or solved a crime. It sounded so far out to me that I told him to forget it, that it would never work.

"Well, he did forget it for a while. But when he started his own Keystone studio he sold himself on the idea that I had turned down. I had turned away what later became one of the world's most enduring comedy ideas, the Keystone Kops.

"We returned to New York in late April and I resumed my friendship with Owen Moore, who I had missed dreadfully."

Afraid that her mother would stop her seeing Moore, Pickford decided to elope with him to New Jersey, where getting married in a hurry was commonplace for performers and socialites of the early 1900s.

On January 7, 1911, the happy couple rode the ferry from Manhattan Island to Jersey City, New Jersey. Pickford was carrying a long white dress that she had borrowed from the studio wardrobe on the pretext that she was going to a party. Her mother was told the same tale.

Pickford had doubts about her decision to marry Moore even before the justice of the peace in Jersey City County Courthouse officially tied the knot.

In her book, *Sunshine and Shadows,* Pickford remembers the marriage this way. "It was a cold and drizzly January day, and as Owen and I walked down the hall to the magistrate's office I wondered what on earth I was doing there. Why, I scarcely knew him … I don't love him at all … If I get up and run very fast I may get to the subway before he catches me."

She said in 1960 that the only thing that stopped her running away was the realisation that she didn't even have the subway fare. "Five cents," she said, "might have saved me a lot of later heartache."

After the wedding Mr. and Mrs. Moore returned on the ferry to New York, where Moore delivered her to the doorway of the Pickford home. "I couldn't say anything to mother, I daren't," she said. "It was almost a month later when the story came out. One of the New Jersey papers was tipped off by the Justice of the Peace, and the story was picked up by the *New York World.* Then the smoke really hit the fan. I had mother and Lottie and Jack standing screaming at me for being so stupid.

"Mother kept me locked in my room for more than a week, only opening the door to let me out to the bathroom or to eat," she said. "Owen banged on the front door of our house and kicked up such a noise that finally the police came and took him away. It was a disastrous time in my life, and I still shudder a little to think of those terrible weeks."

Just before news of the marriage leaked out, Pickford had signed a big contract with the Independent Motion Picture Company (IMP). Carl Laemmle, later to be the founder of Universal Studios in Hollywood, had joined forces with a wealthy industrialist, Robert Cochrane, to create IMP. "We just weren't getting the amount of good films we needed for our growing movie distribution company," said Laemmle to the *Los Angeles Times* in 1927. "So we decided to make our own."

"Mr. Laemmle talked to mother and pointed out that he didn't think my importance in the film industry would be harmed by my marriage to Owen, even suggesting it might well be enhanced. He pointed out that Owen and I were now the hottest couple on the movie screens and were obviously very much in love," said Pickford, "and she relented enough to let us take an apartment together."

Laemmle had already lured the Biograph Girl, Florence Lawrence, away from Griffith's studio and had made her the first actress to receive billing in her real name on the film credits and posters.

"Thomas Ince, who was directing many of the IMP films, was turning out some excellent pictures at the company's studio in Philadelphia, and when they offered me $250 a week I decided not to sign a new contract with Biograph and join IMP," she said. "No, I never was the Biograph Girl, as historians say, but sometimes the papers would refer to me as Little Mary, but that was as near as I got at Biograph to getting any personal acclaim."

Owen Moore, an excellent actor, had ambitions to become a director. He had appeared as Pickford's leading man in several films, but Griffith refused to give him a chance to direct. When she went to IMP, Pickford insisted that Moore be given a contract to act and direct.

"Owen never knew I demanded that he be hired," said Pickford. "We made it look as though Mr. Laemmle needed him as much as he needed me."

IMP was filming in Philadelphia because it was the only way the company could use, without a license, the patented camera belonging to the major studios. "We were too far enough away, at first, from New York, for the majors to send their goons out to smash our cameras, but after about six months they found us," said Laemmle.

"When things got too hot in Philadelphia I decided to send Pickford and Moore to Havana with Thomas Ince and a group of ten other actors and technicians to get them out of reach of the thugs hired by the major studios. They were getting very persistent despite the efforts of the Philadelphia police department."

Charlotte, Jack, and Lottie were to have stayed in New York, or so Mary hoped, but they insisted on going along on the Havana trip, which Pickford and Moore had planned to be a honeymoon trip. Laemmle told the *New York Daily News* in 1923 that "Jack Pickford had by then grown into the most obnoxious person it was my misfortune to meet. Add to that the fact that Charlotte and Lottie were weeping their eyes out at what they considered was the desecration of Mary, and we had a trip I would rather forget."

In the last three months of 1911 and the first three months of 1912, Pickford made a series of films with the Majestic Film Company, which was formed specifically to make films with her as the star.

"I had no contract. I negotiated a price for each individual film," she said. "My popularity was peaking, and I asked for, and received, not only a salary but a share of all the company's profits. I even convinced George Tucker, who was Majestic's principal director, to let Owen direct a couple of the films.

"But by then he was drinking heavily, and on both films George Tucker had to take over. Owen was not finding it easy to accept that I was now earning about ten times as much as his salary. He was abusive to me on the set, and sometimes he never came home at night. Our marriage was falling apart."

Pickford's stay with Majestic was short and the company was wound up. After a brief shouting match on the set between Moore and Pickford, he struck her in the stomach. Others on the set overpowered Moore and threw him off the lot. Pickford, though in some pain, managed to finish the last scene before collapsing on the set. "That was the nearest I ever came to losing shooting time through illness in my entire career," she said.

"I was rushed to hospital and the doctors, after giving me sedatives for a few hours, said they had to give me an emergency appendectomy. I told mother not to tell Owen as I was afraid of what he might do. But he found out somehow and pushed his way into the hospital yelling that no one could operate on his wife without his permission. Doctors convinced him that my life was in no danger, but he had been drinking and apparently threatened one of the doctors so the hospital attendants threw him out. It was obvious our marriage was over. When I left the hospital I had a police escort to gather my things from our apartment and I moved back home with mother, Jack, and Lottie."

Sidney Olcott and his wife Valentine Grant listened to Pickford's story of her visit to hospital, and later told a rather different version.

"We had been aware for a little while in 1912 that Mary had been putting on quite a bit of weight," said Olcott. "She was always a small and slim girl, and we chided her about the extra pounds. She told us she just needed a bit of exercise and when spring arrived she would work it off by walking to and from the studio each day."

"But when we heard that she had fainted a couple of times on the set, we put two and two together and decided she was going to have a baby," said Grant. "When we heard she was taken to hospital we knew it wasn't time for the baby to arrive so wondered if perhaps she was having an abortion."

"That was in the era when hundreds of young hopefuls in the film studios were rushed to hospitals for what the studios announced was an 'appendectomy.' In most cases it was for an abortion," said Olcott. "At Kalem we actually had a fund set aside to pay the hospital bills of contract actresses who got pregnant, more often than not without the benefit of a wedding ring."

"In those days," said Grant, "people having real appendectomies were kept in hospital at least a week. Mary was out and back on the set in three days. I should add that even in the best hospitals in that era many abortions were badly botched with the result that the girl involved was never again able to get pregnant. Both Sidney and I believe that is why Mary, who loves children, never did have any of her own."

D. W. Griffith welcomed Mary back to the Biograph fold after Majestic ceased production. "I'll never forget his kindness," she said. "He offered me $500 a week to make a series of twelve films. And he guaranteed that mother, Lottie, even Jack, would be given parts in the films. He clinched the deal when he told me that Owen would not be allowed inside the studio."

Sid Olcott says Pickford repaid that kindness four decades later when Griffith was a forgotten man. "Although he never knew where the money came from, Griffith accepted a fine apartment in Hollywood and a weekly salary for reading scripts and giving an opinion on their suitability. The dummy company set up to provide this genius of the silent era with all his needs was created by lawyers on the instructions of Mary Pickford. The day he died in 1948 the company was dissolved."

"But I couldn't give him the acclaim he deserved," said Pickford in 1960, confirming for the first time her involvement in his later life. "He had lost his touch, perhaps he hadn't moved with the times, and the thing he wanted most, to be back in the studio, in total command, I couldn't give him. He died a bitter and almost forgotten man. I tried many times to get him to visit me, even to live here at Pickfair if he wished, but he wouldn't understand that I didn't have the power to put him in charge of films that by the forties were costing millions of dollars."

Adolph Zukor, head of Famous Players, and later to be the founder of Paramount Pictures, made Mary an offer, in 1912, that she couldn't refuse. "I want you to move to California where I will star you in films of four and five reels or even longer," he said.

Pickford had been enthusiastic when Griffith had directed her, in 1912, in her first film longer than one reel. "I suddenly realised how much more we could do in twenty minutes than ten," she said in 1943. "It was as though the flood gates had opened up and given me a totally new range of emotions. No longer did we have to rush a scene. We could use close-ups much more effectively. My first two-reeler was *A Pueblo Legend*. It was Mr. Griffith's first two-reeler, too."

Griffith, in an article in *Pictorial Review* in 1939, said, "I was scared to move into two-reelers. I had mastered the art of getting everything into 1,000 feet of film, and I was far from sure that I could make the transition, that I could stretch my stories out to twenty minutes without them looking padded with unnecessary material. So when I decided, let's say I was pressured, to make the two-reeler I knew I could only do it with Mary Pickford. She made directing so easy.

"The film was a great success, everyone loved seeing more of Mary, and I moved into a new dimension of my career. Had it not been for Mary's return to Biograph for those few weeks I may never had had the courage, or the opportunity, to make my big films like *Birth of a Nation* and *Intolerance*."

But first, Pickford had to keep a promise she had made in 1908. "I had told Mr. Belasco, after the two-year run of *The Warrens of Virginia* ended, that I had enjoyed myself so much that if ever he needed me for another play I would give up whatever I was doing and accept whatever role he offered me," she said in 1960.

Belasco called Pickford in January 1913. "Mary," he said. "I have the most wonderful part for you in *A Good Little Devil*. I want you to play Juliet, the young blind heroine of the play. How much are you making a week now?" he asked.

"I told him I was averaging $500 a week, but that I had signed with Adolph Zukor for a minimum of $1,000 a week plus a share of the profits," Pickford recalled. "There was a silence, then he said, 'I guess I'll have to let you pass on this one. There is no way I can afford more than $200 a week.' It took me three seconds to tell him to get the contract ready. I told him I had given my word in 1908 and I never went back on my word."

The play opened in Philadelphia for a two-week run before coming to Broadway. "I'll never forget that opening night as long as I live," said Pickford. "I may have been playing a blind girl but I could clearly see, through the footlights, Mr. Griffith and all my friends from Biograph and IMP filling the first three rows of seats. I nearly lost my composure, and would have been in trouble if a veteran actor on stage had not said, 'Juliet, for a moment there I thought you could see.' I ad-libbed something and was then able to get on with the play.

"We were a big success on Broadway, and I got rave reviews from all the critics. I'll always believe my drop to $200 a week was one of the most satisfying decisions of my career. And it certainly enhanced my reputation. Very few of the movie people in those early days had the experience or ability to star in any stage play, much less at the Belasco Theatre, one of New York's finest."

Adolph Zukor, many years later, said that his promise to pay Mary Pickford $1,000 a week, plus a share of the profits, was not based on his available capital, but on his belief that Pickford was destined to become the world's greatest actress. "As a matter of fact," he told *Variety* in 1973, on his 100th birthday, "I had to pawn my wife's jewellery, sell my house in New Jersey, and borrow heavily from a bank on the strength of my contract with Mary to get sufficient money to make the first film."

When *In the Bishop's Carriage,* a four-reeler directed by Edwin S. Porter, was released both the critics and moviegoers acclaimed it. It made stars of Pickford's choice of principal actors, David W. Hall and House Peters. Both their careers continued well into the sound era.

House Peters, living at the Motion Picture Country Home in 1960, said, "I was totally flabbergasted when Mary chose me to be in the film. I couldn't think what I had done to deserve such an honour. Years later she told me she chose me because I had humility. Imagine that. An actor with humility. But as the years went by and I saw all her films I understood. It was her own humility that had made her so loved by everyone."

Pickford had been separated from Owen Moore for more than a year when he suddenly appeared in Hollywood. "He pleaded with me to give him another chance," said Pickford. "I must have been soft-hearted because I asked Mr. Zukor to give him some parts in a few of my films. I made it clear he was not to be the leading man, because I wanted no clinches that might get me back in his power again.

"He did a good job in my second Famous Players film, *The Caprice,* and I asked the director, Searle Dawley, to have someone watching to see if he was drinking. He wasn't, so I had Mr. Zukor get him some parts with other companies, and then late in 1914 I had him offered a part in *Cinderella.* We had no contact outside the studio, and I was almost feeling sorry for him when Mr. Dawley pointed out that he had started drinking quietly at the side of the set. He finished the film but I told him we must never work together again, nor meet in public or privately."

It was in 1915 that Pickford was able to hire, for the first time, Allan Dwan, a director whose work she had much admired. "When we made *A Girl of Yesterday,* I asked that he give Jack a part. He had been running wild and badly needed taming. Allan is the only person I ever met who was able to control him. He cleverly asked Jack if one day he might like to direct, and Jack jumped at the chance. Dwan sat him on his right side, in a second director's chair, and explained every move he made. They became good friends, but Jack, unfortunately, had too much time on his hands and Allan, one of the busiest directors in Hollywood, couldn't be with him all the time. But it got Jack to seriously think about being a director, and Allan let him sit with him on the set wherever he was filming. For a while we believed he was reforming."

Moore continued working quite steadily, but reports filtered back to Pickford that he was once again drinking heavily. "I didn't see him again until the end of 1915 when I was making my first film with Sidney Olcott as director, *Madame Butterfly.* I wasn't having too easy a time with Sidney. He knew what he wanted and didn't want. I also knew what I wanted and didn't want. So we clashed frequently, and Sidney nearly always won the disputes.

"One morning, just after we had started filming, Owen crashed the set, dishevelled and drunk. He looked old enough to be my father. He started swearing at me until something strange happened. Sidney pushed him away and just stared at him. Within a minute Owen was as meek as a lamb. Sidney told him to leave the set and never come anywhere near me again. He just nodded and walked off the set, and I never saw him again.

"Sidney will tell you that he has never used hypnosis to convince actors how to say their lines, and that may be so, but what I saw that day was hypnosis, whether he likes it to be said or not."

Mary Pickford received a $300,000 signing bonus in January 1916 when she re-signed with Adolph Zukor's company, which was by then affiliated with the Jesse Lasky company. She was to make no more than five films in the year, and would receive $10,000 a week for the entire fifty-two weeks.

Among her directors was Cecil B. DeMille. He had been a stage actor and director before moving, with a gentle push from David Belasco, into the motion picture world. He linked with Jesse Lasky, and when Lasky teamed up with Adolph Zukor he was offered to Pickford as a directing possibility. "I watched two of his first films; he had only done about five before 1916," said Pickford, "and was so impressed that I told them to put him on my next film, *A Romance of the Redwoods.* This turned out so well we teamed up again on *The Little American.*"

In 1918 Mary Pickford met Douglas Fairbanks, Sr., and the greatest romance in the history of Hollywood began. "We had to be very discreet in our meetings," she said. "I was still married to Owen Moore, and to risk the wrath of a man whose antics on and off the set had caused me considerable pain would have been disastrous to my career. We met at friends' homes and planned a strategy to get my divorce."

Convincing Moore to grant Mary her freedom took almost eighteen months. "Finally my lawyers reached an agreement with his lawyers and the divorce went through early in 1920."

Unfortunately for Pickford newspapers started to question the legality of the Nevada divorce, which was granted in Lake Tahoe. Pickford's residential qualifications were said to have been falsely stated. The furor went on until Pickford's lawyers produced a deed of property transfer in the State of Nevada, conveniently dated several months earlier. "My lawyers arranged that," she said. "I had nothing to do with it."

Stories in the newspapers suggested that Pickford had paid Moore in excess of half-a-million dollars for agreeing to the divorce, an immense sum when Moore was perhaps averaging $300 a week from the ever-decreasing work he was able to get. Moore somehow managed to pull his life together and by 1923 was once again a competent and in-demand actor. His last film was in 1937, when he appeared in a strong supporting role with Janet Gaynor and Fredric March in *A Star Is Born*. Something happened to drive him back to drugs, and by 1939 he was dead.

Mary Pickford with Douglas Fairbanks Sr. (left) and
Douglas Fairbanks Jr. (right).

Several months before the Pickford-Moore divorce became final, residents of Beverly Hills noticed a flurry of construction activity on a twenty-acre site at the top of Summit Drive. Pickford and Fairbanks were building their renowned mansion, Pickfair, so that it would be ready when they married in March 1920.

Charlie Chaplin, whose own home bordered on the construction site, was said by Pickford to have spent hours each day sitting on a small platform he built so he could see over the Pickfair fence. "He sat there as if in a trance, only occasionally coming to life to call out suggestions to the workers. He actually jumped over the fence on one occasion and had a heated argument with our architect over where we should build our swimming pool."

Chaplin remembered it, in 1943, somewhat differently. "Mary hadn't told me she was building a house next door, and naturally I was curious as to what was going on. I had the workers put a gate between my property and hers, and at lunch times I invited them over to play tennis on my courts or join me in a lemonade. I had three indoor staff at that time and sometimes they were kept busy from noon to two p.m. just serving lemonade, never any liquor, and delivering sandwiches to the workers.

"I actually knew every nook and cranny in Pickfair long before it was named and months before Mary and Doug moved in. I tried to get the architect to build an underground passage from Pickfair to my house, but I believe Mary vetoed the idea."

In 1960 Pickford claimed she had never heard any suggestion of a tunnel and denied that Chaplin had access to her home before she and Fairbanks moved in. "But I do remember very clearly an occasion just after we moved in and had a house-warming party that we were talking about the number of stairs from the drawing room to the first floor. Chaplin had, I thought, never been in the house before, but he shouted out instantly that there were twenty-four steps and there were fourteen more going to the downstairs bar. We didn't argue, because no one could argue with Chaplin in those days. He was utterly obstinate. Later that night, when everyone had gone home, I counted the stairs and Chaplin was right. Was it a guess, or had he been in the house earlier? I wouldn't put anything past him."

The Pickford-Fairbanks wedding was a quiet one, in the home of the Reverend Whitcome Brougher, a friend of the family. Only a few guests were invited. The happy couple hired a complete Pullman railway car and, together with four servants, went to New York on business. Once the work was completed, Pickford demanded that Fairbanks take her on an eight-week honeymoon tour of Europe.

Alexander Woollcott, the renowned American writer, described the honeymoon in the *New York Times* as being "the most conspicuous in the history of the marriage institution. They were mobbed everywhere they went and at one time had more than twenty bodyguards hired to get them through the crowds who stood night and day outside the Ritz-Carlton Hotel where they were staying."

The newlyweds stopped at the Ritz Hotel in London. In her book, *Sunshine and Shadows,* she recalled the visit to England. "Outside our window we saw them, thousands and thousands of them just waiting for a glimpse of us. I felt so inadequate and powerless to show my gratitude that it actually made me feel ill."

George Grossmith, the celebrated author, hosted a luncheon party for them in London. When asked by Fairbanks if he had arranged for police protection when they left his home, Grossmith answered: "My dear chap, you don't seem to realise that the English are a civilized people, they are not going to harm Mary, depend on it."

At an outdoor garden party that same afternoon in Kensington Gardens, both Pickford and Fairbanks discovered that at least some English people were perhaps not as civilized as Grossmith believed.

"Word of our arrival must have spread," she said. "I was seated in the back of an open Rolls-Royce. The car was almost brought to a halt by the thousands of people. Someone reached out a hand and asked me to shake it. I tried to do so, and found my other hand grasped by someone else. When the car started to move I was slowly but surely being dragged over the back of the car. Douglas turned and saw what was happening and grabbed my ankles. I was in the middle of a tug-of-war that Douglas was slowly losing until two policemen came and freed my hands so I could slide back into the car. I sat on the floor for the rest of the journey."

Two days later they sneaked aboard a cross-Channel boat and landed in Holland, where the scenes of adoration were much more subdued. "Just before we crossed the border into Germany we were warned that we should expect a cold reception since the First World War had only been over for a few months. We had rented a car in Holland but were stopped at the German border by the Dutch authorities. We were determined to see Cologne so we took a streetcar into the city. All our baggage stayed in Holland."

Someone, Pickford says she never found out who, cleared their car at the border and they were reunited with their baggage for the rest of the trip through Germany and Italy, from where they sailed to New York.

Before they left on their honeymoon, Pickford and Fairbanks had set up a new production company they called United Artists. "I brought in D. W. Griffith as a third partner," said Pickford, "and Doug brought in his good friend Charlie Chaplin.

"The latter was a grave mistake. He had no head for finance and only rarely could we get him to attend company meetings. When we decided to hold one on his front lawn, to let him see how serious we were, he refused to come out of the house. But we could see him all the time peeping between some upstairs curtains. I got terribly frustrated with him. He wanted his share of the profits but never did a thing for the company.

"Gloria Swanson was allowed to buy some shares in the late twenties, but she got so fed up with Chaplin's behaviour that she sold the shares back to us. If I remember rightly, at fifty times what they had cost her. We weren't lucky with our partners. Mr. Griffith was winding down his career and many of his later films just didn't have the quality we needed so we had to distribute them through an offshoot company we formed.

"We formed United Artists because we wanted to have total control over all the films we made. Through United Artists we could produce, finance, and distribute not only our own films but others from independents who were producing movies up to the high standard we set for ourselves."

In 1923 Pickford paid the fare of a German director to the United States. "I saw some of his great German films and loved how he controlled his actors," she said. "So I invited him to direct me in *Rosita*. He didn't have the money for the fare so I advanced it for him. When he arrived he lived at Pickfair for several months, until the film was complete. He went on to become one of Warner Brothers' greatest directors. His name? Ernst Lubitsch, of course.

"Throughout the twenties and thirties Chaplin made *The Gold Rush, City Lights,* and *Modern Times.* I made successes like *Pollyanna* and *Tess of the Storm Country.* Doug's films included *Robin Hood* and *The Three Musketeers.* We sometimes took months planning and making a film. We had budgets and we stuck to them, but we never cut corners by building cheap sets or making costumes that were not of the best materials. It was a great time of my life. A lot of important people asked us to distribute their films, and we handled productions from Sam Goldwyn, David Selznick, Alexander Korda, and Walt Disney, yes, Walt Disney was making his cartoons as early as 1923."

In 1927 she made her final silent film, *My Best Girl,* with Sam Taylor directing. It wasn't the director who caught her eye, but a handsome young leading man Taylor had recommended for the role. Though neither Pickford nor her leading man, Charles "Buddy" Rogers, ever admitted it, gossip columnists said over the years that her romance with him began on the set of *My Best Girl.*

Rogers, who was an orchestra leader in addition to being a competent actor, never denied that he wrote a song, *My Best Girl,* and dedicated it to Pickford wherever he appeared with his band. Pickford is also reported to have scheduled many personal appearances she had to make to promote the film, to coincide with Rogers's band engagements.

If there was any disharmony in the marriage of the century, it was well hidden. But when Pickford's world came crashing down in 1928 Fairbanks was nowhere to be seen to comfort her. On March 21, her mother Charlotte died at age fifty-five. In her later years, friends reported, she had become quite erratic in her behaviour and towards the end Pickford had been forced to hire round-the-clock medical help to control her outbursts. She left in excess of $2 million, most of which went to Mary Pickford.

"Something that is not generally known," said Pickford in 1960, "is that Charlie Chaplin and I were once all set to co-star in a silent film called *Bread.* Adolph Zukor was to produce the film and I was to get $10,000 a week, which was just about twice what I was getting elsewhere at that time. But Chaplin said if I was to get $10,000 he wanted $20,000 and Mr. Zukor finally told him where he could put his film, so we never did get together in a movie.

"Perhaps that is not quite true. In Chaplin's *City Lights,* if you look very closely, you will see me in the background in a crowd scene. I was visiting the set and for the heck of it joined the extras. I believe I am on screen for three full seconds."

In 1929, Pickford made her debut in sound films. With Fairbanks she made *The Taming of the Shrew*, which is perhaps best remembered for its writing credits. It read, "By William Shakespeare, with additional dialogue by Sam Taylor." Mr. Taylor's addition cannot have been very good, because one critic claimed "Shakespeare was murdered and his murderer had the audacity to compound the crime by rewriting this revered author's lines. Miss Pickford is not shrewish at all, and was obviously tamed by the swashbuckling Fairbanks long before the film began."

But Pickford survived the critics' blasts, and made a second sound film in 1929, *Coquette.* Even though Pickford's trademark golden curls, which she had continued to wear although she was almost thirty-six, were bobbed, her performance was so good that it won her the coveted Academy Award for 1929. Although most of Pickford's early films have long since been destroyed, *Coquette* probably stands out as an example of why her fame continued long after her retirement.

(It is interesting to note that Pickford's Academy Award victory in 1929 was followed by two more Canadian-born actress winners, Norma Shearer in 1930, and Marie Dressler in 1931. This was a remarkable achievement when you consider the thousands of fine actresses from all over the world who were working in Hollywood movies at that time.)

One more sound film followed in 1931. Shakespeare's rewrite man, Sam Taylor, directed her in *Kiki*. Reviews were generally good for Pickford, although the film itself was not a financial success.

By the end of 1931 items in the gossip columns announced the break-up of the Pickford-Fairbanks marriage. Although Fairbanks was rarely seen around the Summit Drive mansion, it was not until 1935 that the official announcement came that they would be divorced.

In the spring of 1933, Mary Pickford entered a film studio to work for the final time. Frank Borzage and Pickford had gathered around her perhaps the greatest supporting cast of her life. *Secrets* featured England's romantic star, Leslie Howard, Aubrey Smith (shortly to become Sir C. Aubrey Smith), Blanche Frederick, Ned Sparks, Sam De Grasse, Ethel Clayton, and Bessie Barriscale.

The film was not a critical or commercial success despite its sterling cast and within months Mary Pickford announced her retirement from the screen.

The year 1933 was a rough one for her. Her farewell movie was panned, an added blow while she was still recovering from the death of her brother, Jack, who had died in sordid circumstances in a Paris hospital. Although she had spent almost all her working years keeping him out of trouble, and bailing him out when his financial problems grew around him, she always blamed herself for his problems.

"Jack was a talented actor, probably much more talented than me or Lottie, but he didn't seem to want to make himself into the star he could have been. I believe now that he knew several years before he died that his life span was to be short and he no longer had the will to work.

"He could have made a fine director if he had only concentrated more on what he was doing. The sad thing about Jack is that he pulled down so many other people when he fell to his final oblivion. Allan Dwan told me he could make Jack into a great director, but Jack wasn't interested. After working with Allan for just one film he thought he knew everything there was to know."

In 1980, Allan Dwan said, "Jack Pickford could never have made a good director or good anything else. I hate to contradict Mary, but I told her I wasn't prepared to work with him after we made *A Girl of Yesterday* in 1915. He was a useless nobody, a leech on his family since the day he was five, and a man who lived far too long in reaching thirty-six."

Sam De Grasse echoed Dwan's words. "Had there not been a death penalty at the time for murder, I and several hundred more people would gladly have shot him. I often wish one of us had the courage to do just that before he destroyed the lives of dozens of young girls who he infected with his vile disease.

"As an actor he was so-so. In *The Litte Shepherd of Kingdom Come* he showed signs of brilliance but there were too many other distractions and too much money available to him to make him buckle down to work. Douglas Fairbanks tried to control him but gave up in disgust. I have often felt that Mary's break-up with him was caused by her refusal to see that Jack needed discipline."

The Motion Picture Country Home in Woodland Hills, California, was founded by substantial donations from Mary Pickford and Louis B. Mayer. The Motion Picture Relief Fund, set up to help older performers in financial difficulties, was Pickford's great love after she retired. She raised millions of dollars and, again with Mayer, she provided the funding to start the drive for the Motion Picture Hospital that now stands alongside the country home.

In 1936 Pickford married her orchestra leader-actor, Charles "Buddy" Rogers. He moved into Pickfair and they became a popular couple at the film industry's important events.

Pickford tried her hand at writing. She published two books, *Why Not Try God* and *My Rendezvous With Life*. In 1936 she authored a novel, *The Demi Widow*, but there is no record that any of the three became big successes.

That same year her four-time married sister, Lottie, died following a heart attack. At the inquest it was said that she had been following in the footsteps of her mother, and had become irrational at times. She was only thirty-six. Some gossip columns hinted at suicide, but the inquest said it was a heart attack.

Pickford became tireless in her work for good causes. Whatever anyone asked her to do, she and Buddy offered their services. She produced two films with Jesse L. Lasky for United Artists release and was still vice-president of the company.

When CBS asked her to host a radio show she agreed, provided her fee was given to the Motion Picture Relief Fund.

Mary Pickford and Family, 1944: Ronnie, Buddy Rogers, Roxanne, and Mary.

In 1937 she and Buddy formed the Mary Pickford Cosmetic Company and launched a number of beauty products on the North American market. Unfortunately, she had left it too late. The name Pickford was not forgotten, but it hadn't the same sales power of a decade earlier. In late 1938 the company was wound up.

When the United States entered World War Two she threw open Pickfair to servicemen and women visiting Hollywood. Parties were held three and four nights a week. Mary attended every one, dancing with soldiers, sailors, airmen, and marines. In the quiet of the evening following the parties she would sit and reminisce of her days in motion pictures, the talks often going on until daylight streamed into the room. "Time for breakfast," she would say. Everyone present, usually just three or four, would pitch in to make a breakfast of scrambled eggs, sausage, bacon, toast, and coffee. Before the meal was over the guests realised that Mary and Buddy had slipped away and gone to bed.

In 1951 Stanley Kramer announced that he would star Mary Pickford in a film, *Circle of Fire*. Pickford, then fifty-eight years old but looking no more than thirty, appeared at the news conference with Kramer. Asked why she had decided to make a comeback, she snorted, "Really, I've never been away." And she added, "I want to appear in a Technicolor film at least once in my career. Mr. Kramer has given me the opportunity."

The film was never made. The Technicolor Corporation, which controlled every Technicolor camera in existence, refused to give Kramer a date on which he could have the camera he needed to satisfy Pickford. After six months of wrangling, the film was cancelled. Kramer made a simple announcement: "It has taken such a long time trying to get a camera commitment that Miss Pickford has lost interest."

In 1976 she made her last public appearance at the annual birthday party that had been a ritual at Pickfair since she and Fairbanks had moved in. She and Buddy agreed to be photographed with columnist May Mann, who had been trying for several years to convince her that people were still interested in her.

That same year the Academy of Motion Picture Arts and Sciences honoured her with a special award to commemorate her achievements in the industry. Until one day before the ceremony she was expected to attend the Oscar ceremonies, but had to back out at the last minute as she was said to be suffering from a severe cold.

But she did allow the television cameras into her home to record the presentation. She sat in her wheelchair in the large and opulent drawing room of Pickfair and said a few words of thanks in a trembling voice filled with emotion.

In 1978 surprise invitations went out from Mary and Buddy to 500 of the top people in the film industry. The invitation called it the "Last Great Hollywood Party." It wasn't to be free; guests accepting the invitation had to pay $1,000 for the privilege of visiting Pickfair for the last time. All the money was to go to the City of Hope charity, a project Pickford had supported over the years. Pickford and Rogers said they would pay for the cost of an orchestra for dancing, and all the drinks and food the guests could eat. In her final public gesture, Mary Pickford raised $500,000 for a very worthy cause.

But the guests who had expected to meet Pickford were to be disappointed. Buddy Rogers was there to greet them. He posed for pictures in front of a life-sized picture of Mary in the downstairs drawing room. He even conducted the orchestra and sang a few songs, later playing miniature golf with the guests on the immaculate lawns of Pickfair.

But Mary Pickford did not appear. She was, said Rogers, suffering from exhaustion. During the dining hour, her voice was heard over loud speakers that had been placed through the house and in the grounds. She thanked everyone for coming and regretted she was not well enough to greet them in person. No one ever found out if the message had been pre-recorded, or whether Mary was giving her last live performance.

Over the next year she was heard from less and less. She was reported by friends to be staying in bed all the time. Only people she knew would not talk about how she looked in those last days, were allowed into her bedroom to talk with her. She celebrated her eighty-sixth birthday with six carefully chosen guests. Buddy Rogers told everyone present that "Mary selected you because she enjoys your company."

Pickford spoke only a few sentences before falling asleep. Asked if she had any regrets in life, she smiled and answered: "Only one, that I never made a film with Clark Gable. My, he was so handsome." She looked through her thick-lensed glasses at Buddy, and added, "But not as handsome as you, my dear."

A month later she was dead. Though her fame was of generations earlier, obituaries made the front pages of the major newspapers around the world. The funeral service was private. Only family members were permitted to attend. The interment was in the Pickford family crypt in Forest Lawn Memorial Park. It is kept locked at all times and never opened to the thousands of visitors who each year ask permission to enter.

Buddy Rogers tried hard to keep Pickfair intact. He offered it to a number of charitable organizations for the sum of one dollar, complete with many of the treasures Pickford, Fairbanks, and Rogers had accumulated over the years. But the annual upkeep of the house and grounds, estimated at around $300,000, kept anyone from accepting the offer.

The Canadian government was urged to buy the house and turn it into a museum to tell the history not only of Pickford but all other Canadians who had been a part of Hollywood's glory, but declined. "We couldn't afford to keep it," said an aide to Prime Minister Trudeau.

The house was later purchased for $6 million by the owner of a sports arena in California. He sold it three years later for $10 million to actress/singer Pia Zadora and her husband, and in doing so erased the last traces of Mary Pickford's long reign in Hollywood.

Charles "Buddy" Rogers, then seventy-five, married a forty-year-old beauty one year after Pickford's death, and built himself a new, smaller home, on two acres of land that once were part of the Pickfair grounds. He lived there until his death at age ninety-four in 1999. It is reported that he still played golf every day until the last few months of his life and, with his new wife, was seen around town at all the best places until weeks before his death. "What I hate," he said in 1992, "is seeing people point at me and say in a loud whisper that can be heard a mile away, 'That's Mr. Pickford!'"

MARIE PREVOST

"It is unforgivable that she is not billed as the number one star of my film. Marie Prevost is one of the few actresses in Hollywood who know how to underplay comedy to achieve the maximum effect. She stole every scene in my film."

(Ernst Lubitsch, 1924)

Ernst Lubitsch, perhaps the greatest of the many competent film directors from Europe who made their way to Hollywood after World War One, did not endear himself to many with his comment. At the opening night party for *The Marriage Circle*, the stars with top billing on the film's posters were far from happy.

Jack Warner, whose Warner Brothers studio had financed the production, told Lubitsch very bluntly that he, and he alone, decided who were, and were not, the stars of any Warner production.

Adolphe Menjou, a very popular actor of the 1920s and 1930s, whose name was most prominent on the posters, told Lubitsch that he should remember it was the Menjou name that would bring the paying customers to the movie theatre box-offices.

Florence Vidor, another of the "top-billed" stars of the film, was so offended that she threw a drink in the face of Lubitsch and left the party in a huff.

Only Monte Blue, the handsome young male lead of *The Marriage Circle*, agreed with Lubitsch. "I think Marie is sensational," he said. "Working with her is like having a dream come true." To a visibly angry Jack Warner he added, "I hope you will see that she and I appear in many films together in the future." Years later Blue told a magazine writer that Warner made no reply before turning on his heel and leaving the party.

Lubitsch may have thought he was doing Marie Prevost a favor by pointing out that she had, as anyone who had seen the opening night of *The Marriage Circle* knew, indeed stolen every scene in which she appeared. Unhappily, history shows that it was from that day that her career began to go downhill.

Warner did not forget. Less than two years later, when her contract with his studio ended, he failed to pick up the option he held on her services for five more years. This, despite the fact that she had drawn critical acclaim for every role she played in the ten films she made under the Warner banner. Some of these were second-rate features that Warner had pushed her into, but however bad the film, Marie Prevost was continually praised by the public and film reviewers.

It was well known in the industry that her studio fan mail count was much higher than most of Warner's well-established stars of that era. When her success story was printed in a Hollywood trade paper, Warner took out a full-page advertisement in the next issue naming eight stars he claimed were more popular with the public than Marie Prevost.

Monte Blue was teamed with Prevost in three more films, but all were second-rate. Blue, like Prevost, found his option at Warner's was not picked up when the time came for renewal.

Blue's career also started to slide, and by the early 1950s he was reduced to playing a clown in a touring circus. In a 1954 interview with *Circus World* he spoke of his days as a well-respected and popular actor. "Warner Brothers studio destroyed the careers of many people," he said. "I vividly recall the lovely Marie Prevost, who could have been one of the world's great comedy stars. But Ernst Lubitsch said the wrong thing at the wrong time and embarrassed Jack Warner. Warner never forgot things like that. After he dropped her contract, he interfered with her career at other studios and finally drove her to oblivion. I, too, was destroyed by Warner. After leaving the studio I found many directors were afraid to hire me. Warner drove me to where I am today."

Marie Prevost was born Mary Bickford Dunn on November 8, 1898, in Sarnia, Ontario. There are many conflicting stories of her early days in Canada, most being the figments of imagination of different studio publicity writers.

Early Mack Sennett releases said she was of "Anglo-Irish" parentage, had a "French-Canadian" background, and, on one occasion, was of "Scottish-English" parentage. Her father, said Sennett, was "an amateur athlete of world class" and "a skier who had represented Canada at international meets." Her mother, said Sennett, was "a former ballerina" who taught her daughter "grace and poise." Universal studio releases said Mrs. Prevost was "an important business executive" who had taught Marie "her highly developed business sense to ensure she invested her earnings wisely."

Marie was, according to Sennett, "educated at a convent in Montreal, Canada," and it was there she achieved her "fluency in the French language." In fact, apart from a few phrases which Sennett, himself from Montreal, taught her to drop into conversations with journalists, she knew no French at all.

Although there is no record of her ever having visited Montreal, Warner's writers picked up on that angle, saying she was a champion swimmer in her home town in Quebec, Canada, and "still holds a number of Canadian diving records." Warner even had his prop department make up some phony gold medals for her to display to visiting journalists.

Universal obviously read the early Sennett "Scottish" story and told the world that Marie Prevost "is one of only a few who know how to prepare the Highlands delicacy, haggis, the well-kept secret of the Scottish nobility." It went on to say that she learned the secret "from her grandfather, the laird of a titled Scottish family."

All this might have been a little confusing had it not been for a number of stories published in the *Sarnia Observer*, stories that are still maintained on microfilm in the Sarnia Public Library. They tell how Marie Prevost (then Mary Dunn) lost her father when she was only six. Arthur (Teddy) Dunn, a railroad car conductor working for the Grand Trunk Railroad, died, along with five other railway workers, when gas seeped into the St. Clair Tunnel that ran from Sarnia, Ontario, to Port Huron, Michigan.

Mrs. Dunn, the former Marion Bickford, was left to look after Mary and her four-year-old sister, Marjorie (usually known as Peg). A report on the aftermath of the tunnel tragedy, printed a year after the accident, told how the Dunns had moved to Alameda, California, to join Mrs. Dunn's sister, Ethel. Mrs. Dunn had, said the story, "moved to give her family a better life." Working as a waitress in the evenings and washing and ironing laundry for wealthy Sarnia families in the area "had proved too much."

In a 1953 interview with the *San Francisco Chronicle*, Peg Dunn, then Mrs. Peg Halliday, said the family's life in Alameda "was wonderful. We attended St. Mary's School there and soon made new friends."

Both girls changed their surnames to Prevost when their mother went to live with a bank manager, Eric Prevost, in Los Angeles. Mary changed her name to Marie, said Peg, "because it sounded better with the name Prevost."

"Mr. Prevost was a wonderful man," said Peg, "and we were all very happy. Marie went into Manual Arts High School when we moved, and I joined her there two years later."

In 1913, when she was fourteen, Marie graduated with honors from high school. "Her excellent marks got her a good job as a clerk at a Los Angeles law firm," Peg recalled. "She worked there quite contentedly for three years until the day her life changed. It was the day she first visited a film studio.

"The law firm she worked for represented Mack Sennett in many financial matters, and one day in 1917, when Marie was just eighteen, she was asked to take a contract to the Keystone Studio in Edendale for Sennett's signature. Marie was waiting for Sennett when a fat man rushed over and pointed to Marie. "You," he said, "stand over here, and when I give you a signal run to the table over there and sit down on the chair. And remember to smile for the camera." Marie tried to protest, but the director, Ford Sterling, later to become more famous as one of Sennett's Keystone Kops, refused to take "no" for an answer.

"Marie did what she was told. Nobody bothered to tell her that the chair and table would collapse when she sat down. I saw the scene many months later and Marie just bubbled. All you could see when the chair and table gave way were her legs waving in the air. Sterling shouted that it was a good take and without saying another word stalked off into a nearby building. Marie, rather red-faced, brushed herself off and waited for Sennett to see her."

Sennett came down from the tower that he had built to oversee the entire studio lot, signed the contract, and handed it back to Marie who headed back to Los Angeles on a streetcar. "She told me she giggled all the way back," said Peg. "But she still had no thoughts of acting as a career. She thought her experience was fun, but that was the end of it."

Next morning Marie was called into the office of the law firm's senior partner. He looked serious. "I don't know what escapade you got up to yesterday," he said, "but you had better get back to Edendale immediately. Mr. Sennett says he needs you urgently."

"Marie was afraid she was going to lose her job," said Peg. "She sat poker-faced on the streetcar until she reached the studio, very frightened."

Marie Prevost told what happened next in an interview with the *Motion Picture World* in 1923. "I asked for Mr. Sennett and was ushered in right away. He looked very stern as I walked into his office. I was ready to cry. Suddenly, he smiled. 'I want your signature today,' he said. 'Sign right here.' I suddenly realized the paper he pushed in front of me was a contract. I was to be one of his Sennett Bathing Beauties. Best of all I was to be paid $15 a week. I signed without reading a word. Fifteen dollars was a lot of money."

"Mama was not very pleased when Marie arrived home and told her story," said Peg. "There were a few tears but Marie finally got her approval when Mr. Prevost said he thought the industry was a respectable one and Mr. Sennett an honourable man."

Two weeks later Mr. Prevost had a heart attack and died. Marie's $15 suddenly became very important. "Mama had to get a job in a flower shop and we had to move out of the bank house into a smaller home. It was a sad time and yet in memory it was a wonderful time because I was so glad for Marie," said Peg.

As one of Sennett's Bathing Beauties, Marie had little opportunity to show if she had any acting ability. "We took part in a different film every day," Marie told the *Motion Picture World*. "Usually we were just in the background, occasionally we were given small parts, but most of the time we were photographed romping around on the Venice beach, which was near Edendale."

Sennett first realized he had a potential star on his hands when he and the girls were "mugging" for the camera on Venice Pier. "He told us to do anything funny we could think of," Marie recalled. "He was dressed in a swimming costume, making faces, and generally adding to the scene. As I was one of the few Bathing Beauties who could swim and dive, he asked me to pretend to fall off the pier and wave my arms and legs until I hit the water. That didn't sound too funny to me so I pretended to slip and pushed him off the pier instead.

"Everyone looked horrified. They thought I'd be fired. But the camera kept rolling and when he climbed back on the pier he walked up to me and said, 'Marie, your salary is increased to $25 a week.' From then on I got lots of funny things to do in dozens of Keystone films."

Marie Prevost

In his autobiography, Sennett claims to have watched Marie do her "collapsing table and chair" routine from his tower. "When I saw those gorgeous legs waving in the air I knew I had another Bathing Beauty," he recalled. But he claimed not to realize the "legs girl" and the "girl with the contract from his lawyer" were one and the same until he saw, next morning, all the film that had been shot the previous day.

Whether this story is true or not is put in doubt by his memory of how the name Marie Prevost came into being. "I thought Mary 'G'unn [not Dunn] was no name for a beautiful girl," he said, "so I decided to call her Marie Prevost." Since the original contract with Marie is made out in her Prevost name and signed Marie Prevost, this memory of Sennett's seems not to ring true. "It is absolute rubbish," said Peg in a 1963 interview. "We had used the name Prevost for several years before Marie met Sennett. And she was Marie Prevost all through high school."

Shortly after Marie became a Sennett Bathing Beauty, he hired another girl from Manual Arts High School. Phyllis Haver and Marie had become great friends at school, and at the Sennett studio they became inseparable. There is nothing in files on Sennett at the Academy of Motion Picture Arts and Sciences in Los Angeles to suggest Marie had anything to do with the hiring of her friend, but Peg Halliday could never be convinced. "It was too much of a coincidence for it to happen without a push from Marie," she said.

Marie loved her stay with Sennett. "We had a lot of fun," she recalled in a 1925 interview. "Making comedies in those days was sheer enjoyment. The more crazy things we could invent the more Mr. Sennett loved it. He was a gentleman and a 'gentle man' at all times."

In 1919 Marie convinced Sennett to give her sister, Peg, a contract with Keystone. "It was nice of Marie," said Peg in the 1968 interview, "but I wasn't really interested. It was fun, but I didn't have the inventive mind that Marie had. I played a lot of small parts in Keystone comedies but I was glad when the contract expired. I think Sennett was glad when I told him I didn't want a new contract. I'm quite sure, by that time, he realized I had absolutely no talent."

Marie Prevost received her first fan mail after she made *Her Nature Dance* in 1917. The two-reeler gave her screen credits for the first time. "There had been lots of mail addressed to the Sennett Bathing Beauties, and occasionally some 'to the girl with curly hair who wore a bathing suit with stars on it' or something like that. But even if the studio could have identified us, all the mail went to a central office where secretaries sent out group photographs to the writers," she told *Photoplay* in an interview. "When the first letter came addressed to me I was so excited. I still have it and wouldn't part with it. In fact, I kept up a long friendship with the writer by mail, and only after four years did I discover he was sixty-eight, married, with seven children and six grandchildren. But it was a beautiful letter, that first one. You remember things like that."

Sennett, in his memoirs, called Marie Prevost "the most talented actress I ever discovered." In a later chapter he remembers vividly the day she came running to him in tears. It was 1919. "My husband has left me," she said. "Husband?" I said, "How can you have a husband? You aren't even married." "Yes, I am," she said. "I've been married six months and we haven't even had a honeymoon. Now he's left me."

When Sennett had calmed her down and got all the facts, he discovered she had been married secretly one night after a party to a socialite named Sonny Gerke. "I always called him Gerke the Jerky," said Sennett. "He must have been to leave a lovely girl like Marie."

Marie told her sister the full story of her marriage in 1924. "I should have realized what he was like," she said. "Immediately after the wedding he said he had to go home to his mother because she was expecting him. He promised to find a way to break the news to his mother before too long, but he never did."

In a 1954 interview, Sennett suggests that he, Marie, and the two witnesses at the wedding were the only ones who knew she was married. He added: "I suppose Gerke the Jerky must have had some idea, too!"

Marie told Sennett that Sonny had never dared tell his mother that he was married to an actress, much less a Sennett Bathing Beauty, and when she visited the Gerke family mansion in Los Angeles her occupation was never mentioned. So when Mrs. Gerke was out exercising her poodles one day and saw Marie being hauled out of a bar by what appeared to be police officers, she failed to see the camera hidden behind a truck, and immediately thought the worst. Returning home she told Sonny that Marie must never again darken their doorway. That was the end of the marriage. That night Marie received a phone call from Sonny telling her the marriage was over and she must never again contact him.

"Sonny couldn't get a divorce because his mother didn't know he was married and Marie was afraid to get one in case the publicity ruined her career," said Peg. "So they stayed married until 1923 when she wanted to marry Kenneth Harlan, an actor who had worked with her."

In 1919, Marie was offered a $750-a-week contract by William Randolph Hearst, who was assembling a group of players for his new

Cosmopolitan Production Company. "It seemed like a fortune," Marie told *Photoplay*, "but I didn't think I was ready. I had made nine films, all two-reelers, and here was Mr. Hearst talking about five- and six-reelers. I wasn't stupid enough to think I was as good an actress as others he had hired so I went to Mr. Sennett and asked for his advice. He said he would let me out of my contract if I wished, but felt I would be wise to wait until I had more experience. I told him I would turn Mr. Hearst down, so he immediately told me he was raising my salary to $250 a week."

Her contemporaries at Keystone at the time included Gloria Swanson, Bebe Daniels, Charlie Chaplin, and her good friend Phyllis Haver. Sennett's records show Swanson was earning $65 a week, Daniels only $45, Haver $125, and Chaplin, who had yet to create his "little tramp" character, took home $185.

In the *Photoplay* story Marie gave the following as an example of Sennett's refusal to waste not one single foot of film more than was absolutely necessary. "We were filming around a Hollywood pool when our prop man slipped and fell in," she said. "King Baggott, who was directing, was a good swimmer so he dived in to save the prop man, who was obviously drowning. Unfortunately, Baggott hit his head on the bottom of the pool and lay there unconscious. I have always been a good swimmer so I jumped in to get him to the surface while others rescued the prop man. It all ended happily. Baggott had a headache for a few hours, the prop man needed an hour to recover, and a few of us got very wet, but that was all. Next day, Sennett, when he heard what had happened, watched the rushes of the scene — camera operators always kept their cameras running — and rewrote the rest of the script so the rescue, which looked very funny, could be used in the film."

Sennett added more to the story many years later. "I was more than a little embarrassed when the story got out," he said. "Only a week earlier we had sent out a press release saying Baggott was a champion diver!"

Perhaps realizing that Prevost's days with Keystone were numbered, Sennett gave her the lead role in a 1919 five-reel comedy. *Yankee Doodle Dandy in Berlin*, subtitled *The Kaiser's Last Squeal*, was directed by Richard Jones. The film was a box-office success, and paved the way for her to leave Keystone for Universal Studios. Phyllis Haver had moved out a few months earlier, and Marie felt the atmosphere on the Sennett lot was no longer that of one big happy family.

"A lot of the fun had gone," she told *Photoplay*. "Now everything was ruled by money. Money was the bottom line and we no longer had the time to think up ideas or improvise. So when King Baggott, by then a major director, convinced Universal to offer me a thousand-dollar-a-week deal, I went to Mr. Sennett and told him it was time for me to move on. He was very kind. 'All my stars leave me eventually,' he said, perhaps a little wistfully. 'But I wish you well.'"

The majority of film histories of the silent era list Marie Prevost's first film away from Sennett as a comedy, The *Ole Swimmin' Hole*, at Universal. "That is quite incorrect," said Peg in 1968. "It was me who played the lead opposite Charles Ray in that film. It was my one and only big role and Marie got it for me as part of her Universal deal. Charles Ray, a fine actor, was very patient with me, but I really couldn't act. The film was a success mainly because of Mr. Ray. I wasn't offered any more roles and that was the end of my career."

Marie Prevost's first film at Universal was a romantic comedy, *Kissed*, in which she received top billing over Lloyd Whitlock, Frank Glendon, and Lillian Langdon, all big names in the 1920s and 1930s. The film established her as a star. Universal had to hire a special secretary just to answer Marie's mail and send out photographs that Marie signed in every spare moment between shooting.

Two more films directed by Baggott in 1921 cemented her popularity with audiences all over the United States. Every film she made was a moneymaker. Many years later, when Universal was rescued from near bankruptcy by the musical films starring Winnipeg-born Deanna Durbin, Carl Laemmle, Jr., son of the founder of Universal, told *the Los Angeles Times*: "So what else is new? Back in 1921 another Canadian girl did the same thing! Remember Marie Prevost?"

Apparently the reporter did not remember and figured his readers wouldn't either, because he added, as a footnote: "Marie Prevost was an actress in silent films who did not survive the move into sound. She committed suicide in 1939." He was wrong on three counts. She did survive to become a very successful performer in the sound era, she did not commit suicide, and she died in 1937.

Jack Warner had been watching her rise to fame at Universal, and when her two-year contract was due to expire he invited her to sign with Warner Brothers.

"Marie was, by this time, deeply involved with a young actor named Kenneth Harlan," said Peg in the 1968 interview. "Her final film at Universal, in 1922, was *The Flapper* in which she and Harlan played the leads. When Warner said he would sign both she and Harlan to $1,500-a-week contracts, Marie was delighted. The contracts were for two years and Warner's had an option for five additional years at $3,000 a week.

Jack Warner loved publicity. It never mattered to him whether the people he publicized knew what he was doing or whether the facts of the story were correct. All that concerned Warner was that another of his stars was in the headlines. When Prevost and Harlan arrived at the studio and requested side-by-side dressing rooms, Warner decided he had a story to tell. "They will be married on the set of *The Beautiful and the Damned*," he announced. The public loved the story. Thousands of letters and hundreds of gifts for the "bride and groom" arrived at the studio. Warner was in seventh heaven. Until the bombshell landed!

MARIE PREVOST WILL BE A BIGAMIST
IF SHE MARRIES KENNETH HARLAN

This was the headline in the *Los Angeles Mirror* that faced Jack Warner when he arrived at the studio. The story told of Marie's 1918 wedding.

An irate Warner called Marie into his office for an explanation. Her story failed to pacify him. Despite the fact that the wedding publicity story was his own creation, he fired the publicist he had made write the story. He threatened to cancel the contracts of both Marie and Harlan, but wiser and calmer studio lawyers made him withdraw this threat. They pointed out that Warner himself was totally responsible for the bad publicity.

No one ever discovered who tipped the *Mirror* to the wedding, but Peg Halliday is convinced it was Mack Sennett. "He was like an old woman at times," she said. "If he was peeved at something or someone he would react like a jilted suitor."

When he calmed down, Warner pulled a lot of strings to get the Prevost-Gerke marriage annulled quickly. The fuss soon died down and the moralists who had deluged newspaper editors with letters were silenced. The wedding of Prevost and Harlan did take place, but it was not the big event that Warner had planned.

Sonny Gerke never became involved in the divorce, which was granted on the grounds of desertion. He and his family had left Los Angeles several years earlier and "Marie believed they were living in Europe," said Peg.

For two years the marriage was happy. The couple bought a large home on seven acres of land in the Hollywood Hills. Their careers continued to rise despite Warner's resentment of everything they did that was successful.

Marie Prevost (left), Ford Sterling, and Mae Griffin.

Frustrated, he announced cancellation of several films scheduled for Prevost and Harlan. Harlan was given inferior parts on the Warner lot and Marie was offered to small studios on a loan basis.

"Marie was devastated," said Peg Halliday. "Warner refused to talk to her or Harlan. She was given no part in the selection of scripts, no control over who was to star with her, or which studio she was to be loaned to. It became an effort for her to go to work. What had been fun was now almost torture."

Despite her fears, Marie's success continued. *Red Lights*, produced by Sam Goldwyn for Hearst's Cosmopolitan Studio, brought her so much mail that she had to hire two secretaries to cope with the avalanche. *The Wanters*, another big success, produced by Louis Mayer at First National, was so annoying to Warner that he recalled her to the Warner lot and ordered Ernst Lubitsch, in a memo, to "give her something to do that won't create such a fuss."

But *The Marriage Circle*, written by Paul Bern, gave her a chance to succeed beyond all her wildest dreams. Warner was furious when he came back from a four-week overseas vacation to find the film was tailor-made for Marie. Lubitsch said many years later that "Warner threatened to fire me, fire Bern, fire everyone. It made me doubt his sanity when he announced he was going to burn every reel of the film. We talked him out of that, but he used to stand in the shadows of the set and if Marie made a good take he would send his secretary over to me to demand I shoot the scene again. I did what he said, of course, but it was always the best take I used. He had a wonderful star and he wanted to destroy her career."

It was the scene at the first night party for *The Marriage Circle* that probably dictated the rest of her career. "Warner sent her to Principal Pictures, a very small production company, for a run-of-the-mill drama, and followed this with three more badly scripted films," said Peg. "But Sam Goldwyn, who didn't like Warner, fooled him. He sent Warner a third-rate script with the title *Tarnish*. When Warner saw how poor it was he agreed it was ideal for Marie, and the contract was signed. Goldwyn then produced the real script, a blockbuster by writer Frances Marion. Warner was furious but could do nothing and Marie had another big hit."

Lubitsch, solidly entrenched at Warner's by the profitable films he was making, told Jack Warner that he intended to star Marie in two more films, *Three Women*, with Ronald Colman, and *Kiss Me Again*. When Warner refused, Lubitsch pointed out that his contract gave him the right to select any Warner contract player for his films.

Three Women is still acclaimed as one of Lubitsch's finest films. It made Marie Prevost a major box-office attraction.

Although Warner received $5,000 a week for her services from Sam Goldwyn and other studios, he refused to hand over one extra cent to Marie. "Your contract says $1,500," he said in a memo. "And that is what you will get."

In 1926 Marie and Kenneth Harlan were both advised by Warner that he did not intend to pick up their options. Phyllis Haver told a fan magazine in 1937 she believed this rejection caused the first rift in the Prevost-Harlan marriage, and this was the trigger that led to Marie's downfall. "In 1927 Harlan was drinking and staying out all night," she said. "He lost thousands of dollars gambling and more than once forged Marie's name to a cheque when he ran out of money in his own account."

Harlan was one of the few actors who fought and beat Warner's blacklist. He moved into sound with ease and retired in 1940 a wealthy man. In the eleven years that followed his divorce from Prevost, Harlan went through six more marriages and six more divorces. He later operated a theatrical agency and owned and operated a very popular Hollywood restaurant.

In November 1927 Marie was shocked to hear of her mother's death in a New Mexico car accident. "Mama and actress Vera Steadman were driving from Los Angeles to Florida to see me, as my husband and I were living there at the time," said Peg Halliday. "Al Christie, who owned, with his brother Charles, the Christie Studios, offered to drive them across country as he had to oversee some shooting plans in Jacksonville. The accident was nobody's fault. The axle broke and the car crashed. Vera and Al were not badly hurt. Mama died instantly. Marie took this as just one more slap in the face from a cruel world."

Two weeks before Christmas, Marie was again in shock. "She was driving to a friend's home for dinner when a young girl walked in front of her car," said Peg. "She was able to put on the brake and the girl was only bruised, but for a year she wouldn't drive. When she had to go to the studio she went by streetcar. Imagine, earning more than a thousand dollars a week, riding on a streetcar!"

In 1929 Marie filed for divorce from Kenneth Harlan. The news media had a field day. Marie was in the headlines, but in a way she didn't like.

"Only one good thing came out of the court hearings," said Peg. "A witness brought in by Marie's lawyer to explain why she was never at home, as Harlan had alleged, told how Marie spent most evenings, many nights, and every day when she wasn't filming, working as an unpaid nurses' aide at a Los Angeles hospital."

Nurse Evelyn Walker said, "She was there from eight in the morning to ten at night whenever she wasn't wanted at the studio. She did every job she was asked, no matter how dirty or disagreeable. Few of the patients knew who she was but everyone loved her. We called her 'the angel.' She told me helping others helped her forget her own troubles."

Harlan, who did not attend the hearings, or contest the divorce, perhaps read in the papers that the judge, in granting the divorce, called him "a cruel, uncaring, and uncivilized man."

Marie consoled herself with work at the studio and the hospital. Her best friend, Phyllis Haver, now only rarely making films, had time to help her get through the tough times.

But this major prop in her life was removed late in 1929 when Haver married a New York millionaire and left Hollywood for good. "For several years they kept in touch," said Peg, "but making films kept Marie busy and Phyllis seemed so happy in her marriage that the two just drifted apart. It was the beginning of the sound age in Hollywood and Marie, like others, wondered how the public would react when they heard her voice. She saw many old friends released from their contracts by the studios, and she knew her own career was slipping. She made only three films after the divorce and these were with independent companies."

It was Cecil B. DeMille who came to her rescue. He planned to make *The Godless Girl* in 1929 as his first venture into sound film. The list of stars signed was impressive, including Noah Beery, Eddie Quillan, Dick Alexander, Lina Basquette, and George Duryea. "One day the phone rang in her home," said Halliday. "It was DeMille. 'I've been trying to find you,' he said. 'I have a fine role for you in my new film. Are you available?' Of course she was thrilled and DeMille was so delighted with her performance that he blew up her role. She got nine weeks work at $2,000 a week. Her voice came through extremely well. It was a major film, a twelve-reeler, and the reviewers singled her out and praised her role as a reformatory prisoner."

Two more films came along the same year, *The Flying Fool* and *Divorce Made Easy*. But the parts were getting smaller and the money she received was getting less with each film.

By 1936 Marie was existing on handouts from friends. She had sold the home she bought in Malibu after her divorce and moved into a small apartment at 6230 Afton Place, close to the Hollywood studios.

"I wrote her several times in 1936 but never got anything more than a brief postcard in reply," said Halliday. "She sent me a card at Christmas with a note telling me to go and see her latest film, *13 Hours By Air*. I did go, but was shocked to find she had only a tiny part as a waitress in one scene. Not even a speaking part. I told my husband we should drive down to see her in the new year and I wrote asking when would be a good time to visit."

The Hallidays never did receive a reply. And they never again saw her alive. On January 23, 1937, Harry Jenks, manager of the apartment block in which Marie lived, received a number of complaints from other tenants that Marie's dog had been barking for hours. He found a note on the door that read: "Please do not knock on this door more than once as it makes my dog bark. If I am in, I will hear you. I am not deaf."

When his repeated knocks were unanswered, and the dog continued to bark, the manager used his passkey to open the door. Getting no answer when he called he looked in the bedroom. "There she was," said Jenks, "lying face down on the bed. I touched her and she was very cold, so I called a doctor at once."

The newspaper headlines next day screamed "Silent Star Suicide." But this was quickly toned down when an autopsy suggested she had simply starved herself to death trying to get her weight down to a level producers would accept.

An undelivered promissory note was found on a table beside her bed. It read: "Joan Crawford, I.O.U. $100. Thank You. Marie Prevost." It was dated January 21, 1937.

Joan Crawford gave a brief statement to reporters. "We were good friends," she said. "She had only to ask and I would gladly have given her help, money, or other assistance that she needed. She was a wonderful friend and a great comedy actress."

Phyllis Haver, unable to reach Los Angeles from her New York home in time for the funeral, told the *New York Times* that she was "shocked and saddened. I had no inkling of her need. I am ashamed to say that after my marriage I isolated myself from those who mattered most."

A magazine story some months later revealed that she had sent 1,000 red roses to the hospital in which Marie had continued to work as a volunteer. "They are to be distributed to those persons in the hospital who have no flowers and few friends with a card saying they came from Marie Prevost," she said.

In addition, she sent $5,000, asking that a room be named after Marie and the money used to buy whatever equipment was needed to make older people in the hospital more comfortable.

A brief graveside ceremony was all Peg Halliday wanted for her sister, but Joan Crawford, who had purchased the cemetery plot and had paid for all costs of the funeral, had different ideas. "I offered to pay," said Peg in 1968, "but she wouldn't consider it. She seemed to think she was in some way responsible for Marie's death and was inconsolable. She had to halt shooting for two weeks because she was too distraught to be on the set."

The funeral at Hollywood Memorial Cemetery, from which all press were excluded, drew many of the film community's elite. "They were all there," said Peg Halliday. "Joan, of course, and Barbara Stanwyck, Mack Sennett, King Baggott, Douglas Fairbanks Jr., Franklin Pangborn, Lewis Milestone, Wallace Beery, Clark Gable, Andy Devine, Ralph Bellamy, Fred MacMurray, Robert Young, Mervyn LeRoy, and so many more that I can't remember. But where were they when she needed them? And where was I?"

Marie's gravesite is marked with a simple bronze plate bearing her name and date of birth and death. Few stop to read it. Very few of today's tourists who flock daily to the cemetery even remember her name.

The vaults of Hollywood film studios probably contain prints or negatives of many of the films in which Marie Prevost appeared. Only three have been considered worthy of release on videocassette. *The Marriage Circle*, the Lubitsch silent that angered Jack Warner in 1924, is available for film buffs. So are two sound films, *The Flying Fool*, in which she starred with William (Hopalong Cassidy) Boyd in 1929, and *The Sin of Madelon Claudet*, which won Helen Hayes an Oscar in 1931.

The home in which she lived in Sarnia was pulled down years ago to make way for widening of the road. But the apartment block in which she died in Hollywood is still standing. Today's tenants are either young performers looking for that elusive break, or older actors who have dropped out of the limelight.

There is an interesting footnote to the Marie Prevost story. In 1977, when evaluators were listing the contents of the home of Joan Crawford, who had died several weeks earlier, a locked box, when opened, was found to contain hundreds of IOUs from more than twenty different Hollywood personalities of the past who had fallen on hard times. Crawford, often maligned in news stories and later in a book written by her own daughter, had quietly handed out more than $50,000 to performers in need. Thirty of the IOUs, totalling more than $3,000, were signed by Marie Prevost!

Mack Sennett

"Mack Sennett had a feeling for comedy that has never been equalled. He knew precisely what the audiences in those early days wanted. Unhappily, his inability to sense the subtle changes that were taking place in public tastes, led to his downfall. If we could have had only silent movies forever he would still be the world's King of Comedy today."

(Charlie Chaplin, 1956)

Ironically, only eleven years after making his comment about Mack Sennett's inability to keep up with the public's needs, Chaplin made a similar statement about himself. Two sound films, *A King in New York* and *Countess from Hong Kong*, which he made in England after his exile from the United States, were failures at the box office.

"I should have learned how to change with the times," he told the London *Daily Mail*. "I had some of the finest actors in the world [Marlon Brando, Sophia Loren, Margaret Rutherford] at my command in these films but I didn't know what to do with them when words counted more than actions!"

Silent films where actions counted more than words were also Mack Sennett's forte. No one ever disputed his ability to produce the best comedy films when slapstick was the thing. More than 1,000 silent films, mostly one- and two-reelers that lasted only ten or twenty minutes, bore his name in the credits. He also made many two- and three-reel sound films, and a few full-length features. Some of these longer films were successful but most, unfortunately, were not.

Certainly no one today can question Sennett's ability to unearth potential talent. Chaplin said many times that it was Sennett's wisdom and vision of what might be that took him out of Fred Karno's British revue, *A Night in a London Music Hall*, touring the United States in 1912. It was at Sennett's Keystone Studio in Hollywood where Chaplin made his first thirty-five short films and where he created the "tramp" character that became his trademark for more than four decades.

The list of stars, of both silent and sound eras, given their first opportunity by Sennett can be gauged from this partial list of former Sennett discoveries who attended a party he gave, in 1932, to celebrate his twentieth year in Hollywood. Those present included actors Edgar Kennedy, Wallace Beery, Chester Conklin, Slim Summerville, Harry Langdon, Bing Crosby, W. C. Fields, Louise Fazenda, Monte Blue, Mae Busch, Eddie Quillan, Oliver Hardy, Stan Laurel, Edna Purviance, Gloria Swanson, and Charlie Chaplin.

Directors and producers present, who learned their trade under Sennett's guidance, included Lloyd Bacon, Eddie Cline, Wallace McDonald, Del Lord, Frank Capra, Roy Del Ruth, and Eddie Sutherland.

But when Sennett died at the age of eighty, in 1960, he had spent most of his last ten years living alone in a small apartment overlooking Hollywood Boulevard. Only occasionally did a few of the friends he had made in his days of glory pay him a visit.

Mack Sennett was born Michael Sinnott, in Danville, a small town close to Montreal, Quebec, on January 17, 1880. His father was the manager of a small hotel. His great grandparents had emigrated from Ireland a century before Sennett was born. His mother, he used to tell people proudly, provided the rich people of Danville with the "finest and whitest laundry in all of the Province of Quebec."

His education was far from being as limited as many writers have suggested in magazine articles and biographies over the years. He graduated from school at sixteen, top of his class, with honours in mathematics and English. "I was quite a whiz at chemistry, too," he said. "In fact, when I left school I had two ambitions. One was to be a research chemist. The other was to be a singer."

He never pursued the first dream, but by seventeen, although his speaking voice was normal for a boy his age, his singing voice was a robust bass, and he was often featured as a soloist in church and other choral groups around the

Mack Sennett with his mother.

Montreal area. "There was such a dearth of entertainment in Danville that we quite looked forward to one of the old-timers of the town dying," he said. "The wake could sometimes last a week and I always got to sing."

His second dream received a boost when his father received a lucrative job offer from a construction company in East Berlin, Connecticut. "I have never been quite sure what his qualifications as a hotel manager had to do with building, but he got the offer and we moved."

"I think everybody sang in East Berlin," he told *Film Weekly* in 1928. "I was in big demand with my bass voice. So I renewed my dream of becoming not only a professional singer, but a professional singer in opera, perhaps even at the Metropolitan Opera House."

But singing at concerts and in choral groups wasn't making any money for the Sennett (Sinnott) family, so he found another job. "I was over six feet tall, weighed 220 pounds, so where do you think the labour exchange sent me? Where else but the American Iron Works in East Berlin, where I quickly learned to move iron castings, which weighed two hundred pounds, from place to place. I also learned not to go too close to the smelting areas. I still have scars on my hands to show where I got burned," he said.

In East Berlin Sennett got a big boost for his operatic ambitions. The family purchased a large house so that his mother could take in boarders. "We had six or seven at a time and one of these boarders was a big contrast to the rough labourers who were the standard fare. The little man who arrived at our door one evening and stayed until we left town introduced himself as Signor Fontana. He wore a frock coat and, on occasions, a top hat. I earned his undying gratitude when I used my size and weight to stop the other boarders from kicking his hat around the room."

Signor Fontana turned out to be a vocal coach. "I imagine his real name was Joseph Brown, or something like that," said Sennett. "But it didn't matter to me what he was called when he offered me free voice lessons in exchange for free meals. We couldn't rehearse in the house because of the other boarders. I should mention that my bass voice when fully let loose is something rather like a bull moose in heat. So we went into the woods away from the houses and I received my first training there."

Rehearsals had to be moved to the local church hall when Sennett and Fontana heard rumours that some of the locals were planning a moose hunt in the woods near the town. "One of the boarders said they had heard several times the call of a female moose and where there was a female there must be a male."

The church hall belonged to the Baptists of the community, much to the dismay of Sennett's parents. "We were good Roman Catholics," recalled Sennett. "And to step foot in even a Baptist Church hall at that time was enough to get the entire family thrown out of our regular Sunday place of worship. Fortunately, we had a very understanding priest who agreed I could train in the Baptist building if he was permitted to say a few prayers in the hall to ensure my soul wouldn't go you know where."

The Sennett (Sinnott) family moved to Northampton, Massachusetts, in 1900. "We had a bit of money saved from the boarding house, my foundry work, and my father's construction job, so he decided on the move because he had a chance of a partnership in a contracting firm there. I wasn't aware at the time that Signor Fontana was eagerly pushing for the move. He had quietly told my mother, perhaps rather sarcastically, that 'Michael needs a much more experienced coach than me if he is to sing at the Met.'"

Years later the priest from East Berlin, visiting Hollywood at the invitation of Sennett's mother, told him, "The good signor told me his ear drums were bursting from your bellows and he would be totally deaf if he had to listen to your singing much longer. And I fully understood, Michael. You will recall that we had to place you on a platform in the church, slightly higher than the rest of the choir. That was because so many of our singers were reporting constant earaches after the services. So we solved that by letting your voice rise gently, if that is the correct word, over their heads."

Sennett said that the remark was one of the most upsetting he had ever experienced. "Thank you, father," he told the priest. "I thought I was being chosen to stand out because my voice was so magnificent."

In Northampton Sennett chose the Northampton Iron Foundry as a place of employment. It may well have been the most important move in his career. "The manager of the foundry was also a part-time actor in one of the local amateur companies," he said. "He used to rehearse his lines in the lunch break and he would ask any of us around at the time to read the lines of the other characters. I enjoyed playing the different roles and one day he invited me to join him at the theatre, where they were casting for the next play."

Before he knew it, Sennett was on stage playing role after role in everything from comedy to melodrama.

"I loved every minute of it," he said. "I soon found myself playing the lead comedy parts. I learned the art of timing my lines in that little theatre.

"In the melodramas I rarely got a line unless it was as a butler announcing a guest. Even then the audiences laughed because it came naturally to me to create bits of business that weren't in the script. The director encouraged me, and the audiences liked my style so well that week after week I got a round of applause when I made my first entrance in a play, often before I'd said a word."

Sennett was quick to point out that it was an amateur company and no one got paid. "We always got full houses for the plays," he said. "There was only one other place of entertainment in the town, the Academy Theatre, where sometimes the shows were first class, more often than not they were third-rate. We often outdrew the professionals at the box office, but that may have been something to do with our prices. Our top was 15 cents, compared to the Academy's dollar or even $1.50."

The money taken at the door was used to provide summer picnics for local children. "We spent a few bucks on a party at the end of each play, but most of the money went where it was needed most," he recalled. "I used to dress up as a clown and go to the summer picnics. I shall never forget the looks of delight on the faces of the children when I made them laugh."

In 1902 a chance encounter with one of the most renowned entertainers of the day led him to the start of a career in New York. "Marie Dressler, who had been appearing on Broadway for several years, was on a national tour with one of her plays, *Lady Slavey,* when she was booked into the Academy Theatre," he said. "You can judge her importance from the fact that her play was advertised as staying two weeks. Most of the companies staying only one week had to provide a different play every second night."

Sennett was playing the lead in a very funny play when he heard an unusual noise from the audience. "I thought I had a loud voice but all through the play I could hear a raucous laugh high above all the others coming from the back of the theatre. It was so infectious it had everyone else roaring with laughter and I had the most successful night of my amateur career.

"I asked one of the company to see who this loud-voiced person was, and he came back and said, 'You're never going to believe it, Mike. It's Marie Dressler from the Academy Theatre show.' I was stunned. Marie Dressler, laughing at me? She was only the best comedienne in the country at that time. I had heard that the Academy was having heating problems and might have to close for a day while the trouble was fixed, but I never dreamed Marie Dressler would come to see our little show. I couldn't imagine I'd ever meet her, but after the final curtain came down she came backstage and asked to meet me. Me, can you imagine? She asked to meet me.

"I was rather overwhelmed by the presence of the great actress, but she quickly put me at ease. 'You gave a wonderful performance,' she said. 'Have you ever considered becoming a professional actor?' I told her I hadn't, but I would from that day on. She handed me her calling card. On the back she wrote the name and New York address of one of Broadway's most important producers, David Belasco. 'Go and see him,' she said. 'Tell him I sent you. Tell him I want him to find you work in the professional theatre.' On the front she had written, 'This will introduce my friend, Mack Sennett.' That's how she must have heard my name when she asked who the comic in the play was. I didn't like to tell her she had my name wrong. I figured I could tell Mr. Belasco if I ever got to meet him."

The young Northampton lawyer who accompanied her to the show handed over his business card and urged Sennett to let him read any contracts before he signed them. "When I saw the name on the card I realized it was the man everyone was suggesting would be the next mayor of the town. When I was ready to have him read my contracts he was no longer in business as a lawyer, having become the governor of Massachusetts. He went on from there to become the president of the United States. His name was Calvin Coolidge."

Dressler gave Sennett a great big smile, kissed him on the cheek, and wished him well. "Then she swept away with all the majesty and dignity only a really big star, like she was, could exhibit," he said. "Let me tell you something, all my life I've remembered that exit and longed to make just one, somewhere, sometime, like it. But I never will now. Every exit I make has to have a pratfall in it so the audiences will laugh."

Dressler's visit had Sennett hooked. Two weeks later he told the foundry manager he was leaving to try for fame and fortune on the Broadway stage. "Everyone wished me luck, even gave me the door take from the last night of our show. I can't remember, but I think it was about ten dollars. I'd saved about thirty more, so I headed for New York."

David Belasco was out of New York when Mike Sinnott, soon to be Mack Sennett for the rest of his life, arrived at his office three weeks later. "I'll make you an appointment to see Mr. Belasco next week, Mr. Sennett," said his friendly receptionist. "If Miss Dressler sent you I know he'll want to meet you." And she added, "Mr. Sennett, if you don't mind my suggesting this, I think you should buy a new suit for the interview. Mr. Belasco likes his actors to be well dressed."

Sennett spent a few dollars from his meagre savings as the receptionist suggested. "I even went to a first-class barber, close to the theatrical boarding house where I had found a room, and got myself a real stage haircut. When I looked at myself in one of the store windows on 42nd Street I felt I was already on my way to becoming a Broadway star.

"One of the actors in the house where I was staying, a gruff-looking character actor, brought me down to earth with a bump when he looked me over and told me my Massachusetts shoes just weren't good enough for Broadway. I must have looked a little taken aback, for I was already running rather low on funds. I'm sure he could tell. 'Here,' he said. 'I've got a spare pair. You can have them.'"

Sennett recalled retiring to his own room to put on the shoes. "I had to get away," he said. "I was so overwhelmed by his generosity that tears were streaming down my face."

Mack Sennett was to meet up again with his benefactor some fifteen years later in Hollywood and was able to repay the kindness without the actor ever realizing that he had met Sennett before in New York.

Sennett kept his appointment with Belasco. The renowned producer looked him over. "Miss Dressler says you are a good comedy actor," he said. "She has impeccable taste, so I must believe her. But I think you need some solid grounding in the art of comedy before you will be ready for Broadway."

"He directed me to the burlesque houses that were plentiful in New York at that time. I had never seen burlesque, didn't have any idea what it was, but presumed that if it was endorsed by Mr. Belasco it had to be legitimate. So I went to the Bowery Burlesque Theatre and had my eyes opened. If this was New York theatre I could be a star very quickly. In fact, I could even teach the comics a thing or two!"

Sennett returned to his boarding house and buttonholed several of the residents. "How do I get into burlesque?" he asked. "Easy," said one haughty actor, "you lower your standard of morals to theirs, you walk in the stage door, trip over the stage door keeper's outstretched leg, and when you get up there'll be someone waiting to give you a contract."

"It was quite a while before I realized he was just being sarcastic and couldn't possibly imagine why anyone would sink low enough to want to be in burlesque," he said. "But I had enjoyed what I saw. The comics were funny. The 'bump-and-grind' strippers were appealing, though rather fat. But I just couldn't understand why the sopranos and tenors were booed. To me they sounded quite good enough to be at the Metropolitan Opera House."

One story Sennett told that never varied over the years is the tale of his New York debut. "I found out where the Bowery Burlesque actors ate and haunted these places, picking up bits of conversation and quite a few new friends who were not unhappy when someone bought them a sandwich and coffee. I was getting down to my last few dollars when one of my new friends told me there was a job opening at the Bowery. I raced over to the theatre and asked for the man my friend said could give me a part in the next week's show.

"He told me they were looking for a dumb-looking character who would walk across the stage several times each show brushing imaginary dirt off the floor. I used my deepest voice when he asked me to try out my one line. It got me the job. I had to say, looking at the audience, 'and they call this a one-horse town.' I was astounded how the audience loved the line so I started adding bits of business to my character. After I'd said my line I pretended to trip over some invisible horse droppings and did a somersault into the wings. When they applauded I sneaked back and showed my head around the scenery. How many other people can say they stopped the show in their New York debut?"

The second week was rather a letdown for Sennett. "The only thing they had for me was the hind end of a horse," he recalled in 1943. "I needed the money so I got dressed up every night for the role. Even though my face was never seen I joined the rest of the gang in the big dressing room every night before the show and put on my make-up. Why not! I was in the professional theatre."

Unfortunately for Sennett, his second week in the "big time" was the week the police decided to raid the Bowery Burlesque Theatre. "Every last one of us was herded into paddy wagons and away we went to the police station. They kept us in cells all night without charging us. Next morning we were called up before the judge. He listened to the evidence of police officers who had obviously been thoroughly enjoying the show since they didn't raid us till the final curtain came down. The strippers were fined a dollar or two. Some of the comics were fined for 'lewd jokes.' But when I arrived in the dock in my horse's-ass costume the judge was obviously rather bewildered."

"And what do you do for a living?" he said.

"I'm an actor," I replied. "A character actor, sir."

"And what character are you supposed to be in that get-up?" he asked.

"I'm part of an animal, sir," I said.

"What part of what animal?" he asked.

"The ass-end of a horse, sir," I said.

"Now make up your mind, Mr. Sennett. Are you an ass or a horse?" he enquired.

"A horse's ass-end," I replied.

Sennett always swore that he saw a glimmer of a smile on the judge's face, and decided to play the moment for all it was worth.

"Actually, I'm going to be an opera singer, sir," I said.

"I can't quite see the point in this type of training," said the judge, "but then I have never been to the Bowery Theatre."

To the arresting officer he said, "Is there any evidence that this man spoke lewd or indecent lines on stage?"

"No, sir," said the officer, "but he did fart twice rather loudly during his second on stage appearance as the horse."

"Could you distinguish, officer, between the front and rear ends of a horse, and which of the two actors expelled the air?"

"Well," said the officer, "not really, sir. It's simply my judgement."

"I'm afraid your judgement isn't enough to convict this man," said the judge. "Not guilty," he said, and added, "If I were you, Mr. Sennett, I would try to find a more suitable place in which to enhance my singing career. Case dismissed." Sennett later swore the judge winked at him as he left the dock.

Sennett's ventures into the world of burlesque kept the wolf from the door. "I had to eat," he said, "and if it meant doing pratfalls on the burlesque stages that were plentiful in New York at the time, I never argued and in fact learned a lot of stage tricks I used many times later in films. A lot of great comics came out of burlesque, as did so many of the great comedy routines. Some of them will last as long as there is any comedy left in the world."

At this stage in his career Mack Sennett was still determined to become an opera singer. When he had a few dollars saved up he used it on singing lessons. "More than one studio threw me out," he recalled in 1943. "I was loud, I admit, but to throw me out without giving me my money back, that hurt."

In 1906 he said farewell to his dreams of becoming a vocal star. "I was in a Professor Valmar's studio one day and heard him finishing his tuition of another singer. I listened and was bewitched by the superb tone and range of this unknown tenor. When the professor came out to me I commented on the magnificence of his earlier pupil's voice. It was, I said, surely good enough to have won him a place in the Metropolitan Opera Company. 'No,' said the professor. 'As a matter of fact he works every night in a restaurant, just off Broadway, as a singing waiter.'

"It was at that moment I decided to abandon my voice training. If he, with a voice like that, could reach no greater heights than a cafe, what hope had I?"

For two years Sennett stayed in the world of burlesque. "Frank Sheridan, who ran a touring burlesque show, gave me my first chance to become a real comedian. I was allowed to put my own ideas into well-worn skits and before I knew it I was actually writing comedy skits of my own," said Sennett. "I travelled with Sheridan's Burlesque company as far west as Chicago before we headed back east. I dreaded the day when we would reach Boston. I knew all my relatives would all be there to see me perform. By now I had convinced them, in my letters, that I was a big star. I dreaded what they would think."

The day finally arrived. "Before we opened in Boston I asked Frank if he could tell all his comics to play down the crude jokes just for one night, and ask his 'bump-and-grinders' not to be quite as suggestive in their movements as usual. I even rewrote my own skits to take out anything that might offend my family," he recalled.

Everyone co-operated but the audience. They sat on their hands and there wasn't a single belly laugh that night. "My own skits went totally flat," Sennett remembered. "I waited after the show for my family to come back stage, but no one arrived. Oh, my, I thought, has even this tame show offended them? I went back to my theatrical boarding house almost in tears."

Next night the word went out from the theatre management to Frank Sheridan. "No more white-washed shows," they said. "We won't have an audience by Saturday if you put Monday's show on again tonight."

"So we all went back to our regular routines, and the audience laughed and cheered everything we did. After the final curtain I went off stage and was stunned to find my parents and sister waiting for me. For a minute I was horrified at what they must be thinking. Then my mother spoke. 'Michael,' she said. 'That was surely the funniest show we have ever seen. We have never laughed so much in our lives. And those beautiful dancing girls [the bump-and-grinders] were so delightful. You must have a very difficult job deciding which one to choose as your girlfriend.'"

Sennett said he was relieved when his parents left to go home to Northampton. "I kept waiting for the bubble to burst or that I'd wake up and find I'd been dreaming. But it didn't happen.

"Next night Frank Sheridan and his wife stopped me on the way to the dressing rooms. Frank asked how my parents had enjoyed the show. I told him their reaction, and he laughed. 'It was the same when my parents first came to see me,' he said. 'They loved the show and I've come to the conclusion that everyone, no matter what their upbringing, will laugh at down-to-earth comedy.' I remembered that many times, years later, when I questioned the prudence of some comedy routine I wanted to put in my movies."

Sennett hung around New York for the next five years. Occasionally he got small parts in the legitimate theatre and by 1905 was auditioning for parts in Broadway musicals.

"One of my first attempts to get into the big time was at an audition for the musical, *King Dodo,* starring Raymond Hitchcock. The director liked my voice but said he had only one thing to offer, a place in the dancing and singing chorus. Chorus boys with deep bass voices were then, as they are now, hard to find and I was told I had the part until Hitchcock saw me rehearsing one of the dance routines. 'Remove that bumbler,' said Hitchcock. The director protested. 'We can improve his dancing, but just listen to his voice.' 'Fire him,' said Hitchcock. 'We don't need singers that badly. With him in the show Broadway's very existence is in peril.'"

Years later, when Sennett's New York partners insisted that he hire Hitchcock at $2,000 a week for the movies, he protested but was overruled. But Sennett got his revenge. After a week at the Keystone Studios Hitchcock asked to be released from his contract.

"I made his life so miserable," recalled Sennett, "that he said he hated and despised filmmakers. I accepted his resignation and as he left the studio I yelled after him, 'If you'd been able to dance, Mr. Hitchcock, I wouldn't have let you go.' He had no idea what I was talking about."

Hitchcock didn't make another film for seven years, and his movie career was short and unspectacular. But he did return to Broadway for considerable success.

Sennett persevered with his attack on Broadway. He took dancing lessons and eventually made his Broadway debut. "After spending all that money on dancing instruction I was hired as a singer," he said. "The show was *A Chinese Honeymoon*, with Thomas Seabrooke as its star. All my vocal coaches had complained that my diction was poor, but it stood me in good stead in *A Chinese Honeymoon* because all the singing had to be done with a Chinese accent. Seabrooke commended me for the authenticity of my delivery, and recommended that all the rest of the singers should listen carefully and try to reach my perfection."

He worked in a number of other Broadway plays, often as a minor comic, but his great moment arrived when he was chosen to read for a part in the play, *The Boys of Company B.* The play starred John Barrymore, then in the early stages of a great career that was to last until his death at the age of sixty in 1942.

Sennett got a two-line part in Barrymore's play. "He was just back from a tour of Australia and from the look of him he'd celebrated far too much and far too often while he was down there. He was only about twenty-five but he looked like a man of fifty. After having me parade across the stage two or three times he asked me only two questions. 'Are you Irish?' he asked. I told him my ancestors were. 'Do you drink the hard stuff?' he added. I told him I did not, which was a lie. 'Good.' he said, 'you'll only be on stage for a few minutes at each performance so I'll expect you to make a note of all my exits and have my glass filled and ready every time I leave the stage. Can you do that?' I needed the money so I told him I could. 'Very well,' he boomed. 'Then you've got the part.'"

On the last night of the play Sennett recalls tripling the quantity of liquor in the glass for each of Barrymore's many exits. "By the final scene he was rolling about the stage like a drunken sailor and for one night, at least, we had a comedy hit."

When the Barrymore play closed after twelve weeks, Sennett decided to try David Belasco's office once more. "I was surprised that he remembered me," said Sennett to *Film Weekly* in 1925. "He seemed pleased to see me, even got out of his chair and greeted me like I might have been one of Broadway's biggest stars. 'Well, Mr. Sennett,' he said. 'You haven't been setting the world on fire since I last saw you, but you couldn't have come in at a better moment. I have something for you.' I thought for certain I was about to be given the starring role in one of his plays, but my ego was sadly deflated when he told me he would like me to go out to the Biograph moving picture studio. 'They need actors out there with Broadway experience,' said Belasco. 'Just tell them I sent you and that you've just completed a twelve-week season with Barrymore. Tell them I consider you an actor with great potential for the pictures industry.'"

In 1909 few of the actors at Biograph could claim to have had Broadway experience, or any experience at all, for that matter, and he discovered Belasco was right when he arrived at the studio at 11 East 14th Street. "I arrived there at ten o'clock in the morning and at ten thirty I had completed my first part in a film," recalled Sennett. "By the end of the afternoon I had played three more characters. I have no idea if they were part of the same film or three different ones. I lined up at the end of the day with all the others and was paid five dollars for my efforts."

"Can you come back tomorrow? In fact we can probably use you every day this week," said the director. He added, "We only pay $20 for the five-day week, is that acceptable?" "I told him it was," said Sennett. "It wasn't until Friday when I lined up for the $15 balance of my salary that I learned his name was D. W. Griffith.

"The first night I rode back into the city on a streetcar with another young Canadian who was just getting her feet wet at Biograph," he said. "Her name was Mary Pickford. I discovered David Belasco had also sent her to Biograph."

Within weeks of his arrival at Biograph, Sennett was playing important roles as the villain opposite some of the most important actresses on the studio payroll. They included Linda Arvidsen (then D. W. Griffith's wife), Mary Pickford, and Florence Lawrence. It was at Biograph that he first met Mabel Normand, who was soon to become the most important woman in his life.

Between 1908 and 1911 Sennett sold more than 100 script ideas to Griffith, mostly comedies. In 1910 Griffith pushed him into his first directing job when another director became ill. That same year he travelled with Griffith and a small group of actors to California where he stayed six months before finding he missed Mabel Normand too much. "I told Griffith I was heading east," he said, "and he didn't protest too much."

Talking to *Film Weekly* in 1928, D. W. Griffith saw Sennett in a different light. He said, "It was Sennett's great curiosity about everything to do with motion pictures that made him so indispensable to me. He would investigate the lighting, even help put sets together. On occasions, he actually advised me how to shoot a scene. I wouldn't have told him so at the time but I actually listened. He told other actors how to stand, where to stand, and what moves to make to get the maximum effect. It was especially obvious that he knew instinctively what would be funny and what would not. When I decided to give him a chance to direct a film by himself he showed remarkable maturity for one who had been in the industry such a short time."

Billy Bitzer was probably the greatest cameraman from the silent era. He worked with Griffith from the early days of Biograph and stayed with him to the end of his career, filming his major successes including *Birth of a Nation* and *Intolerance*. Bitzer said in a *Film Weekly* article in 1940 that he had once considered leaving Griffith to go with Sennett when he left Biograph to form his own company.

"Griffith rarely gave other directors an opportunity to work on their own, and when he offered Sennett a chance to direct some comedies, he asked me to be his cameraman," said Bitzer. "I was very impressed by the way he coaxed the humour out of actors who didn't look like they had an ounce of humour in them. It was obvious that he was going to be a great director, different in style completely from Griffith, but he had a quality that could not be denied. I enjoyed working with him. He stood no nonsense from anyone. He wasn't afraid to tell actors or technicians, including me, if he thought we weren't getting the most out of a scene.

"When he told Griffith in 1912 that he was planning to form his own company I considered quite seriously accepting the offer he made me to join his Keystone Film Company. The money he offered was more than Griffith was paying, but I had a gut feeling somehow that my career would be more memorable with Griffith, so I stayed, and, of course, I have never regretted that decision."

To finance his new company, Sennett entered into an association with two former racetrack bookmakers who were, in 1912, running a successful film distribution house. In Sennett's autobiography he claims that he was forced into taking the two as his partners because he owed them a $100 gambling debt.

Many people, including the two former bookies, Charles Bauman and Adam Kessel, have denied this. "Sennett needed money," said Kessel, "so Bauman and I agreed to finance his new company. He agreed that he would use our old Bison studio, near Los Angeles, where we had been making western films for our distribution house.

"He took a third share in Keystone, and we each took a third. Sennett didn't put any money in the pot, he got his share for contributing his knowledge and experience in film production. We even agreed to buy the rail tickets from New York to Los Angeles for himself, Mabel Normand, the Biograph actress who was now his girlfriend, and actors Fred Mace and Ford Sterling."

Sennett said in 1943 that he, Sterling, Mace, and Normand didn't waste a minute of the six-day rail journey across the United States. "Even though I was the only one who had ever seen California I was able to describe the wonderful scenery to them, and by the time we arrived in Los Angeles we had the basic ideas prepared for more than fifty different films."

One of Sennett's favourite stories, which he told many times over in the years that followed, was that they started shooting their first film fifteen minutes after they stepped off the train. "There was a big Shriners parade going by the railway depot so I dashed into a store, bought a doll, and wrapped it in a shawl belonging to Mabel. I made her run up and down the line of Shriners as if she was desperately trying to find the father of her baby," he said.

"The Los Angeles police joined in the chase, trying to catch Mabel. That was where I got my idea for the Keystone Kops. Two days later we finished the film in the Bison studio and had it ready for the film exchanges a week later. We never dared show it in Los Angeles. Too many Shriners and city cops might have recognized themselves."

Several film historians have doubted the truth of this story, and Adam Kessel said many years later that he agreed that Sennett's memory was faulty. "The story is a figment of Sennett's imagination. They had no camera with them and couldn't have got hold of one until the next day when they arrived at the Bison studio," he said.

The old Bison Films studio, located at 1712 Allesandro Street [now part of Glendale Boulevard] in Edendale, a suburb of Los Angeles, was discovered by Sennett to be nothing more than an old grocery story that Bauman and Kessel had bought two years earlier.

Mabel Normand told *Film Weekly* in 1929 that Sennett brought in construction workers twenty-four hours after they arrived in Los Angeles. "He had no money to pay the workers or even buy the materials for the buildings he planned, but somehow he charmed the workers into waiting until the end of the month for their money and got all the wood he needed on credit. By then Bauman and Kessel had arrived and everyone got paid on time."

The Keystone Studio sign went up on the rather dilapidated former store within a few days. Once the new buildings were ready, it was hoisted to the top of the biggest structure.

"Mack strutted around like a peacock on the road in front of the store," Normand told *Film Weekly* in 1929. "He waved at everyone who passed, yelling out to passing streetcars that this was his studio."

Sennett issued instructions to everyone in the studio that there were certain taboos that must never be broken by any director, actor, or writer. "We will never make sport of religion, politics, race, or mothers," he said. "A mother must never get hit by a custard pie. Her daughter, yes, as often as possible. Mothers-in-law are fair game, but mothers, never."

"I don't believe anyone at Keystone ever broke those rules," he said in 1959. "My own mother had come out to California to join me, and I wouldn't have embarrassed her for any amount of money. She used to object, at first, to the girls we dumped in swimming pools. Their wet, clinging, rather revealing clothes used to upset her, but when Mabel Normand, who she adored, told her it was alright, it was alright!"

Once the basic Keystone buildings were in place, Sennett built his own office in a tower on top of the biggest structure. "I could see what was going on in every corner of the studio. I used a megaphone to move anyone I saw sitting around doing nothing into some action or other." Presumably that is why Indians in full dress and warpaint can be seen as background extras in scenes supposedly taken in downtown Los Angeles.

By the time the studio was functioning, the Sennett-Normand romance was in full swing. Charlie Chaplin said, in 1958, that "one morning Sennett was in a wonderful mood and we knew the romance was functioning as romances should. Other mornings he would stomp around the studio scowling at everyone. Mabel would arrive late, also in a black mood, and we knew they had been fighting.

"At the beginning of 1913 everyone in the studio was part of a gambling syndicate that tried to estimate the day and month when Mack and Mabel would get married. I, and Slim Summerville, the actor, were the only ones who said they would never get married. Long after I had left Keystone I had a visit from one of the studio technicians. He gave me a wad of money and said they'd decided to wind up the pool. Summerville and I shared the kitty.

"Months later I bumped into Sennett and he jokingly asked why I had bet he would never marry Normand. Equally jokingly, I replied, 'Because we think you are queer [homosexual], Mack.' He went as white as a sheet and looked down at the ground. 'How did you know, Charlie, how did you know?' He dashed away and left me wondering. I recall Ford Sterling once said, 'How come none of Mack's girlfriends get pregnant, like ours do? Maybe the chasing is all show and he is trying to fool us.' And I have wondered from that day on!"

Sennett and Mabel Normand spotted Chaplin a week before they left New York for California in 1912. "We decided to wait until we were settled in Los Angeles before hiring him," said Sennett in 1943. "When we were ready to put him under contract we couldn't find him."

It took Adam Kessel a month to locate him, playing in a small vaudeville theatre in Altoona, Pennsylvania. "Kessel wasn't at all enthused by the idea of signing this unknown to a year's contract. 'Frankly, Mack,' he wrote me, 'I don't think he has any talent at all.' But I insisted, so Kessel bought him a ticket on the train to Los Angeles. His contract was for $125 a week, a lot of money, but you see I believed he would be a big name, and eventually he was."

Chaplin never reached his full potential at Keystone. "I didn't create the tramp costume until I'd been there a month or two," he said. "Sennett often claimed he devised it, but the basic costume was similar to one an old actor, Fred Kitchen, had used in our Fred Karno stage show. I got his permission to copy it. The moustache was the idea of director Del Lord. The big shoes also came from Fred Kitchen. Long after the "little old tramp" became famous I paid Kitchen an annual sum of money for the rights, and I wouldn't have done that if Sennett created the costume."

The Keystone Kops had not been created when Chaplin arrived at the studio, but Sennett claimed to have put him in a Kops uniform on his first day at Keystone. "But he just didn't seem to fit in with the rough-and-tumble of the Kops, so we never used him a second time."

Chaplin tells a different story in his autobiography. "I was never, at any time, in a Keystone Kops outfit or film. I was there in 1912 and the Kops didn't exist until 1913. Their first film was called *The Bangville Police*. I remember it being made, because I didn't find it very funny. How wrong I was!

"By that time I was nearing the end of my one-year contract with Sennett and had developed my own tramp character which used subtlety, not slapstick. I can never say I was anything other than bored with slapstick."

In 1913 Mack Sennett repaid his debt to Marie Dressler. "Few females had achieved fame in comedy by 1913," he recalled. "So when I told Bauman and Kessel that I wanted to make a six-reel film of Dressler's Broadway hit *Tillie's Nightmare,* using her as the star, they pointed out that such a venture would cost around $200,000 and that Dressler would want at least $10,000 a week. 'I doubt,' said Kessel, 'if Miss Dressler would be interested in making a film even if we paid her that much.' I casually mentioned that I was acquainted with the great actress and felt I could convince her to come to California.

"I talked to Dressler on the long-distance phone and was getting nowhere until I mentioned that I owed my entire career to her. 'You do?' she asked. 'I don't recall you appearing in any of my plays.' I reminded her of the episode in Northampton and she roared with laughter. 'I often wondered where you ended up,' she said. 'So what do you want me to do?'

"Ten minutes later I had convinced her that we had a film version of *Tillie's Nightmare* that we proposed to call *Tillie's Punctured Romance*. It was ready for shooting, I told her. 'If you are ready, Mr. Sennett, so am I,' said Dressler. But could you afford my price of $2,500 a week? I told her we would pay $3,000 and throw in a first-class ticket from New York to Los Angeles, plus all her hotel expenses and the use of a car and driver while she was here.

"'How do I know you can afford that sort of money, Mr. Sennett?' she asked. 'How did you know, Miss Dressler, that one day I would become famous?' 'That's enough,' she said. 'When do you want to start?' 'In two weeks,' I said, knowing that the script I had said was ready hadn't even been started. 'Make my reservations,' she said. 'I shall be at your disposal for four weeks.'"

Sennett worked through the night, sleeping only briefly, for almost a week. "Then I knew I had a great story. I decided to give her the greatest film cast yet assembled. Dressler was to have top billing. I used every big name on the lot: Chaplin, Normand, Mack Swain, Chester Conklin, Minta Durfee, Edgar Kennedy, Charlie Chase, Alice Davenport, Wallace MacDonald, and the entire battalion of Keystone Kops. What a cast!"

Tillie's Punctured Romance took three weeks and four days to film. It cost, according to Sennett, $180,000 to make. "It was a huge success and made us more than half-a-million, and it launched Marie Dressler on a film career that only ended with her untimely death in 1934. She was the most co-operative star I ever worked with," he said.

There are many different stories of Gloria Swanson's arrival at Keystone. The most popular is that Sennett was enchanted by her beauty and immediately signed her to a six-month contract. Others suggest that he wasn't impressed with her at all but decided her husband, who had already made a few films at other studios, had great potential.

The husband was Wallace Beery. Copies of their wedding certificate have been printed with many stories over the years, but in her autobiography Swanson talks extensively of her Keystone days, but makes no mention of the presence of Beery or that she was his wife.

Sennett's own version of their arrival on the lot seeking work is probably, for once, the truth. "Immediately Wally Beery walked into my office I recognized him as the man who had given me his second pair of shoes in New York fifteen years earlier. I didn't remind him, but gave him a contract at the studio immediately. He seemed surprised at the speed in which I made up my mind and suggested I might also like to engage his wife, as they often worked together. I took one look at Swanson and was stunned by her beauty. I signed her, too. Beery never did find out I was the actor with 'Massachusetts shoes' in New York."

Sennett denied vehemently printed reports that Swanson was ever one of his Bathing Beauties. "The story got around because I asked her to pose in a bathing suit with the girls to promote the third film she made with us. She agreed, providing it was only a one-shot deal to help sell this one particular film. And that is a fact, she never was a Sennett Bathing Beauty."

Apart from the final few films Chaplin made before he left in 1913 for the Essanay Studio at a salary of $2,000 a week, Sennett's first non-slapstick features were those made by Gloria Swanson. "She was just too dignified to use in slapstick, so we tried a few light romantic comedies. Universal had been making them for at least a year and they were very profitable. Of course, Swanson was a gigantic hit and the films made a great deal of money. By this time she had divorced Beery and he had gone on to better things with some other studio."

Keystone Studio was, by now, turning out four or five two-reel films every week. Sennett's contract actors included Roscoe "Fatty" Arbuckle, soon to be disgraced in a sordid sex trial that cost the life of young actress Virginia Rappe, and his wife Minta Durfee. Others included Louise Fazenda, Mae Busch, and Buster Keaton. Charlie Chaplin's brother Sydney, who never achieved fame and later became Charlie's business manager and is credited with making him a multi-millionaire, also worked for Keystone.

Sennett commented on Sydney Chaplin in 1959. "He was useless as a comic, had none of Charlie's talents, but if only I could have realized his abilities as a business manager I would own this apartment block I live in, instead of renting this one-room shack."

After Arbuckle was exiled from Hollywood, all his unreleased films were destroyed since no one would show them. His wife, Minta Durfee, stayed on at Keystone. Later, when her acting career was over, she greeted customers daily at a small store she ran in Hollywood for many years until her death in 1975.

At the end of 1917, Sennett decided to sever all connections with Keystone. He, Kessel, and Bauman came to an agreement by which they retained the name Keystone and Sennett was given the right to select forty of the company's best films of which he would be the sole owner. Most important to Sennett was the fact that he would have ownership of the Keystone Studio. "I had the Keystone name down in twenty-four hours," he said. "Within another twenty-four hours I had my own sign, 'Mack Sennett Comedies,' high in the sky."

In 1917 Sennett was probably one of the wealthiest men in California. "My accountant told me I was worth about $12 million," he said in 1943. "I owned two hotels, a movie theatre, and two studios. Keystone was making a million dollars a year profit with all taxes paid. It was time to move on."

Sennett took the contracts of only a few of the Keystone directors and stars he felt would fit in with the new style of productions he had agreed with Paramount to produce. Paramount, in turn, agreed to give all Sennett productions maximum distribution under their banner.

The Sennett-Normand romance was on one day and off the next. After one serious battle between the two, in 1918, when bottles and knives were thrown around in Normand's home, she arrived at the studio the next day with a black eye. Sennett announced he was setting up a completely independent company for her, to be called the Mabel Normand Picture Company. He paid all the costs of building a completely new studio for her films alone. Sennett told friends he would have "lost her love" if he hadn't given her the freedom to choose her own scripts and co-stars.

The venture was initially successful. Normand's achievements under the Sennett banner had made her into one of the most popular actresses in the country. Fan mail came in from all over the world, and four secretaries were kept busy ten hours a day answering the queries and mailing out photographs. "Of course, she couldn't sign every one of those photographs herself, so we hired an ex-con, a forger, to do nothing else but sign her name. That worked well until he began to work overtime forging Mabel's name and my name on company cheques he had stolen." One of the photographs, dated 1917, quite likely signed by the forger, was recently sold to a collector in London, England, for more than $5,000.

In 1919 Sennett and Normand came very close to marriage. Del Lord recalled the occasion in 1960. "We had all been invited. The party was set for 500 guests. The wedding was to take place at her studio. At ten in the morning, with the wedding scheduled to take place at noon, everyone was told the ceremony was cancelled. Sennett and Normand were nowhere to be seen. I asked him the following Monday what had gone wrong, and he simply answered, 'You know Del, I really can't imagine myself being married to a woman.'"

The artistic freedom given to Normand let to a deterioration in film quality. Before they knew it, her studio was in debt. Sennett, determined not to lose Normand, found a script he felt ideal for her. He invested $500,000 of his own money in *Molly O*, a film which took almost a year to make, an almost unheard of time when most films were still being made in less than a week.

Then tragedy struck. On the night of February 1, 1922, film director William Desmond Taylor was shot and killed in his home at 404 South Alvarado Street, one of the area's better residential districts.

Mabel Normand was one of the chief suspects from the start. It was quickly suggested that she had been having an affair with Taylor, and she admitted, when questioned, that she had been at his home early in the evening of the night he was killed. Others implicated were the seventeen-year-old actress Mary Miles Minter, whose nightdress was found in Taylor's bedroom. A hand-embroidered handkerchief bearing her name was on the floor of the murder room.

Sennett, who was interviewed by police along with other Taylor acquaintances, said he first heard of the incident early in the morning of Friday, February 2. "I read the story in the newspapers," he said. He was asked no further questions.

Sennett told many interviewers that had it not been for the half million dollars he had invested in Normand's film, *Molly O,* he probably would never have been declared bankrupt. His biggest worry after Taylor's death, or so he claimed two decades after the murder, was not who was guilty but of the $500,000 he had spent on the unreleased film. "I remembered what had happened after the Fatty Arbuckle scandal and all I could think of was the half million dollars I would lose. Naturally I was concerned for Mabel, but I didn't have the same strong feelings for her then."

Douglas MacLean, a well-known film comedy actor, who lived with his wife next door to the Taylor home, told police he went to the window immediately after hearing what he thought was a gunshot. He said that Davis, Normand's chauffeur, and her car, which he had seen at the Taylor house about seven o'clock, had gone when he looked out. "It would have been impossible for someone to leave the house following the shots, get into the car, and drive away before I looked from my window," he said.

Although Taylor's pocket watch, presumed to have been struck by the bullet, had stopped at exactly 7:21 p.m., MacLean claimed the gun shots were much later, probably shortly after eight, suggesting the 7:21 time was set by the killer to mislead the investigators. "I glanced at my watch as I turned away from the window," he told the police. "It was several minutes after eight."

Convinced that what he had heard was a car backfiring, MacLean said he thought no more of the incident until next morning when the police arrived at Taylor's house. MacLean's wife, Faith, told police investigators that she saw a rough looking man leaving Taylor's home at about nine o'clock. "He had a cloth cap down over his eyes and a scarf that seemed to cover part of his lower face," she said. "I wondered why he needed to be so muffled up because it was not a cold evening. It was quite dark and I only saw his outline."

Edna Purviance, Charlie Chaplin's leading lady, who lived two doors further down the road, confirmed Mrs. MacLean's story. "I, too, saw this rough man," she said. "I can't be sure of the time, but think it was a little later than Faith said. It was quite dark and impossible for me to recognize the man. If I must describe him I will say he looked like my idea of a motion picture burglar."

The investigation dragged on and finally reached the coroner's court. The names of Mabel Normand, Mary Miles Minter, and Minter's mother, who had openly said she disapproved of her daughter's relationship with a forty-five year old man, were bandied about in a manner that suggested the police were convinced one of them was guilty of the crime.

Normand's chauffeur testified that he and Mabel had left the Taylor home at about 7:15. "I saw Henry Peavey, Desmond's servant, leave just after seven, a few minutes before we left," said Davis. "He spoke to me as he passed the car. Apart from him I saw no person other than Miss Normand enter or leave the house." Questioned about gunshots, he denied hearing any. "And I don't see how I could have failed to hear them had they occurred while I was waiting for Miss Normand."

Davis claimed that Taylor came out to the car with Normand, kissed her on the cheek, waved, and returned to his house. "Then I drove her home, where she dismissed me for the night," he said. "I was home with my wife before eight-thirty."

This evidence should have cleared Normand, but other evidence suggesting that she had been Taylor's lover destroyed her career. The film, *Molly O,* was shelved indefinitely. When it was finally released, several years later, it was a big success. But by that time all rights to the film had passed from Sennett's hands.

Normand's career went steadily downhill. She was reported a year later to have been involved in a rather odd shooting incident at her home. A revolver bullet injured one of her guests, but he told police it was an accident and nobody was to blame. The matter was dropped despite the fact that neighbours claimed to have heard at least four shots and a lot of screaming.

That same year she was involved in a drug scandal, and newspapers reported she was addicted to cocaine. She died on February 23, 1930, after a long illness said to have been caused by her drug use.

Mary Miles Minter's career also ground to a halt. Nobody wanted to see her films. Newspaper readers were convinced that she, too, had been one of Taylor's sleep-in girlfriends. Her squeaky clean image was totally destroyed by the scandal.

Sennett's agreement with Paramount survived until 1929, but his output declined and with the first sound films being made, they mutually agreed to end the contract. He joined Educational Pictures that same year and announced he would now only be making sound motion pictures. Despite its name, Educational Pictures produced a wide variety of films, few of which could even be remotely called educational.

In November 1933, creditors of Mack Sennett, Inc., asked for the appointment of a receiver to wind up his studio and film production. Mack Sennett was declared bankrupt a few months later.

"He didn't stop working," said Del Lord in 1960. "But now he was just an employee of other companies. He turned out a few sound films but it seemed as though the spark had gone. He told me he had 'exhausted all the possible tricks of the fun factory' and planned to retire to write screenplays for other directors."

In 1937 the Academy of Motion Picture Arts and Sciences honoured Sennett with a special Oscar. The citation read: "For his lasting contribution to the comedy technique of the screen, the Academy presents this special award to that master of fun, discoverer of stars, the sympathetic, kindly, understanding genius, Mack Sennett."

Sennett had little to say on this auspicious occasion. Tears were streaming down his face as he said simply, "Thank you. Thank you, everyone." The audience, consisting of the biggest names in the film industry, rose to its feet and applauded the weeping Sennett for five minutes.

Little was heard of Sennett over the next decade. He attended parties given by the biggest names in Hollywood, entertained friends at his Hollywood Boulevard apartment, but produced no new films. In the early 1950s he dropped out of sight.

In 1959, at an interview with the author, in the presence of Reece Halsey, an old friend who visited the King of Comedy every day, Sennett, after more than a few glasses of Scotch, started crying and said he wanted to get something off his mind before he died. Halsey told him to relax, that he had drunk too much. But Sennett persisted.

"I want you both to know that I killed Bill [William Desmond] Taylor," he said. "It was me they saw leaving the house. I stayed there for about an hour after I shot him, looking for things that might incriminate Mabel. I found some letters she had written but I daren't tell her I had them. I was at the end of the road about seven thirty when I saw her leave in her car, then I went down to the Taylor house. I got my cap and scarf from the studio wardrobe. I kept them on all the time until I got on the streetcar, then shoved them under the seat when no one was looking. The driver looked at me when I climbed on board and I've often wondered why, after Faith

MacLean and Edna Purviance spoke up, he didn't come forward to say I'd been on his streetcar. But he couldn't have identified me; I kept my head down. I got off where I had left my car and drove home."

Reece asked him why he had killed Taylor, Sennett opened his eyes wide and said clearly, "Because he was a bloody queer [homosexual] and stole Mabel by giving her drugs," he said. Then he closed his eyes and fell asleep. When he woke up he claimed to have no memory of what he had said. "I know nothing about the murder," he said. "Absolutely nothing."

In the latter days of his life, Sennett had elaborated on many stories to make them more glamorous and interesting to the few people he could get to listen. Was this just one more of his fairy tales? Reece Halsey thought so. And there the matter ended. "He has never said anything like this before," he said. "Mack has always had a vivid imagination."

Marshall (Mickey) Neilan, a long-time resident of the Motion Picture Home, said before his death in 1958 that he often discussed the Taylor murder with Sennett because he had believed for a long time that Sennett might have committed the crime. "I hated Taylor for what he did to me and dozens, maybe hundreds of others, while pretending to head the industry drive against drugs. Only once did Sennett look me straight in the eyes, and from what we had been discussing, I knew he was about to confess to the murder. But a visitor came in and distracted Mack and that is the end of the story. Dozens of us believed it was Mack but we all hated Taylor and loved Mack so nobody even hinted this to the investigators. If only I had found the courage to kill Taylor myself I might have spent my final days on earth a much better person."

In 1957 Sennett had been hospitalized for a prostate operation, but when he recovered he refused to go to the Halsey's home in Beverly Hills to recuperate. "He demanded to go back to his apartment in Hollywood, so that's where we took him," said Halsey.

"He started writing again and tried to interest Jackie Gleason in starring in a film of his novel, *Don't Step On My Dreams,*" he said. "But as far as I know he never received a reply from Gleason."

The one-time King of Comedy lived alone, only venturing out to buy groceries at a nearby market. He drank a lot, slept a lot, and cooked all his own meals. Any spare time, when he was not sketching out ideas for comedy films, he spent feeding the pigeons that were always waiting on his windowsill.

Early in 1960, just after his eightieth birthday, when Reece Halsey realized that Sennett was no longer able to look after himself, he arranged for his transfer to the Motion Picture Country Home in Woodland Hills. He had to be carried to the car, protesting loudly that he didn't want to leave his home.

Once there, however, he became delighted with his surroundings and the attention he was given. "He found many of his old friends from the silent era were also residents," said Halsey. "He even arranged showings of some of his silent films for the residents. They curtailed his drinking and his health recovered for a short while."

Mack Sennett, in his last few months on this earth, had once again become an important person. He was idolized by those who he had helped in the past but who, until he arrived at the Motion Picture Home, had no idea he was still alive.

Until only a few days before he underwent further prostate surgery on November 4, 1960, he was in contact with actress Shirley MacLaine. "He wanted me to play Mabel Normand's role in a remake of *Molly O*," she recalled in 1970. "It was obvious that he would never be well enough to undertake such a task, but I visited him and sent him flowers. It was the least I could do for one of the founders of our industry."

Sennett didn't survive the November 4 surgery. He died peacefully in his sleep just before midnight.

Roscoe "Fatty" Arbuckle's widow, Minta Durfee, talked to reporters after Sennett's death. "He kept me on at the studio after the trial destroyed Roscoe's career. He paid me double my usual salary because he knew we had little money. And, without any fanfare, he paid all the lawyers' fees for the three trials my husband had to endure.

"Although Roscoe was supposed to be barred from all the studios, Mack brought him in to Keystone and actually let him direct several films behind closed doors. He couldn't credit him as the director so he said 'Direction by Will B. Good,' a most appropriate name. Unfortunately, someone talked and that was the end of his directing career, too.

"Later, when he was releasing films through Paramount, he gave Roscoe a lot of small roles. He had lost a lot of weight through the worry, and few people recognized him. He paid a lot more than the parts deserved, but that was Mack Sennett. He never forgot a friend. It's a pity so many of his friends so quickly forgot about him.

"He would come into my store in Hollywood and buy some trinket worth about two dollars. Then he would offer me a $50 or $100 bill in payment. He knew well I couldn't change bills of that size, so he told me he'd get the change next time he was in. But when next time came he claimed he couldn't remember that I owed him anything and that I must be mistaken."

Minta Durfee said she visited Sennett in his apartment between 1950 and 1958 at least once a week. When he was moved to the Motion Picture Home in Woodland Hills, quite a distance from Los Angeles, she visited as often as she could. "I didn't have a car and it was a difficult place to get to, so I just wrote him long letters," she said. "How this wonderful man could be forgotten by the industry is beyond my understanding."

The funeral service, at the Church of the Blessed Sacrament in Los Angeles, proved that more than just a few people had not forgotten his contribution to the early days of motion pictures. The church was crowded with stars from both silent and sound eras. Among the pallbearers were his Keystone stars, Chester Conklin, Jack Mulhall, and Tom Kennedy. Del Lord, who had suffered a heart attack some months before Sennett died, climbed out of his wheelchair to place a custard pie on the casket. It was a solemn occasion, but the unexpected gesture brought gales of laughter and applause from those attending the funeral.

Sennett's last request, made to Reece Halsey at the Motion Picture Home before he went into surgery, was that all his papers, photographs, letters, and contracts be handed over to the Academy of Motion Picture Arts and Sciences.

Sennett was buried in Holy Cross Cemetery. For some years the grave had no marker until a Los Angeles newspaper story, stating this fact, created considerable concern in the film community. Many offered to pay for a large monument, but Reece Halsey urged that whatever be placed on the grave be simple. And that is how it is today.

DOUGLAS SHEARER

"Douglas Shearer is the only person I know in the world of motion pictures who has received twelve Academy Awards without ever having been seen on the screen. He knew about sound when sound hadn't been invented. He has made many stars by his achievements in the development of studio and theatre sound equipment. I wonder where I would have been today if it wasn't for the genius of this man. He is a star himself, but he will never admit it!"

(Spencer Tracy, 1963)

T he film industry in Hollywood knew Douglas Shearer as a quiet man who shunned the nightlife of the community, and only rarely could be found at any of the many house parties that were the life-blood of the film industry in the 1930s, 1940s, and 1950s. He was never known to raise his voice, no matter what the provocation. And no one, in the forty-one years he was employed by Metro-Goldwyn-Mayer, could ever remember him being angry about anything.

But there was nothing quiet about his remarkable achievements. He was, and is, seventy years after the arrival of sound, still considered to have been the greatest soundman the motion picture industry has ever known. He was piping synchronized sound into theatres in California two years before Warner Brothers were said, in 1927, to have created "talking pictures" when they released *The Jazz Singer*.

A year before he retired, in 1968, Shearer was asked by a reporter for the *Los Angeles Times* if he was concerned that Warners got all the credit for "talking films" when MGM had actually been showing a sound movie for six months before *The Jazz Singer* was shown. "No," he said. "I knew what the studio and I had achieved, and that was all that really mattered. I was working for the best studio in the world, Metro-Goldwyn-Mayer, so why should I be concerned about the claims of an upstart studio like Warners?"

Douglas Shearer was born in Westmount, Montreal, Quebec, in 1899. His grandparents came across the Atlantic to Canada from England. His father, Andrew, was born in England but was only four years old when his parents chose to cross the ocean to the New World in an old-fashioned sailing ship.

He loved to tell and retell a story about the ocean voyage his grandfather, a clergyman, his grandmother, and the four-year-old who grew up to be his father, made to Canada. "My grandparents arrived at the dock in London to board the ship with my father and a milking goat. No one blinked an eye as the quartet boarded the vessel. Probably they thought that men of the church were strange people," said Shearer. "That the goat was to live in their cabin apparently upset no one."

But on the eve of Good Friday, the day before the fourteen-day voyage ended, with the Reverend James Shearer scheduled to conduct a special church service for passengers and crew, he was approached by the ship's captain. "Will it be a very messy service, Reverend?" he asked. "Messy," said Reverend Shearer, rather puzzled, "why should it be messy?" "When you sacrifice the goat on the altar, will the blood fly very far?" "Sacrifice the goat! Is that what you people thought I'd brought it on board for?" roared Shearer. "Good heavens, captain. I brought it so my young son would be able to have fresh milk every day of the journey. He has a rather weak stomach."

"Grandfather used to tell us it was the most undignified Good Friday service he had ever conducted. 'I had a hard job to keep from laughing,' he said. 'For a joke I decided to tie the goat to the altar, and no one would sit in the first three rows of the chapel. Obviously, the captain had not been able to advise them of the real reason for the presence of the animal.'"

When Douglas Shearer was growing up, his parents lived in a beautiful home on a road his grandfather built himself and named Shearer Lane in Westmount, Montreal. It is still there today, much wider and longer, renamed Shearer Street, befitting its new importance. His father, who was the owner of a building and contracting company, built many of the houses there. A lumberyard he owned at the end of Shearer Street, where it joins St. Patrick Street, was later sold to the Northern Electric Company, still stands on the same site today.

When he was only in his teens, Shearer first became interested in what he described to his sister, Norma, as "the seemingly unlimited miracles of sound and light." His father was a member of a syndicate that built one of the first power-generating plants in the Province of Quebec. Electricity was soon a very important thing in his life.

While attending Rosslyn School in Westmount, he used to run over to the power plant at the end of each school day to learn the secrets of electricity from plant engineers. His father provided him with a special room in the basement of the family home so he could experiment with the variety of electrical gadgets he continued to create.

An early success, or failure, depending on where you lived, was the building of a set of telegraph wires that ran across neighbouring properties and ended in the basement of a house almost half a mile away, where an equally enthusiastic young friend and experimenter lived. He hooked the wires up to the electrical system in his home and sent messages to his friend. Unfortunately, more than once he knocked out all the power circuits in an area covering several blocks around his house. Fortunately for young Douglas Shearer, no one but his father ever found out the cause of the blackouts.

After the fifth blackout, Shearer, Sr., bought Shearer, Jr., a camera. The younger Shearer soon became fascinated with light and lenses, and in 1915 had set up his own basement photographic studio and was producing some remarkable pictures of his pet dog and those of the neighbouring children who could be persuaded to pose. Unfortunately, all these achievements didn't make him too popular at home since he invented his own evil-smelling chemicals to develop and print the photographs.

Reminiscing many years later, he recalled that the house "often smelled like rotten eggs. My father told me years later that some of his friends stopped coming to the house because the smell was almost overpowering. I can see why it might have been a little embarrassing, and why they finally built me a little hut in the garden where I could experiment alone."

Shearer dropped out of high school half way through his graduating year. "I got the highest possible marks for mathematics," he said, "as that was the only subject I could imagine would help me become an electrical engineer. In those days it wasn't hard for a fourteen-year-old to get work, especially if, like me, you were prepared to do all the dirty jobs to learn a trade."

Supervisors at the Northern Electric Company plant in Montreal were the first to realize that Shearer was not just a run-of-the-mill employee. Soon he was upgraded to experimental work in the use of electricity for carrying signals over long distances.

At eighteen he entered McGill University to study physics and engineering. "How did a high school dropout get into such a prestigious university?" asked a newspaper reporter in 1930 after he had just received his first Academy Award. "By persuading my old headmaster that I deserved a second chance," he said. "He gave me a phony graduation certificate that could have got me elected prime minister of Canada."

At McGill University Shearer joined the Officers' Training Corps. World War One was raging in Europe and he hoped the things he learned would bring him an offer from the British Royal Flying Corps. But in 1918 his world came crashing down. "I had been accepted by the Royal Flying Corps, forerunner of the Royal Air Force, when probably the greatest flu epidemic of all time hit Montreal. I was one of its first victims. I was ill for nearly six months and when I was fit enough to rejoin the corps the war was over and they didn't need any more Canadians. Which is perhaps just as well, for war records show that the average life span of a pilot in those days was less than one month."

Plans to return to McGill University in September 1918 were halted when he discovered there was no money to pay his fees. "My father had suffered a number of major financial setbacks so, at nineteen, I had to go to work to provide some additional money for the family." The Shearer family, at that time, consisted of his father and mother, himself, and two sisters, Norma, born in 1902, and Athole, born in 1903.

"I spent about two years in a machine shop, and the luckiest break in my life came when the company took on, as an experiment, a line of industrial power plant equipment. I learned very quickly all I needed to know about the principles of mechanics. Often I was sent out to talk to the top mechanical engineers of Canada working in a variety of industries from coast-to-coast. They became my teachers. I asked lots of questions and they were more than willing to answer and explain the mysteries of the many new discoveries that had arrived through wartime research. I doubt if I could ever have got this vast work experience if I had been able to return to McGill. That is why, at MGM, I have always preferred to hire young people with a smattering of knowledge, but willing to learn, rather than older more experienced technicians who have become set in their ways and feel they knew everything there is to know!"

In 1920 Shearer added a sideline to his now lucrative engineering work. "A friend was planning to buy a Ford dealership but was afraid to go ahead until he was sure he had the right man to handle the mechanical work in the dealership repair shop. 'How about me?' I asked. 'Fords don't break down often. I could do it in my spare time.' He was delighted to think he would get a qualified engineer at part-time rates, so we went into business. I got no salary, but twenty-five percent of the profits."

That same year his sister, Norma, then nineteen, convinced her mother, Edith, that she, Norma, and Athole should move to New York to further the singing, acting, and modelling career she had successfully started in Montreal, like Douglas, to earn money for the family.

"I went down by train to New York a couple of times in 1921 to see her work," he said. "Father had decided to join them. We sold the house and I moved into an apartment. In New York I watched the photographers, where Norma was modelling, struggling to get good results with inadequate lighting. But when I suggested a few ideas from my own photography experience, I was gently ejected from the studio."

It was a different story at the Biograph Studio, where Norma got a few small roles. Shearer found directors much more willing to listen to his ideas. "They actually offered me a contract to design a new lighting system for the studio," he said, "but I had commitments in Montreal so reluctantly had to say 'no.'"

He had been back in Montreal for two weeks when an unexpected letter arrived from Florenz Ziegfeld inviting him to New York "to explore the possibilities of making lighting more exciting for the Ziegfeld Follies."

"Apparently a day electrician at Biograph, who worked nights in Ziegfeld's Broadway theatre, told him some of the things I had suggested at the studio. I liked the idea of going back to New York, especially since it meant I would be reunited with my family, but I just couldn't see myself letting my partner in the Ford dealership down. I am not too shy to say there were few engineers as good as I was at that time in Montreal. The dealership flourished as people got to know that cars from our salesroom were always in tip-top shape before they were sold, and if any problem did develop we fixed it expertly and promptly."

By 1922 Norma was becoming well known in the many small film studios that had sprung up in New Jersey and New York City. "Irving Thalberg, working as a production assistant at Universal Studio in Hollywood, saw some of her work and was impressed enough to convince the studio head, Carl Laemmle, to offer her a twelve-month contract in California. When she decided to accept the offer, the whole family decided to move with her. Father thought he might be able to get back in the lumber business down there, and later did, very successfully, providing, often on a minute's notice, any kind of wooden product the studios needed for sets.

"Athole got a few small roles in films at the Biograph studio in New York, but had no real ambition to become an actress. But when Mr. Laemmle offered her a position in his script department in California she jumped at the chance."

Two years later, the Ford dealership owner decided to sell the franchise. "He had a very large offer and since I would get twenty-five percent of the money he received, I agreed with him that it was too good a chance to miss. I had long since left the machine tool company as the Ford job rapidly became a full-time operation. I had quite a lot of money in the bank so decided to visit California to see my family again."

Shearer bought a return rail ticket, first class, packed his special belongings, sold his furniture, and gave up the lease on his apartment. "Why a return ticket, you may ask?" he said. "Well, I wasn't really sure I wanted to leave Canada for good and with the ticket in my pocket I knew I could go home any time I wanted."

Six months later he tucked the return half of his rail ticket deep down in the bottom of a box of souvenirs and decided to forget about returning to Montreal. "By that time Norma had moved over to Metro-Goldwyn-Mayer studios. Irving Thalberg, who had first realized her potential when he was at Universal, told Louis Mayer, when he was invited to join MGM as a producer, that he would accept if the studio put Norma Shearer under long-term contract as an actress."

At a party given by Thalberg in his home, Shearer met Jack Warner, head of Warner Brothers Studio. "All the studio heads were friendly in those days," he recalled. "Warner asked if I planned to stay in California and I said 'yes' if I could find a job. He told me that in his studio everyone started at the bottom, and if I really wanted to learn the film industry I could have a job in the studio prop room. I accepted on the spot and started work the next day."

For more than six months, Shearer moved props on and off the many sets at Warners. "I saw Jack Warner quite often, but any attempt to talk him into giving me a better job was fluffed off. 'You need much more experience,' he said. 'In a year or two we'll talk.'"

Any spare time he had, Shearer spent at MGM where Thalberg encouraged him to learn techniques that might improve the rather primitive cameras still in use in the industry. "In those days there were no unions and MGM, in particular, used to work from six in the morning and end sometimes as late as midnight, so I had lots of time to dabble in electrical and camera things at MGM.

"Something I have never forgotten, and have used as a guide throughout my career, was the example set by Louis Mayer. If the first set was opened at six, he was there. If the last lights were shut off at midnight, he was there. A lot of people don't like him, but that is usually jealousy because of his success. It should be made clear that everyone who works for him respects him. He never asks anyone to do anything he wouldn't do himself."

In July 1925 Thalberg spoke the magic words Shearer had been waiting to hear. "We need you here at MGM," he said. "Some of the things you have been doing are remarkable. I have talked with Mr. Mayer and you can start whenever you like. Your job will be to experiment with lighting, film, cameras, anything you want to do."

"And sound?" asked Shearer. "That's a long way off, if it ever comes," said Thalberg. "But, yes, sound if you wish."

Shearer's first MGM contract was for one year at $150 a week. "Three times what Warner had been giving me," he said, "so I marched in his office and asked when I could leave."

"Today, if you wish," said Warner. "I only gave you a job to keep you happy. If someone else in the industry thinks you have more talent than you have shown working in the prop room, I wish them well with you."

Warner rose, shook hands with Shearer, and signalled that the interview was over. Louis B. Mayer later said, "That was just one of the many mistakes Warner made. He couldn't see talent even when it was right under his nose. Thalberg and I had been watching Shearer from day one, and we knew he was going to be a force to be reckoned with in the industry."

Within six months Douglas Shearer's name was on everyone's lips in the industry. During the filming of *Slave of Fashion*, which starred his sister Norma, he approached Thalberg with a startling proposal. "I know we can't make the entire film talk," he said, "but let's make a talking two-minute trailer that goes to the theatres the week before the film is shown."

Many years after the moment he surprised Thalberg with his proposal, Shearer laughed about the producer's shock when he heard the idea. "He was literally stunned," he said. "When he recovered he said, 'Are you really still talking about sound Douglas? How can we possibly make the trailer speak. No, I don't want to hear about it, the idea is too ridiculous.' He walked away, about ten feet, then he turned and walked back to me. 'Can you really do it, Douglas?' he asked."

Knowing that his career could possibly be on the line from his answer, Shearer replied, "Yes, Irving, I can."

Thalberg clapped him on the back and said, "Then do it, Douglas, do it!" Shearer discovered later that the usually unflappable Thalberg ran over to Mayer's office and gave him the news. Mayer, whose greatest asset was his ability to make instant decisions, looked at Thalberg and smiled. "Then why are you wasting time over here when you should be working on the project," he said. He indicated the discussion was over by dismissing Thalberg with a wave of his hand before turning away to talk to Ida Koverman, his secretary.

Shearer's revolutionary idea was to add sound, both music and dialogue, to the *Slave of Fashion* trailer at each of the fifteen theatres where the film was to be presented the following week.

"The most important thing in the success of this idea was for the actors to speak their lines clearly during filming so the camera picked up every movement of their lips," recalled Shearer. "When the pieces of the film to be used in the trailer were chosen, spliced, and edited, we stood the actors in a line, with their scripts, and they "dubbed" the words they were saying silently on the screen, as we do today with foreign language films. We recorded the dialogue on a regular record machine, and when we played it back synchronized with the trailer the result was quite startling.

"When Mayer saw the film he stopped work on every set and invited everyone to see what we had created. He warned the whole group that if they mentioned what they had seen they would be fired. There was great applause, and we felt as though we had cleared a major hurdle toward the creation of talking pictures."

The initial recording was only the first step for Shearer. "I knew we needed more than just the dialogue so, with Mayer's blessing, I had a studio arranger compose music to complement the two minutes of film. We added a music leader of ten seconds so the projectionist would have ample warning when to start his machine. Thirty musicians recorded the sound on a separate disc while the conductor watched the film on the screen so the music would be loud for the opening and ending, but subdued during the spoken dialogue. Remember, we hadn't at that time discovered how to combine the dialogue and music on one disc."

Douglas Shearer

Originally, it was Shearer's intention to make fifteen copies of each sound recording and ship them, with two record players, to each theatre. "This worried us quite a bit," he recalled. "We would need thirty reliable people able to synchronize the sound with the film, and we just didn't have those people. We weren't concerned about the projectionists, because the ten seconds lead music gave them a cue when to roll the film."

For a while it was decided that the sound venture would only be risked at one of the fifteen theatres.

"Then I had an idea," said Shearer. "I asked Irving Thalberg to give me one more day to come up with a solution. I drove to downtown Los Angeles and talked to the manager of one of the two radio stations then broadcasting in the area.

"I proposed that they should have the recorded sound and music in their studio and at a predetermined time they would put both discs, synchronized, on the air. We would provide each of the theatres with the best quality radio receivers available and I devised speakers, rather like the old megaphones the band singers used, to increase the volume of the reception.

"The radio station's owners were enthusiastic about the idea, and agreed they would do it if MGM would invest quite a few thousand dollars they badly needed to buy new equipment for their studio. Mayer gave the OK and we started making plans and setting a date. We tried it out at one of the theatres in the middle of the night when there was no audience and the radio station wasn't supposed to be broadcasting, and it worked beautifully."

Mayer, Thalberg, Norma, and most of the studio heads went to one of the fifteen theatres and sat quietly at the back awaiting what they hoped would not be too much of a shock for the audience. "Well, it worked beautifully in all fifteen theatres," recalled Shearer. "It was so successful that audiences stood and cheered and asked for it to be repeated. I had to telephone the radio station and set a time for a replay. They held us to ransom for a lot more money but Mayer agreed it was worth the expenditure. I have never seen so many excited people."

The theatre owners demanded that MGM repeat the sound effects every night for the rest of the week. "Once again I had to negotiate with the radio station and MGM paid over another fistful of dollars," said Shearer. "Theatre managers called to tell us their theatres were packed every night of the week. A sample survey we made suggested many were people who had heard the 'sound miracle' once and went to hear it again and again.

"Everyone at MGM was stimulated and ecstatic with the result of the experiment. But the big letdown came the following week when *Slave of Fashion* was shown in its entirety. Unfortunately we had obviously not made it clear that only the trailer would have sound. Patrons started booing when the complete film was as silent as all the others they had seen until that time were. We had to take the film off after the Monday showing. It was a good film but we had to shelve it for awhile, only releasing it months later, with a silent trailer, to other theatres across the United States."

Two years later, there was a sequel. MGM became the owner of a radio station in Los Angeles. The original owners had declared bankruptcy, and the courts decided that MGM, with its sizeable financial involvement, was the legal owner and must pay all the bills. The studio owned the broadcasting station for twelve years before selling it for a large profit to one of the national radio networks.

By 1926 sound was obviously going to be the big thing in the motion picture industry. Warner Brothers mortgaged their studio and joined forces with Western Electric, soon to become the elite of the sound world in American theatres, to win the race.

But the newsreel companies beat them all. Early in 1927 a Fox Movietone News film was shown in New York to a startled audience who heard people like Calvin Coolidge, Babe Ruth, and Charles Lindbergh speak to them from the screen. The Fox studio equipped about 100 theatres with equipment designed to amplify the voices and music of its newsreels.

The Warner and Fox methods of sound were to use disc recordings separate from the film, as MGM had with its radio and theatre experiment. Warner's experiment with more than 100 Vitaphone short subject films was, at times, far from successful. If the film broke and had to be spliced, there was no way to change the sound on disc and often the pictures and voice were a long way from being synchronized.

Although it is always called the first talking film, Warner Brothers' *The Jazz Singer* was not true sound on film; most of the film was silent with only a musical background, but at the end Al Jolson startled his audience by facing them and providing a brief vocal interlude.

Meanwhile, Douglas Shearer was busy at MGM. Thalberg, in his memoirs, talks about a meeting between himself, Mayer, and Eddie Mannix, the latter sent in by the New York head office of Loew's Inc., owners of MGM, to be comptroller in Los Angeles. "Mannix asked Mayer what he was doing about sound film production," he said. "Mayer looked flustered for a second and said, 'Eddie, we're ahead of everyone, we have the most advanced and informed sound man working for us. He has been here two years now and you can take my word for it that we will be first when the real sound on film is created.' Mannix congratulated Mayer and left the room, no doubt to advise New York that everything was under control. I turned to Mayer and asked who this genius was. 'You brought him here, you should know,' said Mayer. 'Young Shearer, that's who I mean. Let's give him a title, and double his salary before Mannix asks too many questions. Tell him I say he has freedom to experiment with sound any way he wishes and to hire a staff if he needs them. What shall we call him?'"

After some discussion, Douglas Shearer was called to Mayer's office and advised, first that his salary had been increased to $300 a week, and second that he now had an official title, Director of the Metro-Goldwyn-Mayer Sound Research Department.

Shearer laughed about this many times. "For almost a year I was the entire sound department. I knew the secret to sound films could only be found by putting the words and music on a strip of magnetic tape that ran with the film, but how to get it to work was the problem. I could find no one else who agreed with me so I hired no one."

In 1928 Irving Thalberg married Norma Shearer. "You might have imagined I would be greatly enthused over the marriage," said Shearer, "but it did nothing to help my career. Few of the people at MGM had any idea where my experiments were leading and I'm sure, for a while, most of the studio employees thought of me as someone being shunted off to a dead end job because I was Norma's brother."

But Shearer persevered and got permission to hire Professor Verne Knudson, an expert on acoustics employed at the University of California in Los Angeles, to design the new sound stages he knew would soon be needed. The resulting buildings were so solidly built that they have withstood several earthquakes and are still in use today by the Sony Corporation, which took over MGM in 1991. They are now used to house the production sets of many popular TV shows, including "Jeopardy" and "Wheel of Fortune."

By now Shearer had, with the help of the Victor Recording Company, devised a method of recording sound on film. "Of course," he said, "the soundtrack was recorded separately on a different film to that in the camera, and later we had to marry the two together to provide the complete picture. This allowed us to edit each separately and finally add a music track to the finished film, a much superior method to that used by other studios."

When Shearer started work on his sound research there was no method existing to make the transfers of sound to the actual film. "My research department had by now about twenty employees; working in groups of four they tackled different problems that faced us," he said. "I went from group to group, working with them and suggesting ways that hold-ups could be overcome."

Little by little, Shearer and his team solved all the problems, and when it came time for MGM's first complete musical, *The Broadway Melody*, to be filmed in 1928 for 1929 release, the sound department had the answer to all the difficulties that had faced them.

But Shearer didn't devote all his time to sound. "I realized that if we were to get quality sound we had a lot of other things to eliminate first," he said. "The cameras of that time were quite noisy. It hadn't mattered while producing silent films, but now the primitive microphones picked up the whir and the soundtrack produced something like a cat purring continuously. First we tried putting the camera in a soundproof box, but the cameramen almost suffocated and the cameras soon became dangerously overheated in the closed area. The obvious solution was to build a more silent camera, so I devised that. At first the cameras were placed in one spot and were not movable. It quickly became obvious that this greatly limited photographic possibilities, so I devised a camera dolly that could follow the action.

"Most of the early sound films were just reproductions of stage plays with the camera planted where the audience would have been. There were no opportunities for long-distance shots or close-ups. Then there were the microphones. We tried hiding them in the clothing of the actors, but mikes were big and couldn't be easily hidden. I produced a small microphone that was used in clothing for awhile but every time the actor moved the rustle of clothing was picked up."

Shearer finally decided on using a static microphone hanging over the heads of the actors, just out of camera range. "This worked beautifully when the actors were able to stand still, but the sound faded in and out when they had to move. We already had our camera dollies and the obvious solution to record moving actors was a moving microphone, on a boom.

"It sounds so easy now, but at the time we had a hundred difficulties. The camera dolly and mike booms often collided. Shadows of the mike boom were constantly crossing the faces of the actors or could be clearly seen on the wall behind the action."

At this point, Shearer decided to once again enter the lighting field. "I remembered what I had done in my small Montreal studio to eliminate shadows and convinced Mayer that he should put me in charge of all set lighting. I was fortunate to be associated with Cedric Gibbons, the art director. Before each film we discussed the light and sound difficulties and he came up with innovative set designs that eliminated almost every problem." The credits "Sound by Douglas Shearer" and "Art Direction by Cedric Gibbons" appeared on hundreds of MGM films until 1960, when Gibbons died.

Louis B. Mayer was one of the founders of the Academy of Motion Picture Arts and Sciences, which annually awards Oscars to those people in the film industry considered to be the best in their own particular field. The first Academy Award for excellence in sound was awarded in 1930. The winner was Douglas Shearer for the soundtrack of *The Big House*. Jack Warner was so incensed by Shearer's win, expecting his own studio to take the honours, that on the night of the awards he started a feud with Mayer that lasted, with the exception of one single day in 1943, until Mayer's death in 1957.

The Big House, which starred Chester Morris, Wallace Beery, and Robert Montgomery, is available for film buffs to see on video. It is remarkable for its clarity of sound and consistency of volume, so often lacking in early sound films.

Shearer told the *New York Times* after the awards ceremony that few people had any idea of the problems sound recordists faced. "For example," he said, "it took us a long time trying to discover how to record a simple thing like raindrops. At first they sounded like marbles dropping on a wooden floor. After many tries we came up with the answer. We learned to 'damp' the sound by putting several layers of blotting paper on window sills, or placing heavy layers of felt on the ground just out of camera range."

On June 6, 1931, when Shearer was deep into his studio experiments, tragedy hit his life. His wife, distraught over the death of her mother, killed herself in front of hundreds of horrified spectators on Venice Pier, not far from the Shearer home in Santa Monica.

Venice police reported that Mrs. Shearer had approached one of the shooting galleries on the pier. The attendant told the police that she "played with the pistol for a few seconds before taking two wild shots at the targets, then she put the pistol to her head and fired." Mrs. Shearer died instantly, said the doctor who was called to the scene.

Shearer testified at the inquest. "We all tried very hard," he said, "but she was unable to recover from the shock of her mother's unexpected death in

May. One day I found her examining a revolver I kept at home, and I removed it from the house to my office as a precaution against what I feared. I hired a full-time nurse to stay with her at all times when I was not at home, but on June 6 my wife somehow slipped away."

The Shearers' next-door neighbour, Mrs. Waldo Waterman, told the inquest that Shearer had asked her, and her husband, to visit Mrs. Shearer as often as possible to keep her mind occupied, "but every conversation we had seemed to turn to her mother's death and she would start weeping uncontrollably." A verdict of suicide while of unsound mind was returned.

Immediately after the funeral Shearer returned to his research. "He even had a bed installed in his office," said Martin Marsh, who worked with him. "He moved some clothes and toiletries in and it wasn't unusual for him to stay there for several nights on a run."

On August 20, 1932, just a little over a year after his first wife's death, Shearer's friends were surprised to read in the papers a brief announcement from Las Vegas. "Douglas Graham Shearer, 32, motion picture sound technician and brother of Norma Shearer, screen star, was married here today to Ann Lee Cunningham, 28, of Los Angeles. Immediately after the ceremony they left in Shearer's private airplane to return to Hollywood where they will make their home."

"He returned to work the next day as though nothing had happened," said Marsh. "Perhaps he hadn't realized that the story of his wedding had been printed in the Los Angeles papers, and when we got together to go in and congratulate him, he told us not to make a fuss about it. 'I was lonely,' he said. 'And Ann has turned out to be a perfect companion to alleviate that loneliness.' And that is all he ever said about the marriage. Only a few of his closest friends ever met his new wife. They kept to themselves and were rarely seen at any of the opening nights or at house parties. I never did meet her."

In the early 1930s Shearer was named director of technical research at MGM. This position gave him total control over all the studio's scientific and technical advancement work in film production, from camera to laboratory to projection and sound.

In 1935 he won two more Academy Awards. The first was for sound recording of the Jeanette MacDonald and Nelson Eddy film, *Naughty Marietta*. Available on videotape, it is a great example of the early work of Douglas Shearer. His other award was for his research and development in perfecting a method of automatic control of film cameras and sound recording machines.

Despite all the advancements with less noisy cameras, improved lighting, and better microphones in the studios, a big problem remained unsolved in the theatres themselves.

"Not only was the sound distorted in the theatres with the primitive amplification of those early days, but seats in certain parts of the theatres were never full. People just wouldn't sit there because the sound was so loud and harsh. We needed good sound in the theatres just as much as we did in the studio if moviegoers were not to get tired of what was still considered by many to be nothing more than a fad. After all, Charlie Chaplin was still making silent films and packing the theatres with his genius.

"So I spent six months devising a two-horn system of sound reproduction that made it possible for music to come out of one speaker and voices out of another. You might say the concept was a forerunner of stereophonic sound." The two-horn method was improved by Shearer over the years, and was still the basis of all theatre sound equipment in use forty years later when he died.

This system won him his fourth award at the 1936 Oscar ceremonies. The film about the 1906 earthquake, *San Francisco*, gave him a second Academy Award for the year; he always considered it his finest work.

"For this film we tried something different that has now become standard practice," he said in 1943. "The director shot his scenes complete with dialogue. Then he turned over the film to me. We had devised a master film soundtrack that could be divided into eight individual tracks. Track one carried the studio dialogue. Track two the rumble of the earthquake. Track three falling walls. Track four crashing timbers. Track five the crackle of flames. Track six the screams of panic-stricken people. Track seven the sirens of fire engines. Track eight the discord of a piano as it crashed to the ground, and all other background musical effects."

As the film was run off in the projection booth, Shearer's creation, the first sound "mixer" used in the film industry, brought in the tracks individually, regulating their volume at a control board at which Shearer sat. "You might say I was a little like a conductor of a symphony orchestra as I blended the different sounds together on one single track," he said.

When it was released, *San Francisco* had everyone hanging on to their seats in theatres around the world. At the 1936 awards ceremony, Clark Gable, one of the film's stars, told the news media that he hadn't seen the completed film until the premiere night in Hollywood. "It was incredible," he said. "With only dialogue in the studio it seemed very tame, but with Douglas Shearer's sound and John Hoffman's earthquake sequences, it had me gasping for breath with its realism. The people around me were screaming as loud as those on the screen. I probably let out a few yelps myself."

The year 1937 brought Shearer two more Academy Awards, for technical achievements in advancing the use of sound and for the development of a new camera drive system that guaranteed absolute camera speed accuracy at all times.

In 1940, one of the most enduring musicals of all time, *Strike Up the Band*, starring Judy Garland and Mickey Rooney, with its complicated musical score, earned him another Oscar.

At the awards banquet of that year he modestly told an interviewer from the *Los Angeles Times* that he never actually invented anything. "All I did," he said, "was to take existing principles established by voice-reproduction techniques and use a little of my own skills in adapting these essentials to the new needs of sound reproduction by way of the screen."

Three years after he made that statement Douglas Shearer, when he re-read it, roared with laughter. "I hope he and his readers understood what I was saying. I'm not sure that I did!"

In 1941 he showed his amazing command of all aspects of motion picture production by devising a fine-grain film that provided greater clarity and crispness when magnified many times on the huge screens then being used in the bigger theatres. This put one more Oscar in his trophy case.

Little was heard of Shearer from October 1943 until early 1945. Those enquiring about his absence from the studio were told he was working on a major development for location work, and there was no set date for his return. It was some years before his absence was fully explained.

This was the story he told in 1947. "In September of 1943 I received a visit at the studio from the British ambassador to the United States. He had flown from Washington with a personal letter to me from the British Prime Minister, Winston Churchill. The letter explained that development of radar was a number one priority in the European war, and Mr. Churchill felt that my knowledge of sound and cameras might be useful in solving some of the problems that were plaguing them.

"Of course, I was flattered, but I felt any work of this sort should be done in conjunction with the United States government. I asked the ambassador if I could fly back with him to Washington so we could discuss how both our two governments could become involved."

The British ambassador was more than willing to utilize the vast research facilities of the United States and a meeting was arranged at the

White House with President Franklin Roosevelt and the United States' military chiefs of staff.

"The rest is easy to explain," said Shearer. "With the president's blessing and support I started work at a location that is still top secret and we were able to perfect the radar that I believe helped shorten the war."

He was offered a civilian award for his military achievements but declined the opportunity to have his work recognized. "I didn't do it for personal glory," he told President Roosevelt at a White House dinner he and his wife attended. "I did it to help save lives and get the war over and done with." But he always kept, in his study with pride, a framed letter from Winston Churchill congratulating him on his work.

In 1947, *Variety* wrote a short article telling of a visit by Shearer to the Office of Naval Research (ONR) in Washington, where a special tribute was paid to him for his wartime achievements. "Among Shearer's discoveries," said an ONR spokesman, "were ways to reduce the complex mathematical computations required in methods developed by such scientists as Einstein and Dr. Robert Millikan, so they could be utilized much easier in a number of naval projects."

Years later it was also revealed that his radar research had continued at a site close to Los Angeles into the 1950s. Using his radar and sound knowledge, he invented a device that allowed the United States to determine when and where nuclear explosions were taking place anywhere in the world. The principles of his findings are still in use today, probably by every major country in the world. At no time did he receive one cent for his work with the government, or for his discoveries.

Back in Hollywood in 1945, Shearer continued with his experimental work at MGM. *Thirty Seconds over Tokyo*, showing the first attack by the United States on Japan, starring Spencer Tracy, earned him another Oscar for his sound recording expertise.

Green Dolphin Street in 1947 and *The Great Caruso* brought him to the podium twice more to receive Oscars for his ever-improving sound methods.

Cinemascope was all the rage in the late 1950s, but audiences soon got tired of seeing the lines down the screen where the images from three projectors overlapped. With *Ben Hur* being prepared for production at MGM, Shearer concentrated his efforts on finding a way to produce wide-screen films using only one camera.

His invention, known as Camera 65, because of its use of sixty-five millimetre film instead of the standard thirty-five millimetre stock, and the creation of the film it used, brought Douglas Shearer his twelfth and final Academy Award in 1959. He also got rid of the curved screen, characteristic of Cinerama, and showed how Camera 65 could be shown on a flat, but wide, screen. It became known as Panavision. After the ceremonies he told the newsmen present that "thirteen might be an unlucky number, so I won't try for any more awards. From now on I'll be in the background letting the creative young minds at MGM take full credit for their achievements."

In May 1961 he was once more in the news, but not in a way he enjoyed. Papers nationally printed a brief item that said, "Douglas Shearer, winner of many Academy Awards at MGM for his engineering expertise, was today divorced by his wife of twenty-seven years, Ann, fifty-six. 'He was never at home,' she said. 'It was no longer a marriage.' The court approved an agreed settlement dividing community property valued at $800,000 between them."

In 1963 his name was on yet another award announced by the Academy. It was given to recognize the engineering work done by MGM in the creation and development of a background projection system that permitted exteriors to be shot indoors, with even studio technicians finding it difficult to tell which was the real outdoors and which was filmed in the studio. As the award was given to Shearer and the entire MGM research department, he declined to attend, saying, "It is time the department as a whole got the credit."

Accepting the award, a young researcher at MGM said, "Mr. Shearer may not be here in person, but his inspiring presence was felt on many occasions during the development of this system."

In 1965, when he was sixty-six, he married for a third time. There was only a brief announcement in the *Hollywood Reporter* that his new wife was named Avice and that the couple would live in Shearer's Santa Monica home.

Three years later, in 1968, he retired. "I am no longer young," he said. "At sixty-nine I am slowing down and at times it becomes difficult to get up in the morning and drive to work. The industry is not the same as it was when I first came to Hollywood in the late 1920s. A lot of the fun has gone from making films. There cannot be too many things now left to invent. Or, if there are, I can't think of them. So what better time for me to retire."

He was not seen in public again. A few months later, friends calling his home were told by his wife that Shearer was in a convalescent home due to a progressive and terminal illness. He allowed only his wife and two grown sons from his second marriage, Stephen and Mark, to visit him during the two years he remained under medical care.

In January 1971 Douglas Shearer died, leaving a huge legacy of advancements in a wide variety of technical fields associated with the motion picture industry.

He would have been very happy to see the prominence given to his death in the obituaries that were printed in national and trade papers. The *New York Times* gave his passing fifteen inches of space on its front page, an honour usually only offered to the giants of industry and politics and a few of the more important film actors and actresses.

At seventy-one, Douglas Shearer had earned his place in the sun. Many of his films that won awards, and even more of those that didn't, are available today on videocassettes. Mark Warner, a film buff in Beaumont, Texas, was reported in a newspaper story printed in 1991 to have collected more than 100 of the feature films in which the credits listed "Sound by Douglas Shearer." "He was the ultimate sound man," said Warner. "There will never be another Douglas Shearer."

NORMA SHEARER

"If we had royalty in the film industry, Norma Shearer would undoubtedly be Queen of Hollywood. She has a dignity that few other actresses have, she has a sense of serenity that few other actresses have, and she has the natural ability to convey emotions on the screen that few other actresses seem to be able to achieve. In my opinion she is one of the great stars of our time."

(Louis B. Mayer, 1931)

L ouis B. Mayer, head of Hollywood's largest film studio, Metro-Goldwyn-Mayer, was a proud man on the night of the 1930 Academy Awards banquet. MGM had been named as winner of three of the seven awards presented that year. Douglas Shearer had won the Best Sound Recording award for his work on *The Big House*. Frances Marion, Mayer's favourite writer on the MGM lot, had taken the Best Writing award for the same film.

Both these awards had sent Jack Warner, one of the three brothers who headed the Warner Brothers studio, into a frenzy. He shouted at Mayer after the banquet. "We were robbed by your cheap manipulations," he yelled.

Mayer let the tirade ride over his head, for hadn't his favourite actress, Norma Shearer, also won the Best Actress award for her role in *The Divorcée,* proving, as he loudly stated, "that Mayer knows quality when he sees and hears it."

Nobody dared tell the triumphant Mayer on the occasion of the second annual Academy Awards, of which he had been the founding father, that Shearer was only at MGM because Irving Thalberg, production chief at the studio, had brought her there and convinced her to sign a long-term contract.

Eighteen months before the awards that so delighted Mayer, Thalberg had cemented his relationship with Shearer by marrying her in what the press described as "the film capital's social event of 1928." Thalberg, at the best of times a shy individual, stood with his wife and listened to Mayer stealing what should have been his thunder.

Eight years later, just a year after the untimely death of Thalberg, Mayer was singing a different tune. "Norma Shearer is a traitor to MGM," he told a press conference. "She is behaving in a most unprofessional manner. When she came to me looking for work she was a simple girl from a poverty-stricken Canadian family. We taught her all she knows and now, at the height of her success, she wants to desert us and retire. This, regardless of a contract she signed with us. You can be assured I, and Metro-Goldwyn-Mayer, will not allow this to happen."

Norma Shearer was born on August 15, 1902, in Montreal, Quebec. Some movie history books suggest the year was either 1900 or 1904, but 1902 is the date the Motion Picture and Television Hospital said, at her death, was the date on her Canadian birth certificate.

When she was born, the Shearer family home was a large mansion. Her father, Andrew, a successful building contractor, was able to provide the family with a much higher standard of living than was enjoyed by the average family living in Montreal at that time. While her brother, Douglas, three years older than Norma, was experimenting with light and sound at the age of fourteen, Norma was receiving deportment, drama, and voice classes and piano lessons from the best available teachers.

A few years later, when her father's business had to be sold due to bad investments he made in other unconnected industries, training or teaching that cost money had to be discontinued.

In the 1930s, when her fame had reached its highest peak, she told the Los Angeles *Evening Times* that she took her first job at fourteen. "I accepted a job offer from Mr. Ramsperger, owner of the International Music Store in downtown Montreal," she said. "I sat in the window of the store playing popular music of that time for six hours a day. There were no outside amplifiers at that time, although I do recall Douglas volunteering once to rig up some sort of a system, but the store declined. To hear what I was playing the people who used to gather outside the window had to come into the store and once they were in they rarely went out without buying a copy or two of the songs they had heard.

"I even sang a few of the songs. But I was only good on the slow ballads and the store owner thought the livelier music made customers more anxious to spend their money, so I was allowed to play very few songs I could sing.

"I'd only been there a couple of weeks when the store owner introduced me to a Mr. Morris, who ran one of the city's silent movie houses. He asked if I would be interested in playing, every evening, as accompaniment to the movies. Since we needed every cent we could get, I told him I'd give it a whirl.

"Well, it was very successful. I knew so many songs from playing them all day long, and Mr. Morris gave me a book provided by the movie companies. It had marches, gallops, everything you could think of that would be suitable accompaniment for scenes that ranged from a wild west posse chasing the Indians to a sad death scene, of which there were so many in those early days.

"I worked at the store from ten a.m. to five in the afternoon. They gave me an hour for lunch, without pay of course. Then I dashed home for the hot meal mother had waiting, then back to the movie theatre in time to be playing when the first members of the audience arrived at around seven. Some nights I didn't get home till eleven o'clock."

By the time she was seventeen, Norma Shearer was also a model, and considered one of the best in Montreal. Somehow she had found time to act in more than half-a-dozen community productions staged at one of the city's largest theatres, and she was singled out on several occasions as the actress with most ability.

Fortunately for her schedule, she had given up the movie theatre job after one year. "It was hard to concentrate, night after night, on the quick changes happening on the screen. And from where I sat, in front of the screen, I had to almost break my neck to see what was being shown. I put up with the boos when I played a tune the audience thought was inappropriate, but when they started throwing oranges and apples, even tomatoes once, when the film broke down, as it did quite often, I'd had enough. You'd think I broke the film from the way they behaved."

When Norma was eighteen, her mother, Edith, decided her daughter had sufficient talent to satisfy a much larger audience than that provided by Montreal. "She told Dad that she was going to New York with me, and Athole, my sister, to seek my fame and fortune. She had me believing that I really did have the talent she thought I had.

"When Dad agreed, and he told me years later that he said 'yes' because he felt we were tired of seeing him brooding all day in his misery without a job, I decided to set out on this great adventure mother had planned.

"We got a couple of rooms at a really good price just behind one of New York's elevated streetcar lines," she told the *Los Angeles Times* in 1935. "The rooms were spotless and we wondered why we had got such a bargain until we tried to sleep at night. Every time the streetcars ran past, pictures on the wall jumped up and down like jack-in-the-boxes. Add to that the summer heat and no air-conditioning in those days and you have some idea of what hell is like. Those trains seemed to run every few minutes and after ten that was pretty frustrating. We didn't notice them during the day, but at night, wow! We finally bought ear plugs and that helped. Since we didn't have a telephone we weren't missing much."

Mrs. Shearer believed in starting her daughter's career at the top. She wangled an introduction to the great Florenz Ziegfeld, then casting for his next Ziegfeld Follies. "He was charming," said Shearer, "although I noticed his roving eye checking out much more extensive ground than what I hoped was my pretty face. 'Hoist up your skirt,' he said. 'Now, higher, much higher. What are you trying to hide?' Then he stopped smiling, told me to drop my skirt. 'I see what you are hiding,' said the great man. 'Those legs. My dear, they just aren't good enough for the Ziegfeld Follies.'"

Mrs. Shearer and her daughter marched out of Ziegfeld's office feeling very downcast. "I remember turning round as we reached the door and making a very rude sign to Mr. Ziegfeld. I don't even know where I learned it, but I did it. He looked at me as though I was a worm and smiled broadly."

That, for some years, was Shearer's only contact with the impresario. When they next met it was a very different story.

Norma Shearer played a few small roles in Broadway plays in 1920. "But I didn't select my plays too well," she recalled in 1943. "One only lasted three days, and the other two ran less than a month."

Mrs. Shearer decided that films might be the thing for her daughters, and she hustled both girls to every little movie studio in New York. It was a young David Selznick, then working for his father, Lewis J. Selznick, and his older brother, producer Myron Selznick, just starting his career in the motion picture industry, who offered Norma and Athole extra work in a film he was making, *The Flapper.*

"Mr. Selznick was very nice to us," she recalled. "He liked the way we handled ourselves on the set and he sent us over to Biograph to see the great director, D. W. Griffith. Mr. Griffith immediately cast us in his film, *Way Down East.*

"Once we got started it was easy. I can't remember the names of the half-dozen more films we made before Athole decided acting was not for her. I remember the day very clearly because it was the day I was offered my first speaking role in a film. Speaking role sounds strange today, because of course the lines we spoke were never heard by movie-goers. The film was *The Stealers.*"

There are two versions of what happened next. Twenty-one-year-old Irving Thalberg, then working as an assistant to Carl Laemmle in the New York office of Universal Films, claims he saw *The Stealers* the day before he left for California to become a producer at Universal's West Coast studio. "I fell in love with this gorgeous girl and sat through the film twice," he told *Picturegoer* in 1930. "I had just time to find out her name from the cameraman I knew on the picture before I had to hop aboard the train to Los Angeles. I thought about her all the way across America, and knew that if I succeeded as a producer I would send for her and make her a star. I also knew that I wanted so very desperately to marry her."

Shearer's own story runs like this. "I was making *The Stealers* when a young man, impeccably dressed, came over to me and asked my name. He introduced himself as Irving Thalberg, and said he was working with Universal Films. He asked if I had considered moving to California where the weather was better, and said he was leaving in a few days to become one of Universal's junior producers. He gave me his card, on which he crossed out Universal's New York address, and wrote in the Los Angeles studio address. He told me to call him if I got to California.

"He was quite a small man, perhaps an inch or two higher than me at the most, and I'm only five-feet three, and I don't think I was very impressed. But I took the card and gave it to mother that evening. I think this was the first nudge to us that we should move to California."

That same year, Norma's father, Andrew Shearer, decided to join his family in New York. He sold the house, which was heavily mortgaged, and left half the money with his son, Douglas, who had chosen to stay in Montreal and move into an apartment.

In 1921 the Shearer family had a lean time in New York. "I worked in only one film in which I had a real part," she recalled. "Herbert Brenon was producing the film, *The Sign on the Door,* at First National's studio. He paid me $25 a day for a small part that stretched over several days, as I was not necessarily in the foreground but had to be present in a lot of scenes. He gave mother, Athole, and even my father, extra parts. They each got $5 a day, and their participation lasted several days, too."

Work, for some reason, became difficult to find. Shearer had to settle mainly for modelling jobs, and was named "Miss Lotta Miles" for Kelly-Springfield tire advertisements. With funds running low, Shearer managed to win small roles in 1923 in *The Bootleggers* and *The Man Who Paid.* "We were grateful for the crumbs, but I actually had to take a job playing piano in one of the dingier New York movie houses for $5 a day to keep the wolf from the door. But it was the best thing that ever happened to me. David Selznick, who had got my film career started, came to the theatre to see the first night of one of his movies.

"He came down to the front, where my piano was set up, to give me some music that had been specially composed to fit the action on the screen. Suddenly he recognized me. 'Miss Shearer,' he said. 'I can't believe you aren't working in one of the studios. You have a great talent, and now I find you are a musician, too. Can you report to my studio next Monday? I have a part for you in my new film.'

"Could I report? I'll say I could! I was there at seven thirty in the morning hoping to be ahead of him. I wanted to show my enthusiasm by being in his office when he arrived. But when I walked in at seven thirty he was already there. 'What kept you?' he asked. 'Don't you remember, we start at seven?'

"Mr. Selznick gave me a great part in his film *Channing of the North West*. He paid me $60 a day for five days. At the end of the first day we all went out and had steak for supper to celebrate. I'd never dreamed I could earn $300 in one week. Was I in the big-time!

"When the film was completed, I got several other small roles that kept me busy. We were able to afford to have a telephone installed, and when the phone rang and mother told me Mr. Selznick was on the line, I was thrilled. 'I'd like you to come to the studio to see the movie you just made,' he said. 'I think you're going to like what you see.' We set a time and I hopped on a streetcar to the studio.

"It was the first time a producer had asked me to sit with him to watch a movie I had made. David Selznick was charming. I think he must have only been twenty, the same age as me. Well, we watched the film and if I say so myself, it was good, very good. Selznick stood up, took both my hands, and said the words I'll never forget, 'You are going to be a very big star, my dear. I am going to Hollywood to start my own company and one day I will be the person to make you into that big star.' He kissed me on the cheek and wished me luck."

But it was Irving Thalberg who created the incentive for the Shearer family to move to Hollywood. Thalberg wrote her from Universal studio to say he was leaving to join Louis Mayer, as production head of Mayer's film company. "It was obvious the real action in the movie world was now in Hollywood," said Shearer. "So we took a vote and it came out four to nothing in favor of going west. It took a week to get things sorted out, and, of course, we asked Douglas to come with us, but he said he was doing well in Montreal, but might visit us in a year or two.

"We had a bumpy train ride in coach class to Los Angeles. After the third day I felt like one of the pioneers bouncing along in a covered wagon. My rear end was so sore from sitting that Athole and I decided that at every stop, even if only for a minute or two, we would race up and down the station platform for exercise. Twice we nearly missed the train but a porter hauled us on board just in time.

"As soon as we arrived in Los Angeles, we found a small apartment and I was allowed to go first at having a much needed soak in the bathtub. Then I went out to the nearest drug store and called Irving Thalberg at Universal. I was horrified to learn that he had already left, but a kind telephone operator found me the number of the Mayer Company. There were so many Mayers in Los Angeles at the time that it took her several minutes to find the right one.

"I called and a voice answered, 'The Mayer Film Company, Louis Mayer speaking.' Can you imagine today getting right through to 'the' Louis B. Mayer? Unless you had the right password you would never get past the seventeenth secretary.

"I asked for Irving Thalberg, and Mr. Mayer said he was out at the moment but should be back in a short while. 'I'll have him call you,' said Mayer. 'Oh, dear,' I said, 'we don't have a telephone yet, we just arrived from New York.' 'Very well,' said Mayer, 'give me your address and he'll get in touch with you.' I told him my name, and he said, 'Name sounds familiar. Have I heard it before? Oh, yes, I know, you're the girl Irving is raving about. Perhaps you'd better come and see us. Right away, if you can. I'll make sure Irving stays here when he returns to the office.'

"I raced back to the apartment and changed into my prettiest dress, while I told everyone what Mayer had said. 'You think I should come with you?' said mother. 'No,' said my father, 'I should go with her.' I told them both that I was twenty-one and quite able to take care of myself. I pointed out that there would probably be twenty or thirty men on the streetcar and I was sure I would come to no harm there either.

"I arrived at the Mayer studio with my heart pounding. I was so excited that I almost didn't notice a large grease stain on the front of my dress. Mayer's receptionist pointed it out but told me not to worry, 'Lots of people who don't know our streetcar system come here with grease on their clothes. You'll learn how to miss it as time goes by.'

"But how will I explain it to Mr. Thalberg, and Mr. Mayer? I'm sure I was almost in tears when a quiet voice behind me said, 'You won't have to explain, Miss Shearer. I've been on the streetcars, too.' I whirled around and there was Mr. Thalberg. He put out his hand and greeted me warmly. 'Come into my office,' he said. 'Let's start discussing how we can best make you into a star.'"

Thalberg had already convinced Mayer that he had a potential future star on his hands, and less than an hour later Shearer was signed to a five-year, $110-a-week contract with the Mayer Company.

In 1943 Mayer remembered her arrival at his studio differently. "I could hear her cry of horror in my office when she spotted a big grease stain on her dress, even though the door was closed. I looked out and saw this delightful young woman. Grease or no grease she had a sense of nobility about her that I couldn't remember any other actress having. Thalberg came out of his office right then, and he introduced me to Norma Shearer.

"I told our receptionist to help get some of the grease off Shearer's dress while Thalberg and I had a short talk. I told him to sign her to a long-term contract, at once. I suggested we offer $100 a week, but Irving said that wouldn't do. 'In New York she was getting $25 a day, and the least we could hope for is that she will accept $125 a week.' We compromised on $110 and I told my secretary to type in her name, the five year term, and the amount on one of our standard printed contracts."

Thalberg then returned to his office and informed Shearer that he had convinced Mayer to offer her a five-year contract. "Will $100 a week be acceptable?" he asked. Shearer nodded happily. "Then I'll make it out for $110," he said.

Shearer remembered the meeting differently. "First he offered me $80 a week, but I said it wasn't enough. Then he offered $90, and I still said 'no.' I reminded him that I had earned $300 a week in New York, and he reminded me it was for just one week and that I was probably out of work for the next five weeks so that made the $300 a week average out to about $50 a week. He tried offering $100 so I told him to stop quibbling, it would be $110 or nothing. He laughed and said, 'I'd better go and stop Mr. Mayer's secretary from typing the contract out for $100.'

"He went out, and in a few minutes brought the contract back for my signature. I signed it without reading a single word. Something I would never dare do today. Only when I read it next day did I discover that it included a clause that would give me fifty percent of everything the Mayer Company got over and above my $110 a week if I was loaned out to other studios. I once estimated that small clause earned me more than $90,000 over the life of the contract.

"I remember telling him, as I raised the pen to sign, that I was twenty-one and didn't need my parents' approval. 'So am I,' he said, 'I don't need mine either, so what say we go out to dinner tonight at the poshest restaurant we can find?' I said 'yes,' without thinking, and began a most wonderful relationship that lasted for thirteen years until he was taken away from me much too early by God."

The Mayer Company had not too many parts to offer her in 1923, but Thalberg used connections he had made while at Universal, and pushed to get Shearer the lead role in a First National film, *The Wanters*. "I finally listened to reason and accepted director John Stahl's suggestion that I was moving too fast with Norma," said Thalberg to *Picturegoer*. "So I settled for a smaller role for her in the film and was eternally grateful to John for his wise advice. I was too eager to put her on top of the tree when she hadn't even tested out the lower branches."

Warner Brothers spotted Shearer in *The Wanters,* and cast her in a good supporting role in *Lucretia Lombard.* "I remember that Irving talked them into paying $400 a week for me, so when fifty percent of the portion over $110 was added to my pay check it came to $255. Suddenly I knew that Irving was very much on my side. I think that was when I first really knew he was in love with me and I with him."

Shearer played in three more films away from Mayer Pictures before Louis Mayer announced to her that he now had the ideal part for her to start her career with his company. Mayer was right. *Pleasure Mad,* in which she played the lead as a 1920s flapper, drew great reviews from all parts of the country.

Norma Shearer's marriage to Irving Thalberg, September 8, 1928: from left, Andrew Shearer and Edith Shearer (parents of the bride); Douglas Shearer (brother of the bride); Bernice Ferns (friend of the bride, from Montreal); Norma Shearer; Irving Thalberg; Sylvia Thalberg (sister of the groom); Louis B. Mayer; Irene Mayer and Edith Mayer (daughters of Louis B. Mayer); Rabbi Edgar F. Magnin.

Shearer recalled in 1943 that it was her insistence that she play second leads wherever possible. "I told Irving and Mr. Mayer that I needed more experience before tackling the big roles. They finally agreed that they would be patient with me until I felt I was ready. They agreed to let me read every script that came into the studio so I could get a better idea of what was suitable and what was not."

Mayer, that same year, recalled how he had urged both Shearer and Thalberg to take their time in grooming her for stardom. "She wasn't ready," he said. "I know how anxious she must have been, but rushing things never helped. I told the same thing to many others including Jean Harlow and Joan Crawford, and look what big stars they became."

There were more loan-outs to Warner Brothers, Fox, Paramount, and a film being made on location in Saint John, New Brunswick. "I was feeling a little homesick for Canada, and when they said *Blue Water* was going to be filmed in Saint John I jumped at the chance providing they agreed I could take a train when the film was complete to see my brother, Douglas, in Montreal. Mother, father, and Athole came with me on location. I have often wondered why the people of New Brunswick seemed so very much friendlier than those in California. Perhaps it was because none of them were looking for anything. In Hollywood everyone you meet is wanting you to do something for them."

Blue Water was produced for New Brunswick Films Ltd. by Ernest Shipman, the man who — nineteen years earlier — had given another Canadian, Joe De Grasse, his first role as a professional actor in a Boston play.

The Shearers enjoyed a week in Montreal. "Some of my films had already been shown in the city and it was exciting to be written about in my old home town. A newspaper editor got me to go back to Frank Ramsperger's music store so they could take a picture of me with the owner. I'll swear it was that same piano that I had played years before still there, but playing it was a pianist, far more talented than I had been.

"The photographer and I went inside and I introduced myself to Mr. Ramsperger and the pianist. Both of them recognized me from my films, but the owner didn't remember me from when I played in his store. He asked me to play a duet with the current pianist, which I did, and a crowd gathered in the store. The pianist said he hoped our meeting would bring him luck and one day he, too, would have his name in the spotlight like mine. As far as I know he never did. His name was Billy Eckstein but he was not the Billy Eckstine who went on to great renown as a singer, recording artist, and bandleader.

"After I left, a friend wrote to tell me that Mr. Ramsperger had put the photograph the newspaper took, of him watching me play on the piano, with a handwritten card that read 'Montreal's own star of the motion pictures was once employed in our store.'

"I was terribly reluctant to leave Montreal, but Irving called me every night I was away and I knew that was where my heart really was."

By 1924 the Shearer family was living in a beautiful home in Beverly Hills. They also maintained a beachfront home, almost as large, at Santa Monica. Andrew Shearer, remembering his construction expertise from Montreal, had started a small lumberyard, specializing in providing the highest quality wood to the studios for their sets. In the three years it had been operating, it had grown to be a massive operation employing more than 100 carpenters.

"We pride ourselves that we can supply whatever any studio needs within a few hours. We have exotic woods from India and Burma, maple from Canada, and oak from England, just to mention a few," he told the *Los Angeles Examiner* in 1925.

In 1924 the headline news was the merger between Louis Mayer's company and Metro-Goldwyn, a growing company that had been founded by Sam Goldwyn.

"But Sam had left to go on his own before the merger, and although Metro-Goldwyn-Mayer ballyhooed both their names, Goldwyn was never a part of MGM. Suddenly I was part of the largest, most important studio in Hollywood — we should really say Culver City — for that is where the MGM empire was built."

Shearer's first MGM film was the silent, *He Who Gets Slapped,* in which she co-starred with John Gilbert, the great screen lover of that time, Conrad Nagel, and Lon Chaney, Sr., the "man of a thousand faces."

The trade papers, perhaps with a little push from both Mayer and Thalberg, gave her a front page story. The headline read "Metro-Goldwyn-Mayer Has Made Its First Star." Mayer took all the credit for Shearer's discovery, and ended the story by saying, "She is just the first of many who will come from nowhere through our star-making program. Before we finish there will be more stars at MGM than there are in the heavens." He obviously liked what he had said so much that almost immediately he began calling MGM the studio "where there are more stars than in the heavens." It became a catch-phrase on all publicity handouts and was the studio's slogan until the late 1950s, when it was quietly put to sleep.

The Shearer family was shocked in 1926 when Andrew and Edith Shearer announced their separation. Within weeks he had sold his lumber company, divided the assets equally, and Edith had returned to Montreal. "I can't live in this country without my husband," she told the *Los Angeles Times*.

When the two studios merged, Thalberg became production manager at MGM with responsibility for every film made on the lot. In addition, he had artistic control of the careers of several of the company's up-and-coming performers, including Norma Shearer.

"Irving guided my career every step of the way," she said in 1943. "Isn't it ironic, when you think of the tremendous output of feature films the studio produced, that not one film ever left MGM with his name on it. Directors, producers, writers, stars, technicians, you name it, got screen credit for their work. Irving never got a single credit. It's hard to believe, but that's a fact."

Despite her new-found fame, Shearer often said that she was happier playing supporting roles. "I would have got out of the lead parts if I could, but Irving and Louie were insistent. I think I had a lot of insecurity in those late twenties that I couldn't shake off. It was a nagging inside that was very puzzling to me. It didn't go until September 8, 1928, when Irving and I were married. I can only conclude that I was afraid what I looked forward to would never happen. Irving was never, any of the time I knew him, in really good health and he used to drive himself to the limits working ten, twelve, sometimes fifteen hours a day at the studio. His mother used to tell him constantly that marriage wasn't for him because of his frailty. But it happened, and from that day my whole life changed."

Norma Shearer's brother, Douglas, had made the move to California in 1925, married, and set himself up in a seafront home at Santa Monica. By 1927 he was prospering at MGM, experimenting with sound, which had not yet officially arrived.

Athole had married producer-writer-director Howard Hawks, and they too settled down in Beverly Hills. They lived together until his death in 1977, when he was eighty-one. Hawks received an honorary Oscar in 1974 for his many years of notable achievements in the film industry, and was still using all his skills until a few years before he died.

The Irving Thalbergs built a mansion on Summit Drive, close to the homes of Mary Pickford and Charlie Chaplin. Shearer lived in it for many years after her husband's death, selling it in 1957 to director William Wyler, who remained there until his death in 1981.

The Thalberg home was the scene of many of Hollywood's most notable parties in the early 1930s. The happy couple were seen in the best restaurants and at the liveliest night clubs in town. Thalberg and Shearer were such good dancers that often everyone else cleared the floor when they got up to dance at places like Hollywood's famed Coconut Grove. The other dancers stood around and applauded the Thalbergs' intricate footwork.

Shearer's pleasure was destroyed only nine months after the wedding when American immigration authorities ordered her mother, who had come down from Montreal for the wedding, to leave the country within fourteen days. "She is not welcome here," said the immigration official who visited the Thalberg home where she was staying. "She had been informed that we did not want her to try to return to Los Angeles but she slipped across the border illegally."

"Mother claimed she had no idea why she was not wanted but agreed to go back to Montreal," said Shearer in 1960. "We didn't find out until many years later the real reason for her deportation order. We had even appealed to the White House, but nobody was willing to help. The order had to be carried out.

"In the late 1950s I received a lot of personal correspondence and other things after mother died. It seems that when she returned to Montreal after she and father separated she wrote a lot of rather unpleasant letters to newspapers in Canada about the United States. She suggested that it was time the British came back again to end the terrible corruption that was sweeping the United States. She even called for the overthrow of the president and his cabinet. In one letter she offered a sum of money to any Canadian willing to shoot the president. No wonder our appeal to the White House for a stay in her deportation was refused! Looking back now, all I can think is that the divorce must have unhinged her for awhile. The things she wrote were totally opposed to her normal self."

In 1929 Norma Shearer made her first sound film. *The Trial of Mary Dugan* also starred Raymond Hackett and H. B. Warner. Warner, a renowned British stage and screen actor, spoke about Shearer in 1958. "I was charmed by her very presence," he said. "The coarseness of many other actresses was totally lacking in her make up. Like many others, I had wondered how these beautiful ladies of the silent screen would appear to their audiences when there was a voice to go with the face. In Norma's case I need not have had any fears; her voice was beautifully modulated and had the depth necessary to bring out the beauty of the lines with which she was provided.

Norma Shearer

"Her brother, Douglas, who was the MGM sound chief — still is, I believe — hovered around the set from morning till night. If performers were going to be destroyed by the creeping giant, sound, his sister was not going to be one of them. But I must say, in all fairness, that he was equally careful with the recording of even the smallest actor on the set. The result, as everyone knows, was a superb film, one of which I am very proud and which I know was a source of satisfaction to Norma. Do you know, she still comes to visit me in my old age?"

But it was not *The Trial of Mary Dugan* that made Norma Shearer into the top rank star she became only a few months later. She made two more films in 1929, *The Divorcée* with Robert Montgomery and Chester Morris, and *Their Own Desire*. Both films brought her Best Actress nominations for the 1928-29 awards ceremony held late in 1929. *The Divorcée* won her the Academy Award statuette, which one year later became officially known as the Oscar.

Louis B. Mayer, the man who approached all the other major film companies with his proposal to create the Academy of Motion Picture Arts and Sciences, and spearheaded the plans to bring it to fruition, had not won a single award for MGM at the 1927-28 awards ceremony. He was a disappointed man when he drove home after the banquet. "But 1929 is going to be different," he told the trade press. "I promise we shall win at least two awards. Perhaps even three!"

MGM and its performers and creative technicians did take home three Academy Awards. Norma Shearer spoke to the press after the banquet. Asked if she had ever feared the arrival of sound, she said: "I met the talkies with ignorant bliss. I wasn't afraid to talk, I'd been on the Broadway stage, so I didn't really think about it. It offered a new way for me to express emotion." She smiled at the newsmen. "But, of course, I would have murdered my brother, Douglas, if he hadn't made me sound so good."

In 1930 she made only two films, *Strangers May Kiss,* a frothy little film of no consequence, and *Let Us Be Gay,* in which she was starred with Rod La Rocque, Sally Eilers, Marie Dressler, and Hedda Hopper. Hopper, then an actress, was later to become one of the most vitriolic showbusiness columnists the industry ever had to face.

Marie Dressler, in her first talkie, stole all the rave reviews, but Shearer was a close second in critical approval. "I made two friends in that film," she said. "One, Marie Dressler, I lost tragically only four years later. In that short time we had become so close that it was like losing a mother when she died. The other, Hedda Hopper, gave up her acting career very quickly and became a columnist. People used to scream names at her when she came on the set. Others told terrible stories of her vicious attacks on them, but I found her to be a great companion and even greater friend. Thinking back to all the bad stories she wrote, I have to think, knowing the people involved, that they often didn't get as much as they deserved."

Irving Thalberg, Jr., was born in 1930. "I took the rest of the year off to be with him at all times," said Shearer. "It was important that he knew his mother from day one. He was much more important than my career."

In 1931 Shearer was nominated for an Academy Award for *A Free Soul,* but she didn't win. The film had a great cast including Clark Gable, Leslie Howard, and Lionel Barrymore. She also made Noel Coward's *Private Lives* with Robert Montgomery, and *Strange Interlude* with Clark Gable.

Shearer was asked in 1960, when Gable died, if she would like to comment on the films she made with him. "After those two films I made with the gentleman in 1931, I didn't see him again until we worked together on *Idiot's Delight* in 1939. He kept out of my way because he had tried the usual hands-on approach he used with all his leading ladies. I gave him an excellently placed knee in the spot that really dampened his ardour for several weeks. And I remember, too, that he had bad breath and a cap on one of his teeth that kept coming off at most inconvenient moments.

"But he was, however, a fine actor, and a joy to team up with, once those initial problems were taken care of. I remember just before we started *Idiot's Delight* he came over to my dressing room carrying a strange looking metal object with straps hanging from it. 'Norma,' he said. 'I just thought I should let you know that I have had this object created so that I can withstand your worst assaults on my manhood.' So I kicked him very hard on the left leg and he was limping for days. He never did worry me again and we became quite good friends."

It was in 1931 that Florenz Ziegfeld arrived in Hollywood. He and Louis B. Mayer were said to be discussing making a film telling Ziegfeld's life story. It was to include many new musical numbers and, of course, the great Ziegfeld Girls.

"There is only one person I can think of to personify the grace, magnificence, and beauty of the Ziegfeld girl, and you have her here at MGM," said the Broadway producer. "She must be the star of the film."

"And who is that?" asked Mayer.

"Norma Shearer, of course," said Ziegfeld.

Shearer was called in to meet Ziegfeld, for what Mayer, and Ziegfeld, believed was for the first time. The impresario showed no signs of remembering their previous meeting years earlier in New York. He told her of his desire to star her in a Ziegfeld Follies on film, and that she was the only person in the world who could fulfill his dream.

"I listened to all his prattle for about ten minutes," Shearer remembered. "As usual I could see him undressing me with his beady eyes. Then I turned to him, lifted up my skirt very high, and watched his eyes goggle. Then I dropped the skirt, and said, 'Mr. Ziegfeld, I just don't have the legs to be a Ziegfeld girl.' As I turned to leave the room I gave him the same rude sign I'd given him in New York a decade before. Did it ring a bell? I doubt it. He'd seen too many legs and probably got far too many rude signs in his life to remember mine."

Shearer went over to Irving Thalberg's office and requested him to tell Mayer to advise Mr. Ziegfeld that he could 'go to hell.' And that put an end to negotiations for almost five years, when the great showman's estate talked Mayer into making *The Great Ziegfeld,* without Shearer, of course.

In 1932 Shearer told Mayer and her husband that she would, in future, only appear in films adapted from books considered to be classics. She advised them, and presumably her husband had been warned in advance, that the first one must be *Smiling Through* and her leading man must be the popular British actor, Leslie Howard.

Mayer, realising that whatever Shearer made would bring money into MGM's coffers, agreed. The film was made and it did make a profit, but its rather slow action did nothing to enhance the career of the woman now known as the Queen of Hollywood.

It was in 1934 that Shearer made another classic, *The Barretts of Wimpole Street,* with Maureen O'Sullivan, Charles Laughton, and Fredric March. She didn't want the role at first, but heard through the grapevine that publisher William Randolph Hearst was using pressure on Mayer to get his girlfriend, Marion Davies, the part.

"When I heard that trollop might get the role I told Irving I'd do the film," she said in 1943. "Looking back now I am convinced that Louie and Irving had started the rumour to get me to agree to do the film. But anyway, it brought me another Oscar nomination, so I mustn't complain." The Thalbergs' second child, Katharine, was born in 1935. As with her son, Irving, Shearer took a full year off work to be at home with the new arrival.

In 1936 she demanded to play the role of Juliet in *Romeo and Juliet.* Once more she asked for and received Leslie Howard as her leading man. The cast featured many more of MGM's top contract artists including John Barrymore, Andy Devine, and Reginald Denny.

When the studio publicity department put out the word that Norma Shearer was to play Juliet, thousands of letters came in opposing the idea. The gist of most of them was that a thirty-four-year-old woman shouldn't be playing a sixteen-year-old girl. Mayer countered with a release that said Mary Pickford and the Gish sisters had been doing just that for years and he was adamant that Shearer would play Juliet.

The film was acclaimed by the critics. Hedda Hopper, her friend, wrote that "Shearer must be accepted as the epitome of natural high breeding and the final word in feminine sophistication in a film that denotes quality in its highest form."

Regardless of great reviews, the film was not a box-office success, and despite the tremendous promotion it received from the studio, it came nowhere near recouping its gigantic production costs.

By then Shearer was not too concerned about the film or whether it was loved or hated. Her beloved Irving had suffered a heart attack. Looked after at home by a round-the-clock team of doctors and nurses, he was said to be recovering when he developed pneumonia. Within days he was dead. On September 14, 1936, Mayer announced the news as he dabbed tears from his eyes. "We had our differences," he said, "but this good man was the genius who provided Metro-Goldwyn-Mayer with many of its greatest films. I will miss him like I would miss a son." Then he broke down and had to be helped back to his car.

Less than a month later it was revealed that Thalberg had been secretly working toward a complete break from MGM. "He had planned to take with him, to a new company he had already formed, his wife Norma Shearer and about a dozen of MGM's actors, actresses, and technicians, all of whom had been stalling on negotiations for new contracts with Mayer," said *Variety*.

Shearer, when approached for a comment, said "I had no knowledge of any such plan. He certainly never told me, and we have never had any secrets in our lives together." She added, "In fact, I signed a new contract with MGM only a few months ago. It will allow me to make six films, of my own choice, over the next four years."

Contract or not, Shearer announced in 1937 her total retirement from the film industry. "Irving left me very well provided for, and I have my own money, of course. I have Irving's shares in Metro-Goldwyn-Mayer but shall probably negotiate with the company for a fair settlement of their value."

Mayer went through the roof. "We have spent more than half-a-million dollars preparing for her appearance in *Marie Antoinette,* a role she has been looking forward to playing. It is to be, and will be, the highlight of her entire career." After ranting about her ungratefulness to the studio that made her a star, he pointed out that MGM held a watertight contract that guaranteed her appearance in six films before the end of 1943 at $150,000 each. "We intend to hold her to that contract," he said.

Years later it was revealed that Mayer had blackmailed her into honouring her contract by threatening to hold up settlement of the Thalberg estate by refusing to assign a price to the MGM shares she had inherited from Thalberg. Shearer's lawyers warned her that it was possible he could stall for several years and that she needed the money, which was estimated to be around $6 million, to pay his death duties.

Sheared capitulated and made the film. But *Marie Antoinette* was not the big hit everyone expected. W. S. Van Dyke, one of Hollywood's most distinguished directors, was in control of a cast that included Tyrone Power, Anita Louise, and Robert Morley. It recouped its costs, but just barely. Seen today, the film is slow and stodgy, with dialogue that at best can be called trite.

Shearer issued a statement to the press saying that "we failed because we did not have Irving Thalberg's meticulous eye for script doctoring."

Another man from her past returned into her life that same year. David Selznick, by this time a major producer in Hollywood, asked her if she would like to play Scarlett O'Hara in his planned production of *Gone With the Wind*. "I promised in New York that I would one day make you the most important actress in the industry," he told her. "This is the film that will never be forgotten, it will still be around long after you and I are gone."

Mayer quickly approved the deal, which was to pay Shearer one million dollars and MGM another half-million for allowing her to work away from her home studio.

"It would have been the only film I would ever have made away from MGM," she recalled. "From the day the studios merged in 1924 I had never worked away from the Culver City studios." But it wasn't to be. If there were thousands who thought she was too old to play Juliet, there were ten times as many who protested to Selznick that she was far too old, at thirty-six, to play Scarlett. Mayer and Selznick talked. They then called in Shearer and told her their decision was that she should withdraw from the film.

"I was quite happy," she said. "I really only agreed to play Scarlett so David Selznick could keep his promise to make me into the greatest star of all time. I'd always thought I was too old and, besides, I didn't believe I had the fire to play Scarlett. In addition, I thought I was already as important as I ever wanted to be. Why push things?"

In 1939 she accepted a role opposite Clark Gable in *Idiot's Delight*. "There was total harmony on the set after our earlier confrontation," she said. "I enjoyed working with Gable, who had decided he was not going to get anywhere with me."

She also made *The Women*, with Paulette Goddard (the Charlie Chaplin discovery), Mary Boland, Rosalind Russell, and Joan Crawford. "That one was a breeze. I've often felt I got on better working with women than men, although I can't ignore the genius of our director, George Cukor, who handled us like a bunch of silly children, which perhaps we were to his eyes."

Escape, with Robert Taylor, was her only film in 1940. It was successful and made MGM a lot of money.

"In 1941 I was tired," she said. "So I asked Louie if I could do the final two films of my contract in 1942. He was gracious, and agreed. The war, of course, was on in Europe so I could not do any travelling as I had hoped, so I just sat at home and did some knitting. Didn't know I could knit? I've knitted every sweater that I've worn since I was fifteen."

Shearer was seen around town in 1940 with actor George Raft. Both protested they were "nothing more than good friends" and after a romance that lasted two years they broke up and decided to be occasional companions for lunch or dinner.

We Were Dancing, with Melvyn Douglas, was well received in 1942, but her swan song, *Her Cardboard Lover*, again with Robert Taylor, was disappointing to her fans who had hoped for a big one from their favorite's last appearance before the camera. "On these two films," she said a year later, "no one but me was trying to destroy my career. I just didn't have the heart to play any more."

When the final "cut" had been called on the set of *Her Cardboard Lover*, Louis B. Mayer called the press together to announce the completion of her MGM contract and her immediate retirement. Shearer gave him a big hug and a kiss. "I will always count Mr. Mayer as one of my best friends and advisors," she said. "We have had disagreements, it is true, but when I needed someone to count on, he was always there for me. Once, when he was quite ill with laryngitis, and I needed urgent advice, he got up from his sick bed and drove into the studio just because I needed him. He couldn't talk, so he scribbled answers to my problems of a piece of paper. Friends like Louis B. Mayer are hard to find."

An avid ski enthusiast, Shearer spent a lot of time in the winter months in Colorado. But everyone in the film capital was amazed, when in December 1942 she announced that she had married her ski instructor, twenty-eight-year-old French-born Martin Arrouge.

"They say life begins at forty," she told the news media. "Well, I'm forty, I have lots of life left, and I intend to enjoy it with the man I am very much in love with. I have talked this over with Katharine and Irving Jr., the two children from my marriage to their father [Irving Thalberg], and they are both totally supportive of my attempts to make my life fulfilling. I have made full provision for their future lives and they have wished me well."

It was revealed in Hedda Hopper's column that Arrouge had signed a legal document, at his insistence, renouncing all his community property rights to Shearer's substantial fortune.

Shearer and Arrouge never sought the limelight in the years that followed. Mary Pickford said, in 1962, "I often see Norma and Martin walking past my house, hand-in-hand, obviously very happy together." She added: "But they don't drop in to see me anymore, they seem to have forgotten the world around them exists."

In 1946 a brief announcement in the *Hollywood Reporter* said that Enterprise Productions, Inc., was planning a series of films to star Norma Shearer. It reminded readers of her past successes and said she had told the paper that "at forty-four I still have a lot left in me to offer to the public."

But nothing was ever heard of the plan after the initial announcement. She is reported as telling one of her friends that the company was one she had incorporated herself, and the announcement was just to test the waters. "Martin and I wanted to see if there was any favourable reaction, but there was none of any kind so we didn't continue with the idea."

When the war ended in Europe and Asia, Shearer and Arrouge travelled around the world. They were reported to be in Russia where Shearer was mobbed by crowds who were only just seeing her films for the first time, dubbed into Russian. She was said to have spent hours signing thousands of autographs. Actress Irene Dunne, who lived in Paris for some years in the late 1940s, told *Variety* in 1950 that she had enjoyed many walks, talks, and breakfasts, lunches, and suppers with Shearer and her husband. "They were obviously deliriously happy," she said.

There was no more news from the couple for more than thirty years. If friends knew where they were living, no one was prepared to betray that knowledge. Letters sent to her through the Academy of Motion Picture Arts and Sciences were obviously forwarded to her, because the writers would receive a letter or phone call out of the blue months later. The letters and calls came from just about every corner of the world.

In 1981 came the news that seventy-nine-year-old Norma Shearer had suffered three major strokes, was unable to see, and was partially paralysed. At the request of her husband, said a news item in the *New York Post,* she had been moved to the Motion Picture and Television Home and Hospital in Woodland Hills. Her husband Martin Arrouge, it continued, had rented a small home near the hospital so he could be with his wife every day.

On June 13, 1983, the *Los Angeles Times* announced her death, the previous day, at the age of eighty-one. She had developed bronchial pneumonia, said a hospital spokesman, and in her frail state she could not combat it.

Benny Rau, an executive at MGM when Shearer was the idol of Hollywood, also a patient in the Motion Picture Home and Hospital, told a reporter that although most of the time she didn't recognize him, and speech had been difficult for her, there were periods each day when her memory came back. "Martin and I shared every waking hour with her," he said. "Just in case she needed company."

"When she was able to recognize me, we used to reminisce about the old days," he said, "and I used to read to her from some of the scripts I had kept. Early on the morning of June 12 she asked me to read my copy of the *Mrs. Miniver* script. I had read it to her before but this time, when I had finished, I noticed tears running down her cheeks. 'What's the matter Norma? Have I upset you?' I asked. 'No,' she said. And she spoke clearly and distinctly for the first time in many months. 'But I wanted to hear that again before I died. You see I was the one Louie chose for that part long before he considered Greer Garson. But I turned it down. That is the only regret I have in my entire life.'"

Three hours later she passed away peacefully in her sleep. Her husband, Martin Arrouge, was at her side.

The funeral service was private, with only half-a-dozen people present. She was interred in Forest Lawn Cemetery with a simple marker on the grave bearing nothing more than her name.

EPILOGUE

"There are some things that should never end. But, alas, time catches up with all of us and only memories remain of the wonderful days of our youth, those carefree days when we faced the world with a smile and a wonderment at what might lie ahead in our lives. If you can look back at those days with pleasure mixed, at times, with a little sadness, as I do in this, my seventy-fifth year, your life has not been in vain."

(Mary Pickford, 1968)

This book has been a labour of love. If any good things can come out of a conflict as terrible as World War Two, I count one of them the privilege I was given, while training in Canada to fly with the Royal Air Force, to visit the paradise then known as Hollywood.

I consider myself very favoured to have met the real stars of Hollywood, the ones who made its name synonymous with all that was good in the world of entertainment. To have lived briefly in the city of glamour, when it really was glamourous, is something I wish I could offer to each of you.

To have had the doors of the biggest names in show business opened to me, and have the studios welcome me in as though I was a "Very Important Person," is something I look back on with awe, even now, fifty-seven years after my adventure of a lifetime happened.

That I am able to write my memories of so long ago in such detail is because of the help I received from one of Hollywood's most important names in sound, Douglas Shearer. When he heard me asking so many questions, and saw me trying to scribble notes as fast as my pen would write, he presented me, for the duration of my stay, with one of his inventions, the first wire tape recorder I had ever seen.

Although it weighed more than thirty pounds, I carried it everywhere I went, from studio to studio and house to house. Like me, many of the people

I talked to had never seen a wire recorder before, and perhaps for the sheer
novelty of using it they talked much more than they originally intended. The
wire recorder was rather like today's reel-to-reel tape recorders except the
much larger spools held magnetic coated wire. The microphone, which
Douglas Shearer loaned me, added another few pounds to the already weighty
machine, but I wouldn't have left for any appointment without it.

I owe a permanent debt of gratitude to a young secretary at Metro-
Goldwyn-Mayer studio. MGM's boss, Louis B. Mayer, loaned Ann Howard
to me. Every night at around eleven, she arrived at the Sidney Olcott and
Valentine Grant home in Mayer's own chauffeur-driven car to collect the
reels I had filled with conversation. She took them back to the studio, leaving
me new wire reels for next day's taping.

At the studio she had a duplicate of my machine, and using this she
worked through the night transcribing the contents into readable copy on
her typewriter. Since my recording continued for eighteen days without a
break she too worked for eighteen nights without a break.

I should tell you that she came over from England to the United States
around the same time as Elizabeth Taylor, and hoped, at one time, for a
career in acting. She had a few parts when she was around fifteen or sixteen,
including one in the *Prince and the Pauper* that looked like it might be her
stepping stone to stardom. But for some reason fame never came. A wise
mother told her to stop dreaming and find another line of work. Fortunately
for me, she did, at MGM. She may not have been a star on the movie screen
but she always will be in my heart.

When I returned to Hollywood after the war I renewed my friendship
with many of my wartime friends and found the warmth of their hospitality
had not waned. I tried to locate Ann Howard, but had no luck. Louis B. Mayer
said she had married and moved away, but no one knew her married name or
where she had gone. Even an item in the *Hollywood Reporter* failed to locate her.

It is sad now to think that the only way I had thanked her in 1943 was to
buy her a hamburger and coke in the commissary at MGM. This was a poor
repayment for a magnificent job that made this book possible.

I have not told in this book all the things my Hollywood friends told me,
because some of the stories were too personal, too sad, or too frightening to
be put on paper all these years later. And I have omitted the ultimate ending
to the Florence La Badie story because, when I finally uncovered it by
accident a few years ago, I found the truth very hard to believe and
impossible to put into words on paper.

Many other Canadians who were in Hollywood in the creative years deserve to be mentioned, but it is impossible to cover the lives and careers of everyone so many wonderful people had to be omitted. You will find a list of a few of them at the end of the book.

I must mention one in particular, although I met him, not in Hollywood, but fifteen years ago in his beautiful home in North Vancouver. Osmond Borradaile, awarded the Order of Canada some years ago (an honor in which I am happy to say I was involved), was one of the world's great directors of photography who made permanent history with his work on the Alexander Korda films made in England.

The story of how he earned the Oscar that sat in the window of his study is worth a chapter to itself, but I have left it out because this great Canadian asked to keep the story for the autobiography he was at the time writing. Borradaile started in the early silent studios of Hollywood, sweeping the floors, and rose to the top as one of the greatest cinematographers who ever lived. Sadly, he died in 1999 when he was 100 years young. I don't believe his autobiography was ever completed.

And so my story ends. Hollywood today is nothing like the Hollywood I knew in 1943. Even the stars who lived in beautiful mansions rarely locked their doors in those days. Bars on windows and regular armed security patrols today testify that many things have changed, unhappily, not for the better!

I hope you have enjoyed joining me for this look at Hollywood when it was the Hollywood we once dreamed about, and I trust it will have given you some small indication of the vital role Canadians played in the early days of motion pictures in both New York and Hollywood.

Charles Foster
145 Leonard Street
Riverview, New Brunswick
Canada E1B 1K7
(506) 386-8749
e-mail retsofcharles@webtv.net

Gone ... But Not Forgotten!

Here are a few more names of Canadians who were part of the creative years of the movies. Only those actors born in 1900 or earlier, and who participated in the silent film era, are included. The names marked with an asterisk* are ones I was privileged to meet in 1943 or while doing research for this book.

Hugh Allen, Toronto, Ont., 1886-1986
Julia Arthur,* Hamilton, Ont., 1869-1950
William Bertram, Walkerton, Ont., 1880-1933
Genevieve Blinn,* Saint John, N. B, 1900-1956
Donald Brian,* St. John's, Nfld., 1871-1948
Clifford Bruce, Toronto, Ont., 1885-1919
Richard Carlyle, Guelph, Ont., 1879-1942
Frazer Coulter, Smiths Falls, Ont., 1849-1937
William Courtleigh Jr., Guelph, Ont., 1869-1930
Edward Earle,* Toronto, Ont., 1882-1972
Roy Emerton, Toronto, Ont., 1892-1944
Herbert Fortier, Toronto, Ont., 1867-1949
Robert Fleming, Toronto, Ont., 1878-1933
Rockliffe Fellowes, Ottawa, Ont., 1885-1930
Pauline Garon,* Montreal, Que., 1900-1965
Clarence Geldert, Saint John, N. B., 1867-1935
Huntley Gordon,* Montreal, Que., 1897-1956
Edna Gregory,* Winnipeg, Man., 1900-1963
Harry Hamm, Napanee, Ont., 1891-1943
Del Henderson,* St. Thomas, Ont., 1883-1956
Rapley Holmes, Fredericton, N. B., 1868-1928
Kathleen Howard,* Hamilton, Ont., 1879-1956
Joseph Kilgour, Ayr, Ont., 1864-1933

Matheson Lang,* Montreal, Que., 1879-1948

Wilfred Lucas, Niagara Falls, Ont., 1871-1940

Willard Mack, Morrisburg, Ont., 1873-1934

Charles Hill Mailes, Halifax, N. S., 1870-1937

James Rennie, Toronto, Ont., 1889-1965

John S. Robertson, Toronto, Ont., 1878-1964

Andrew Robson, Hamilton, Ont., 1867-1921

Ned Sparks,* Toronto, Ont., 1883-1957

Ben Taggart,* Ottawa, Ont., 1889-1947

Angus D. Taillon, Barrie, Ont., 1888-1953

Eva Tanguay,* Marbleton, Ont., 1878-1947

Gus Thomas, Toronto, Ont., 1865-1926

Harold Vosburgh, Penetanguishene, Ont., 1870-1926

Lucile Watson,* Quebec City, Que., 1879-1962

George White,* Toronto, Ont., 1890-1968

INDEX